P9-AFZ-409

WITHDRAWN

A Garland Series

AMERICAN INDIAN ETHNOHISTORY

North Central and Northeastern Indians

compiled and edited by
DAVID AGEE HORR
Brandeis University

Indians of Northern Ohio and Southeastern Michigan

AN ETHNOHISTORICAL REPORT

Erminie Wheeler-Voegelin

THE LOCATION OF INDIAN TRIBES
IN SOUTHEASTERN MICHIGAN
AND NORTHERN OHIO

Helen Hornbeck Tanner

Garland Publishing Inc., New York & London
1974

78284

Copyright© 1974

by Garland Publishing, Inc.

All Rights Reserved

Library of Congress Cataloging in Publication Data

Voegelin, Erminie Wheeler, 1903-
    An ethnohistorical report.

    (American Indian ethnohistory: North central and
northeastern Indians)
    At head of title: Indians of northern Ohio and
southeastern Michigan.
    E. W. Voegelin's report presented "before the Indian
Claims Commission, docket nos. 13-E et al."
    1. Indians of North America--Michigan--History.
2. Indians of North America--Ohio--History. I. Tanner,
Helen Hornbeck. The location of Indian tribes in south-
eastern Michigan and northern Ohio. 1974. II. United
States. Indian Claims Commission. III. Title.
IV. Title: Indians of northern Ohio and southeastern
Michigan. V. Series.
E78.M6V63   970.4'74   74-2283
    ISBN 0-8240-0800-6

LIBRARY
LEWIS-CLARK
STATE COLLEGE

Printed in the United States of America

Contents

5

*Garland Publishing has repaginated this work (at outside center) to facilitate scholarly use. However, original pagination has been retained for internal reference.

6

Publisher's Preface

The Garland American Indian Ethnohistory series presents original documents on the history and anthropology of many American Indian tribes and groups who were involved in the Indian Claims actions of the 1950s and 1960s. These reports were written to be used as evidence in legal proceedings to determine the aboriginal rights of various Indian groups to certain geographical regions or areas within the United States. In each case, the Indian Claims Commission issued a set of findings which are an important historical outcome of the proceedings and of the reports.

The Garland volumes include, as background material, introductory sections on the Indian Claims actions and the gathering of the ethnohistorical materials by Ralph A. Barney, Chief of the Indian Claims Section of the Department of Justice since its inception in 1946, and Robert A. Manners, Professor of Anthropology at Brandeis University. Both were professionally involved in several cases and Dr. Manners has published on the Claims actions.

Each volume also contains a brief introductory historical sketch of the tribe or group which is representative of the kind of information available at the time of the Claims actions. Much of this material was summarized in a 1650-page document (House Report No. 2503), published in 1953 by order of the House of Representatives committee investigating the Bureau of Indian Affairs. In addition to summaries on history and population, the massive government report included maps which gave the 1950 location of the various American Indian groups, largely on reservations, as well as the estimated original range occupied by the group or tribe in question. This material appears in the Garland volumes in abridged form, since it gives a picture of the kind of information available to the United States government in the 1950s on which it might have based decisions concerning the

PREFACE

American Indians had the Indian Claims actions not taken place. In addition, these brief introductory sections will help orient the general reader to the groups covered by the ethnohistorical reports.

The reports in this series have been organized into logical groupings for maximum efficiency of use. Short reports have been bound together into single volumes by tribe or by geographical area when several tribes are represented by a single report, with Commission findings bound at the end of the pertinent volume. In those cases where many reports pertain to the same group or area they may comprise several volumes which are numbered consecutively. When several volumes deal with the same set of claims, the findings appear in the final volume of that set of interrelated reports. It should be noted that, since this series is intended to present these ethnohistorical materials as documents, the reports are reproduced *verbatim*, with no additions, deletions, or other editing by the compiler of the series or the original authors.

Within the body of the reports, reference is often made to exhibit numbers. These refer to other material accepted as evidence, often in the form of excerpts from existing publications or other documents pertaining to the tribes in question. This material is not included in the volumes themselves, although a bibliography of these items usually appears in the report. These exhibits are on file in the Indian Claims Commission offices in Washington, D.C., or in the National Archives.

General Nature and
Content of the Series

The formal reports contained in this series represent only part of the evidence amassed in the 370-odd court actions assigned separate docket numbers by the Indian Claims Commission. Almost since the outset, those involved with the Indian Claims' activities have voiced the opinion that the specifically researched ethnohistorical studies should not simply be filed away in some federal depository though this did become the case with these reports. The present series is the result of careful searching through more than 600 unindexed file drawers in the Indian Claims Commission, the National Archives, and elsewhere, sometimes even in the papers of the originally participating scholars.

Each claims action was an adversary proceeding with a particular Indian tribe or group as plaintiff and the United States Government, represented by the Indian Claims Section of the Justice Department, as defendant. Each side collected evidence on the nature of aboriginal use and occupancy of particular areas in order to determine which Indian groups were entitled to compensation for lands taken by the United States, either by treaty or otherwise, and just what lands were in question. Once this phase of the action was settled, the proceedings moved on to the question of the value of the lands at the time they were taken from the Indians. It is with the title phase of the Claims proceedings that the present series is concerned. Therefore the numerous appraisals of economic value are omitted.

Claims to title were settled on the basis of several types of evidence presented during hearings before the Indian Claims Commission. The expert testimony submitted included verbal and written reports by anthropologists, archaeologists, and historians. During the early days of the Commission, virtually all such testimony was oral and is preserved only in the official court transcripts. Later on, the Government required its expert witnesses to submit formal written reports. The lawyers for the plaintiffs did not initially make this a requirement so that, for some cases, reports are available on the Government side but not for the Indians. Finally, the Commission did require all ethnohistorical reports to be submitted by both sides in written form. The title page of each individual report indicates whether it was submitted as an exhibit for the plaintiff (sometimes called claimant, petitioner or intervenor) or the defendant.

Since the formal reports were subject to examination by the Commissioners and by the opposing lawyers, they were carefully prepared. The specific nature of the reports did mean that some topics often included in an ethnography might be excluded. In the California cases, for example, some well-researched reports on pottery making and other craft industries were not used. On the other hand, data on political structure, kinship and property inheritance rights, and many other such topics, were often considered because they did bear upon how rights to property and power were determined within a group and the question of how the Indians originally used the land. Once the evidence was submitted and examined in the hearings, the Commissioners issued a set of Findings and Opinions, which, by themselves, are important historical documents.

The Garland series includes only the formal ethnohistorical reports and the title findings of the Commission since the entire documentation of the Claims actions is so voluminous. The lengthy hearing transcripts are uneconomic to reproduce without editing and our purpose is to present unedited documents as actually *used*. The transcript of the Kiowa-Comanche case is included because of its unique nature. The transcripts are all on file either in the Indian Claims Commission or the National Archives, and may be consulted there.

The content of this series was determined solely by those ethnohistorical reports submitted to the Commission. Therefore, American Indian tribes and groups not involved in Claims actions are not represented for various reasons. For example, the Indians of the northeastern and eastern United States had lost most of their lands prior to the establishment of the country in 1776. In other instances, the tribe no longer existed in 1946 or did not submit a claim. In some cases claims were submitted, but were denied before a report was commissioned for that tribe.

The reports for the various areas covered by the Claims Act have been approached in somewhat different ways. When possible, they deal with individual tribes or named groups. This does not mean that in such cases there were no overlapping claims; however, the overall tribal situation was not so complex as to prevent an initial identification of tribal groups with specific geographic areas. By contrast, in some areas such as the eastern and north central regions, reports tend to focus on Royce areas rather than individual tribes because the aboriginal claims situation often involved recurring movement through the region by many different tribes over a relatively short time period. In these regions treaties ceding certain lands to the United States were often signed by several different tribes or perhaps only by certain parts of some of the tribes involved. Here the area reports *in toto* form an almost jigsaw-puzzle-like solution to the enormously complex tribal relationships. The Royce Area maps and designations were published in Bureau of American Ethnology, Annual Report, vol. 18, no. 2, 1896-7.

David Agee Horr

11

12

The Indian Claims Commission

Prior to the creation of the Indian Claims Commission by the Act of August 13, 1946 (60 Stat. 1049; 25 U.S.C. § 70 et seq.), no tribe of Indians could bring a suit against the United States without the special permission of Congress. This was a cumbersome and wholly unsatisfactory procedure. By the 1946 Act, Congress created a special judicial tribunal to "hear and determine" claims by Indian tribes in an effort to settle, once and for all, the claims of the Indians. The Act is unique in the true sense of the word. Never before has any government generally opened the doors of its courts to the claims of its aborigines. The Commission is authorized to consider claims by any "tribe, band or identifiable group of American Indians" that the United States in its previous dealings had not always carried out its treaty obligations, had imposed treaties upon them against their wishes, had failed to pay them adequately for their land, had failed to account properly for the expenditure of their tribal funds and, in many instances, had not been "fair and honorable" in their dealings with them.

The tribes had five years within which to file their claims and, after adjudication, they could have the Commission's decisions reviewed by the United States Court of Claims and by the Supreme Court of the United States. The Congress imposed one important limitation: the Commission could render only a money judgment in favor of the tribes. It could not return any land to them which might have been taken wrongfully, nor could it give them any land to supply a land base.

The present volumes deal with only one of the multi-faceted aspects of Indian claims litigation: the area of land occupied by the tribes prior to the coming of the white man into the area in general, or the area occupied by a particular tribe for "a long time" prior to its acquisition by the United

States, or their dispossession by the whites.

The land problem was confounded by different concepts inherent in the nature of the disparate cultures. The culture of the Europeans who discovered and later settled this continent was basically legalistic, particularly where land was concerned. Land was the subject of "ownership" either by the monarch or his subjects, and "titles" were the capstone of such ownership. "Ownership" in the sense of a legal right was unknown to the Indian. As Justice Black said in *Shoshone Indians* v. *United States*, 324 U.S. 335, 357 (1945):

> ... Ownership meant no more to them than to roam the land as a great common, and to possess and enjoy it in the same way that they possessed and enjoyed sunlight and the west wind and the feel of spring in the air. Acquisitiveness, which develops a law of real property, is an accomplishment only of the "civilized."

When the Europeans "discovered" the North American continent they found it inhabited by the Indians and the question of their rights aroused a great moral debate. Charles V of Spain sought the advice of the theologian Franciscus de Victoria, primary professor of sacred theology in the University of Salamanca, who suggested that since the aborigines "were true owners, before the Spaniards came among them, both from the public and private point of view," they should be treated with to secure cessions of their lands. This view obviously could not prevail if the European monarchs owned the land and could parcel it out to their subjects.

The matter came to a head in 1823 when Chief Justice John Marshall decided the famous case of *Johnson* v. *McIntosh*, 21 U.S. (8 Wheat.) 453. In 1775 the Piankeshaw Indians had sold a tract of land to various individuals. However, in 1818, the United States sold and patented the same land to William McIntosh. Thus the contest was which deed was valid. From a long and detailed examination of the history of Indian relations in this country, Chief Justice Marshall concluded that the legal title was in the United

States Government and that the tribes had no right to sell and convey the land (at least, without governmental consent).

However, the Indians could not be ignored, particularly in the early days when they were numerically far stronger than the few settlers huddled along the coast. From this developed the theory that while the legal "title" was in the discovering nations and later in the United States, the Indians had a right of possession based on what was characterized as their "aboriginal title."

More than thirty years ago, long before the creation of the Indian Claims Commission, the Supreme Court had occasion to lay down the rule, which was later adopted by the Commission, as to what was necessary to establish Indian title. In *United States* v. *Santa Fe Pacific R. Co.*, 314 U. S. 339, 345 (1941), the Court said:

> Occupancy necessary to establish aboriginal possession is a question of fact to be determined as any other question of fact. If it were established as a fact that the lands in question were, or were included in, the ancestral home of the Walapais in the sense that they constituted a definable territory occupied exclusively by the Walapais (as distinguished from lands wandered over by many tribes), then the Walapais had "Indian title". . . .

15

The determination of the "question of fact" of the aboriginal or original Indian title is what the ethnographic studies in these volumes, and the findings and the opinions of the Commission are all about. The anthropologists have dug up the facts to the extent that they were able to do so. Based on these facts the Commission has made its determination of the areas of land occupied by the various tribes under their original title or their later occupancy, and it is on the basis of these determinations of the areas of aboriginal title that these cases then go forward to determine the amount of recovery by the several tribes.

Quite understandably much of the "evidence" consists of deductions made by the witnesses from the frequently meager hard facts available and, of necessity, the determinations of the Commission are based on this type of evidence. While the boundaries of the areas exclusively and actually used and occupied may not always be correct, they represent in most instances a fair approximation of the areas occupied by the various tribes aboriginally or for "a long time" on the dates when the United States acquired the land or they were permanently dispossessed of it. All in all, it has been a difficult job well done.

I cannot close this brief introduction without expressing my admiration for the many scholars on both sides who so diligently sought out the facts to present to the Commission. They did a magnificent job for which all other scholars and interested laymen should be grateful. My personal acquaintance with them has been an outstanding experience.

I am also personally happy to see these ethnographic studies and the decisions of the Commission published instead of being buried in the National Archives. They will contribute greatly to our knowledge of the American Indian.

Ralph A. Barney

Introduction to the Ethnohistorical Reports on the Land Claims Cases

The research reports and the findings contained in this compilation may prove, in the long run, to have contributed little to resolving the massive economic and social problems which confront today's Native Americans. However, it is most unlikely that any of the diligent and often dedicated sponsors of the movement that led, in 1946, to the passage of the Indian Claims Commission Act ever had such lofty expectations. What is more likely is that the proponents of the legislation, as Ralph Barney observes in his introductory remarks, had simply hoped to "clean up the mess," to put an end to the stream of suits and claims against the federal government, each of which had required Congressional approval before it could be brought to trial. But the "mess" was not so easily resolved. Some cases have been settled. Others have been heard, adjudicated and appealed to higher courts. A few, like that of "the Indians of California," may be reopened.

But when, and if, all of the claims have been resolved in the courts, the government will not have succeeded in pacifying the claimants nor in satisfying their demands for decent compensation. In short, the Act has not fulfilled even the minimal goal of putting an end to Native American claims against the United States Government.

In light of the relatively meager benefits that have so far accrued to Native Americans as a consequence of the Act of 1946, it might seem almost callous to draw attention now to the richness of the by-product of that Act as represented in the 118 volumes in this series. For whatever one may feel about the intended benefits of the Act, it is clear that the scholarly fallout is stunning indeed. The materials presented in these volumes include a concentrated body of ethnohistorical research data and adversary findings unique in the record of cultural historiography and, so far as I know, in the annals of jurisprudence.

Literally hundreds of people were involved in the research and litigation that led to these reports and findings. Thousands of interviews were conducted. Extensive archaeological surveys were made. Large quantities of previously "unknown" or unexamined agency and other files, personal correspondence, photographs, diaries, and so on were uncovered and their contents incorporated in the reports. Regular archival and library resources were examined and reexamined with a thoroughness that would not have been possible without the support that both claimants and the defendant were able to provide. Then there were the adversary proceedings, which, though patently unpleasant to most of the experts, did provide an even more effective check on the quality of the research product than the customary scholarly scrutiny of one's colleagues. For where there is litigation, the experts on both sides have probably reviewed much, if not all, of the same data. Moreover, the litigous circumstances place a premium on revealing inaccuracies and/or slipshod research methods.[1]

Finally, I would like to emphasize that another apparent by-product of the Act and the research and hearings that followed its implementation may be detected in the effect that this research and its attendant litigation have had on the thinking of many Native Americans now pressing for improved economic, social and political conditions for *all* Indians in the United States. Thus, if the working-out of the Act has made only minor contributions to the welfare of a

18

[1] Some ethnohistorical and legal problems confronted by the plaintiffs' and defendant's experts and attorneys were explored at a 1954 symposium on the Claims Act (see *Ethnohistory* 2,4, pp. 287-375). The participants were Ralph A. Barney, Chief of the Indian Claims Section, Lands Division, Dept. of Justice; Donald C. Gormley of the law firm of Wilkinson, Boyden, Cragun & Barker; and anthropologists Verne Ray, Julian Steward, A. L. Kroeber, J. A. Jones and Nancy Oestreich Lurie.

handful of American Indians, it has apparently had a much more salutary effect on their thinking about the welfare of *all* Native Americans. For the "time immemorial" and the "exclusive occupancy" strictures of the Act resulted, in many ways, in pitting group against group to the detriment of all.[2] In most cases, the occupancy and/or use claims of one group conflicted, at least in part, with those of another or several other groups of Indians.[3] Where such joint use or occupancy was proved to the satisfaction of the Commission, none of the claimants benefitted, thus demonstrating (as I have been told by several Native Americans) the perils of division and intra-Indian competition and, by implication, the likely advantages of pan-Indian cooperation in future endeavors, political as well as legal.

This "unforeseen consequence" of the research and litigation, of the claims and counter-claims, has certainly been among the factors that have helped to persuade those Native Americans who were not already convinced of the pitfalls as well as the potential virtues of a revived "tribalism" of the need for a more unified, a pan-Indian approach to their problems. These volumes can only help to bolster the case for such unity and, thus, perhaps to enhance the political impact of Native Americans in the United States.

Robert A. Manners

---

[2] In this respect, the claim of "The Indians of California" is exceptional because an earlier case had laid the groundwork whereby a number of different groups (culturally and linguistically) were permitted to combine all of their separate land-use-and-occupation claims into one. If the Act had allowed *all* American Indian plaintiffs to combine their claims in this manner (and to share equally in the awards), and if they had been willing to do so, the resultant claims, litigation and decisions might have been, at the very least, quite interesting. . . . i.e., "The Indians of the United States vs. the United States Government for just compensation for the taking of all lands (less land held in existing reservations) between the Atlantic and the Pacific Oceans."

[3] A striking example, with which I am familiar, are the overlapping Navaho, Hopi, Walapai, Havasupai claims.

Editor's Note

In terms of the numbers of tribes involved in overlapping claims, the area of the upper Great Lakes and Ohio Valley is the most complicated of all the Indian Claims Commission actions. At the time of the founding of the new United States government following the Revolution, many Indian tribes and groups had been dislodged from their earliest locations along the lower Great Lakes and the Eastern Seaboard, and many of these groups had moved across the mountains into the old Northwest Territories. Here, they encountered already existing Indian groups, and by the time of the Treaty of Greeneville in 1795 many Indian tribes and groups were contesting these lands with the advancing whites and with each other. By the mid-1800s, most of the Indians in this area had moved west of the Mississippi River, though some groups remained.

In trying to sort out this most complicated Claims situation, reports were written around Royce areas, in an attempt to determine exactly which Indian groups had how much claim to particular regions. It will therefore be useful for the reader to refer to the volume containing the Royce report, although recent scholarship has shown that some of Royce's original boundaries were incorrectly drawn.

In general, then, the individual reports for this area do not concentrate on the history of a particular tribe. However, taken together, they provide the most detailed study available of the history and interrelations of the many Indian tribes in this area. It should be noted that the Chippewa claims were so extensive that most of the reports concerning their lands have been grouped in a series of volumes.

D.A.H.

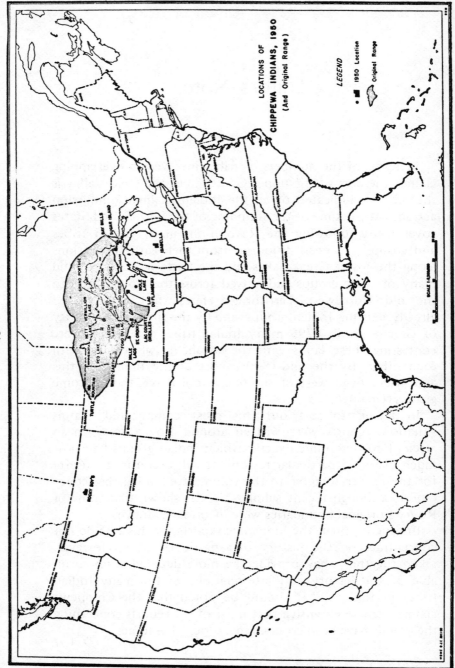

LOCATIONS OF
CHIPPEWA INDIANS, 1950
(And Original Range)

LEGEND

• ■ 1950 Location

〰 Original Range

22

"Chippewa (popular adaptation of *Ojibway*, 'to roast till puckered up,' referring to the puckered seam on their moccasins; from *ojib* 'to pucker up,' *ub-way* 'to roast'). One of the largest tribes n. of Mexico, whose range was formerly along both shores of L. Huron and L. Superior, extending across Minnesota to Turtle mts., N. Dak. Although strong in numbers and occupying an extensive territory, the Chippewa were never prominent in history, owing to their remoteness from the frontier during the period of the colonial wars. According to tradition they are part of an Algonquian body, including the Ottawa and Potawatomi, which separated into divisions when it reached Mackinaw in its westward movement, having come from some point n. or n. e. of Mackinaw. Warren (Minn. Hist. Soc. Coll., v, 1885) asserts that they were settled in a large village at La Pointe, Wis., about the time of the discovery of America, and Verwyst (Missionary Labors, 1886) says that about 1612 they suddenly abandoned this locality, many of them going back to the Sault, while others settled at the w. end of L. Superior, where Father Allouez found them in 1665–67. There is nothing found to sustain the statement of Warren and Verwyst in regard to the early residence of the tribe at La Pointe. They were first noticed in the Jesuit Relation of 1640 under the name Baouichtigouin (probably Bawa tigowininiwug, 'people of Sault'), as residing at the Sault, and it is possible that Nicollet met them in 1634 or 1639. In 1642 they were visited by Raymbaut and Jogues, who found them at the Sault and at war with a people to the w., doubtless the Sioux. A remnant or off-shoot of the tribe resided n. of L. Superior after the main body moved s. to Sault Ste Marie, or when it had reached the vicinity of the Sault. The Marameg, a tribe closely related to if not an actual division of the Chippewa, who dwelt along the n. shore of the lake, were apparently incorporated with the latter while they were at the Sault or at any rate prior to 1670 (Jesuit Rel., 1670). On the n. the Chippewa are so closely connected with the Cree and Maskegon that the three can be distinguished only by those intimately acquainted with their dialects and customs, while on the s. the Chippewa, Ottawa, and Potawatomi have always formed a sort of loose confederacy, frequently designated in the last century the Three Fires. It seems to be well established that some of the Chippewa have resided n. of L. Superior from time immemorial. These and the Marameg claimed the n. side of the lake as their country. According to Perrot some of the Chippewa living s. of L. Superior in 1670–99, although relying chiefly on the chase, cultivated some maize, and were then at peace with the neighboring Sioux. It is singular that this author omits to mention wild rice (*Zizania aquatica*) among their food supplies, since the possession of wild-rice fields was one of the chief causes of their wars with the Dakota, Foxes, and other nations, and according to Jenks (19th Rep. B. A. E., 1900) 10,000 Chippewa in the United States use it at the present time. About this period they first came into possession of fire-

23

arms, and were pushing their way westward, alternately at peace and at war with the Sioux and in almost constant conflict with the Foxes. The French, in 1692, reestablished a trading post at Shaugawaumikgong, now La Pointe, Ashland co., Wis., which became an important Chippewa settlement. In the beginning of the 18th century the Chippewa succeeded in driving the Foxes, already reduced by a war with the French, from n. Wisconsin, compelling them to take refuge with the Sauk. They then turned against the Sioux, driving them across the Mississippi and s. to Minnesota r., and continued their westward march across Minnesota and North Dakota until they occupied the headwaters of Red r., and established their westernmost band in the Turtle mts. It was not until after 1736 that they obtained a foothold w. of L. Superior. While the main divisions of the tribe were thus extending their possessions in the w., others overran the Peninsula between L. Huron and L. Erie, which had long been claimed by the Iroquois through conquest. The Iroquois were forced to withdraw, and the whole region was occupied by the Chippewa bands, most of whom are now known as Missisauga, although they still call themselves Ojibwa. The Chippewa took part with the other tribes of the N. W. in all the wars against the frontier settlements to the close of the war of 1812. Those living within the United States made a treaty with the Government in 1815, and have since remained peaceful, all residing on reservations or allotted lands within their original territory in Michigan, Wisconsin, Minnesota, and North Dakota, with the exception of the small band of Swan Creek and Black River Chippewa, who sold their lands in s. Michigan in 1836 and are now with the Munsee in Franklin co., Kans.

*   *   *   *   *   *   *

"It is impossible to determine the past or present numbers of the Chippewa, as in former times only a small part of the tribe came in contact with the whites at any period, and they are now so mixed with other tribes in many quarters that no separate returns are given. The principal estimates are as follows: In 1764, about 25,000; 1783 and 1794, about 15,000; 1843, about 30,000; 1851, about 28,000. It is probable that most of these estimates take no account of more remote bands. In 1884 there were in Dakota 914; in Minnesota, 5,885; in Wisconsin, 3,656; in Michigan, 3,500 returned separately, and 6,000 Chippewa and Ottawa, of whom perhaps one-third are Chippewa; in Kansas, 76 Chippewa and Munsee. The entire number in the United States at this time was therefore about 16,000. In British America those of Ontario, including the Nipissing, numbered at the same time about 9,000, while in Manitoba and the Northwest Territories there were 17,129 Chippewa and Cree on reservations under the same agencies. The Chippewa now (1905) probably number 30,000 to 32,000—15,000 in British America and 14,144 in the United States, exclusive of about 3,000 in Michigan."

Source: *Handbook of American Indians, Part 1*, pp. 277–280.

"This is the largest of the Algonquian tribes and the fourth largest Indian tribe within the boundaries of the United States. The Chippewa were woodland Indians and originally occupied much of the present State of Michigan and parts of the northern shores of Lakes Superior and Huron. Many of the tribe moved westward after their first contact with Europeans and are at present scattered over a large area, in a number of reservations, and mixed with the white population. The number of Chippewa Indians showed an increase in Minnesota, Wisconsin, North Dakota, and Montana, but a considerable decrease in Michigan. The decrease in Michigan, however, was probably due to failure to return the Indian population of many areas by tribe. The Chippewa have had a large admixture of white blood ever since the early days of French settlement in the region of the Great Lakes. As compared with 34.5 percent in 1910, only 18.7 percent are now reported as full blood. Even this probably includes as full blood many who are only predominantly of Indian blood."

Source: *The Indian Population of the United States and Alaska*, 1930, p. 38.

SELECTED REFERENCES ON THE OJIBWAY
AS OF 1952

(Including the Bungi, Chippewa, Missisauga, Plains Ojibway, and Saulteaux)

Barnouw, Victor. Acculturation and Personality among the Wisconsin Chippewa. Memoir No. 72, American Anthropological Association, 1950.

Cavell, C. Great Lakes Agency Ten Year Program Report. 1944. 257 pp. (Bureau of Indian Affairs).

Consolidated Chippewa Ten Year Program Report Summary. 1944. 8 pp. (Bureau of Indian Affairs).

Densmore, F. Chippewa Customs. Bulletin of the Bureau of American Ethnology, Vol. LXXXVI, pp. 1–204, 1929.

Diddock, Joseph A. Turtle Mountain Ten Year Program Report. 1944. 34 pp. (Bureau of Indian Affairs).

Farver, Peru. Tomah Ten Year Program Report. 1944. 93 pp. (Bureau of Indian Affairs).

Fisher, Margaret W. The Chippewas of Minnesota. 105 pp. no date. mss. (Bureau of Indian Affairs).

Great Lakes Agency Ten Year Program Summary. 1944. 54 pp. (Bureau of Indian Affairs).

Holst, J. H. A Survey of Indian Groups in the State of Michigan. 1939. 21 pp. (Bureau of Indian Affairs).

Holst, John H. The Evolution of the Turtle Mountain Chippewa Tribal Roll. 1941. 25 pp. (Bureau of Indian Affairs).

Krzywicki, Ludwik. Primitive Society and its Vital Statistics. London, 1934. Ojibway pp. 503–5, Missisauga pp. 416–17.

Landes, R. Ojibway Sociology. Columbia University Contributions to Anthropology, Vol. XXIX, pp. 1–144, 1937.

Landes, R. The Ojibway Woman. Columbia University Contributions to Anthropology, Vol. XXXI, pp. 1–247, 1938.

McCullough, H. D. Rocky Boys Ten Year Program Summary. 1944. 8 pp. (Bureau of Indian Affairs).

McCullough, H. D. Turtle Mountain Ten Year Program Summary. 1944. 12 pp. (Bureau of Indian Affairs).

Mekeel, H. S. Report on the Michigan Indians. 1937. 11 pp. mss. (Bureau of Indian Affairs).

Murdock, Geo. P. Ethnographic Bibliography of North America. 1941. p. 101.

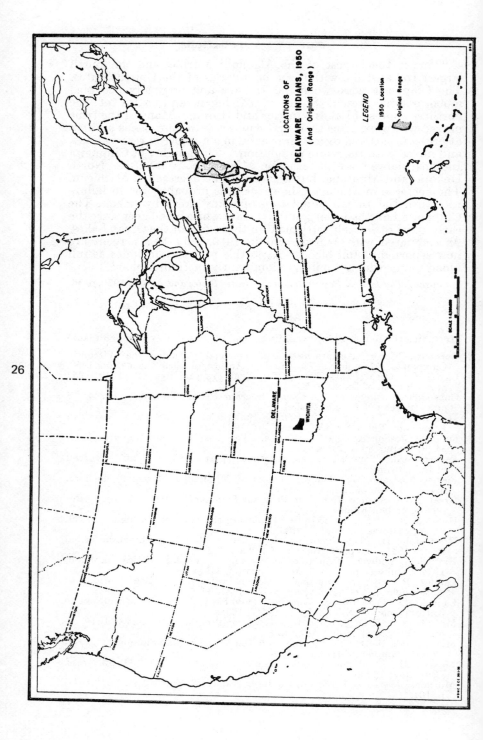

LOCATIONS OF
DELAWARE INDIANS, 1950
(And Original Range)

LEGEND

■ 1950 Location

Original Range

SCALE 1:13,000,000

DELAWARE

WICHITA

26

THE HISTORY OF THE DELAWARE

"The early traditional history of the Lenape is contained in their national legend, the Walam Olum. When they made their first treaty with Penn, in 1682, the Delawares had their council fire at Shackamaxon, about the present Germantown, suburb of Philadelphia, and under various local names occupied the whole country along the river. To this early period belongs their great chief, Tamenend, from whom the Tammany Society takes its name. The different bands frequently acted separately but regarded themselves as part of one great body. About the year 1720 the Iroquois assumed dominion over them, forbidding them to make war or sales of lands, a condition which lasted until about the opening of the French and Indian war. As the whites, under the sanction of the Iroquois, crowded them out of their ancient homes, the Delawares removed to the Susquehanna, settling at Wyoming and other points about 1742. They soon crossed the mountains to the headwaters of the Allegheny, the first of them having settled upon that stream in 1724. In 1751, by invitation of the Huron, they began to form settlements in E. Ohio, and in a few years the greater part of the Delawares were fixed upon the Muskingum and other streams in E. Ohio, together with the Munsee and Mahican, who had accompanied them from the E., being driven out by the same pressure and afterward consolidating with them. The Delawares, being now within reach of the French and backed by the western tribes, asserted their independence of the Iroquois, and in the subsequent wars up to the treaty of Greenville in 1795 showed themselves the most determined opponents of the advancing whites. The work of the devoted Moravian missionaries in the 17th and 18th centuries forms an important part of the history of these tribes (see *Gnadenhultten, Missions*). About the year 1770 the Delawares received permission from the Miami and Piankishaw to occupy the country between the Ohio and White rs., in Indiana, where at one time they had 6 villages. In 1789, by permission of the Spanish government, a part of them removed to Missouri, and afterward to Arkansas, together with a band of Shawnee. By 1820 the two bands had found their way to Texas, where the Delawares numbered at that time probably at least 700. By the year 1835 most of the tribe had been gathered on a reservation in Kansas, from which they removed, in 1867, to Indian Ter. and incorporated with the Cherokee Nation. Another band is affiliated with the Caddo and Wichita in w. Oklahoma, besides which there are a few scattered remnants in the United States, with several hundred in Canada, under the various names of Delawares, Munsee, and Moravians."

Source: *Handbook of American Indians, Part 1*, pp. 385–386.

DELAWARE POPULATION

"The Delaware confederacy at the time of white settlement, occupied a large area in Delaware, eastern Pennsylvania, New Jersey, and southern New York. They moved successively west

27

to Ohio, Indiana, Missouri and finally to Kansas, Oklahoma, and Texas. The great majority of the remaining members of the tribe are now in Oklahoma, mainly in Craig, Nowata and Washington Counties. The number enumerated in 1930, including the related Munsee, was 971, as compared with 985 in 1910. Only 20.2 percent were reported as full blood, as compared with 29.7 percent in 1910."

Source: *The Indian Population of the United States and Alaska*, 1930, p. 38.

Selected References on the Delaware
AS OF 1952

(Including the Munsee, the Unalachtigo, and the Unami, collectively known as the Lenape)

Heckewelder, J. G. E. An account of the History, Manners, and Customs, of the Indian Nations, who once inhabited Pennsylvania and the neighboring States. Transactions of the Historical and Literary Committee of the American Philosophical Society. Philadelphia, Vol. I, pp. 1–348, 1819.

Hulbert, A. B. and Schwarze, W. N. eds. Zeisberger's History of Northern American Indian. Ohio Archeological and Historical Quarterly, Vol. XIX, 1–189, 1910.

Kiowa Ten Year Program Summary. 1944. 11 pp. (Bureau of Indian Affairs).

Krzywicki, Ludwik. Primitive Society and its Vital Statistics. London, 1934. pp. 528–30.

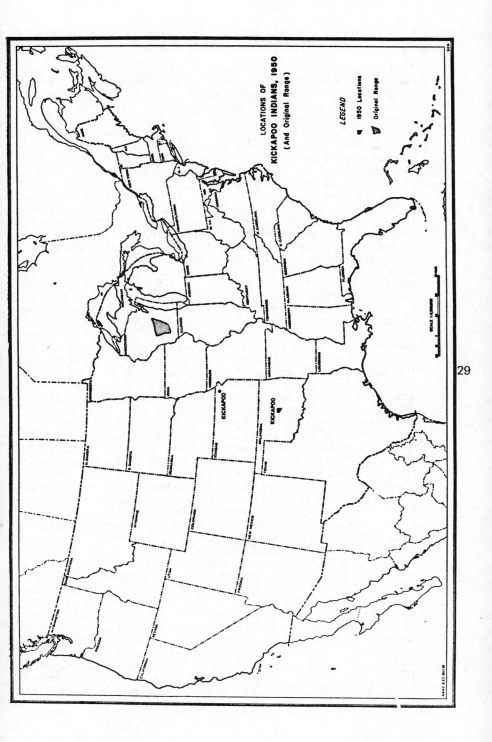

LOCATIONS OF
KICKAPOO INDIANS, 1950
(And Original Range)

LEGEND

■ 1950 Locations

◪ Original Range

SCALE 1:6,000,000

29

"The people of this tribe, unless they are hidden under a name not yet known to be synonymous, first appear in history about 1667–70. At this time they were found by Allouez near the portage between Fox and Wisconsin rs. Verwyst (Missionary Labors, 1886) suggests Alloa, Columbia co., Wis., as the probable locality, about 12 m. s. of the mixed village of the Mascouten, Miami, and Wea. No tradition of their former home or previous wanderings has been recorded; but if the name Outitchakouk mentioned by Druillettes (Jes. Rel. 1658, 21, 1858) refers to the Kickapoo, which seems probable, the first mention of them is carried back a few years, but they were then in the same locality. Le Sueur (1699) mentions in his voyage up the Mississippi, the river of the Quincapous (Kickapoo), above the mouth of the Wisconsin, which he says was 'so called from the name of a nation which formerly dwelt on its banks.' This probably refers to Kickapoo r., Crawford co., Wis., though it empties into the Wisconsin, and not into the Mississippi. Tock r., Ill., was for a time denominated the "River of the Kickapoos," but this is much too far s. to agree with the stream mentioned by Le Sueur. A few years later a part at least of the tribe appears to have moved s. and settled somewhere about Milwaukee r. They entered into the plot of the Foxes in 1712 to burn the fort at Detroit. On the destruction of the Illinois confederacy, about 1765, by the combined forces of the tribes n. of them, the conquered country was partitioned among the victors, the Sauk and Foxes moving down to the Rock r. country, while the Kickapoo went farther s., fixing their headquarters for a time at Peoria. They appear to have gradually extended their range, a portion centering about Sangamon r., while another part pressed toward the e., establishing themselves on the waters of the Wabash, despite the opposition of the Miami and Piankashaw. The western band became known as the Prairie band, while the others were denominated the Vermilion band, from their residence on Vermilion r., a branch of the Wabash. They played a prominent part in the history of this region up to the close of the War of 1812, aiding Tecumseh in his efforts against the United States, while many Kickapoo fought with Black Hawk in 1832. In 1837 Kickapoo warriors to the number of 100 were engaged by the United States to go, in connection with other western Indians, to fight the Seminole of Florida. In 1809 they ceded to the United States their lands on Wabash and Vermilion rs., and in 1819 all their claims to the central portion of Illinois. Of this land, as stated in the treaty, they 'claim a large portion by descent from their ancestors, and the balance by conquest from the Illinois nation, and uninterrupted possession for more than half a century.' They afterward removed to Missouri and thence to Kansas. About the year 1852 a large party left the main body, together with some Potawatomi, and went to Texas and thence to Mexico, where they became known as 'Mexican Kickapoo.' In 1863 they were joined by another dissatisfied party from the tribe. The Mexican band proved a constant

30

source of annoyance to the border settlements, and efforts were made to induce them to return, which were so far successful in 1873 a number were brought back and settled in Indian Ter. Others have come in since, but the remainder, constituting at present nearly half the tribe, are now settled on a reservation, granted them by the Mexican government, in the Santa Rosa mts. of e. Chihuahua."

Source: *Handbook of American Indians, Part 1*, pp. 684–685.

KICKAPOO POPULATION

"This is a small but well-known tribe formerly living in Wisconsin, but now located in the Kickapoo Reservation in Brown County, Kansas, and in Lincoln and Pottawatomie Counties, Oklahoma. The number enumerated in 1930 was 523, as compared with 348 in 1910. Perhaps as many more are located in the State of Chihuahua in Mexico. Of the Kickapoo in Kansas, only 14.7 percent were returned as full blood, but of those in Oklahoma, 95.0 percent were so returned."

Source: *The Indian Population of the United States and Alaska*, 1930, p. 38.

SELECTED REFERENCES ON THE KICKAPOO
AS OF 1952

Affairs of Mexican Kicking Kickapoo Indians. Report. (To accompany S. Res. No. 261, 59th Cong.) (Washington, Govt. Print. Off., 1907.) (60th Cong., 1st sess. Senate. Rept. 5.)

Affairs of the Mexican Kickapoo Indians. Hearings before the subcommittee of the Committee on Indian Affairs, United States Senate. Washington, Govt. Print. Off., 1907.

Affairs of the Mexican Kickapoo Indians. Hearings before the subcommittee of the Committee on Indian Affairs, United States Senate. Washington, Govt. Print. Off., 1908. (60th Cong., 1st sess. Senate. Doc. 215.)

Affairs of the Mexican Kickapoo Indians. Hearing before the subcommittee of the Committee on Indian Affairs, United States Senate. (Washington, Govt. Print. Off., 1908.)

Bruce, H. E. Potawatomi (Kansas) Ten Year Program Report. 1944. 62 pp. (Bureau of Indian Affairs).

Gilmore, Thos. R. Shawnee Agency Ten Year Program Report. 1944. 17 pp. (Bureau of Indian Affairs).

Jones, W. Kickapoo Ethnological Notes. American Anthropologist, n. s. Vol. XV, pp. 332–5, 1913.

Krzwicki, Ludwik. Primitive Society and its Vital Statistics. London, 1934. pp. 406–7.

Mooney, J. and Jones, W. Kickapoo. Bulletin of the Bureau of American Ethnology, Vol. XXX, i, pp. 684–6, 1907.

Murdock, Geo. P. Ethnographic Bibliography of North America. 1941. p. 89.

Spaulding, R. Potawatomi Ten Year Program Summary. 1944. 11 pp. (Bureau of Indian Affairs).

Treaty stipulations with Kickapoo Indians. Feb. 13, 1908. (Washington, Govt. Print. Off., 1908.) (60th Cong., 1st sess. Senate. Doc. 350.)

Wright, Muriel H. A Guide to the Indian Tribes of Oklahoma. Norman, 1951. Kickapoos pp. 166–9.

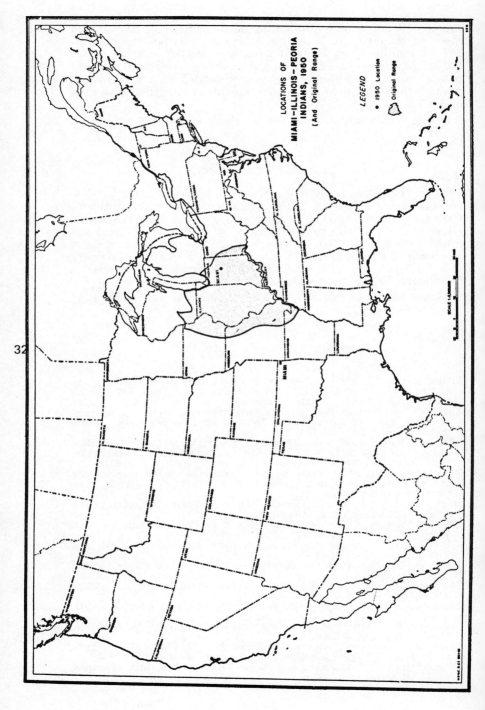

LOCATIONS OF
MIAMI–ILLINOIS–PEORIA
INDIANS, 1950
(And Original Range)

LEGEND

• 1950 Location

○ Original Range

SCALE 1:9,000,000

32

"MIAMI (? Chippewa: *Omaumeg*, 'people who live on the peninsula'). An Algonquian tribe, usually designated by early English writers as Twightwees (twa^{n}h twa^{n}h, the cry of a crane.— Hewitt), from their own name, the earliest recorded notice of which is from information furnished in 1658 by Gabriel Druillettes (Jes. Rel. 1658, 21, 1858), who called them the Oumamik, then living 60 leagues from St Michel, the first village of the Potawatomi mentioned by him; it was therefore at or about the mouth of Green bay, Wis. Tailhan (Perrot, Memoire) says that they withdrew into the Mississippi valley, 60 leagues from the bay, and were established there from 1657 to 1676, although Bacqueville de la Potherie asserts that, with the Mascoutens, the Kickapoo, and part of the Illinois, they came to settle at that place about 1667. The first time the French came into actual contact with the Miami was when Perrot visited them about 1668. His second visit was in 1670, when they were living at the headwaters of Fox r., Wis. In 1671 a part at least of the tribe were living with the Mascoutens in a palisaded village in this locality (Jes. Rel. 1671, 45, 1858). Soon after this the Miami parted from the Mascoutens and formed new settlements at the s. end of L. Michigan and on Kalamazoo r., Mich. The settlements at the s. end of the lake were at Chicago and on St Joseph r., where missions were established late in the 17th century, although the former is mentioned as a Wea village at the time of Marquette's visit, and Wea were found there in 1701 by De Courtemarche. It is likely that these Wea were the Miami mentioned by Allouez and others as being united with the Mascoutens in Wisconsin. The chief village of the Miami on St Joseph r. was, according to Zenobius (Le Clerq, 11, 133), about 15 leagues inland, in lat. 41°. The extent of territory occupied by this tribe a few years later compels the conclusion that the Miami in Wisconsin, when the whites first heard of them, formed but a part of the tribe, and that other bodies were already in n. e. Illinois and n. Indiana. As the Miami and their allies were found later on the Wabash in Indiana and in n. w. Ohio, in which latter territory they gave their name to three rivers, it would seem that they had moved s. e. from the localities where first known within historic times. Little Turtle, their famous chief, said: 'My fathers kindled the first fire at Detroit; thence they extended their lines to the headwaters of the Scioto; thence to its mouth; thence down the Ohio to the mouth of the Wabash, and thence to Chicago over L. Michigan.' When Vincennes was sent by Gov. Vaudreville in 1705 on a mission to the Miami they were found occupying principally the territory n. w. of the upper Wabash. There was a Miami village at Detroit in 1703, but their chief settlement was still on St Joseph r. In 1711 the Miami the Wea had three villages on the St Joseph, Maumee, and Wabash. Kekionga, at the head of the Maumee, became the chief seat of the Miami proper, while Ouiatenon, on the Wabash, was the headquarters of the Wea branch. By the encroachments of the Potawatomi, Kickapoo, and other northern

33

78284

tribes the Miami were driven from St Joseph r. and the country n. w. of the Wabash. They sent out colonies to the e. and formed settlements on Miami r. in Ohio, and perhaps as far e. as the Scioto. This country they held until the peace of 1763, when they retired to Indiana, and the abandoned country was occupied by the Shawnee. They took a prominent part in all the Indian wars in Ohio valley until the close of the war of 1812. Soon afterward they began to sell their lands, and by 1827 had disposed of most of their holdings in Indiana and had agreed to remove to Kansas, whence they went later to Indian Ter., where the remnant still resides. In all treaty negotiations they were considered as original owners of the Wabash country and all of w. Ohio, while the other tribes in that region were regarded as tenants or intruders on their lands. A considerable part of the tribe, commonly known as Meshingomesia's band, continued to reside on a reservation in Wabash co., Ind., until 1872, when the land was divided among the survivors, then numbering about 300.

*   *   *   *   *   *   *

It is impossible to give a satisfactory estimate of the numbers of the Miami at any one time, on account of confusion with the Wea and Piankashaw, who probably never exceeded 1,500. An estimate in 1764 gives them 1,500; another in the following year places their number at 1,250. In 1825 the population of the Miami, Eel Rivers, and Wea was given as 1,400, of whom 327 were Wea. Since their removal to the W. they have rapidly decreased. Only 57 Miami were officially known in Indian Ter. in 1885, while the Wea and Piankashaw were confederated with the remnant of the Illinois under the name of Peoria, the whole body numbering but 149; these increased to 191 in 1903. The total number of Miami 1905 in Indian Ter. was 124; in Indiana, in 1900, there were 243; the latter, however, are greatly mixed with white blood. Including individuals scattered among other tribes, the whole number is probably 400.

The Miami joined in or made treaties with the United States as follows: (1) Greenville, O., with Gen. Anthony Wayne, Aug. 3, 1795, defining the boundary between the United States and tribes w. of Ohio r. and ceding certain tracts of land; (2) Ft Wayne, Ind., June 7, 1803, with various tribes, defining boundaries and ceding certain lands; (3) Grouseland, Ind., Aug. 21, 1805, ceding certain lands in Indiana and defining boundaries; (4) Ft Wayne, Ind., Sept. 30, 1809, in which the Miami, Eel River tribes, and Delawares ceded certain lands in Indiana, and the relations between the Delawares and Miami regarding certain territory are defined; (5) Treaty of peace at Greenville, O., July 22, 1814, between the United States, the Wyandot, Delawares, Shawnee, Seneca, and the Miami, including the Eel River and Wea tribes; (6) Peace treaty of Spring Wells, Mich,. Sept. 8, 1815, by the Miami and other tribes; (7) St Mary's, O., Oct. 6, 1818, by which the Miami ceded certain lands in Indiana; (8) Treaty of the Wabash, Ind., Oct. 23, 1826, by which the Miami ceded all their lands in Indiana, n. and w. of Wabash and Miami rs.; (9)

Wyandot village, Ind., Feb. 11, 1828, by which the Eel River Miami ceded all claim to the reservation at their village on Sugar Tree cr., Ind.,; (10) Forks of Wabash, Ind., Oct. 23, 1834, by which the Miami ceded several tracts in Indiana; (11) Forks of the Wabash, Ind., Nov. 6, 1838, by which the Miami ceded most of of their remaining lands in Indiana, and the United States agreed to furnish them a reservation w. of the Mississippi; (12) Forks of the Wabash, Ind., Nov. 28, 1840, by which the Miami ceded their remaining lands in Indiana and agreed to remove to the country assigned them w. of the Mississippi; (13) Washington, June 5, 1854, by which they ceded a tract assigned by amended treaty of Nov. 28, 1840, excepting 70,000 a. retained as a reserve; (14) Washington, Feb. 23, 1867, with Seneca and others, in which it is stipulated that the Miami may become confederated with the Peoria and others if they so desire."

Source: *Handbook of American Indians, Part 1*, pp. 852–854.

MIAMI AND ILLINOIS POPULATION

"This is 'a group of small Algonquian tribes made up of the Miami 'and the remnants of the Wea, Piankashaw, and Peoria. The number enumerated in 1930 was 284, as compared with 360 in 1910. Of these, 173 in 1930 were located in Ottawa County, Oklahoma, and 47 in Indiana. Only 21 of this group of tribes (17 in Oklahoma and 4 in Indiana) were returned as full blood."

Source: *The Indian Population of the United States and Alaska*, 1930, p. 38.

SELECTED REFERENCES ON THE MIAMI
AS OF 1952

(Including the Miami proper, the Piankashaw, and the Wea)

Andrews, H. A. Quapaw Subagency Ten Year Program Report. 1944. 31 pp. (Bureau of Indian Affairs.)
Kinietz, W. V. The Indian Tribes of the Great Lakes. Occasional Contributions from the Museum of Anthropology of the University of Michigan, Ann Arbor, Vol. V, pp. 161–225, 1940.
Krzywicki, Ludwik. Primitive Society and its Vital Statistics. London, 1934. pp. 460–1.
Murdock, Geo. P. Ethnographic Bibliography of North America. 1941. p. 89.
Trowbridge, C. C. Meearmeear Traditions. Ed. W. V. Kinietz. Occasional Contributions from the Museum of Anthropology of the University Michigan, Ann Arbor, Vol. VII, pp. 1–91, 1938.
Wright, Muriel H. A Guide to the Indian Tribes of Oklahoma. Norman, 1951. Eel River Indians, p. 155, Miami pp. 182–3, Wea pp. 254–5.

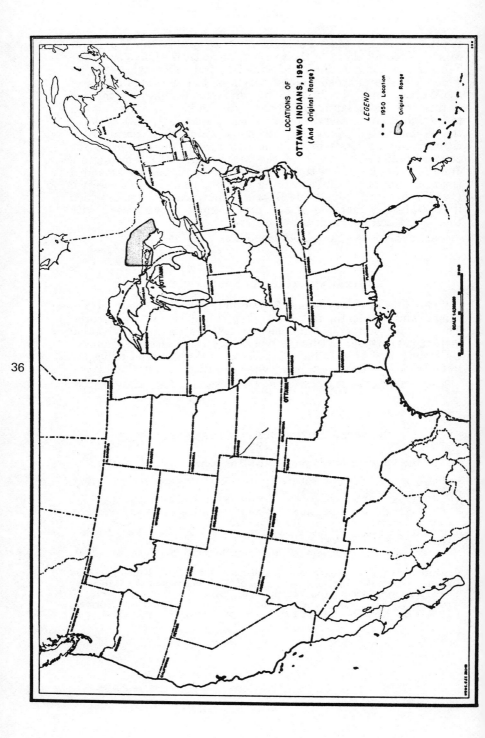

LOCATIONS OF
OTTAWA INDIANS, 1950
(And Original Range)

LEGEND

• • 1950 Location

⬡ Original Range

SCALE 1:6,500,000

"The two tribes (i. e., the Ottawa and Hurons) lived together until about 1700, when the Hurons removed to the vicinity of Detroit, while a portion of the Ottawa about this time seems to have obtained a foothold on the w. shore of L. Huron between Saginaw bay and Detroit, where the Potawatomi were probably in close union with them. Four divisions of the tribe were represented by a deputy at the treaty signed at Montreal in 1700. The band which had moved to the s. e. part of the lower Michigan peninsula returned to Mackinaw about 1706. Soon afterward the chief seat of a portion of the tribe was fixed at Waganakisi (L'arbre Croche), near the lower end of L. Michigan. From this point they spread in every direction, the majority settling along the e. shore of the lake, as far s. as St. Joseph r., while a few found their way into s. Wisconsin and n. e. Illinois. In the n. they shared Manitoulin id. and the n. shore of L. Huron with the Chippewa, and in the s. e. their villages alternated with those of their old allies the Hurons, now called Wyandot, along the shore of L. Erie from Detroit to the vicinity of Beaver cr. in Pennsylvania. They took an active part in all the Indian wars of that region up to the close of the War of 1812. The celebrated chief Pontiac was a member of this tribe, and Pontiac's war of 1763, waged chiefly around Detroit, is a prominent event in their history. A small part of the tribe which refused to submit to the authority of the United States removed to Canada, and together with some Chippewa and Potawatomi, is now settled on Walpole id. in L. St. Clair. The other Ottawa in Canadian territory are on Manitoulin and Cockburn ids. and the adjacent shore of L. Huron.

All of the Ottawa lands along the w. shore of L. Michigan were ceded by various treaties, ending with the Chicago treaty of Sept. 26, 1833, wherein they agreed to remove to lands granted them on Missouri r. in the n. e. corner of Kansas. Other bands, known as the Ottawa of Blanchard's fork of Great Auglaize r., and of Roche de Bouef on Maumee r., resided in Ohio, but these removed w. of the Mississippi about 1832 and are now living in Oklahoma. The great body, however, remained in the lower peninsula of Michigan, where they are still found scattered in a number of small villages and settlements.

*　　　*　　　*　　　*　　　*　　　*　　　*

"The Ottawa entered into numerous treaties with the United States as follows: Ft. McIntosh, Jan. 21, 1785; Ft. Harmar, Ohio, Jan. 9, 1789; Greenville, Ohio, Aug. 3, 1795; Ft. Industry, July 4, 1805; Detroit, Mich., Nov. 17, 1807; Brownstown, Mich., Nov. 25, 1808; Greenville, Ohio, July 22, 1814; Spring Wells, Mich., Sept. 8, 1815; St. Louis, Mo., Aug. 24, 1816; on the Miami, Ohio, Sept. 29, 1817; St. Mary's, Ohio, Sept. 17, 1818; L'Arbre Croche and Michilimackinac, Mich., July 6, 1820; Chicago, Ill., Aug. 29, 1821; Prairie du Chien, Wis., Aug. 19, 1825; Green Bay, Wis., Aug. 25, 1828; Prairie du Chien, Wis., July 29, 1829; Miami Bay, Ohio, Aug. 30, 1831; Maumee, Ohio, Feb. 18, 1833; Chicago, Ill.,

Sept. 26, 1833; Washington, D. C., Mar. 28, 1836; Council Bluffs, Iowa, June 5 and 17, 1846; Detroit, Mich., July 31, 1855, and Washington, D. C., June 24, 1862.

"The population of the different Ottawa groups is not known with certainty. In 1906 the Chippewa and Ottawa on Manitoulin and Cockburn ids., Canada, were 1,497, of whom about half were Ottawa; there were 197 Ottawa under the Seneca School, Okla., and in Michigan 5,587 scattered Chippewa and Ottawa in 1900, of whom about two-thirds are Ottawa. The total is therefore about 4,700."

Source: *Handbook of American Indians, Part 2*, pp. 170–171.

OTTAWA POPULATION

"The habitat of the Ottawa when first met by Europeans was along the northern shore of Georgian Bay in Canada. In consequence of Indian wars in the 17th century, the Ottawa moved west into Wisconsin, but later many of them moved back into the Lower Peninsula of Michigan. They are now mainly located in Emmet, Charlevoix, and Leelanau Counties, Michigan. A smaller band is located with the Quapaw in Ottawa County, Oklahoma. Another small band was enumerated in Vilas County, Wisconsin. The total number of the Ottawa enumerated in 1930 was 1,745, as compared with 2,717 in 1910. There were also 359 Indians with tribe not reported in Emmet, Charlevoix, and Leelanau Counties, who should probably be added to the number of Ottawa. There has, however, undoubtedly been a definite decrease in the Ottawa population in 20 years. The Ottawa, like the Chippewa and Menominee, are largely mixed with white blood."

Source: *The Indian Population of the United States and Alaska*, 1930, p. 38.

SELECTED REFERENCES ON THE OTTAWA
AS OF 1952

Andrews, H. A. Quapaw Subagency Ten Year Program Report. 1944. 31 pp. (Bureau of Indian Affairs).

Holst, J. H. A Survey of the Indian Groups in the State of Michigan. 1939. 26 pp. (Bureau of Indian Affairs).

Kinietz, W. V. The Indian Tribes of the Western Great Lakes. Occasional Contributions from the Museum of Anthropology of the University of Michigan, Vol. X, pp. 226–307, 1940.

Krzywicki, Ludwik. Primitive Society and its Vital Statistics. London, 1934. pp. 464–5.

Mooney, J., and Hewitt, J. N. B. Ottawa. Bulletin of the Bureau of American Ethnology, Vol. XXX, ii, pp. 167–72, 1910.

Murdock, Geo. P. Ethnographic Bibliography of North America, 1941. p. 104.

Perrot, N. Memoir on the Manners, Customs, and Religion of the Savages of North America. Indian Tribes of the Upper Mississippi Valley. Ed. E. H. Blair. Cleveland, Ohio. Vol. I, pp. 25–272, 1911.

Wright, Muriel H. A Guide to the Indian Tribes of Oklahoma. Norman, 1951. Ottawa, pp. 200–2.

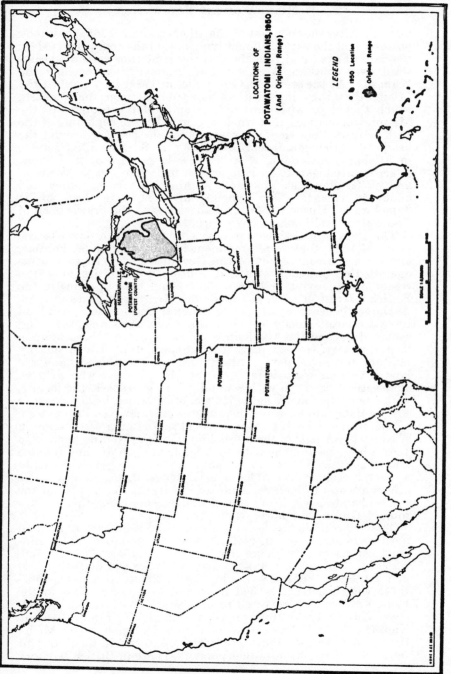

LOCATIONS OF
POTAWATOMI INDIANS, 1950
(And Original Range)

LEGEND
• 1950 Location
▓ Original Range

HANNAHVILLE
POTAWATOMI
(FOREST COUNTY)

POTAWATOMI

POTAWATOMI

SCALE 1:5,000,000

39

". . . After the conquest of the Illinois, about 1765, they took possession of the part of Illinois lying n. e. of the country seized by the Sauk, Foxes, and Kickapoo, at the same time spreading eastward over southern Michigan and gradually approaching the Wabash. At the treaty of Greenville, in 1795, they notified the Miami that they intended to move down upon the Wabash, which they soon afterward did, in spite of the protests of the Miami, who claimed that whole region. By the beginning of the 19th century they were in possession of the country around the head of L. Michigan, from Milwaukee r. in Wisconsin to Grand r. in Michigan, extending s. w. over a large part of n. Illinois, e. across Michigan to L. Erie, and s. in Indiana to the Wabash and as far down as Pine cr. Within this territory they had about 50 villages. The principal divisions were those of St Joseph r. and Huron r., Mich., Wabash r., and the Prairie band of Potawatomi in Illinois and Wisconsin.

The Potawatomi sided actively with the French down to the peace of 1763; they were prominent in the rising under Pontiac, and on the breaking out of the Revolution in 1775 took arms against the United States and continued hostilities until the treaty of Greenville in 1795. They again took up arms in the British interest in 1812, and made final treaties of peace in 1815. As the settlements rapidly pressed upon them, they sold their land by piece-meal, chiefly between the years 1836 and 1841 and removed beyond·the Mississippi. A large part of those residing in Indiana refused to leave their homes until driven out by military force. A part of them escaped into Canada and are now settled on Walpole id. in L. St Clair. Those who went w. were settled partly in w. Iowa and partly in Kansas, the former, with whom were many individuals of other tribes, being known as Prairie Potawatomi, while the others were known as Potawatomi of the Woods. In 1846 they were all united on a reservation in s. Kansas. A part of them was known as the Keotuc band. In 1861 a large part of the tribe took lands in severalty and became known as Citizen Potawatomi, but in 1868 they again removed to a tract in Indian Ter. (Oklahoma), where they now are. The others are still in Kansas, while a considerable body, part of the Prairie bands, is yet in Wisconsin, and another band, the Potawatomi of Huron, is in lower Michigan.

The tribe probably never greatly exceeded 3,000 souls, and most estimates place them far below that number. The principal estimates give them about 1,500 in 1765, 1,750 in 1766, 2,250 in 1778, 2,000 in 1783, 1,200 in 1795, 2,500 in 1812, 3,400 in 1820, and 1,800 in 1843. The last estimate does not include those who had recently fled to Canada. In 1908 those in the United States were reported to number 2,522 distributed as follows: Citizen Potawatomi in Oklahoma, 1,768; Prairie band in Kansas 676; and Potawatomi of Huron, in Calhoun co., Mich., 78. A few besides these are scattered through their ancient territory and at various other points. Those in British territory are all in the province of Ontario and number about 220, of whom 176 are living with Chippewa and Ottawa on Walpole id. in L. St. Clair, and the remainder (no longer officially reported) are divided between Caradoc and Riviere aux Sables, where they reside by permission of the Chippewa and Munsee.

The Potawatomi have participated in the following treaties with the United States: Ft Harmar, Ohio, Jan. 9, 1789; Greenville, Ohio, Aug. 3, 1795; Ft Wayne, Ind., June 7, 1803; Ft Industry, Ohio, July 4, 1805; Grouseland, Ind., Aug. 21, 1805; Detroit, Mich., Nov. 17, 1807; Brownstown, Mich., Nov. 25, 1808; Ft Wayne, Ind., Sept. 30, 1809; Greenville, Ohio, July 22, 1814; Portage des Sioux, Mo., July 18, 1815; Spring Wells, Mich., Sept. Sept. 8, 1815; St Louis, Mo., Aug. 24, 1816; Miami, Ohio, Sept. 29, 1817; St Mary's, Ohio, Oct. 2, 1818; Chicago, Ill., Aug. 29, 1821; Prairie du Chien, Wis., Aug. 19, 1825; Wabash, Ind., Oct. 16, 1826; St Joseph, Mich, Sept. 19, 1827; Green Bay, Wis., Aug. 25, 1828; St Joseph River, Mich., Sept. 20, 1828; Prairie du Chien, Wis., July 29, 1829; Camp Tippecanoe, Ind., Oct. 20, 1832; Tippecanoe River, Ind., Oct. 26 and 27, 1832; Chicago, Ill., Sept. 26, 1833; Lake Maxeeniekuekee, Ind., Dec. 4, 1834; Tippecanoe River, Ind., Dec. 10, 1834; Potawattomie Mills, Ind., Dec. 16, 1834; Potawattimie Mills, Ind., Dec. 16, 1834; Logansport, Ind., Dec. 17, 1834; Turkey Creek Prairie, Ind., March 26, 1836; Tippecanoe River, Ind., Mar. 29 and Apr. 11, 1836; Indian Agency, Ind., Apr. 22, 1836; Yellow River, Ind., Aug. 5, 1836; Chippewanaung, Ind., Sept. 20, 22, and 23, 1836; Washington, D. C., Feb. 11, 1837; Council Bluffs, Iowa, June 5 and 17, 1846; Kansas River, Kan., Nov. 15, 1861; Washington, D. C., Feb. 27, 1867."

Source: *Handbook of American Indians, Part 2*, pp. 290–291.

41

POTAWATOMI POPULATION

"This tribe, when first known, inhabited what is now the Lower Peninsula of Michigan. Later they moved to the Upper Peninsula and then gradually to the south and west to their present locations in Kansas and Oklahoma. The tribe is widely scattered. The greatest concentration is in Jackson County, Kansas, where 573 were enumerated. There were 347 Potawatomi in Pottawatomie County, Oklahoma, and 288 in Forest County, Wisconsin. Indians were returned as Potawatomi from 19 different states, from New York to California. The total number enumerated in 1930 was 1,854, as compared with 2,440 in 1910. Of the total number in 1930, 38.0 percent were returned as full blood. The largest proportion of full bloods was in the Wisconsin band, the Oklahoma and Kansas Potawatomi being mainly of mixed blood."

Source: *The Indian Population of the United States and Alaska*, 1930, p. 39.

SELECTED REFERENCES ON THE POTAWATOMI
AS OF 1952

Bruce, H. E. Potawatomi Agency Ten Year Program Report. 1944. 62 pp. (Bureau of Indian Affairs).

Cavell, C. Great Lakes Agency Ten Year Program Report. 1944. 257 pp. (Bureau of Indian Affairs).

Gilmore, Thomas R. Shawnee Agency Ten Year Program Report. 1944. 17 pp. (Bureau of Indian Affairs).

Great Lakes Ten Year Program Summary. 1944. 54 pp. (Bureau of Indian Affairs).

Kryzyicki, Ludwik. Primitive Society and Its Vital Statistics. London, 1934. pp. 467–9.

Mooney, J. and Hewitt, J. N B. Potawatomi. Bulletin of the Bureau of American Ethnology, Vol. XXX, ii, pp. 289–93, 1910.

Murdock, Geo. P. Ethnographical Bibliography of North America. 1941. p. 90.

Skinner, A. The Mascoutens or Prairie Potawatomi Indians. Bulletins of the Public Museum of the City of Milwaukee, Vol. VI. pp. 1–411, 1924–1927.

Tiedke, K. E. A Study of the Hannahville Indian Community, Menominee County, Michigan. 1949. 29 pp. (Bureau of Indian Affairs).

Wright, Muriel H. A Guide to the Indian Tribes of Oklahoma. Norman, 1951. Potawatomi pp. 214–18.

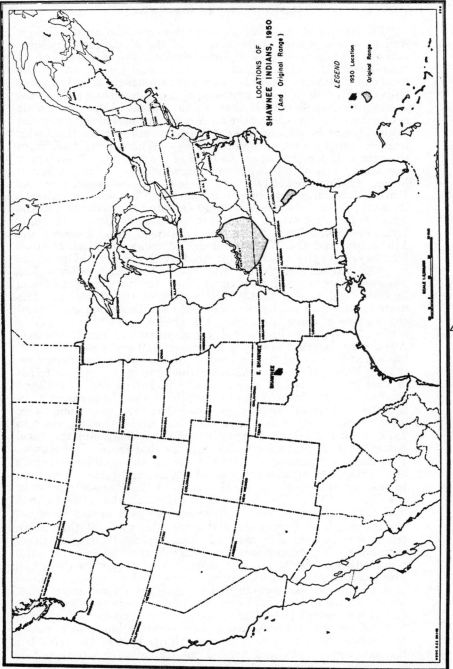

LOCATIONS OF
SHAWNEE INDIANS, 1950
(And Original Range)

LEGEND

1950 Location

Original Range

43

"The history of the Shawnee after their reunion on the Ohio is well known as a part of the history of the Northwest territory, and may be dismissed with brief notice. For a period of 40 years—from the beginning of the French and Indian war to the treaty of Greenville in 1795—they were almost constantly at war with the English or the Americans, and distinguished themselves as the most hostile tribe in that region. Most of the expeditions sent across the Ohio during the Revolutionary period were directed against the Shawnee, and most of the destruction on the Kentucky frontier was the work of the same tribe. When driven back from the Scioto they retreated to the head of the Miami r., from which the Miami had withdrawn some years before. After the Revolution, finding themselves left without the assistance of the British, large numbers joined the hostile Cherokee and Creeks in the S., while a considerable body accepted the invitation of the Spanish government in 1793 and settled, together with some Delawares, on a tract near Cape Girardeau, Mo., between the Mississippi and the Whitewater rs., in what was then Spanish territory. Wayne's victory, followed by the treaty of Greenville in 1795, put an end to the long war in the Ohio valley. The Shawnee were obliged to give up their territory on the Miami in Ohio, and retired to the headwaters of the Auglaize. The more hostile part of the tribe crossed the Mississippi and joined those living at Cape Girardeau. In 1798 a part of those in Ohio settled on White r. in Indiana, by invitation of the Delawares. A few years later a Shawnee medicine-man, Tenskwatawa (q. v.), known as The Prophet, the brother of the celebrated Tecumseh (q. v.), began to preach a new doctrine among the various trives of that region. His followers rapidly increased and established themselves in a village at the mouth of the Tippecanoe r. in Indiana. It soon became evident that his intentions were hostile, and a force was sent against him under Gen Harrison in 1821, resulting in the destruction of the village and the total defeat of the Indians in the decisive battle of Tippecanoe. Tecumseh was among the Creeks at the time, endeavoring to secure their aid against the United States, and returned in time to take command of the N. W. tribes in the British interest in the War of 1912. The Shawnee in Missouri who formed about half of the tribe, are said to have had no part in this struggle. By the death of Tecumseh in this war the spirit of the Indian tribes was broken, and most of them accepted terms of peace soon after. The Shawnee in Missouri sold their lands in 1825 and removed to a reservation in Kansas. A large part of them had previously gone to Texas, where they settled on the headwaters of the Sabine r., and remained there until driven out about 1839. The Shawnee of Ohio sold their remaining lands at Wapakoneta and Hog Creek in 1831, and joined those in Kansas. The mixed band of Seneca and Shawnee at Lewistown, Ohio, also removed to Kansas about the same time. A large part of the tribe left Kansas about 1845 and settled on Canadian r., Indian Ter.

44

(Oklahoma), where they are now known as Absentee Shawnee. In 1867 the Shawnee living with the Seneca removed also from Kansas to the Territory and are now known as Eastern Shawnee. In 1869, by intertribal agreement, the main body became incorporated with the Cherokee Nation in the present Oklahoma, where they are now residing. Those known as Black Bob's band refused to remove from Kansas with the others, but have since joined them."

Source: *Handbook of American Indians, Part 2,* pp. 535–536.

Shawnee Population

"This is the southernmost tribe of the Algonquian stock. The history of the tribe is very complicated and in some details uncertain. It is probable that they had moved from the north to the habitat on the Cumberland River where they were first known to Europeans. Later, a part of the tribe settled on the Savannah River. Some of the Shawnee were in Pennsylvania early in the nineteenth century, and others among the Creeks in the South. All were eventually pushed west across the Mississippi River. The greater part of the tribe is now in Oklahoma, mainly in Cleveland, Craig, Ottawa, and Pottawatomie Counties. The number enumerated as Shawnee in 1930 was 1,161, as compared with 1,338 in 1910. In 1930, 412 or 35.5 percent of the Shawnee were returned as full blood."

45

Source: *The Indian Population of the United States and Alaska, 1930,* p. 39.

Selected References on the Shawnee
AS OF 1952

Andrews, H. A. Quapaw Subagency Ten Year Program Report. 1944. 31 pp. (Bureau of Indian Affairs).

Gilmore, Thomas R. Shawnee Ten Year Program Report. 1944. 17 pp. (Bureau of Indian Affairs).

Krzywicki, Ludwik. Primitive Society and its Vital Statistics. London, 1934. pp. 472–4.

Mooney, J. Shawnee. Bulletin of the Bureau of American Ethnology, Vol. XXX, ii, pp. 530–8, 1910.

Murdock, Geo. P. Ethnographical Bibliography of North America. 1941. p. 91.

Spencer, J. The Shawnee Indians. Transactions of the Kansas State Historical Society, Vol. X, pp. 382–402, 1908.

Trowbridge, C. C. Shawnese Traditions. Ed. W. V. Kinietz and E. W. Voegelin. Occasional Contributions from the Museum of Anthropology of the University of Michigan, Vol. IX, pp. 1–71, 1939.

Wright, Muriel H. A Guide to the Indian Tribes of Oklahoma. Norman, 1951. Shawnee pp. 240–5.

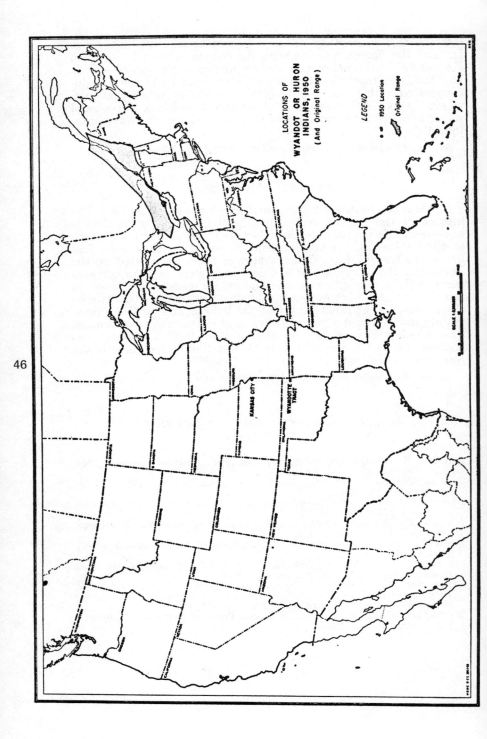

LOCATIONS OF
**WYANDOT OR HURON
INDIANS, 1950**
(And Original Range)

LEGEND

•• 1950 Location

Original Range

SCALE 1:41,000,000

"In 1745 a considerable party of Hurons under the leadership of the war chief Orontony, or Nicholas, removed from Detroit r. to the marsh lands of Sandusky bay. Orontony was a wily savage whose enmity was greatly to be feared, and he commanded men who formed an alert, unscrupulous, and powerful body. The French having provoked the bitter hatred of Nicholas, which was fomented by English agents, he conspired to destroy the French, not only at Detroit but at the upper posts, and by Aug., 1747, the "Iroquois of the West," the Hurons, Ottawa, Abnaki, Potawatomi, 'Ouabash,' Sauteurs, Missisauga, Foxes, Sioux, Sauk, 'Sarastau,' Loups, Shawnee, and Miami, indeed all the tribes of the middle W., with the exception of those of the Illinois country, had entered into the conspiracy; but through the treachery of a Huron woman the plot was revealed to a Jesuit priest, who communicated the information to Longueuil, the French commandant at Detroit, who in turn notified all the other French posts, and although a desultory warfare broke out, resulting in a number of murders, there was no concerted action. Orontony, finding that he had been deserted by his allies, and seeing the activity and determination of the French not to suffer English encroachments on what they called French territory, finally, in Apr., 1748, destroyed his villages and palisade at Sandusky, and removed, with 119 warriors and their families, to White r., Ind. Not long after he withdrew to the Illinois country on Ohio r., near the Indiana line, where he died in the autumn of 1748. The inflexible and determined conduct of Longueuil toward most of the conspiring tribes brought the coalition to an end by May, 1748.

"After this trouble the Hurons seem to have returned to Detroit and Sandusky, where they became known as Wyandots and gradually acquired a paramount influence in the Ohio valley and the lake region. They laid claim to the greater part of Ohio, and the settlement of the Shawnee and Delawares within that area was with their consent; they exercised the right to light the council fire at all intertribal councils, and although few in number they joined all the Indian movements in the Ohio valley and the lake region and supported the British against the Americans. After the peace of 1815 a large tract in Ohio and Michigan was confirmed to them, but they sold a large part of it in 1819, under treaty provisions, reserving a small portion near Upper Sandusky, Ohio, and a smaller area on Huron r., near Detroit, until 1842, when these tracts also were sold and the tribe removed to Wyandotte co., Kans. By the terms of the treaty of 1855 they were declared to be citizens, but by the treaty of 1867 their tribal organization was restored and they were placed on a small tract, still occupied by them, in the n. e. corner of Oklahoma."

Source: *Handbook of American Indians, Part 1*, pp. 589–590.

47

"Wyandot: Early in the seventeenth century, the Huron Confederacy was one of the largest and most powerful tribal groups on the North American continent. Champlain estimated their population in 1615 as 30,000, and Hewitt gives a more conservative estimate of 20,000 in 1648. In this latter year, desperate warfare began between the Huron and the Iroquois confederacies, and after two years the Huron power was completely destroyed. The survivors were driven from their habitat in the present Province of Ontario and most of them were adopted into other tribes. A small band fled to northern Michigan and then to Wisconsin, where they were associated with the Potawatomi and the Ottawa. Many years later, they returned eastward and settled around the western end of Lake Erie where they became known as Wyandot. In 1842 they sold the last of their lands in Ohio and moved to Kansas, and in 1867 were finally located in Ottawa County, Oklahoma. The number enumerated in 1930 was 353, exactly the same number as enumerated in 1910. Practically all of these were of mixed blood. Even in 1910, 242, or 68.6 percent were returned as 'more than half white' ".

Source: *The Indian Population of the United States and Alaska*, 1930, p. 42.

SELECTED REFERENCES ON THE HURON OR WYANDOTTE
AS OF 1952

48 (Including the Ataronchronon, Huron Proper, Tionontati or Tobacco, Wenrohonronon, and Wyandot)

Andrews, H. A. Quapaw Subagency Ten Year Program Report. 1944. 31 pp. (Bureau of Indian Affairs.)
Brebeuf, J. de. Relation of the Hurons. 1636. The Jesuit Relations and allied Documents. Ed. R. G. Thwaites, Vol. X, pp. 124–137. Cleveland, 1897.
Kinietz, W. V. The Indian Tribes of the Western Great Lakes. Occasional Contributions from the Museum of Anthropology of the University of Michigan, Vol. X, pp. 1–160, 1940.
Krzywicki, Ludwik. Primitive Society and its Vital Statistics. London, 1934.
Murdock, Geo. P. Ethnographic Bibliography of North America. 1941. P. 109.
Sagard-Theodat, G. The Long Voyage to the Country of the Hurons. Ed. G. M. Wrong. Publications of the Champlain Society, Toronto, Vol. XXV, pp. 1–411, 1939.
Wright, Muriel H. A Guide to the Indian Tribes of Oklahoma. Norman, 1951. Wyandot, pp. 261–4.

Illinois

An Algonquian Confederacy formerly occupying southern Wisconsin and northern Illinois and parts of Iowa and Missouri. It comprised the Cahokia, Kaskaskia, Peoria and others. In 1833 the surviving Kaskaskia and Peoria sold their lands in Illinois and removed west to the Mississippi River to Kansas. These groups are now located in the northeastern corner of Oklahoma.

Selected References on the Illinois
AS OF 1952

(Including the Cahokia, Kaskaskia, Mascouten, Michigamea, Moingwena, Peoria and Tamaroa)

Andrews, H. A. Quapaw Subagency Ten Year Program Report. 1944. 31 pp. (Bureau of Indian Affairs).

Beckwith, H. W. The Illinois and Indiana Indians. Fergus Historical Series, Chicago, Vol. XXVII, pp. 99–106, 1884.

Krzywicki, Ludwik. Primitive Society and its Vital Statistics. London, 1934. Illinois pp. 530–2, Cahokia pp. 394–5 and 531–2, Kaskaskia pp. 405–6 and 530–2, Mascouten pp. 413–15, Michigamea p. 336, Peoria pp. 424–5, and 550–2, Tamaroa pp. 434–5.

Mooney, J. and Thomas, C. Illinois. Bulletin of the Bureau of American Ethnology, Vol. XXX, i, pp. 597–9, 1907.

Murdock, Geo. P. Ethnographic Bibliography of North America. 941. p. 88.

Wright, Muriel H. A Guide to the Indian Tribes of Oklahoma. Norman, 1951. Cahokia pp. 53–4, Illinois pp. 157–8, Kaskaskia p. 160, Michigamea p. 183, Moingwena p. 186, Peoria pp. 207–9, Piankashaw pp. 209–10.

50

BEFORE THE INDIAN CLAIMS COMMISSION

51

Docket Nos. 13-E et al.

An Ethnohistorical Report on the Indian Use and Occupancy of
Royce Area 53, which was ceded "at fort Industry, on the Miami
of the lake" by the "Wyandot, Ottawa, Chippewa, Munsee, and
Delaware, Shawanee, and Pattawatamy nations" to the Connecticut
Land Company and the proprietors of the half million acres of
land lying south of lake Erie, called Sufferers' Land, in a
conveyance bearing date of July 4, 1805, and on the Indian Use
and Occupancy of Royce Area 54, which was ceded to the United
States by the "Wyandot, Ottawa, Chipawa, Munsee and Delaware,
Shawanee, and Pottawatima nations" under the Treaty held "at
Fort Industry, on the Miami of the lake," on July 4, 1805.

51

By

Dr. Erminie Wheeler-Voegelin

Treaty of July 4, 1805 (7 Stat. 87)
Proclaimed April 24, 1806

CONTENTS

53

54

LIST OF DEFENDANT'S EXHIBITS USED IN THIS REPORT

Figures

Foreword

The Great Lakes-Ohio Valley Research Project of Indiana University
was requested by the Honorable Perry W. Morton, Assistant Attorney General, under a directive of February 24, 1956, to prepare a Report dealing with aboriginal use and occupancy of the lands comprising Royce Areas
53 and 54, Ohio 1. The present Report has been prepared in consonance
with Mr. Morton's directive.

Areas Involved. The two contiguous tracts of land in northeastern
Ohio known as Royce Areas 53 and 54, Ohio 1, which are involved, respectively, in (1) a conveyance bearing date of July 4, 1805, made by the
"Wyandot, Ottawa, Chippewa, Munsee, and Delaware, Shawanee, and Pattawatamy nations" to the Connecticut Land Company and to "the proprietors of
the half million acres of land lying south of lake Erie, called Sufferers'
Land," at Fort Industry on the "Miami of the lake [present Maumee River]"[1]
and (2) in the Treaty of July 4, 1805, made between the United States
and the "Wyandot, Ottawa, Chipawa, Munsee and Delaware, Shawanee, and
Pottawatima nations" at Fort Industry on the "Miami of the lake" (7 Stat.
87), are located entirely within the northeastern quarter of the present
State of Ohio. The boundaries of Royce Areas 53 and 54 are shown on the
End Pocket Map of this Report.

55

History of Areas 53 and 54. From ca. 1640 until 1737 little is
known concerning Indian use and/or occupancy of Royce Areas 53 and 54.
Early French maps and brief accounts by the few Europeans who travelled
along the "south shore of Lake Erie" during this period yield meager,

---

1. American State Papers, Class II, vol. 1, p. 696; Dft. Ex. A-252.

albeit in a few instances important, information. However, the detailed history of native use and occupancy of Area 53 only begins in 1737, and that of Area 54 even later--in 1748.

Sovereignty over the lands lying south of Lake Erie, including Royce Areas 53 and 54 was, from around the beginning of the 18th century until 1763, in dispute between France and England. At the end of the French and Indian War sovereignty of the entire Ohio Valley-Great Lakes region passed to Great Britain by the Treaty of Paris of 1763. Control of the Ohio Valley lands had been assumed by Great Britain in 1760, after the capitulation of Quebec (Sept. 18, 1759) and Montreal (Sept. 8, 1760).

British sovereignty over Areas 53 and 54 lasted from 1763 to July 4, 1776. On this latter date sovereignty of the United States became legally attached to the lands constituting present Royce Area 54. Sovereignty over Royce Area 53, which was part of the Connecticut Western Reserve, was however, claimed by the State of Connecticut until May, 1800, when Connecticut renounced jurisdiction over the Western Reserve to the United States, but excepted from the renunciation the right, title and interest to the soil of said Reserve.

The President of the United States by proclamation issued March 2, 1801, released and conveyed to the Governor of the State of Connecticut, and his successors, for the use and benefit of persons holding and claiming under the State of Connecticut all the right, title, interest and estate of the United States in and to the soil of the "Western Reserve," including Royce Area 53.

Organization of the Report. Data on use and occupancy of Areas 53 and 54 are presented in chronological sequence in our Report; the total

time period covered is from 1640 to April 24, 1806. The history of
native use and occupancy falls naturally into several different periods
which we have used as major breaking points for the several chapters of
the Report. The first chapter deals with use and occupancy during the
very early or protohistoric period (1640-1736); the second chapter with
native use and occupancy during the period when the French and the
British were actively contending for control of the lands south of Lake
Erie (1737-1759). The third chapter deals with the period of British
control and subsequent sovereignty over these lands (1760-1776); the last
two chapters deal with use and occupancy within the period of American
sovereignty; Chapter IV covers the years of Indian-American hostilities
(1777-1795), and Chapter V covers the subsequent peaceful period (1796-
April 24, 1806). Each of the five chapters carries its own summary and
conclusions.

57

A large end-pocket map (Fig. 7) of Areas 53 and 54 and environs,
showing all known native villages, camps and hunting locations existent
during the years 1737-1806 which can be either pinpointed or generally
located and dated, accompanies the Report. In case the location is only
generally known it is legended on the Map with a question mark. Many
references to Indian camps, hunting grounds, and even villages which are
contained in the text of the Report, and which apparently relate to Areas
53 and 54, were found to be too indefinite to legend, even questionably;
hence the Report itself contains more data than is summarized on the Map.
If the dates for use of legended sites, or the identity of the group(s)
using them are questionable, this is also indicated on the map.

Key. Throughout the Report all bracketed remarks in quoted material
are ours, except for those which are explicitly credited to the author

or editor of the material quoted. In the running text, parenthetical remarks are ours.

All citations to pages in the Jesuit Relations refer only to odd-numbered pages. The English translation of the Relations is carried on the odd-numbered pages, the French text on the even-numbered pages. Reproduction of the English translation, only, is offered in exhibit.

Defendant's exhibits are referred to by last name of author or editor, short title, volume, page(s) and exhibit number, in the foot-notes. A complete list of all exhibits cited, with author's full name, full title of the work, etc., and notation of all pages offered in exhibit, is to be found at the end of the Report.

Conversion of 17th- and 18th century French leagues to English statute miles is based on the ratio of 1 league to 2.5 miles.

Conversion of population figures given in terms of "warriors" is based on the ratio of 1 warrior to 3 other persons.

The yearly economic round followed by the Great Lakes-Ohio Valley Indians who used and/or occupied Areas 53 and 54 is described in detail in several contemporary accounts, which are quoted or summarized on pp. 67-76, 82-83, and 93-94 of the Report.

Chapter 1. The Early Period: 1640-1736

1. **Earliest Known Occupancy of Royce Areas 53 and 54:**

1640-1660. The earliest known-occupants of present Royce Areas 53 and
54 were apparently the Erieehrononp (Eries) or the "Nation of the Cat,"
a now-extinct Iroquoian-speaking people[1] who are mentioned in a French
Jesuit relation of 1641 as living toward the southwestern part of Lake
Erie.[2] In another early Jesuit account (1648) Father Paul Ragueneau,
Superior of the Huron Mission, locates the Eries a little more definitely:

> This Lake, called Erié, was formerly inhabited
> on its Southern shores by certain tribes whom we
> call the Nation of the Cat; they have been com-
> pelled to retire far inland to escape their enemies,
> who are farther to the West. These people of the
> Cat Nation have a number of stationary villages, for
> they till the soil, and speak the same language as
> our Hurons.[3]

59

In the 1650's the Five Nations Iroquois[4] began a war against

---

1. Hodge, ed., Handbook, pt. 1, pp. 430-432, esp. p. 431; Dft. Ex.
A-1. Lahontan, New Voyages, vol. 2, pp. 732-733; Dft. Ex. A- 9.
Thwaites, ed., Jesuit Relations, vol. 33, p. 63; Dft. Ex. A-4.

2. Thwaites, ed., Jesuit Relations, vol. 21, pp. 187, 189, 191;
Dft. Ex. A-3.

3. Thwaites, ed., Jesuit Relations, vol. 33, p. 63; Dft. Ex. A-4.

4. The Five Nations Iroquois had their villages during the 17th
century in the upper Mohawk Valley-Finger Lakes region of New York. The
"Five Nations" were, severally, progressing from east to west, the
Mohawks, Oneidas, Onondagas, Cayugas, and Senecas. After the Tuscaroras,
a southern Iroquoian-speaking people, joined the Five Nations during the
second decade of the 18th century, the "Five Nations" became known as the
"Six Nations" or "Six Nations Iroquois" (Colden, History, pp. 17-20; Dft.
Ex. A-56. O'Callaghan, ed., Documents, vol. 3, pp. 250-252; Dft. Ex.
A-41. Thwaites, ed., Jesuit Relations, vol. 49, pp. 257, 259; Dft. Ex.
A-169).

(cont'd on p. 2.)

the Eries.[5] Consequently no Jesuit mission was established among the
latter, nor did any missionaries or other Europeans ever visit any of
the Erie villages, although some of the Fathers talked to Erie captives among the Five Nations. In 1654 the Eries reputedly numbered
some three or four thousand warriors, or around 12,000-16,000 souls.[6]
This was at the beginning of the Iroquois-Erie war, when the Eries
were being attacked by, and were also attacking, the Onondagas and
other Five Nations Iroquois. Some six years later, by 1660, the Eries
were among the "different tribes whom they [Iroquois] have conquered,"
according to the Jesuit Father Jerome Lalemant. Five Nations Iroquois
policy, according to Lalemant, was to incorporate conquered peoples
into the Iroquois population, and "the Riquehronnons [Eries] who are

---

4. (continued from page 1.) In 1677 the Five Nations Iroquois numbered "2,150 fighting men" or approximately 8,800 souls (Green and
Harrington, American Population, p. 194; Dft. Ex. A-17).
      The Five Nations Iroquois speak Iroquoian dialects which are,
or were, mutually intelligible with the Huron and Erie dialects of
Iroquois. Surrounding the various Iroquoian-speaking groups during
the 17th, 18th and early 19th centuries were other groups of Algonquian-speaking Indians, such as the Ottawas, Chippewas, Algonkins,
Delawares, Abnakis, Hudson River Indians, Shawnees, etc., whose languages are entirely different from the Iroquoian languages. See
Lahontan, New Voyages, vol. 1, pp. 46-47. 297; Dft. Ex. A-8. Lahontan,
New Voyages, vol. 2, pp. 732-733: Dft. Ex. A-9. O'Callaghan, ed.,
Documents, vol. 7, p. 958; Dft. Ex. A-112. Thwaites, ed., Jesuit Relations, vol. 21, p. 39; Dft. Ex. A-3. Thwaites, ed., Jesuit Relations,
vol. 41, p. 221; Dft. Ex. 168. Thwaites, ed., Jesuit Relations, vol.
18, pp. 233, 235; Dft. Ex. A-170. Thwaites, ed., Jesuit Relations,
vol. 67, pp. 145, 147; Dft. Ex. 171. Thwaites, ed., Jesuit Relations,
vol. 63, pp. 147, 149; Dft. Ex. 172.

5. Thwaites, ed., Jesuit Relations, vol. 42, pp. 49, 53, 57, 85,
87, 97, 129, 137, 177, 179, 181, 183, 191, 201; Dft. Ex. A-5.

6. Thwaites, ed., Jesuit Relations, vol. 42, pp. 111, 113; Dft.
Ex. A-5. This figure may be too high; in another account the number of
Eries in 1654 is given as 2,000-3,000 warriors (Thwaites, ed., Jesuit
Relations, vol. 42, p. 179; Dft. Ex. A-5).

the Cat Nation," were no exception.[7]

This meant that by 1660 the country embracing present Royce Areas 53 and 54 was probably devoid of native inhabitants. Those Eries who had lived in, or used these Areas, and who had escaped death during the Iroquois-Erie war had by 1660 been taken eastward to the Finger Lakes region of New York, to increase the population of Five Nations Iroquois towns.

2. <u>Use and Occupancy of Areas 53 and 54, 1661-1700</u>. No Five Nations Iroquois settlements existed in present Area 53 and/or Area 54 between the end of the Erie-Iroquois war and 1700. Several 17th-century maps, not drawn to scale and badly distorted as all early maps are, but having the virtue of being based on knowledge gained by French explorers who were actually in the Lake Erie region during the last quarter of the 17th century, attest to the lack of any late 17th-century re-settlement of Royce Areas 53 and 54 after the extinction of the Eries. So do some early accounts.

61

The first map, inserted in/work published in 1698 but based on earlier knowledge, is by Father Louis Hennepin,[8] Recollect chaplain and associate of the great French explorer, René-Robert Cavelier, Sieur de La Salle, on La Salle's 1678-1679 Great Lakes expedition. Hennepin, both on his map and in his text, designates Lake Erie as "Lake Erie or

---

7. Thwaites, ed., Jesuit Relations, vol. 45, pp. 205, 207; Dft. Ex. A-6. Incorporation of captives by the Five Nations Iroquois is also noted by a Dutch author writing in 1654 about the Iroquois as of 1642-1651 (Van der Donck, Description, p. 211; Dft. Ex. A-64).

8. Hennepin, A Map of a Large Country; Dft. Ex. A-47.

of the Cat"[9] and locates the "Erieckronois [Eries]" between two unnamed
rivers near the western end of the Lake.

A second map, drawn in 1684 by Jean Baptiste Louis Franquelin,
French cartographer and at that time draughtsman for La Salle, was
made to show La Salle's voyages during the years 1681-1683.[10] This
map has, on the southwestern shore of "Lac Erie," a village of "Antouaronons N Détruite [nation destroyed]." The anthropologist J. N. B. Hewitt,
in the Handbook of American Indians, identifies "Antouoronons" as
Senecas,[11] but this identification is clearly not applicable to the
"Antouaronons" legended on Franquelin's map, since the Senecas were by
no means a "nation destroyed" in 1684. Who the "Antouaronons" were we
do not know; but in 1684 they were, at any rate, extinct. No other
groups are shown on the Franquelin map of 1684 as occupying, or having
occupied the lands south of the western half of Lake Erie.

A third map is one which, although dated 1692, actually relates
to the years 1679-1683.[12] This map is by Father Christian Le Clercq, a
Recollect missionary who from 1675 to 1680 was stationed at Isle Percée

---

9. Hennepin states that the name "Erie" derives from the Huron
name "Erige, or Erike; that is to say the Lake of the Cat. The inhabitants of Canada have softned that Word, and call it Erie..."
(Hennepin, A New Discovery, vol. 1, p. 106; Dft. Ex. A-7).

10. Franquelin, Carte de la Louisiane; Dft. Ex. A-11. Tucker,
Indian Villages, p. 4; Dft. Ex. A-10.

11. Hodge, ed., Handbook, pt. 2, p. 507; Dft. Ex. A-2. See also
Hodge, ed., Handbook, pt. 2, 1026; Dft. Ex. A-2.

12. Le Clercq, Carte Generalle de la Nouvelle France; Dft. Ex.
A-43.

and Gaspé south of the mouth of the St. Lawrence River.[13] Le Clercq's
map is included in his book, First Establishment of the Faith in the
New World, which is a compendium containing in its third part an account
of La Salle's voyages of 1679-1683.[14] Presumably Le Clercq based the
lower Great Lakes section of his map on the 1679-1683 La Salle material,
since Le Clercq himself was never in the interior of New France.

On Le Clercq's map the lands south of the western third of Lake
Erie, which would include present Royce Areas 53 and 54, bear no legend,
thus indicating to us that they were unoccupied and unused, ca. 1679-
1683.

All three maps, Hennepin's, Franquelin's, and Le Clercq's, depict
the Five Nations Iroquois as occupying the lands east of Royce Areas 53
and 54. On Hennepin's map[15] the legend, "Great Villages of the
Iroquois" begins in the lands south of the eastern third of Lake Erie
and extends eastward to the Hudson River. On the Franquelin map,[16]
which is probably the most reliable of the three,[17] the legend "Pays des
Iroquois [Country of the Iroquois]" starts in the present Ontario
Peninsula north of Lake Erie, and extends south of Lake Ontario and
eastward into present eastern New York. On Le Clercq's map, which is

---

13. Shea, Discovery and Exploration, p. 78; Dft. Ex. A-44.

14. Shea, Discovery and Exploration, pp. 79-82; Dft. Ex. A-44.

15. Dft. Ex. A-47.

16. Dft. Ex. A-11.

17. Franquelin not only had direct contact with La Salle, but was
also a professional cartographer. See Tucker, Indian Villages, p. 4;
Dft. Ex. A-10.

the least reliable,[18] the legend, "pais des Iroquois [country of the Iroquois]" begins south of Lake Erie, at what could be approximately the eastern border of present Royce Areas 53 and 54, and extends eastward south of Lake Ontario into present eastern New York.

No primary 17th-century Dutch or English accounts or maps of the Lake Erie country, based on actual exploration of the region, exist to our knowledge. One crude English map, made by a William Hack in Wapping, England in 1684, includes Lake Erie, but obviously the data on the map derive from early French maps.[19]

---

18. Dft. Ex. A-43. Strictly speaking, the Le Clercq map is a secondary rather than a primary source, although it was made at an early date.

19. Hack, Novvelle France; Dft. Ex. A-58. In 1653 Adriaen Van der Donck, A Dutch lawyer at Beverwyck (Albany, New York) from 1642 to 1651, wrote complacently that "Many of our Netherlanders have been far into the country, more than seventy or eighty miles from the river [Hudson] and seashore" (Van der Donck, Description, pp. 126, 128, 138, 221; Dft. Ex. A-64. Emphasis ours). Eighty miles westward from present-day Albany is a little better than half the distance to the eastern edge of the Finger Lakes country of New York, where most of the Five Nations lived.

In 1687 Thomas Dongan, governor of New York, 1682-1688, wrote that until he came to New York in 1683 "no man of our Governm^t ever went beyond the Sinicaes [Senecas'] Country" (O'Callaghan, ed., Documents, vol. 3, p. 395; Dft. Ex. A-41.) Dongan evidently had reference to one Wentworth Greenhalgh's "tour" as far west as the Seneca towns in 1677 (O'Callaghan, ed., Documents, vol. 3, pp. 250-252; Dft. Ex. A-41), and to some New York traders' abortive effort to trade with the Ottawas at Michilimackinac in 1686 and 1687. This latter attempt was stopped by the French (O'Callaghan, ed., Documents, vol. 3, p. 395 and fn. 1; Dft. Ex. A-41. O'Callaghan, ed., Documents, vol. 5, p. 731; Dft. Ex. A-38). Significantly, no English accounts of the country between New York and Mackinac, or maps, resulted from the 1686-1687 venture, as far as we know.

As late as 1700, some 36 years after the English first conquered New York from the Dutch, the Earl of Bellomont, governor of New York, wrote to the Lords of Trade in England concerning the urgent need for English maps to replace French maps of the country. "It were as good a work as your Lordships could do, to send over a very skillfull surveyor to make correct maps of all these plantations [provinces]," Bellomont

(cont'd on p. 7.)

Why Royce Areas 53 and 54 were unoccupied in the 1680's is indicated in a work published in 1703 by a French officer, Louis-Armand de
Lom d'Arce, Baron de Lahontan, who saw much of the Lakes Ontario-Erie-
Huron region between 1683 and 1692.[20] Whatever Lahontan's faults as an
author may have been[21] he was an educated recorder of what he himself
observed, and knew the Lake Erie country well, having travelled twice
along the south shore of that Lake, as well as along its north shore.[22]
Lahontan's book, New Voyages to North-America, contains two maps, "A
General Map of New France"[23] and "A Map of the Great Lakes Region."[24]

On his "General Map" Lahontan legends the Eries as west of Areas
53 and 54, near the extreme western end of "Errie or Conti Lake,"[25] and
in his written account Lahontan remarks that the "Errieronons [Eries]"

---

19. (continued from page 6.) suggested (O'Callaghan, ed., Documents,
vol. 4, p. 796; Dft. Ex. 16).
    By 1701 New York had, we know, one Samuel Clowes as Surveyor,
since there is a map made by Clowes in that year (Dft. Ex. A-23). The
most casual inspection of this map demonstrates how little the English
of New York knew even of the eastern Great Lakes region, and how ignorant
they were of the rest of the Great Lakes country at the opening of the
18th century. Yet this 1701 map, which is discussed in some detail later
in this chapter, was "a draught the most accurate" Lieutenant Governor
John Nanfan to New York "had been able to procure" of the Great Lakes
region (O'Callaghan, ed., Documents, vol. 4, p. 888; Dft. Ex. 16).

20. Lahontan, New Voyages, vol. 1, pp. x-xxix, 25, 264, Dft. Ex.
A-8.   135-149, 152-164,

21. Lahontan, New voyages, vol. 1, pp. xxxvi-xlix; Dft. Ex. A-8.
            139, 155, 163-164;

22. Lahontan, New Voyages, vol. 1, pp.
Dft. Ex. A-8.

23. Dft. Ex. A-48.

24. Dft. Ex. A-49.

25. Dft. Ex. A-48. The Contis represented the cadet, or younger
branch of the House of Bourbon.

were an Iroquoian-speaking people who had been "totally destroy'd" by
the Five Nations Iroquois in former times.[26] No still-existent Indian
groups are indicated as living on the south side of Lake Erie, on
either of Lahontan's maps or in his text.[27] Of interest, however, and
bearing directly on native use of present Area 53 and also possibly
Area 54 in the 1680-1690's is a line drawn on Lahontan's General Map,
extending from Lake Champlain on the northeastern New York-Vermont
border, westward along the southern shore of Lake Erie and continuing
to the Mississippi River. This line is legended as follows:

> This faint line represents ye way that ye
> Ilinese [Illinois Indians] march thro a vast
> tract of ground to make War against ye
> Iroquese; The same being ye passage of ye
> Iroquese in their incursions upon ye other
> Savages, as far as the River Missisipi.[28]

In his text, Lahontan elaborates on the fact that a war road,
used by opposing Indian groups, ran directly across present Royce Area
53, and therefore made this region unsafe for any native groups to
occupy. He writes:

> The Lake Errié is justly dignified with the
> illustrious name of Conti; for assuredly 'tis
> the finest Lake upon Earth...its Banks are
> deck'd with Oak-Trees, Elms, Chesnut-Trees,
> Walnut-Trees, Apple-Trees, Plum-Trees, and
> Vines which bear their fine clusters up to the
> very top of the Trees, upon a sort of ground
> that lies as smooth as one's Hand...I cannot

66

---

26. Lahontan, New Voyages, vol. 1, p. 320; Dft. Ex. A-8.
Lahontan, New Voyages, vol. 2, p. 733; Dft. Ex. A-9.

27. See Lahontan, A General Map; Dft. Ex. A-48; Lahontan, Map of
the Great Lakes; Dft. Ex. A-51; Lahontan, New Voyages, vol. 1, pp. 340-
341; Dft. Ex. A-8.

28. Lahontan, A General Map; Dft. Ex. A-48.

express what vast quantities of Deer and Turkeys
are to be found in these Woods, and in the vast
Meads that lye upon the South side of the Lake...
The Banks of this Lake are commonly frequented
by none but Warriours, whether the Iroquese, the
Ilinese [Illinois], the Oumamis [Miamis], etc.
and 'tis very dangerous to stop there. By this
means it comes to pass, that the Stags, Roe-
Bucks and Turkeys, run in great Bodies up and
down the shoar, all round the Lake...[29]

Each one of the Five Nations Iroquois is specifically located by

Lahontan on both his maps. The villages of all five groups are shown in

the region of the upper Mohawk Valley-Finger Lakes country in present

----

29. Lahontan, New Voyages, vol. 1, pp. 319-320; Dft. Ex. A-8.
    The Illinois Indians, who in the 1680's were living on the
upper Illinois River, and the Miamis, who were on the St. Joseph River
of Lake Michigan, were two of the western Indian groups who in the 1670's
and early 1680's had been subjected to severe Iroquois attacks. In one
Iroquois war expedition alone, in 1680, Iroquois warriors killed or
captured some 700 Illinois Indians (English Translation of Margry, vol. 5,
pp. 245-246; Dft. Ex. A- 61).
    In the latter part of the 17th century, however, the western
Indians began to obtain guns (which the Mohawks had had as early as 1639;
O'Callaghan, ed., Documents, vol. 1, pp. 150, 182; Dft. Ex. A-65; Van
der Donck, Description, p. 211; Dft. Ex. A-64; Megalopensis, Short
Sketch, pp. 153, 157; Dft. Ex. A-63) and help from the French and thus
were able, as Lahontan notes, to start repaying the Iroquois in kind.
    Accounts of late 17th-century retaliatory attacks by French-
allied western Indians against the Iroquois are numerous, but too removed
from our immediate interest to cite in extenso. A few references will
suffice:
    In the summer of 1687 Jacques Réné de Brisay, Marquis de
Denonville, governor of Canada, led a large expedition in which 300
Ottawa, Huron, and Illinois Indians participated, against the Senecas
(O'Callaghan, ed., Documents, vol. 9, pp. 337-338; Dft. Ex. A-22).
    In 1691 Louis de Buade, Comte de Frontenac, governor of
Canada, outlined plans to "set all [the western Indians] in motion"
against the Iroquois (English Translation of Margry, vol. 5, pp. 245-
246; Dft. Ex. A-61).
    By 1694 one western group alone--the Illinois Indians--re-
ported that by exact count they had killed or captured 445 Iroquois between 1687 and 1694 (English Translation of Margry, vol. 4, pp. 100-101,
fn. 1; Dft. Ex. A-60).
    The toll taken on the Iroquois between 1680 and 1700 by the
western Indians was so great that in the latter year the Earl of Bellomont, governor of New York, at "a Private Conference with Two of the

(cont'd on p. 10.)

67

central New York.[30] The country north of Lake Erie and east of Lake
Huron, now known as the Ontario Peninsula, is legended several times
as being the "Beaver hunting [country] of ye Iroquese" on Lahontan's
General Map, but no such legend appears for the lands south of Lake
Erie, which include present Royce Areas 53 and 54. Because of the
existence of the war road, which is mapped along the south side of
Lake Erie, the southern country was too dangerous "to stop there,"
although by virtue of non-use it abounded in game.

(fn. 29, cont'd.) principal Sachems of each of the 5 Nations warned
these chiefs:

> You must needs be sensible that the
> Dowagenhaws [Chippewas: Hodge, ed., Hand-
> book, pt. 2, p. 1051; Dft. Ex. A-2], Twich-
> twees [Miamis: Hodge, ed., Handbook, pt. 2,
> p. 1164; Dft. Ex. A-2], Ottowawas [Ottawas]
> & Diondedees [Tionontatis, a division of
> the Hurons: Hodge, ed., Handbook, pt. 2,
> pp. 755-756; Dft. Ex. A-2] and the other
> Remote Indians are vastly more numerous than
> you 5 Nations, and that by their continual
> Warring upon you they will in a few years
> totally destroy you...(Wraxall, Abridgment,
> pp. 33-34; Dft. Ex. A-18).

Bellomont's remarks as to comparative numbers of the Five Nations
Iroquois and the western Indians are supported by population figures
for these groups, given in Green and Harrington, American Population,
pp. 194-195; Dft. Ex. A-17.

30. Lahontan, A General Map; Dft. Ex. A-48. Lahontan, A Map of
the Great Lakes; Dft. Ex. A-49.
Lahontan designates the five Iroquois groups by the French names
for them, as follows: the "Agnis" (Mohawks; see Hodge, ed., Handbook,
pt. 2, p. 1022; Dft. Ex. A-2); the "Onnontagues" (Onondagas; Hodge, ed.,
Handbook, pt. 2, p. 1109; Dft. Ex. A-2); the "Goyogoans" (Cayugas;
Hodge, ed., Handbook, pt. 2, p. 1057; Dft. Ex. A-2); and the "Tsonontouans"
(Senecas; Hodge, ed., Handbook, pt. 2, p. 1162; Dft. Ex. A-2).

The region south of Lake Erie evidently continued to be un-
populated and unused after Lahontan's time; this is evident from a 1697
map by a French officer, Louis de la Porte Louvigny, who was stationed
at Michilimackinac (present Mackinac) in 1690-1694. Louvigny's map is
based primarily on knowledge gained at Michilimackinac, and on information obtained from Indians, coureurs de bois, and other contemporary
sources.[31] The locations of several native groups are noted on the
Louvigny map, but no peoples or settlements are indicated within the
region between Lake Erie and the Ohio River. The Iroquois are legended
as "cinq villages des Iroquois [five villages of Iroquois]," and the
villages themselves are shown in present central New York on rivers
flowing into the south side of Lake Ontario. A heavy circle, the only
one of its kind on the Louvigny map, is drawn around the Iroquois
villages and was apparently intended to indicate the Iroquois domain as
of the 1690's. The nearest Indian group west of Lake Erie noted on
Louvigny's map is a Miami group, shown as living near the mouth of the
St. Joseph River of Lake Michigan.

Thus we find, for the last four decades of the 17th century, no
contemporary record of any occupancy or economic use of present Royce
Areas 53 and 54. Although around the mid-17th century these lands had
been divested of population by the Five Nations Iroquois, subsequently
the Five Nations did not make any settlements on them, nor are there any
indications that they used the lands for hunting, after the Eries had

69

31. Louvigny, Carte de Fleuve Missisipi; Dft. Ex. A-45. Tucker,
Indian Villages, p. 6; Dft. Ex. A-10.

vacated them.[32] By ca. 1685 the possibility of exclusive use or
occupancy of present Royce Areas 53 and 54 by the Five Nations or any
other Indians had vanished, since from around 1685 onward for several
years these Areas lay adjacent to a war road which was used not only
by Five Nations warriors, but also by war parties of French-allied
Indians from the west who were intent on attacking the Iroquois.[33]

3. Significant Political Events During the Years 1684-1701.
During the last quarter of the 17th century there developed a serious
dispute between the French governors of Canada and New York's Governor Thomas Dongan as to which administration controlled the Five
Nations Iroquois--and their furs.[34] In 1666 the Iroquois had asked

32. Where the Iroquois customarily hunted between 1660 and 1700
is relevant for the light it throws on Iroquois non-use of other lands,
such as Royce Areas 53 and 54. Several primary sources indicate that
during the last three decades of the 17th century the hunting country
of the Iroquois lay north of Lake Erie, between that lake and Lake
Huron, in the Ontario Peninsula. See, for example, Kellogg, ed.,
Early Narratives, pp. 163-166, 178-180, 195-198; esp. p. 197, 208-209;
Dft. Ex. A-54. Franquelin, Carte de la Louisiane; Dft. Ex. A-11.
Lahontan, General Map; Dft. Ex. A-48. Lahontan, New Voyages, vol. 1,
pp. 138-142; Dft. Ex. A-8. O'Callaghan, ed., Documents, vol. 4,
pp. 796-797; Dft. Ex. A-16. O'Callaghan, ed., Documents, vol. 9, p. 80;
Dft. Ex. A-22.

33. The Five Nations Iroquois' loss of any possible control,
during the last quarter of the 17th century, of lands they had pre-
viously depopulated was noted some 20 years ago by the late Clark
Wissler, an eminent American anthropologist (see Murdock, "Clark
Wissler, 1870-1947," pp. 292-304; Dft. Ex. A-12). This loss, Wissler
points out, was due to the fact that the Indians of present-day
Michigan and Indiana were by the late 17th century well-armed, and
under French leadership "were successfully defying the power of the
Five Nations" (Wissler, Indians of the United States, pp. 112-114; Dft.
Ex. A-13). For a recent discussion of this point see Northwest Ohio
Quarterly, vol. 32, pp. 91, 93, 99-100; Dft. Ex. A-59.

34. Wraxall, Abridgment, pp. ix, xxxvi-xxxix; Dft. Ex. A-18.

to be received among the number of the French King's "true subjects," and had been so received.[35] By 1679, however, the Oneidas and Mohawks, specifically, were referring to themselves as "subjects" of the English King.[36] In 1684, two years after he had been appointed as governor of New York, Dongan obtained formal re-affirmation from the Five Nations that they considered themselves subjects of England.[37] Dongan also began to challenge the French rights to control of the lands and Indians to the west of New York, including control of the lands south of Lake Erie. Briefly stated, Dongan's argument was: that the Five Nations Iroquois had previously "conquered" a vast country west of their villages in New York; hence this western country belonged to the Five Nations; hence it belonged to England, since the Five Nations were subjects of England.[38] The French vigorously disputed these claims, and in the summer of 1687 led a large French and Indian expedition against the Senecas.[39] The English King thereupon issued a warrant to Dongan, dated

---

35. O'Callaghan, ed., Documents, vol. 3, pp. 125, 126, 127; Dft. Ex. A-41. O'Callaghan, ed., Documents, vol. 9, pp. 44-46; Dft. Ex. A-22.

36. Wraxall, Abridgment, p. 9; Dft. Ex. A-18.

37. O'Callaghan, ed., Documents, vol. 3, pp. 347, 363, 448; Dft. Ex. A-41. Wraxall, Abridgment, pp. 10-12, 15; Dft. Ex. A-18. Note, however, what an Onondaga speaker told the French that same year: "We are born free. We neither depend upon Yonnondio [French governor] nor Corlaer [New York governor]" (Colden, History, p. 55; Dft. Ex. A-56).

38. O'Callaghan, ed., Documents, vol. 3, pp. 447-449, 464; Dft. Ex. A-41. O'Callaghan, ed., Documents, vol. 9, pp. 263-265, 297; Dft. Ex. A-22.

39. See for example O'Callaghan, ed., Documents, vol. 9, pp. 263-264, 265; Dft. Ex. A-22; O'Callaghan, ed., Documents, vol. 3, pp. 447-449; Dft. Ex. A-41. For the French-Indian expedition against the Senecas see fn. 29, this Chapter.

14

November 10, 1687, instructing Dongan to inform the "Governor of
Canada...that upon mature consideration we [the King] have thought
fitt to own the five nations...as our Subjects..."[40] Dongan did so,
and also informed the Five Nations about the King's warrant, and
about the several demands he had made after receiving it, on the
governor of Canada.[41]

Up to this time, the only reference we have found, made by the
Iroquois themselves, to ownership of lands they had previously
conquered is one that was made in August, 1684 when an Iroquois
speaker referred in a council to "The Susquahanna River wch we won
with our Sword [by our Sweat[42]]..."[43] However, early in 1683 the
Iroquois, in council with Dongan, compared what the French could
claim by conquest and what they the Five Nations could similarly claim,
in the way of lands, in the following speech:

> ...the French can have no title to those places
> which they possesse, nay not to Cadarachqui [Fort
> Frontenac, now Kingston, Ontario] and Mount Royall
> nor none of our lands towards the Ottowawas, Dionon-
> dades [Hurons], Twichtwichs [Miamis]; for by what
> means can they pretend them [sic], because they
> came to the Maquase [Mohawk] country formerly and
> now laterly to the Sinnekes [Seneca] country and
> burnt some bark houses and cut downe our corne--if
> that be a good title then we can claim all Canida,
> for we not only did soe, but subdued whole nations
> of Indians that liv'd there, and demolished there

---

40. O'Callaghan, ed., Documents, vol. 3, p. 503; Dft. Ex. A-41.

41. O'Callaghan, ed., Documents, vol. 3, p. 533; Dft. Ex. A-41.

42. Brackets are Wraxall's.

43. Wraxall, Abridgment, p. 11; Dft. Ex. A-18.

castles in so much, that now great oake trees grow
where they were built...Wee are the just and right-
full owners of all our lands and these which the
French now pretend, which we have long since given
and granted to the King of England, and now his
Excell: who represents His Majsty sacred person is
the owner of those lands and must not suffer any encroachment upon the great King of England's territories.[44]

That Dongan himself, at least until May, 1687 was uncertain about

pushing Irouqois claims to "conquered lands" to an extreme, but that he

had at this time lands west and southwest of New York in mind, is

evident in a letter he wrote dated May 20, 1687 to Father Jean de

Lamberville, Jesuit missionary at Onondaga. Dongan states:

I am sorry that our Indians are soe troublesome
to the Indians of Cannida but I am informed from
Christians that it is the custom of those people,
that what country they conquer belongs to them as
their own, yet I lay no stress on that, but I am
still in doubt whether that land where the Indians
goes to warr belongs to our King or to the King of
France but in all probability if I be truly informed
it must depend on the King of England territories it
lying west and by south of this place and your coun-
treys lye to the northward of us...[45]

73

---

44. O'Callaghan, ed., Documents, vol. 3, p. 534; Dft. Ex. A-41.
    At this same council the Iroquois acknowledged their former
friendship with the French, but claimed that it had been ended when the
governor of Canada had

basely begun an unjust warr upon us--'tis true
we have had in former times a sort of friendship with the French, but it was held by the
left hand, which is now wholly broke by shedding
the blood of so many of our people; but the
covenant chain with your Excell: has always been
kept in our right hand fast and firm...(idem)

45. O'Callaghan, ed., Documents, vol. 3. p. 464; Dft. Ex. A-41.

The opinions of historians vary as to the wisdom of Dongan's policy in respect to New York's Indian relations.[46] There is no doubt, however, as the historian Allan W. Trelease has recently written, that Dongan's efforts, including "the unrealistic claim of sovereignty over the Iroquois and the constant effort to manipulate them against the French, which [Dongan] developed, became the keystone of New York's Indian policy in the years ahead."[47]

The other significant events in the history of New York-Indian claims to the lands south of Lake Erie were three in number. All occurred during the summer of 1701.

The first was a French-inspired, French-dominated peace conference held at Montreal, which was attended by representatives of the Five Nations Iroquois, the French, and the French-allied western Indians--the Hurons, Ottawas, Chippewas, Potawatomis, Sac, Foxes, Winnebagos, Menominees, Mascoutens, Miamis, Illinois, Kickapoos, etc., of present-day Michigan, Wisconsin, northern Indiana, and Illinois.[48] At the conference a peace pact was ratified on August 4, 1701; the signing of this pact marked the end of the long series of disastrous attacks that had been going on during the last quarter of the 17th

---

46. Wraxall, Abridgment, pp. lxi-lxii; Dft. Ex. A-18. Trelease, Indian Affairs, pp. 260, 292-294; Dft. Ex. A-24.

47. Trelease, Indian Affairs, p. 294; see also p. 253; Dft. Ex. A-24.

48. O'Callaghan, ed., Documents, vol. 9, pp. 722-725, also 708-711; Dft. Ex. A-22. For a detailed contemporary account of this conference see English Translation of La Potherie, vol. 4, Letter 12, pp. 193-266; Dft. Ex. A-46. See also English Translation of Margry, vol. 5, pp. 409-411; Dft. Ex. A-61 for the purport of the conference and ibid., vol. 5, pp. 449-450; Dft. Ex. A-61, for a French account of the reaction of the English to the conference.

century between the Five Nations Iroquois and the various western Indian groups. In terms of our immediate interest in Royce Areas 53 and 54, the negotiation of an effective peace in 1701 put a stop to the use of the southern shore of Lake Erie as a war road, either by Five Nations Iroquois warriors, or by war parties of the "Remote" or "Farr Indians," as the English of New York were wont to designate the western groups during the early 18th century.

The second significant event that occurred during the summer of 1701 was the establishment on July 24, 1701 of Fort Pontchartrain du Detroit by Antoine de la Mothe Cadillac, French administrator, at what is now the city of Detroit.[49] This new French fort was northwest of present Royce Areas 53 and 54 some 40 miles plus by water, or over 150 miles by land. Cadillac's purpose was to persuade as many of the French-allied western Indians as possible to settle in the vicinity of Fort Pontchartrain. This meant that in late 1701 and thereafter an active incentive existed for the Great Lakes and other western Indians to locate their summer villages, not in lands south of Lake Erie such as present Royce Areas 53 and 54, but rather in the St. Clair River-Lake St. Clair-Detroit River country between the western extremity of Lake Erie and the southern end of Lake Huron.[50]

75

---

49. Callières, Cadillac Starts for Detroit, p. 107; Dft. Ex. A-20. Callières, Detroit in Charge, pp. 108-110, esp. p. 110; Dft. Ex. A-21.

50. English Translation of Margry, vol. 5, pp. 321-322; Dft. Ex. A-61. Cadillac, Detroit Is Founded, pp. 96-100; Dft. Ex. A-19. Cadillac, Description of Detroit, pp. 133, 136-138; Dft. Ex. A-57. D'Aigremont, Letter, p. 431; Dft. Ex. A-25. Cadillac, Report of Detroit in 1703, pp. 161-163, 170-171, 184; Dft. Ex. A-26. Cadillac Complains of Vaudreuil, pp. 336-341; Dft. Ex. A-30. For the mileage by water from Detroit to the northwestern corner of Area 53 (40 miles) see p 115, this Report.

The erection of a French fort at Detroit, with all its impli-
cations as to which European power, France or England, would control
the Indians and the Indian fur trade in the Great Lakes region, pre-
cipitated the third significant event that occurred during the summer
of 1701. New York colonial administrators, who in 1700 had recommended
that an English fort be built at Detroit,[51] were greatly disturbed when
they learned that Cadillac was to go there. Accordingly in the summer of
1701 John Nanfan, Lieutenant Governor and Commander in Chief of the
Province of New York, hurriedly summoned representatives of each of the
Five Nations Iroquois to Albany, and at a conference with them[52] Nanfan
procured on July 19, 1701 an instrument or deed from the Iroquois to a
tract of land "in length about eight hundred miles and in bredth four
hundred miles," west of the Five Nations villages.[53] This deed, together with a map drafted by one "Samuel Clowes, Surveyor,"[54] which
attempts to show the bounds of the lands ceded and which also shows the
location of each of the Five Nations in present New York outside the
ceded tract, Nanfan forwarded to the Lords of Trade in England. In his
August 21, 1701 covering letter of transmittal for the deed and the map
Nanfan refers to the deed as conveying "A tract of land 800 miles long

76

---

51. O'Callaghan, ed., Documents, vol. 4, pp. 647-652, esp.
pp. 650-651; Dft. Ex. A-16.

52. O'Callaghan, ed., Documents, vol. 4, pp. 896-908; Dft. Ex.
A-16. For a brief French account of the July, 1701 conference Nanfan
held at Albany see English Translation of Margry, vol. 5, p. 449; Dft.
Ex. A-61.

53. O'Callaghan, ed., Documents, vol. 4, pp. 908-911; Dft. Ex.
A-16.

54. Clowes, Map of 1701; Dft. Ex. A-23.

and 400 miles broad including all their [Five Nations Iroquois] beaver hunting [lands]..."[55] Of the Clowes map he remarks that it is "a draught the most accurate I have been able to procure, of the situation of our Five Nations as well as that land conveyed to his Majesty..." The conveyed lands, Nanfan goes on to explain, are shown on the map within a "prick'd [dotted] line..."[56]

Of chief interest to us is the fact that on the Clowes map all of the lands south of Lake Erie to a point in depth midway between the Lake and the Ohio River--which would include all of present Royce Areas 53 and 54--are within the dotted boundary line, and are legended as "Beaver-hunting."[57] This assignment by Clowes of the country south of Lake Erie to the Five Nations Iroquois as a part of their beaver-hunting lands is in direct contradiction to all the information deriving from late 17th-century travel accounts and maps that we have presented in Section 2 of this chapter.[58]

The sole authority a cartographer has in depicting the boundaries of a ceded tract is the document in which the description of the tract is set forth. The validity of Clowes' dotted line showing the boundaries of the tract conveyed by the Iroquois to the English King in 1701 rests,

---

55. O'Callaghan, ed., Documents, vol. 4, p. 888; Dft. Ex. A-16.

56. Idem.

57. Clowes, Map of 1⁻ ⁻; Dft. Ex. A-23.

58. See pp. 3-12, this Report.

therefore, on how accurately Clowes followed, or was able to follow,[59] the description of the ceded tract, as this is set forth in the 1701 deed.

The tract is described twice in the body of the deed;[60] the two descriptions are not identical in their wording, but are quite similar. We quote the first one, with two bracketed emendations and two bracketed additions taken from the second description:

> The land is scituate lyeing and being northwest and by west from Albany beginning on the south [north[61]] west side of Cadarachqui lake [Lake Ontario] and includes all that waste [vast[62]] Tract of Land lyeing between the great lake off [sic] Ottowawa [Lake Huron] and the lake called by the natives Sahiquage and by the Christians the lake of Swege [Lake Erie] and runns till it butts upon the Twichtwichs [Miamis[63]] and is bounded on the right hand by a place called Quadoge [Chicago?[64]] conteigning in length about eight hundred miles and bredth four hundred miles including the country where the bevers the deers, Elk and such beasts keep and the place called Tieugsachrondio, alias Fort de Tret [Fort Detroit] or wawyachtenok and so runs round the lake of swege [Lake Erie]

---

59. See p. 6, fn. 19, this Report.

60. O'Callaghan, ed., Documents, vol. 4, pp. 908, 909; Dft. Ex. A-16.

61. Second description;   ~han, ed., Documents, vol. 4, p. 909; Dft. Ex. A-16.

62. Second description; O'Callag-   ... Documents, vol. 4, p. 909; Dft. Ex. A-16.

63. Hodge, ed., Handbook, pt. 2, p. 1164; Dft. Ex. A-2.

64. See O'Callaghan, ed., Documents, vol. 4, p. 908, fn. 5; Dft. Ex. A-16.

till you come to [a[65]] place called Oniadarondaquat[66]
which is about twenty miles from the Sinnekes Castles.
[including likewise the great falls of oakinagaro
(Niagara)[67]]...[68]

It will be observed that two kinds of descriptions of the tract
are given in the deed. One such describes the tract by metes and bounds;
the other gives its length and breadth in terms of English miles. Neither
description, we conclude, supports Clowes' having drawn the southern
sector of the boundary line where he did.

In terms of metes and bounds, all that the 1701 deed says is that
the southern boundary ran in part from Detroit "round the lake of swege
[Lake Erie]" to Irondequoit Bay on the south shore of Lake Ontario.
Clowes, however, depicts this line as running some 80-90 miles south of
Lake Erie, through lands halfway between the south shore of the Lake and
the Ohio River.

In terms of English miles, the deed describes the ceded tract as
being approximately 800 miles long and 400 miles broad. Such a tract,
plotted on a present-day map drawn to scale (see map 1, facing this page)
extends from the northernmost point on the Ontario Peninsula southward
almost to the Ohio River, and from the northwestern shore of Lake Ontario

---

65. Second description; O'Callaghan, ed., Documents, vol. 4,
p. 909; Dft. Ex. A-16.

66. Irondequoit, on Irondequoit Bay, Lake Ontario, east of the
mouth of the Genesee River near present Rochester, New York. See Kellogg,
ed., Early Narratives, pp. 177-178; Dft. Ex. A-54.

67. Second description; O'Callaghan, ed., Documents, vol. 4,
p. 909; Dft. Ex. A-16.

68. O'Callaghan, ed., Documents, vol. 4, p. 908; Dft. Ex. A-16.
Emphasis ours.

westward across the Mississippi to central Minnesota and western
Iowa.[69] Clowes depicts no such immense tract in his draft.

Evidently, in attempting to show the extent of the ceded lands
Clowes used the most reliable of the two descriptions, namely that by
metes and bounds. But in drawing the eastern sector of the tract's
southern boundary line, and in legending the lands within this line as
Five Nations beaver-hunting country Clowes took, we conclude, un-
warranted liberty with the data at his command. His assumptions are
not confirmed in the deed itself,[70] or supported by other documents.[71]

---

69. The lands conveyed in the 1701 deed were at unat date entirely unsurveyed, had never been mapped to scale, and had barely been
penetrated by any New York traders or travellers. See p. 6, fn. 19,
this Report; also the observations of Cadwallader Colden, surveyor-
general of New York, writing in 1727. Colden remarks on how far the
French of Canada exceeded the English during the 17th century in their
"daring attempts...in travelling very far among unknown Indians, discovering new Countries" and entering upon "Enterprises they would not
attempt if they liv'd in the Province of New-York" (Colden, History,
pp. 19-20; Dft. Ex. A-56. See also O'Callaghan, Documents, vol. 7,
pp. 953-956, 985; Dft. Ex. A-112).
   For recent comment on the political reasons for the English
securing the 1701 deed see Northwest Ohio Quarterly, vol. 30, p. 94;
Dft. Ex. A-59.

70. Not only does the text of the 1701 deed fail to confirm
Clowes' mapping, but positively, it clearly indicates that the lands
the Iroquois were then using and had previously used for beaver-
hunting were lands north (not south) of Lake Erie. The Ontario
Peninsula is the only part of the ceded tract which is unmistakably
described in the deed, and the history of Iroquois depopulation,
use, and later loss of exclusive control of the Peninsula in the 17th
century is narrated in the deed with considerable accuracy (O'Callaghan, ed., Documents, vol. 4, pp. 908-909; Dft. Ex. A-16. Cf. Hodge,
ed., Handbook, pt. 1, pp. 587-589; Dft. Ex. A-1. Hodge, ed., Handbook, pt. 2, pp. 755-756; Dft. Ex. A-2).

71. For late 17th-century references to Iroquois use of the
Ontario Peninsula for hunting see this chapter, fn. 32. Contemporary
reports for 1701 and for February, 1702 show that the Iroquois continued to hunt on the Peninsula during these years also, but no

(cont'd on p. 23.)

23

4. Use and Occupancy of Areas 53 and 54; 1702-1736. A series of
contemporary references to present Areas 53 and 54 relate mainly to lack
of use and occupancy of these two Areas during the period 1702-1736.

         an
The first such/anonymous "List of Indian Tribes in the West,"
probably compiled about 1712, begins thus:

> Lake Erie   there are no tribes
> settled on the coast of this lake[72]

The same list furnishes an indication of the success the French had had
in attracting Indians to settle at or near Fort Pontchartrain during the
first decade of that Fort's existence. In round numbers, some 2,500
Potawatomis, Hurons, Ottawas and Mississagues, a branch of the Chippewas,
had summer villages near present Detroit by 1712.[73]

(fn. 71, cont'd) mention is made of their hunting south of Lake Erie
(English Translation of Margry, vol. 5, pp. 409-411, 413, 450; Dft.
Ex. A-61). For a clear statement of the location of Iroquois beaver-
hunting lands in 1701 see also New York Governor George Clinton's notes,
written in 1755, to show why the Iroquois, in 1701, objected to the
French building a fort at Detroit, which "might, in time, deprive them
[Iroquois] of their Beaver hunting Country, which extends from Cadaragh-
qui Lake [Ontario] to the Northernmost part of the Huron's Lake, bounded
on the Southward by Lake Erie and Detroit" (O'Callaghan, ed., Documents,
vol. 6, p. 736; Dft. Ex. A-39). Actually, it was Lieutenant Governor
John Nanfan of New York, rather than the Iroquois, who in 1701 called
attention to the danger a French fort at Detroit held for the Iroquois,
but nonetheless Clinton's observations on the location of Iroquois
hunting grounds are of interest.

    A detailed English map, unsigned and undated (Brown, Early Maps of
the Ohio Valley, pl. 13; Dft. Ex. A-51), which we conclude was probably
drawn in 1723 by Cadwallader Colden, surveyor-general of New York at the
time (see p. 26, fn. 81, this Chapter), legends the country north of
Lake Erie as "The Country's Conquered by the Five Nations," but no lands
south of Lake Erie are legended thus.

72. List of Indian Tribes in the West, pp. 552-553; Dft. Ex. A-28.

73. *Idem.*

81

Lack of any Indian settlements along the south shore of Lake
Erie in 1718 and 1719 is also either explicitly or implicitly noted
in several documents.

The first such is Secretary of Pennsylvania James Logan's rough
draft of materials for Governor William Keith's memorial to the Board
of Trade relating to the Indians, dated October, 1718. Logan notes
that there were, in 1718,

> No Indians in the French Interest on this [south]
> side of St. Lawrence [River] nearer than the
> Miamis or Twoitthis, as the Iroquoise call them,
> who are about 2000 seated chiefly on the fore-
> mentioned River Miamis flowing into Lake Erie
> [present Maumee River], and on or near the
> branches of Ouabache [Wabash River].[74]

In a letter to Governor Keith dated February 8, 1719, Logan is
even more explicit. He urges that forts be built "as far back [west]"
from the English colonies as possible,

> especially on Lake Erie, where at present there
> are no Indians, and on [Lake] Ontario where the
> 5 nations are settled.[75]

A French map, dated May, 1718, which was drawn by the noted
French cartographer Guillaume Delisle,[76] legends Lake Erie as "Lac
Erié ou Du Chat [Lake Erie or of the Cat]" and locates the "Nation du

---

74. Hazard, ed., Register of Pennsylvania, vol. 3, January to
July 8, 1829, p. 211; Dft. Ex. A-33.

75. Hazard, ed., Register of Pennsylvania, vol. 3, January to
July 8, 1829, p. 212; Dft. Ex. A-33. See also O'Callaghan, ed.
Documents, vol. 5, p. 733; Dft. Ex. A-38.

76. Tucker, Indian Villages, p. 6; Dft. Ex. A-10.

Chat [Nation of the Cat]" on the south shore of the lake, west of Sandusky Bay. Under the legend "Nation du Chat" appears the notation "Elle
a été detruite par les Iroquois [It has been destroyed by the Iro-
quois]."[77] No existent Indians are legended south of Lake Erie.

A detailed and fairly lengthy "Memoir on the Savages of Canada as
far as the Mississippi River," which is endorsed as having been written
in 1718 by Captain the Sieur de Sabrevois, commandant at Detroit (1714-
1717) contains mention of a "Road [path]" along the south side of Lake
Erie, but does not refer to any Indians living or hunting on the south
side of the lake. In the Sabrevois Memoir this is significant.[78]

The route along the south shore of Lake Erie from Niagara to the
west end of the lake was, according to Sabrevois "much more attractive"
than the route along the north shore. "The reason why few people" used
the southern route was

83

> because it Is thirty Leagues [75 miles] Longer
> than that on the North. On either side of that
> Lake [Erie] one is not obliged to fast, on
> account of The abundance of game to be found
> there. On the Southern side are seen buffalo,
> which are Not found on the Northern side.

Sebrevois also notes in 1718 that the Sandusky River, which flows in a
northerly course some 20-25 miles west of the western boundary of Royce
Areas 53 and 54 and empties into Sandusky Bay on its south side, was
being used, in conjunction with the Scioto, which empties into the Ohio,

---

77. Delisle, Carte de la Louisiane (May 1718); Dft. Ex. A-37.

78. Sabrevois, Memoir, pp. 363-376; Dft. Ex. A-29.

by Indian warriors from Detroit and Lake Huron bent on raiding the
Cherokees, Shawnees, and other Indians living south of the Ohio.[79]
Possibly this had something to to with the lack of native population
in Royce Areas 53 and 54 in 1718.

An anonymous, undated map,[80] which we conclude was drawn in 1723
by Cadwallader Colden, then surveyor-general of New York, fails to
legend any Indians living south of Lake Erie.[81]

----

79. Sabrevois, Memoir, p. 364; Dft. Ex. A-29. The Jesuit historian, Pierre de Charlevoix, going from Niagara to Detroit in 1721, went
by the northern route. He too remarks that the south shore road "is
much more agreeable but longer by one half" (Charlevoix, Journal, vol. 2,
pp. 1-2; Dft. Ex. A-40).

80. Brown, Early Maps of the Ohio Valley, pl. 13; Dft. Ex. A-51.
Brown, Early Maps of the Ohio Valley, pp. 84-85; Dft. Ex. A-97.

81. We attribute this anonymous, undated map to Colden for the
following reasons:
(1) A map of the province of New York, "Drawn by the surveyor Gen[ll] Dr. Colden, with great exactness from all the surveys that
have been made formerly and of late in this province, which are in his
hands, and from the French map of the lakes corrected by some late information in those places that lye near this province" was sent to Lord
Carteret in England by Governor William Burnet of New York on December
16, 1723 (O'Callaghan, ed., Documents, vol. 5, p. 704; Dft. Ex. A-38).
(2) The anonymous, undated map is now in the Public Record
Office, Board of Trade Collection, London--where Colden's 1723 map
would expectably be.
(3) The anonymous map states, as part of its title, that it
was taken "from the Map of Louisiane done by Mr. De Lisle in 1718."
(4) The map also carries marginal notations relating to
events occurring at Albany as late as May 23, 1723; this would be the
"late information" mentioned by Burnet as being on the Colden map he was
sending Carteret.
(5) Lastly, a map which is strikingly similar to the
anonymous map was used by Colden as the frontispiece for his History of
the Five Indian Nations, published in London in 1747 (Colden, History,
pp. xviii-xix; Dft. Ex. A-56). It seems to us dubious that a surveyor-
general would use another person's map as the frontispiece for his own
book--especially if he himself had already carefully prepared a map of
the same region.

During the summer of 1726 the French built a fort at Niagara,[82] a site which, as early as 1687, New York's Governor Thomas Dongan had suggested be used as the location for an English fort.[83] As a result of this action by the French, Governor Burnet of New York held a conference at Albany in September, 1726 with seven representatives of the Onondaga, Cayuga, and Seneca Indians.[84]

At this council the seven Iroquois sachems signed an instrument confirming the deed to the Iroquois beaver-hunting lands which the Five Nations had given the English in 1701. In addition, the seven sachems deeded a tract of country 60 miles in depth, "Beginning from a Creek Call'd Canahogue on the Lake Osweego [Lake Erie]" and extending eastwardly to Salmon River in Oswego County, New York.[85]

E.B. O'Callaghan, historian and editor of several volumes in the series, Documents Relating to the Colonial History of the State of New York, identifies the "Creek Call'd Canahogue" as the Cuyahoga River, but cites no sources.[86] The undated, unsigned English map, which we attribute to Cadwallader Colden, surveyor-general of New York, and date

85

---

82. O'Callaghan, ed., Documents, vol. 5, pp. 802-803; Dft. Ex. A-38.

83. O'Callaghan, ed., Documents, vol. 3, p. 394; Dft. Ex. A-41. See also O'Callaghan, ed., Documents, vol. 5, pp. 571-572, 641-642, 727; Dft. Ex. A-38 for other English references to Niagara as a strategic location.

84. O'Callaghan, ed., Documents, vol. 5, pp. 799-800; Dft. Ex. A-38. The Mohawks and Oneidas were not represented.

85. O'Callaghan, ed., Documents, vol. 5, pp. 800-801; Dft. Ex. A-38. For discussion of the 1701 deed see pp. 16-22, this Report

86. O'Callaghan, ed., Documents, vol. 5, p. 801, fn.; Dft. Ex. A-38.

1723,[87] legends "Canahogue" as a region below the middle part of
Lake Erie; possibly this is the basis for O'Callaghan's identification
of Canahogue. Creek as Cuyahoga River.

If we accept O'Callaghan's identification, and we have no reason
not to, the western limits of the tract deeded by the seven Iroquois
sachems in 1726 lay along the eastern boundary of present Royce Areas
53 and 54. This would indicate that any professed interest of the
Onondagas, Cayugas, and Senecas in 1726 in lands south of Lake Erie
extended westward only as far as the eastern boundary of Royce Areas
53 and 54. There is, however, no intimation in the text of the 1726
deed as to what sort of interest the Iroquois had in any lands south
of Lake Erie, including those that they deeded. We know that they had
no settlements on these lands in 1723;[88] furthermore, the hunting
country of the Iroquois is referred to by Governor Burnet in a letter
of December 4, 1726 to the Duke of Newcastle, as still lying "between
the three nearest great Lakes [Lakes Ontario, Erie, and Huron]."[89]

---

87. Brown, Early Maps of the Ohio Valley, pl. 13; Dft. Ex. A-51.
See p. 26, fn. 81, this Chapter for discussion of the probable author
of this map.

88. Brown, Early Maps of the Ohio Valley, pl. 13; Dft. Ex. A-51,
and fn. 81, this chapter.

89. O'Callaghan, ed., Documents, vol. 5, p. 803; Dft. Ex. A-30.
For Iroquois utilization of the Ontario Peninsula as their hunting
grounds prior to 1726 see p. 12, fn. 32, and pp. 22-23, fn. 71, this
Chapter.

Three French despatches for the years 1728, 1730, and 1732 indicate that northern Ohio, including Royce Areas 53 and 54, continued to be uninhabited during these years. However, there is a faint intimation in the latest of these despatches that the Hurons living near Detroit may have been using the country south of Lake Erie for hunting during the 1730's.

The 1728 despatch is concerned with French proposals to encourage 150 families of Shawnees to settle at a location "between Lake Erie and the Riviere d'Oyo [Ohio River]" where they "would form a barrier between the Iroquois and us [French]..."[90] In the second despatch, written in 1730, a French official observes that

> It would be easy to attract them [Shawnees] to the shore of the Lake [Erie]...A considerable trade might be done with them, for between Niagara and Detroit is a hunting district, where they could live in plenty.[91]

By 1732 a third despatch relates that the Shawnees had established their villages elsewhere than in present Areas 53 and 54 - "on the other side of the Belle Riviere d'Oyo." There had been, a French agent reported, "talks" between the Shawnees and

> the Hurons, the Miamis and the Ouiatanons [Weas] to induce the [Shawanees] to light their fire at that place. The Hurons among others maintained that they wanted to live like good brothers with [the Shawnees]; if they [the Shawnees] settled on

---

90. Stevens and Kent, eds., Wilderness Chronicles, pp. 3-4; Dft. Ex. A-32.

91. State of Canada in 1730, pp. 75-76; Dft. Ex. A-31. Emphasis ours.

> this side [west] they would hurt their [Hurons']
> hunting ground, and it would suit them [the
> Hurons] better if they were in a place where
> they could injure no one.[92]

This suggests that the Hurons were accustomed by 1732 to hunt south of
Lake Erie.

Two maps by two English compilers, Daniel Coxe and Henry Popple,
which were published in London in 1726 and 1733 respectively, follow
the Delisle Map of 1718 in noting the extinct "Eries" or "N du Chat"
as the only native group on the southern shore of Lake Erie.[93]

However, a detailed French census of Indian tribes connected
with the Government of Canada, dated 1736,[94] again suggests that some
use was being made of the lands south of Lake Erie by members of a
still-extant Indian group. This 1736 census lists for the "Lake Erie;
Detroit" district 200 Huron men, 100 Potawatomi men, 200 Ottawa
warriors. For another district, "Lake Erie and Dependencies; South
Side" the following brief remarks are entered:

> The Ontationoué, that is those who speak the
> language of Men; so called by the Iroquois be-
> cause they understand each other--may be fifty
> men. I know nothing of them...................[95]

---

92. Stevens and Kent, eds., Wilderness Chronicles, pp. 5-6; Dft.
Ex. A-32. Emphasis ours.

93. Brown, Early Maps, pl. 11; Dft. Ex. A-34. Brown, Early Maps,
p. 83; Dft. Ex. A-97. Popple, Map of 1733; Dft. Ex. A-15. The Delisle
Map of 1718 (Dft. Ex. A-37) is discussed on pp. 24-25 this Report.

94. O'Callaghan, ed., Documents, vol. 9, pp. 1052-1058; Dft. Ex.
A-22. This 1736 census was written at Michilimackinac, and is attributed to M. de la Chauvignerie, a French ensign. The author of the
census states that he obtained his information from French voyageurs
"whom I questioned" (O'Callaghan, ed., Documents, vol. 9, p. 1058 and
fn.; Dft. Ex. A-22).

95. O'Callaghan, ed., Documents, vol. 9, pp. 1057-1058; Dft. Ex.
A-22.

The "Ontationou&" entry in the "Lake Erie...South Side" list is
preceded by one for the "Flathead or Cherakis, Chicachas, Totiris
[Tutelos]" who were situated south of the Ohio, and is followed by an
entry for the Miamis, who lived west of Lake Erie. Since all of the
entries for this "district" are in a more or less recognizable geographical arrangement, the "Ontationou&" are, implicitly, located north of
the Ohio and east of the Miamis; they are, therefore, the census-maker's
"Lake Erie...South Side" group.

The only living Indians in the western Lake Erie region in 1736
who spoke a language similar to that of the Five Nations Iroquois were
the Hurons, based at Detroit.[96] Furthermore, the native name for part
of the Detroit Hurons was Tionontati or Tobacco Nation, which would seem
to be a related form of the name "Ontationou&" used in the census.[97]
It is possible, therefore, that by 1736 some 50 men or around 200 Tionontati Hurons from Detroit had recently moved to the south side of Lake
Erie. But where they were settled cannot be pinpointed from the non-
committal notice accorded them in the 1736 census.

89

5. Summary and Conclusions on Early Use and Occupancy of Royce
Areas 53 and 54: 1640-1736. The data presented in the preceding pages
on use and occupancy of Royce Areas 53 and 54 between 1641, our earliest
known date, and 1736, can be summarized as follows.

---

96. See p.1-2, fn. 4, this Report.

97. O'Callaghan, ed., Documents, General Index, p. 312; Dft. Ex.
A-42. Thwaites, ed., Jesuit Relations, vol. 50, p. 307; Dft. Ex. A-55.
Hodge, ed., Handbook, pt. 1, p. 585; Dft. Ex. A-1. Hodge, ed., Handbook,
pt. 2, pp. 755-756; Dft. Ex. A-2. See p. 47 and fn. 45, Chapter 2, this
Report.

The Eries, an Iroquoian-speaking people, probably used and occupied Royce Areas 53 and 54 from 1641, at least, up to the late 1650's.

By 1660 the Eries were a defeated people. Those who had survived
the attacks of the Five Nations Iroquois lost their identity through
being forced to remove eastward to Five Nations Iroquois villages in
present central New York State. After 1660, therefore, present Royce
Areas 53 and 54 were depopulated, unused Areas. No Five Nations
Iroquois settled south of Lake Erie after they had caused the Eries to
vacate the region, and during the years 1660-1700 the Iroquois are reported as hunting north of Lake Erie in the Ontario Peninsula, rath
than in the country south of the Lake.

Why the Five Nations Iroquois eschewed the lands south of Lake
Erie for hunting is explained in an early source. From about 1685 onward, up to the end of the 17th century, an east-west war road passed
along the south shore of Lake Erie; this war road was used both by war
parties of western, French-allied Indians such as the Illinois, Miamis,
etc., bent on attacking the Five Nations Iroquois of New York, and by
Five Nations warriors travelling west to attack the western Indians.
The existence of such a war path made present Area 53, and possibly
also Area 54, dangerous territory for any Indians to hunt in regularly,
much less to live in.

In 1701 a peace treaty concluded between the Five Nations, the
western Indians, and the French rendered the war road across Area 53
obsolete. The establishment by the French of a fort at present-day
Detroit in 1701 served, however, to focus the attention of the western
Indians on the Detroit region, rather than on the lands south of Lake

Erie, as a living center. And despite the peace treaty, the Five
Nations Iroquois continued to live in their towns in present central
New York, and to hunt in the Ontario Peninsula north of Lake Erie. One
document only, an English map drafted in 1701 to illustrate the 1701
deed the Five Nations Iroquois gave the English to their "Beaver-hunting
country," assigns lands south of Lake Erie to the Iroquois as part of
their beaver-hunting country. The text of the 1701 deed itself does not
support such an assignment on the map. Nor do other contemporary
documents. A detailed English map of 1723, for example, legends the
lands north of Lake Erie, only, as having been "conquered" by the
Iroquois.

During the years 1702-1732 present Royce Areas 53 and 54 continued
to be devoid of any native population. A cession of land which included
country on the south shore of Lake Erie, made by representatives of the
Onondaga, Cayuga, and Seneca Iroquois to the English in 1726, did not
extend farther west than the eastern boundary of Royce Areas 53 and 54.

However, by 1732 hints begin to appear in contemporary accounts
indicating that the Huron Indians of the Detroit region may have been
using the lands south of Lake Erie, including present Royce Areas 53
and 54, for hunting. And by 1736 a small group of Iroquoian-speaking
Indians, who probably derived from the Tionontati Huron group near
Detroit, are reported as living south of Lake Erie. But whether this
group was situated in or near our Areas of particular interest cannot
be definitely determined.

Our conclusions on native use and occupancy of Royce Areas 53 and
54 between 1740 and 1736 are therefore as follows.

At the beginning of the period 1640-1736, and up to about 1660, Royce Areas 53 and 54 may have been used and occupied by the Eries, an Iroquoian-speaking people who became extinct as a group around 1660.

After 1660 and until the early 1730's there is no record of any Indians using or occupying Royce Areas 53 and 54, although between 1685 and 1701 present Royce Area 53, at least, was traversed by Indian warriors from many different groups.

By 1736 some of the Tionontati Hurons deriving from Detroit may have been living in or near present Royce Areas 53 and 54.

Chapter II. Use and Occupancy of Royce Areas
53 and 54: 1737-1759

1. The Hurons and Other Indians in Royce Area 53: 1737-1747.

The long period during which there is no record of use and occupancy of present Royce Area 53 by still-extant Indians ends in the latter half of the 1730's. Possibly during the winter of 1737-1738,[1] but more likely during the winter of 1738-1739 a group of Hurons or, as they later came to be known to the English, Wyandots,[2] from the Huron mission village on Bois Blanc Island at the mouth of the Detroit River, under a chief known as Angouirot, removed to a region referred to as "Sandoské" [Sandusky],[3] south of Sandusky Bay in southwestern Lake Erie. The reason for the removal of these Hurons to Sandusky was a quarrel which had arisen between them and a body of Ottawas who were also domiciled near Detroit.[4]

93

1. Shiels, Jesuits in Ohio, p. 39; Dft. Ex. A-62.

2. See Ontario History, vol. 49, no. 2, p. 75; Dft. Ex. A-269. Hereafter "Huron" and "Wyandot" are used interchangeably in this Report.

3. The Huron of Detroit, p. 286; Dft. Ex. A-66. Shiels, Jesuits in Ohio, pp. 35-36, 42; Dft. Ex. A-62. The Detroit Huron, pp. 328-329; Dft. Ex. A-209. The Detroit Huron, p. 331; Dft. Ex. A-209. De Noyelles to Beauharnois, pp. 163-164; Dft. Ex. A-67.
The name "Sandusky" is used generally for a region bordering on Sandusky Bay, and also, specifically, for the Bay itself, for a sizable river that empties into the Bay, and for various 18th-century Indian villages near the Bay. It is impossible in some documents to know whether the name is being used generally or specifically.

4. The Huron of Detroit, pp. 279-280; Dft. Ex. A-66. The Detroit Huron, pp. 328, 331-332; Dft. Ex. A-209.

Despite unremitting efforts of French authorities at Detroit to induce the Hurons to quit the Sandusky region and either rejoin the remainder of the Hurons settled on Bois Blanc Island in the Detroit River, or else go to Montreal,[5] the emigrant Hurons stayed at Sandusky, living in a forted village at or near present Castalia, Erie County, Ohio in northwestern Area 53, through the years 1738-1747.[6]

Although apparently the dominant group in the Sandusky Bay region from 1738 to 1747, the Sandusky Hurons were not the only Indians there. In 1745 there was at least one cabin of Senecas with them,[7] and in 1747 they are reported as having

> attached to them several families of vagabond
> Iroquois, Loups [Mahicans   ] &c.
> 'Tis even asserted that there are some Saut

5. The Huron of Detroit, pp. 279-288; Dft. Ex. A-66. The Detroit Huron, pp. 328-329, 331-333; Dft. Ex. A-209. Instructions to the Chevalier de Beauharnois, pp. 346-348; Dft. Ex. A-68. Shiels, Jesuits in Ohio, pp. 33-36; Dft. Ex. A-62. For refugee Hurons on the St. Lawrence River from 1648 onward see Hodge, ed., Handbook, pt. 1, pp. 588-590; Dft. Ex. A-1.

6. The location of their village at "Sandusky" is pinpointed in the journal of a French engineer, Lt. Joseph Chaussegros de Léry, who visited the site in 1755; De Léry, Journal, pp. 99-100; Dft. Ex. A-113. For the existence of the village up to the year 1748 see O'Callaghan, ed., Documents. vol. 10. pp. 84, 162; Dft. Ex. A-69.

7. A French traveler at "Sandusky" in 1745 remarks: "we lodged at the home of the great Sonontoin [Seneca]." The next day the same traveller writes: "The Huronts urged us to return by their village." Anonymous Diary of a Trip, p. 2; Dft. Ex. A-75

Indians[8] among them.[9]

Also, according to two 1745 and 1747 reports some Shawnees may have been associated, temporarily, at least, with the Hurons "near Sandusky."[10]

During the decade 1737-1747 other Indians also moved into or very close to Area 53, but on its eastern, not on its western side. In June, 1743 Pierre Joseph Céloron, commandant at Detroit, reported that some "Senecas, Onondagas, and other of the Five Iroquois villages" have "seated themselves of late years, at the White river" and have asked

> for some Frenchmen to supply their wants, under
> promise that if their request be granted, they
> would drive off the English [traders] from that
> quarter and have no dealings with them...

---

8. These "Saut Indians" were French Mohawks from Sault St. Louis, on the St. Lawrence River nine miles above Montreal, who are also often referred to as Caughnawagas or Caughnawaga Mohawks, from the name of their village (see Hodge, ed., Handbook, pt. 1, p. 220; Dft. Ex. A-1. Trelease, Indian Affairs, p. 252; Dft. Ex. A-24. O'Callaghan, ed., Documents, vol. 5, p. 732; Dft. Ex. A-38. Drake, ed., Indian Captivities, p. 234; Dft. Ex. A-95). A Jesuit "Mission of the Sault" was established in 1667 (Thwaites, ed., Jesuit Relations, vol. 63, pp. 141, 143, 145, 147, 149, 151, 153, 155; Dft. Ex. A-172). Because the Caughnawaga Mohawks or "Iroquois of the Sault" were Catholicized Indians, they tended to have rather close relations with the Iroquoian-speaking Hurons near Detroit, who for long had also had a Jesuit mission at their village, and who were to some extent Catholicized (see, for example, Drake, ed., Indian Captivities, pp. 205-206; Dft. Ex. A-95).

9. O'Callaghan, ed., Documents, vol. 10, p. 115; Dft. Ex. A-69.
    The French term for both the Mahicans and the Delawares was Loups, "wolves." The term was probably used by the French for the Mahicans of Hudson River originally, and was later extended to include Delaware groups (Hodge, ed., Handbook, pt. 1, p. 385; Dft. Ex. A-1).

10. [Vaudreuil-Cavagnal], Extracts of Letters, p. 22; Dft. Ex. A-297. Vaudreuil to Maurepas, pp. 13, 21; Dft. Ex. A-79.
    The French were, and had been since at least 1730, interested in having the Shawnees settle near Detroit; see O'Callaghan, ed., Documents, col. 10, p. 138; Dft. Ex. A-69; The Huron of Detroit, p. 285; Dft. Ex. A-66; The Detroit Huron, p. 333; Dft. Ex. A-209.

Céloron had therefore "permitted some residents of Detroit, to carry goods thither," and had also sent Sieur Robert Navarre, intendant at Detroit, to report on "this new Establishment."[11]

There has been considerable, and in our opinion unnecessary discussion as to which river is meant by the "White river," on which various Indians had seated themselves by 1743. The conclusion reached by several historians that the "White river" is the present Cuyahoga River, which bounds Area 53 on the east, is correct, but no historian has referred to an entry in a 1754 document which establishes this. The 1754 document is an account by a French engineer, Lt. Joseph Chaussegros de Léry, of a trip taken by canoe along the south shore of Lake Erie from Presque Isle to Detroit, July 30-August 6, 1754. In it is an entry made by De Léry on August 2, 1754 concerning the "Rivière à Seguin" (at the mouth of which De Léry was then encamped) and a sketch of the mouth of this river. The final sentence of De Léry's entry reads: "Drawing of the Rivière Blanche or Seguin marked C, it is also called Goyahague." This would seem to establish without doubt the White River or "Rivière Blanche" as the Cuyahoga.[12]

96

---

11. O'Callaghan, ed., Documents, vol. 9, pp. 1099-1100; Dft. Ex. A-22.

12. De Léry, Journal, pp. 51-53, 62; Dft. Ex. A-113. Emphasis ours. See also ibid., p. 99; Dft. Ex. A-113. Saguin was the name of the French trader who went to the White River in 1743 (Hanna, The Wilderness Trail, vol. 1, p. 315; Dft. Ex. A-70).
For an elaborate attempt to identify the White River with the Cuyahoga see the historian Charles A. Hanna's, The Wilderness Trail, vol. 1, pp. 320-339; Dft. Ex. A-70, and vol. 2, pp. 167-168; Dft. Ex. A-82. For later identification of this river with the Cuyahoga see Gipson, The British Empire, vol. 4, pp. 169-171, fn. 61; Dft. Ex. A-71; Mulkearn, ed., George Mercer Papers, pp. 487-488, fn. 89; Dft. Ex. A-72; Wainwright, George Croghan and the Indian Uprising, p. 23; Dft. Ex. A-114; Wainwright, George Croghan, Wilderness Diplomat, p. 6; Dft. Ex. A-115. For some erroneous identifications see Raymond,

(cont'd on p. 39.)

In his report for Céloron in 1743 Navarre states that

> There are ten different tribes settled upon
> that river [White river], numbering altogether
> about five or six hundred men, namely, the
> Senecas, Cayugas, Oneidas, Onondagos, Mohawks,
> Loups [Delawares?], Moraignans [Mahicans?[13]],
> Ottawas, Abenakis of St. Francis, and the
> Sauteux [Chippewa[14]] of the lower end of Lake Ontario...
>
> The number of Indians who have settled on this
> river increases every day, since hunting there is
> abundant, while on the other hand at their former
> homes, there is no more game.[15]

Where the "ten different tribes" were specifically located on White

River in 1743 Navarre does not say, but some of the groups, at least,

seem to have been by 1747 on the lower (more northerly) reaches of the

Cuyahoga River, close to or within extreme northeastern Area 53. In

that year one Capt. Raymond, an officer at Quebec, refers to "the

---

(fn. 12, cont'd) Memoir, p. 475, fn. 1; Dft. Ex. A-74; Collections.
of the Illinois State Historical Library, vol. 29, p. 23, fn. 4; Dft.
Ex. A-298; Peckham, Pontiac, p. 33; Dft. Ex. A-319. Hodge, ed., Handbook,
pt. 2, p. 581; Dft. Ex. A-2.
     The initial error in not utilizing De Léry's entry for August 2,
1754 rests with Hanna. In 1910 or 1911 Hanna had a translation of
De Léry's journal of his trip from Presque Isle to Detroit and published
it, but in part only. Inexplicably, he reproduced the journal only
from the entry for August 4, 1754 onward (Hanna, The Wilderness Trail,
vol. 2, pp. 167-168; Dft. Ex. A-82).

13. Hodge, ed., Handbook, pt. 2, p. 1094; Dft. Ex. A-2.

14. Hodge, ed., Handbook, pt. 2, p. 1134; Dft. Ex. A-2.

15. Hanna, The Wilderness Trail, vol. 1, pp. 315-318; Dft. Ex.
A-70. The visit of an Oneida Indian to the mouth of the Cuyahoga around
1740 is related in Whittlesey, History of Cleveland, pp. 345-346; Dft.
Ex. A-78, and seems a fairly plausible incident.

For identification of the "Loups" see p. 37, fn. 9, this Chapter.

Yrocois at the Outlet of la Rivière Blanche," and in 1747 the Pennsylvania
trader, George Croghan, also refers to "a part of ye Six Nations Ingans,
That has there Dwelling on ye Borders of Lake Arey [Erie]."[16]

The number of Ottawas on the Cuyahoga in 1743 was not very great,
according to Navarre. "The merchants of Detroit," he states,

> have made a great mistake in accusing Saguin[17]
> of trying to gain over the Ottawas of Detroit.
> There was found there of that nation five or
> six cabins, who have asked the Iroquois Seneca
> for a small piece of land, in order to light a
> little fire; which has been granted them. The
> greater part of these Ottawas are bad people
> who only establish themselves in this place to
> go more easily to Choueghen [Oswego, New York].
> No one can prevent them. The people of Detroit
> to whom they owe money can never catch them to
> make them pay. Besides, the road from there is
> very much shorter. It is this which likewise
> causes a part of the Hurons to remain in their
> village of Sandoske. On returning from Saguin's
> place [to Detroit] we have seen their [Hurons'
> of Sandusky] preparations for their voyage to
> [trade with] the English.[18]

98

---

16. Raymond, Memoir, p. 474; Dft. Ex. A-74. Pennsylvania Archives,
1st ser., vol. 1, p. 742; Dft. Ex. A-73. A map published in 1755 (Evans,
A General MAP; Dft. Ex. A-93) which is discussed later in this chapter
may show the specific locations of these villages. On the 1755 map a
town legended as "Mingoes T." and a "French House" are shown on the west
bank of the Cuyahoga River, some 20-25 miles above its mouth, in present
Area 53. A "Tawas [Ottawa]" town is shown opposite the French trading
house, on the east bank of the Cuyahoga, just outside Area 53. For a
description of the Cuyahoga and its natural attractions see Heckewelder,
Map and Description, pp. 339-340; Dft. Ex. A-196.

17. The French trader in 1743 on the Cuyahoga.

18. Hanna, The Wilderness Trail, vol. 1, p. 318; Dft. Ex. A-70.

English traders were evidently encroaching on French trade with
the Indians on White River as early as 1744. In June of that year Paul
Joseph le Moyne. Chevalier de Longueuil, commandant at Detroit urged
the Detroit Indians to attack any Englishmen found on White River.
Also, in answer to a message from the "Chiefs of the Post of the White
River" Longueuil charged "Toyaraguindiagué, and Canante-Chiarirou,
Chiefs of the nations on the White River" to protect the flag of their
father the French against English intruders. In September, 1744,
several Englishmen having arrived at the White River to trade, Longueuil
raised a picked force of 35 Ottawas to go from Detroit to the White River
"to plunder and kill the Englishmen, or take them prisoners." In 1745
a group of Shawnee traveling westward "along the Lake Erie & that of
Sandoski" notified Longueuil they had "detained" 15 Englishmen and
offered to deliver them to Longueuil.[19]

The decade 1737-1747 ends with an "incident" indicating that the
Sandusky Hurons, under their chief, Nicolas Orontoni, who were by then
definitely committed to trading with the English, were in contact with
the Indians on the Cuyahoga. The incident was reported from Detroit by
Longueuil in June 1747. and concerned

> some Hurons of Detroit, belonging to the tribe
> of the war chief Nicolas, who, some years since,
> had settled at Sandoské, [and now] have killed
> 5 Frenchmen who were on their return from the
> post at the White river, and stolen their furs...

99

---

19. Raymond, Memoir, pp. 474-476; Dft. Ex. A-74. Pennsylvania
Archives, 1st ser., vol. 1, p. 742; Dft. Ex. A-73. O'Callaghan, ed.,
Documents, vol. 9, pp. 706-708, 1111-1112; Dft. Ex. A-22. [Vaudreuil-
Cavagnal], Extracts in English, p. 23; Dft. Ex. A-297.

> Nicolas' tribe continues...to reside at Sandoské,
> where...they doubtless expect not only to main-
> tain themselves but even to harass Detroit by
> small war parties.[20]

Though the French from this time on generally attributed the killing
of the five Frenchmen to Nicolas' Sandusky Hurons, it seems more likely
that it was done by these Hurons and some Iroquois from the Cuyahoga.
In May, 1747 three Six Nations Indians living on Lake Erie sent a
letter by George Croghan, Pennsylvania trader, to the Governor of
Pennsylvania, stating they had "killd five of ye French, hard by
this fortt which is Call[d] Detreat" and presenting, with the letter,
"one of those Frenchman's Sculps [scalps]..."[21]

The murder of the five Frenchmen led to the discovery soon
afterwards by the French at Detroit of a plot Nicolas and his band
of Hurons had concocted "to destroy all the French of Detroit and
afterward to go to the fort and subject all to fire and sword."
Because some of the Hurons "struck too soon" Detroit was saved,[22]
but late in August, 1747, it was reported that "The Hurons of
Sandosket, and of Nicolas' band, continue insolent."[23]

100

---

20. O'Callaghan, ed., Documents, vol. 10, pp. 83-84, 114-115;
Dft. Ex. A-69. Hodge, ed., Handbook, pt. 1, p. 589; Dft. Ex. A-1.

21. Pennsylvania Archives, 1st ser., vol. 1, pp. 741-742; Dft.
Ex. A-73.

22. Vaudreuil to Maurepas, pp. 32-33; Dft. Ex. A-79. Raymond,
Memoir, pp. 474-475; Dft. Ex. A-74. O'Callaghan, ed., Documents, vol.
10, pp. 83-84, 114-115; Dft. Ex. A-69. This was the so-called "Conspiracy
of Nicolas." As a result of the hostilities the Huron mission village
on Bois Blanc Island was abandoned, and the Hurons there removed nearer to
Detroit (ibid., vol. 10, p. 115; Dft. Ex. A-69).

23. O'Callaghan, ed., Documents, vol. 10, p. 138; Dft. Ex. A-69.

A few weeks later, however, Nicolas signified his willingness to come to Detroit and conclude a peace,[24] but he procrastinated in doing so.[25] According to a September 2, 1747 report from Chabert de Joncaire, French resident among the Senecas, the Cayugas had told Joncaire that

> the [Sandusky] Hurons had sent word to the 5
> Nations that, owing to their small number,
> they considered themselves no longer Hurons,
> but Iroquois, since the greater portion of
> their village were children of Iroquois.
> Should this be so, Sieur Joncaire thinks that
> the Beautiful river [Ohio] will be the route
> which they will proceed to join the village
> of the Five Nations.[26]

Learning of this, the Governor of New France instructed Longueuil, at Detroit,

> particularly to prevent, by all means
> possible, the reception by the 5 Nations
> of the Hurons belonging to that tribe that
> talked of taking refuge among them.[27]

No anti-French Hurons "took refuge" among the Five Nations in 1747. In September of that year

> Nicolas, [sic] Orotoni and Aniotin, chiefs of
> the Huron traitors, came [to Detroit] to sue for
> peace, and to surrender the belts which have been
> the cause of this treason; they have made speeches
> to which Mr. de Longueuil has given an answer, but
> he doubts their sincerity.[28]

101

---

24. O'Callaghan, ed., Documents, vol. 10, p. 141; Dft. Ex. A-69.

25. O'Callaghan, ed., Documents. vol. 10, p. 145; Dft. Ex. A-69.

26. O'Callaghan, ed., Documents, vol. 10, p. 146; Dft. Ex. A-69.

27. O'Callaghan, ed., Documents, vol. 10, p. 148; Dft. Ex. A-69.

28. O'Callaghan, ed., Documents, vol. 10, p. 150; Dft. Ex. A-69.

While Nicolas and Aniotin were at Detroit negotiating some Frenchmen were attacked at Grosse Isle near Detroit by an adopted Onondaga, a
Seneca, and two "Mohegans" (Mahicans), guided by a Detroit Huron. Nicolas
and Aniotin "apprehensive that some of their people might be confounded"
with the attackers, told Longueuil where the raiding party had hidden,
"and offered even to arrest them." The raiders were captured in a
cabin on Bois Blanc Island and four of them "put in irons" at Detroit.[29]
When the Senecas and Mohegans of New York heard of this arrest, they
sent out two war parties. This obliged the Hurons at "Ostandouket
[Sandusky]" in October, 1747

> to collect together at the White river, 25
> leagues [62.5 miles] from Detroit, to entrench
> themselves there and examine in safety the con-
> duct of the Iroquois, which they promise to
> report to us [Longueuil] in case of any movement.[30]

2. Use and Occupancy of Areas 53 and 54: 1748-1754. Of the four
Indians in irons at Detroit late in 1747 one, the Seneca, had either committed
suicide or been killed by a companion on the night of December 28/29,
1747. At the end of January, 1748

> 14 Hurons of Sandosket, with Scotach and Quarante
> Sols at their head, came [to Detroit] to ask for
> the release of the three prisoners confined in irons...

Reluctantly, Longueuil released the trio, "on the advice of the principal
French and Indians in the fort [Detroit]."[31]

---

29. Idem. The Onondaga was killed by the enraged Detroit populace.

30. O'Callaghan, ed., Documents, vol. 10, p. 151; Dft. Ex. A-69.

31. O'Callaghan, ed., Documents, vol. 10, pp. 156-157; Dft. Ex.
A-69. The fact that "Scotach and Quarante Sols" headed this delegation,
and not Nicolas and Aniotin, suggests that the Sandusky Hurons may have
consisted, at this time, of two factions.

In February, 1748 Longueuil wrote from Detroit that

> Nicolas' conduct is not free from equivocation; the
> English [traders] from Philadelphia visited him twice
> during the winter [1747-1748], to trade, and were
> well received.[32]

Where the Philadelphia traders visited Nicolas in the winter of
1747-1748 we do not certainly know, but it was probably at his village
at present Castalia, Erie County, near Sandusky Bay. Early in 1748
the French commandant at Niagara reported that the (Ottawa?) "chief at
the Little Rapid" had told him that "the English had given him some
bad belts [anti-French messages] to transmit to Sandostket." These,
the commandant suspected, the Ottawa chief had actually "sent...to
their destination at the moment he promised to send them back to the
English."[33]

The next news concerning Sandusky comes from one Kinousaki, a pro-
French Ottawa chief of Detroit[34] who in the spring of 1748 went to the
"Miami [Maumee] river" and Sandusky Bay to "bring back the Hurons who
had deserted from the village of Otsandosket."[35] Returning to Detroit
on April 7, 1748 Kinousaki reported that

103

> Nicolas, with 119 warriors of his nation,
> men, women and baggage, had taken the route
> to the White river [Cuyahoga] after having
> burnt the fort and cabins of the village
> [of Otsandosket (Sandusky)][36]

---

32. O'Callaghan, ed., Documents, vol. 10, p. 157; Dft. Ex. A-69.

33. Idem.

34. O'Callaghan, ed., Documents, vol. 10, p. 138; Dft. Ex. A-69.

35. O'Callaghan, ed., Documents, vol. 10, p. 162; Dft. Ex. A-69.

36. Idem.

At about the same time two Hurons who had been sent out by

> Sastaredzy the Huron chief of a loyal tribe
> [at Detroit], confirm[ed] the departure of
> Nicolas and his people for the White river,
> to seek shelter among the Iroquois there, or
> among the Mohegans who are near Orange [Albany],
> and [say] that only 70 men of all their nation
> will come back.[37]

In June, 1748 there is a significant entry in French despatches.
In that month "emissaries from Nicolas and the Chaouenons [Shawnees]
of Sonioto [Scioto]"[38] arrived at Detroit.[39]

This statement, taken in conjunction with an English document,[40]
indicates that by the summer of 1748 the Sandusky Hurons had split
into two groups. All the Sandusky Hurons may (or may not) have gone
to the Cuyahoga ("White River") early in the spring of 1748, as stated.
From there some of them, evidently, appealed to the Senecas, Delawares
and Shawnees of the upper Ohio region "to come and meet [them] in
[their] retreat from the French." The Senecas, Delawares and Shawnees
complied,[41] and by August, 1748 thirty Sandusky Huron warriors and
their families were established NEAR Kuskusky,[42] a series of Six
Nations settlements on Beaver Creek in extreme western

104

---

37. Idem.

38. The Shawnee town of Sonioto or Scioto was at the mouth of
the Scioto River; see Thwaites, ed., Jesuit Relations, vol. 69, pp.
179, 181, 183, 297-299; Dft. Ex. A-90.

39. O'Callaghan, ed., Documents, vol. 10, p. 162; Dft. Ex. A-69.

40. Minutes of the Provincial Council, vol. 5, pp. 348-358; Dft.
Ex. A-76.

41. Minutes of the Provincial Council, vol. 5, p. 353; Dft. Ex.
A-76.

42. Weiser, Notes; Dft. Ex. A-81. Brown, Early Maps, pl. 19; Dft.
Ex. A-96. Brown, Early Maps, pp. 91-92; Dft. Ex. A-97.

Pennsylvania,[43] some 65 miles east of Areas 53 and 54. Near the Kuskusky

settlements, at Logstown, then a mixed Iroquois-Shawnee-Delaware village

on the Ohio River 18 miles below present Pittsburgh,[44] Conrad Weiser,,

Pennsylvania envoy and Provincial interpreter, met these Hurons and

the Senecas, Delawares, and Shawnees of the upper Ohio in council,

August 27-September 15, 1748. Weiser refers to the Hurons by the names

the English used for them, as "Wondots [Wyandots], otherways call'd

Ionontady Hagas."[45] At the Logstown council Weiser queried the "Wondots"

as to why they had left the French, and as to their numbers. To the

latter question they replied that

> there was one hundred fighting Men that came
> over to join the English, seventy were left
> behind at another Town a good distance off,
> they hoped they [the seventy] wou'd follow
> them [to Kuskusky].[46]

43. Hanna, The Wilderness Trail, vol. 1, p. 340; Dft. Ex. A-70.

44. Thwaites, ed., Jesuit Relations, vol. 69, pp. 297-298; Dft.
Ex. A-90. English Translation of Margry, vol. 6, pp. 688, 694; Dft.
Ex. A-88.

45. Minutes of the Provincial Council, vol. 5, p. 350: Dft. Ex.
A-76. The names Huron and Wyandot, or variants thereof, are used in
French and English documents, respectively, for the same Indians. A
third name, Tionontati (of which Weiser's "Ionontady Hagas" is a variant)
was also used by the English and the Six Nations Iroquois for the Hurons.
The Hurons' name for themselves was "Wendat" (Thwaites, ed., Jesuit
Relations, vol. 16, p. 227; Dft. Ex. A-173. Ontario History, vol. 49,
no. 2, p. 75; Dft. Ex. A-269).

46. Minutes of the Provincial Council, vol. 5, p. 350; Dft. Ex.
A-76. The number of men (70) "left behind" is the same number of men
Sastaredzy's envoys, in the spring of 1748, stated would "come back".

Weiser also recorded the names of five of the "Wondots." One of
the names, "Wanduny," may be that of Nicolas Orontoni, but this seems
unlikely, considering other movements of Nicolas in 1748.[47] In June
of 1748, as we have seen, emissaries from Nicolas and from the Shawnee
living at the mouth of the Scioto River arrived at Detroit. Nicolas
would seem to have been somewhere in present central Ohio before sending
to Detroit. Several 1750 and 1755 documents indicate where he and his
band probably were, in the summer and fall of 1748.

A 1750 source states that some anti-French Hurons were hunting
and wintering near the mouth of the "Vermilion [Huron] River"[48] in
present western Area 53, near the spot where Father Armand de la
Richardie, Jesuit missionary at Detroit, had his winter mission during
1750-1751.   These Hurons derived from a Huron town in which Nicolas
resided, known to the French as "Conchaké" (var., Konchake, Couchake)[49]
and to the English as "Moskingum" (var., Muskingum, etc.), located near
present Coshocton, Coshocton County, Ohio, almost 30 miles south of Area

---

47. Minutes of the Provincial Council, vol. 5, p. 355; Dft. Ex.
A-76. Aniotin's name, or any possible variant of it, does not appear
on Weiser's list.

48. The present Huron River in western Area 53 was known in the
1750's to the French as "Rivière aux Hurons, Rivière au Pere [from Father
Richardie?], and Rivière au Vermillon" (De Léry, Journal. p. 53; Dft.
Ex. A-113).

49. Ott, ed., Selections, pp. 260-265; Dft. Ex. A-83. Shiels, The
Jesuits in Ohio, pp. 33-40; Dft. Ex. A-62. Thwaites, ed., Jesuit Relations,
vol. 70, pp. 63, 65; Dft. Ex. A-84. De Léry, Journal, pp. 105; Dft. Ex.
A-113.   71-73,

54 at the "Forks of Muskingum."[50] The French frequently referred to Nicolas' town, Conchaké, in the early 1750's, but we have no record of any Frenchman risking his life to visit this anti-French, pro-English Huron settlement while Nicolas lived there. However, Christopher Gist, a surveyor from North Carolina for the Ohio Land Company, stopped at "Moskingom," as he calls Conchaké, in December, 1750 and found George Croghan, the Pennsylvania trader, established there. Gist describes Muskingum (or Conchaké) as

> a Town of the Wyendotts The Wyendotts or little Mingoes[51] are divided between the French and English one half of them [at Detroit] adhere to the first, and the other half are firmly attached to the latter The Town of Moskingum consists of about one Hundred Families When we came within sight of the Town, We perceived

50. During the 18th century the name "Muskingum" was (1) applied to a town site at the head of the present Muskingum River; (2) to the present Muskingum River; (3) to present Tuscarawas River. The Tuscarawas and present Walhonding Rivers unite to form the Muskingum as it is known today; the locale where the two streams unite was often called "the Forks of the Muskingum" or simply "the Forks." See Ontario History, vol. 49, no. 2, p. 91; Dft. Ex. A-269.

51. "Mingo" was a name often used by the English, and applied variously--for the Six Nations Iroquois generally, or for the Senecas, or for those of the Six Nations, especially the western Senecas, who during the 18th century lived on the upper Ohio River and later during that century moved westward into central Ohio. The term probably derives from mengwe, "stealthy, treacherous," the name used for the Iroquois by various Algonquian-speaking groups such as the Delawares, Shawnees, etc. See Hodge, ed., Handbook, pt. 1, pp. 867-868; Dft. Ex. A-1, and White, ed., Lewis Henry Morgan, p. 53; Dft. Ex. A-103.

The Wyandots, probably because they spoke an Iroquoian language, and also possibly because they were few in numbers compared with the Six Nations, were sometimes referred to as "little Mingoes."

English Colours hoisted on the King's
House, and at George Croghan's; upon
enquiring the Reason I was informed that
the French had lately taken several
English traders, and that Mr Croghan had
ordered all the White Men to come into
this Town...[52]

Other travellers beside Gist furnish information showing that

Nicolas and the majority of the Hurons of Sandusky went to Conchaké

(Muskingum) after leaving Sandusky Bay early in 1748. In August,

1749 Céloron, while on his lead-plate-burying expedition down the

Ohio River, informed the "Ohio Indians" at a council held at Logs-

town that he was

now going down the River in order to whip home
some of our children, that is the Twitchwees
[Miamis] & Wayundotts [Wyandots] & let them
know that they have no business to trade or
traffic with the English...[53]

---

52. Mulkearn, ed., George Mercer Papers, pp. 11, 486, fn. 83; Dft.
Ex. A-72. See also Darlington, Christopher Gist's Journals, p. 105;
Dft. Ex. A-224; Hanna, The Wilderness Trail, vol. 2, p. 145 and fn. 5;
Dft. Ex.C2; Map of the Ohio Company Lands; Dft. Ex. A-85. Muskingum
had been an English traders' depot since March, 1748, at least. At that
date one Thomas Kinton had a "Store House...at Muskinggun" (Bailey, ed.,
Ohio Company Papers, pp. 70-71; Dft. Ex. A-77).
Gist stayed at the Wyandot town of Muskingum for a month. On
January 4, 1751, "One Teafe (an Indian Trader) came to Town from near
Lake Erie" with the news that "it was expected that the other Part of
the Weyendott Nation [at Detroit] would desert the French and come over
to the English Interest, & join their Brethren on the Elk's Eye Creek
[Muskingum River], & build a strong Fort and Town there" (Mulkearn, ed.,
George Mercer Papers, p. 13; Dft. Ex. A-72). This never happened, however.

53. O'Callaghan, ed., Documents, vol. 6, pp. 732, 533; Dft. Ex.
A-39. See also Collections of the Illinois State Historical Library,
vol. 29, pp. 97, 105; Dft. Ex. A-298. Céloron did not visit the Wyandots
at Conchaké during his expedition; he did, however, visit the Miamis.

Later, after he had assumed his duties as commandant at Detroit (1750-
1754) Céloron refers in passing, in a letter written in August, 1751, to
"Conchaké" as "the place to which [the Hurons] retired after killing the
French..."[54]

A "Trader's Map of the Ohio Country, 1750-1752" attributed to John
Pattin, a Pennsylvania trader, shows an unnamed town at the Forks of
Muskingum and "Whitewoman's Town" close to the Forks. However, by
Pattin's own verbal statements there was only one town at or near
the Forks in 1750-1752, the name for which was "Wendawets [Wyandot]
Town."[55]

Some indication of the route Nicolas and his band took in their
removal to Conchaké is provided in the 1755 journal of De Léry, the
French engineer. In March-April, 1755 De Léry went from Detroit to
Fort Duquesne (present Pittsburgh). From Sandusky Bay he took "the
Couchake road" south through the western part of Area 53, and southeastward through Area 54. About 16-17 leagues (40-42.5 miles) northwest of Conchaké, in central Area 54, De Léry notes a location on the
bank of a stream

109

     where some Hurons had taken refuge... ...made

---

54. Céloron to Vaudreuil, August 4, 1751, p. 288; Dft. Ex. A-87.
The Frenchmen were killed in May, 1747.

55. [Pattin], Trader's Map of the Ohio Country, 1750-1752; Dft.
Ex. A-102. Pennsylvania Magazine of History and Biography, vol. 65,
pp. 420-438; Dft. Ex. A-131.

at Detroit. It is called the cabin of the
fugitives.[56]

Farther on, about 10 leagues (25 miles) northwest of Conchaké, De Léry
came to a second "place where fugitive Hurons had taken shelter."[57]
This location is either in or close to extreme south-central Area 54.

"Couchaké" itself is located, in a sketch by De Léry, at the forks
of the "Konchaké [Walhonding]" and the "Naguerreconnon [Tuscarawas]"
rivers, on the north side of the Tuscarawas River. De Léry mentions
Conchaké's past history as a Huron town briefly: "Couchaké is a place
where the Hurons took refuge during the war..."[58]

While they were living at Conchaké the Hurons evidently hunted in
winter through most of Areas 54 and 53. Soon after Céloron came to
Detroit as commandant in the spring of 1750,[59] he addressed some of
these "rebel" Hurons, in an effort "to induce them to return to their
mission [near Detroit]." The Hurons promised to return, but earnestly

110

---

56. De Léry, Journal, pp. 103-104; Dft. Ex. A-113. The version
of De Léry's Journal published by Hanna reads at this point: "Where
some Hurons had taken refuge after the treacherous deed they committed
at Detroit. It is called the Fugitives' Camp" (Hanna, The Wilderness
Trail, vol. 2, p. 176; Dft. Ex. A-82).

57. De Léry, Journal, p. 104; Dft. Ex. A-113. Hanna's version
reads at this point: "Tourieuse is a place whither the Huron fugitives
had withdrawn." (Hanna, The Wilderness Trail, vol. 2, p. 177; Dft.
Ex. A-82).

58. De Léry, Journal, p. 105; Dft. Ex. A-113. "The war" was
King George's War (1745-1748), the American phase of the War of the
Austrian Succession (1740-1748).

59. La Jonquière and Bigot to the French Minister, October 5,
1749, p. 31; Dft. Ex. A-89.

begged Céloron "to leave the land at rest" (i. e., not send any French soldiers into it) "from Conchaké...to the Vermilion [Huron] River... where all the rebel Huron were to gather" prior to going to Detroit. Céloron assented, but warned them that if they allowed any English traders to pass these "bounds" and "come to Sandusky or on the Maumee River [he] would have them arrested." The Hurons agreed to this.[60]

The Conchaké Hurons, however, did not live up to their agreement, and in November or December, 1750 after the French had built a fort on the northwest shore of Sandusky Bay, south of present Port Clinton, Ottawa County, Ohio[61] French troops acting on Céloron's orders arrested three (five?) English traders who were with the rebel Hurons at the latter's winter hunting depot at Sandusky.[62] The arrest of the English traders, and the fact that Céloron insisted on sending the latter in the

---

60. Céloron to Vaudreuil, August 4, 1751, pp. 287-288; Dft. Ex. A-87. Nicolas is not referred to in these negotiations. He died at Conchaké in August or September, 1750, recommending to his people before his death "not only never to return to the mission [opposite Detroit], but also to kill even the Blackrobe [Father de la Richardie] a61; if he came [to Conchaké] to enlist them" (Ott, ed., Selections, p. 260, Dft. Ex. A-83).

61. De Léry, Journal, pp. 54-55; Dft. Ex. A-113. Pennsylvania Magazine of History and Biography, vol. 65, p. 427; Dft. Ex. A-131. Deposition of Thomas Bourke, p. 50½; Dft. Ex. A-207. The fort was called Fort Sandoski. It was evacuated soon after it was built.

62. Ott, ed., Selections, p. 264; Dft. Ex. A-83. Céloron to Vaudreuil, April 23, 1751, pp. 245-246; Dft. Ex. A-86. O'Callaghan, ed., Documents, vol. 6, p. 733; Dft. Ex. A-39. O'Callaghan, ed., Documents, vol. 10, pp. 240-241; Dft. Ex. A-69.

spring of 1751 to Montreal to the Governor of Canada,[63] caused "general consternation" among the Hurons.[64] Although some of the "rebels" returned to Detroit soon after the English traders had been captured, the majority apparently were still at Conchaké in August, 1751.[65]

Before Christopher Gist, on his Ohio trip of 1750-1751 reached Conchaké ("Moskingum") he passed through another Indian town which, we conclude, was a mile or so east of the southeastern tip of Royce Area 54, at or near present Bolivar, Stark County, Ohio. Of this town he writes:

> Friday [Dec.] 7 Set out SW 8 M crossing the said Elk's Eye Creek [present Tuscarawas River] to a

---

63. The names of the arrested men, as given by the French governor, are "Luke Arowin," "John Fortimer," and "Thomas Borke" (O'Callaghan, ed., Documents, vol. 6, p. 733; Dft. Ex. A-39). In a deposition made by Thomas Bourke at the British embassy in Paris in 1752 Bourke stated that he and Luke Erwin and Joseph Faltener were arrested by 50 French soldiers "at a place called Cuyahoga about ten leagues [25 miles] from the fort which the French have built on Lake Sandusky." In extenuation for trading there, Bourke states that the country he was in was within "the territory of the Five Nations which further extends divers leagues about it." Bourke probably falsified in order to disguise the fact that he was in territory which, as Céloron had warned the Hurons, the English should not enter (Deposition of Thomas Bourke, pp. 503-504½ Dft. Ex. A-207; p. 44, this Report).

The English traders were some of Croghan's men, who had been sent to trade "with a party of Indians of the Wayondott Tribe then hunting on the Heads of the Scioto River" (Bailey, Ohio Company Papers, pp. 36-37, 137-138; Dft. Ex. A-77. The dates given in Bailey for the arrest of the traders, 1749, 1751 are both wrong).

64. Ott, ed., Selections, pp. 264-265; Dft. Ex. A-83. Shiels, Jesuits in Ohio, pp. 45-46; Dft. Ex. A-62. Céloron to Vaudreuil, April 23, 1751, pp. 245-246; Dft. Ex. A-86.

65. Céloron to Vaudreuil, August 4, 1751, pp. 288-289; Dft. Ex. A-87. O'Callaghan, Documents, vol. 10, p. 249; Dft. Ex. A-69.

Town of the Ottaways, a Nation of French Indians;
an old French Man (named Mark Coonce) who had
married an Indian Woman of the six Nations lived
here; the Indians were all out a hunting...There
are not above six or eight Families belonging to
this Town.[66]

A "Map of the Ohio Company Lands" by John Mercer, secretary of the

Company, shows the route Gist took in 1750-1751. The Ottawa town Gist

says he visited on December 7, 1750 is not indicated on the map, al-

though other towns he stopped at are. The map has, however one curious

entry on it. Considerably north of "Moskingom Town" at the headwaters of

the same river that "Moskingom Town" is on, a second settlement is in-

dicated, on the east side of the river. North of this is the legend

"Tuscaroras." No "Town" or "T." is included in the legend, as it is in

others, and the dotted line showing Gist's route passes a good distance

south of "Tuscaroras."[67]

Whatever it is intended to be, from its location north of Muskingum   113

"Tuscaroras" was apparently close to the boundaries of Royce Area 54 or

Royce Area 53. The historian Charles A. Hanna, who does not refer to the

"Map of the Ohio Company Lands," accepts the "Ottawa" town Gist visited

---

66. Mulkearn, ed., George Mercer Papers, pp. 11, 487-488; Dft.
Ex. A-72. See Heckewelder, Narrative, p. 114; Dft. Ex. A-53 for
identification of Elk's Eye Creek as the Muskingum (present Tuscarawas)
River.

67. Map of the Ohio Company Lands; Dft. Ex. A-85. Mulkearn,
ed., George Mercer Papers, pp. 143, 225, 237, 411-412, 526-527, 577-578;
Dft. Ex. A-72.
    For the Wyandot and Delaware names of the location known from an
early date as "Tuscarawas" see Ontario History, vol. 49, no. 2, p. 91;
Dft. Ex. A-269.

in 1750 as being "Tuscarawas."[68] We agree with him, and conclude that the Ohio Company Lands Map is in error, for the following reasons. (a) The "Traders Map of the Ohio Country, 1750-1752," attributed to Pattin legends a "Tuscgrawies" town at an unlabelled fork some distance east of the Forks of Muskingum, on what is apparently the upper Tuscarawas River. No other town is legended on this river. (b) A second map, an anonymous compendium published with George Washington's Journal in 1754, also locates "Tuskaroras" northeast of Muskingum on the upper reaches of the Tuscarawas River.[69]

In a 1750-1751 despatch from the French governor of Louisiana it is stated that one band of Shawnees "had gone back to Sandusky," from the Ohio River,[70] but no further details are given.

By 1751 the French were making determined efforts to keep Pennsylvania traders out of the Lake Erie region. In late 1751, according to the report of a half-breed British Indian the French "built a new Fort at a Place call'd Kyhogo [Cuyahoga] on the West [south] Side of Lake Eare [Erie]."[71] The need for their doing this is made plain in a

---

68. Hanna, The Wilderness Trail, vol. 1, p. 334; Dft. Ex. A-70. Hanna, The Wilderness Trail, vol. 2, p. 145, fn. 1; Dft. Ex. A-82.

69. [Pattin], Traders Map of the Ohio Country, 1750-1752; Dft. Ex. A-102. Pennsylvania Magazine of History and Biography, vol. 65, pp. 420-438; Dft. Ex. A-131. Brown, Early Maps, pl. 19; Dft. Ex. A-96. Brown, Early Maps, pp. 91-92; Dft. Ex. A-97.

70. La Jonquière to Rouillé, September 27, 1751, p. 372; Dft. Ex. A-80.

71. Calendar of Virginia State Papers, vol. 1, p. 245; Dft. Ex. A-111. This may have been rumor rather than fact. In 1752 however, the "Castor or Beaver Comp^y of Quebec" petitioned to have a fort erected on "la Riviere Blanche" (Cuyahoga) to support their Indian trade, which was suffering from encroachment by English traders. The petition was granted (O'Callaghan, ed., Documents, vol. 6, p. 825; Dft. Ex. A-39).

despatch from the English trading house at present Oswego, New York, on
the south shore of Lake Ontario. On May 4, 1751 Lt. John Lindesay,
commandant at Oswego, reported he had been told a French army was to
build a fort at Niagara

> and to run off the [pro-English] Shawanahs [Shawnees]
> Chanundadees [Wyandots] and Twigtwee Indians [Miamis]
> (who live at Kyahagah [Cuyahoga] on the Drafts
> [branches] of Ohio and [on] Ohio) with whom the Phil-
> adelphians trade, and to drive them from thence...

The next day a Cayuga chief assured Lt. Lindesay that

> the Five Nations [Iroquois] were determined to assist
> and defend all those Indians who live at Cayahaga
> [Cuyahoga] and to protect the English that traded
> there...[72]

Evidently there were still a number of Indians belonging to
several different groups living on the Cuyahoga River in 1751. An
anonymous map drawn in 1755 indicates what may have happened to this
population on the Cuyahoga by 1752, however. South of Lake Erie, in
what seems to be the extreme eastern part of Area 53, there is a
legend on the map: "Six Nats. moved four years ago to Tiughsoghrun-
tie."[73] Tiisughsobruntie is mentioned by an 18th-century geographer
as the "early seat of the Wyandots," and is identified as a name for

115

---

72. O'Callaghan, ed., Documents, vol. 6, pp. 704, 706; Dft. Ex.
A-39. Parentheses are Lindesay's; brackets are ours.

73. Anonymous Draft of the Ohio from an Indian Account; Dft. Ex.
A-100. For the provenience of this map see Brown, Early Maps, p. 94;
Dft. Ex. A-97. The map can be dated by one of the legends on it:
"Twighttwees [Miami]" town at Pickawillany "destroyed three years ago
by the French." The French razed Pickawillany in 1752 (Minutes of the
Provincial Council, vol. 5, pp. 599-600; Dft. Ex. A-76.

Detroit by Hanna.[74] Assuming this identification is correct, it is likely that the "Six Nats." in the legend on the anonymous map of 1755 refers to the mixed group of Indians (Iroquois, "Loups," Mahicans, Ottawas, etc.) that had settled on the Cuyahoga around 1742. With French influence strengthened by the building of several forts in the Lakes district from 1750 onward, the French were probably able by 1752 to persuade the Indians living on the Cuyahoga to move to Detroit, where Pennsylvania traders could not traffic/them.[75]

By October, 1753, with the French in control of trade in the Ohio Valley-Lake region,[76] we know that the rebel Hurons had left Conchaké (Muskingum) and had "returned to their village"--presumably to their village near Detroit.[77] Their numbers, however, were depleted; in 1752, 120 of them had died of smallpox at Conchaké.[78]

---

74. Evans, Analysis, p. 13; Dft. Ex. A-94. Hanna, The Wilderness Trail, vol. 1, p. 12; Dft. Ex. A-70.
The Clowes Map of 1701 (Dft. Ex. A-23) legends "Tiugh-Taghondio or Wawyachtenok" as the Iroquois name for the western end of the Ontario Peninsula, opposite Detroit.

75. English traders were still attempting, in 1752, to trade with the Indians on the Cuyahoga. A trader's list shows that one James Lowery, in 1752, suffered from "Debts lost at Guahagey by the Wyandott Indians" (Bailey, Ohio Company Papers, pp. 110, 113-114; Dft. Ex. A-77).

76. Minutes of the Provincial Council, vol. 5, p. 684; Dft. Ex. A-76.

77. Duquesne to Rouillé, October 31, 1753, pp. 849-850; Dft. Ex. A-91. The Hurons had been expected back at Detroit in 1752; see O'Callaghan, ed., Documents, vol. 10, p. 249; Dft. Ex. A-69 and also Joncaire, Letter to Baby [March 11, 1752]; Dft. Ex. A-267.

78. De Léry, Journal, p. 105; Dft. Ex. A-119. In the spring of 1752 smallpox was rife in the Ohio Valley (O'Callaghan, ed., Documents, vol. 10, p. 249; Dft. Ex. A-69. Goodman, Journal of Captain William Trent, p. 85; Dft. Ex. A-249).

A map, published in 1755, shows certain towns and Indian groups in present Areas 53 and 54, but as is so often the case with maps, the information is difficult to date. The map is by Lewis Evans, Pennsylvania surveyor and geographer, and is politically oriented to show English rights to the Ohio Valley.[79] On it, as already noted, Evans legends a "French House" and a "Mingoes T[own]" on the west side of the Cuyahoga River 25-30 miles above its mouth, and an Ottawa town opposite the French house on the east bank of the Cuyahoga. It is very unlikely, as indicated by data presented above, that either of the two Indians towns Evans maps on the Cuyahoga were in existence as late as 1755.[80] No Indian village or French house is mentioned in an excellent account by one Col. James Smith, a White captive who, early in 1756, hunted with a party of Ottawas, Chippewas and Caughnawaga Mohawks up and down the Cuyahoga River from its mouth to the rapids on the upper Cuyahoga.[81]

At the junction of Tuscarawas River and "Lamonshikolas Creek" (present Sandy Creek) Evans legends "Tuscarawas," just outside the extreme southeastern corner of present Area 54. No indication is given as to what Indians, if any, occupied it. On the east side of the Tuscarawas

117

79. Dictionary of American Biography, vol. 6, pp. 206-207; Dft. Ex. A-98.

80. Evans, A General MAP; Dft. Ex. A-93. In his Analysis of his map Evans expressly states that "The present, late and antient Seats of the original Inhabitants are expressed in the Map" (Evans, Analysis, p. iv; Dft. Ex. A-94; emphasis ours).

81. See pp. 74-76, this Report.

River below its junction with Sandy Creek, a short distance outside of
Area 54, another site, "Three Legs," is legended, but is also not
identified. Likewise, within Royce Area 54, some distance north of
the Forks of Muskingum and west of the western branch of the Muskingum, in western Area 54, "Mohiccons" are legended, but no village
is specifically indicated. On lower Sandusky River, 12-14 miles west
of Area 53, Evans legends two Wyandot towns, and "Junundot, built in
1754," and Fort Sandusky.

Another 1755 map, an ambitious compendium made by Dr. John
Mitchell, an adopted Virginian, and published in London, is disappoint-
ing for its patent inaccuracies as concern the Lake Erie region. On
his map Mitchell legends a river flowing into what is apparently Sandusky Bay, as the "R. Blanc [White River]." The lands to the east of
"R. Blanc" Mitchell legends grandiosely as "Canahogue The seat of War
the Mart of Trade and chief Hunting Grounds of the Six Nations on the
Lakes."[82] To the east of Canahogue Mitchell indicates "Canahogue Bay
Middle of the Lake," with the "Gwahago R[iver]" flowing into it from
the south. Possibly the "Gwahago" is intended as the Cuyahoga River,
the mouth of which Mitchell expands into a non-existent "Bay." East

---

82. Mitchell, A Map of the British and French Dominions; Dft.
Ex. A-99. Brown, Early Maps, pp. 95-97; Dft. Ex. A-97. Drake, ed.,
Indian Captivities, p. 223   Dft. Ex. A-95. Fite and Freeman, A
Book of Old Maps, p. 181; Dft. Ex. A-150.
  The legend "Canahogue" may have been taken from the Colden map
of 1723, which is discussed on p. 26, fn. 81, this Report.
  Mitchell's Map of 1755, like Lewis Evans' General MAP of 1755,
is politically oriented to show English rights to the Ohio Valley.
(Brown, Early Maps, p. 96; Dft. Ex. A-97. Fite and Freeman, A Book of
Old Maps, p. 182; Dft. Ex. A-150.)

of the Gwahago River are lands legended "Gwahago Iroquois." But the most
obvious of all errors in the section of Mitchell's map under review is
his location of "L[ake] Otsanderket [Sandusky]" which he shows as a land-
locked lake several miles south of Lake Erie. Mitchell gives "L. Otsanderket" as the source for "Elks Eye Creek [present Tuscarawas River]" a
stream on which, lower down, he locates "Tuscaroraas" on the west side
and "Legs T." just below on the east side. Since Mitchell had free
access to all the documents in the London Board of Trade, his map is a
graphic illustration of the ignorance of British colonial officialdom in
1755 about the lands south of Lake Erie, to which the British were laying
claim by virtue of these lands having "belonged" to the Six Nations
Iroquois, and having been put by the latter "under the protection of the
Crown of Great Brittain."[83]

3. Use and Occupancy of Royce Areas 53 and 54: 1755-1759. For 119
the years 1755-1759 there are several contemporary sources relating to
use and occupancy of Areas 53 and 54. The first such is an anonymous
"Draft of the Ohio Valley from an Indian Account," drawn in 1755.[84] A
few miles south of the western end of Lake Erie at the head of a long
river flowing into the Ohio labelled the "Anagarighuone" there is a
village indicated, and a legend, "Mohawks a few yet here." No river
heads near the south shore of Lake Erie and empties into the Ohio, but

---

83. O'Callaghan, ed., Documents, vol. 6, p. 886; Dft. Ex. A-39.
84. Anonymous, Draft of the Ohio; Dft. Ex. A-100. See fn. 73,
this Chapter.

the existence of a few Mohawks somewhere south of the western end of Lake Erie, perhaps in western Area 53, is of interest in connection with a remark made in De Léry's journal of 1755, a document we have already had occasion to refer to,[85] and to which we now turn for a description of Areas 53 and 54 in 1755.

On March 16, 1755 De Léry was at the mouth of Portage River, at present Port Clinton, Ottawa County, Ohio, about six miles west of extreme northwestern Area 53. He had with him two Iroquois companions. From Portage River De Léry went southwesterly that day on a well-established portage trail about two miles long, to reach the north shore of Sandusky Bay, where he and one of the Iroquois fired their guns "several times to make ourselves heard by the French Traders on the southeast shore of Lake Dotsandoské." No response was made to their signals.

120

Having found a leaky canoe on the morning of March 17, 1755, at noon that day De Léry set out to cross Sandusky Bay near its western end, where it was, according to his estimate. "a league and a half" (3.75 miles) wide. His passage of 3.75 miles across the bay brought him slightly east of the mouth of Sandusky River, to a point "three leagues [7.5 miles] above" (west of) "Rivière du Poisson Doré."[86] The mouth of present Pickerel Creek, which flows into Sandusky Bay and is identified by Hanna as De Léry's "Rivière du Poisson Doré," is eight

---

85. See fn. 6, this Chapter.

86. De Léry, Journal, pp. 55, 96, 99; Dft. Ex. A-113.

miles east of the mouth of the Sandusky River. We therefore agree with
Hanna's identification. Pickerel Creek empties into Lake Erie four
miles west of Area 53.[87]

De Léry was eastward-bound. At 4 p. m. on March 17, he arrived "at
the place of Sieur Gouin, a trader." This trading post was, we conclude,
at the mouth of the Rivière du Poisson Doré (Pickerel Creek) since De
Léry mentions, specifically, the distance to this stream from the point
where he had crossed the Bay.

The next day, March 18, 1755 De Léry, then at the trading post at
Pickerel Creek four miles west of Area 53, sent some Hurons to what he
refers to as "the little village," to get a guide and a horse. The
Indians set out from Sieur Gouin's house in the morning and returned by
4 p.m., unsuccessful. De Léry thereupon decided to travel eastward via
Lake Erie, and procured a canoe which he planned to use as far as "the
Rivière à Seguin, which is called Gayahagué [Cuyahoga]."[88]

121

March 19, 1755 found De Léry camped within present Area 53 at the
"foot" (mouth) of Sandusky Bay on the south side, probably near present
Sandusky, Erie County, Ohio, four and a half leagues (11.25 miles) west
of Sieur Gouin's. Bad weather set in, but on March 21, 1755, De Léry
went "a league and a half [3.75 miles]" farther eastward "to the foot of
the swamp, east of Lake Dotsandoské." where he "crossed the portage to

---

87. See pocket map, this Report. Hanna, The Wilderness Trail,
vol. 2, p. 172; Dft. Ex. A-82. For references to the various small
creeks in and near northwestern Area 53 see Firelands Pioneer, vol, no.
3, September 1860, pp. 11-12, 46-48; Dft. Ex. A-242.

88. De Léry, Journal, pp. 97-99, 102; Dft. Ex. A-113.

the great lake [Lake Erie] which we found full of ice."[89] This

> made us decide to retrace our steps [westward] to
> the portage of the Anioton village...at five
> o'clock we arrived at this village, where only
> three cabins and some palisades remained. We
> resolved to take the Couchake route, even though
> it is long, and asked a Huron to guide us...but
> he did not want to...
> We were in the place where the Hurons took
> refuge after they left Isle du Bois Blanc [1738]
> and killed the Frenchmen [1747]. They had built
> a fort here, of which a plan follows.[90]

Anioton, according to De Léry's sketch maps,[91] was on a stream,

one league (2.5 miles) south of Sandusky Bay. As nearly as can be

determined from De Léry's maps, and the distances he gives between

this village and other points, Anioton was at or near the head of

Cold Creek, at present Castalia, Erie County, Ohio, in northwestern

Area 53.[92]

---

89. De Léry, Journal, pp. 100-101; Dft. Ex. A-113.

90. De Léry, Journal, p. 101; Dft. Ex. A-113.
Aniotin was the Huron chief who, with Nicolas, went from S
dusky to Detroit in September, 1747 to sue for peace. The name of th
chief who first went to Sandusky in 1738 was Angouirot. "Anioton" may
possibly be another form of Angouirot's name.

91. De Léry, Journal, pp. 100, 101; Dft. Ex. A-113.

92. De Léry, Journal, pp. 99-102; Dft. Ex. A-113.
Lois Mulkearn, editor of the recently published George
Mercer Papers, locates this early Huron village "in the vicinity of
present Venice, Ohio" (Mulkearn, ed., George Mercer Papers, p. 489
Dft. Ex. A-72.) Venice, however, is at the mouth of Cold Creek, on
Sandusky Bay, whereas Castalia is at the head of the creek, about
four miles inland from the Bay. See Firelands Pioneer, vol. 2, no. 3,
September 1860, pp. 12, 22, 46-47; Dft. Ex. A-242.

While De Léry was at Anioton on March 22, 1755, he observes that:

An Ágnier [Mohawk] wintering three day's march
from this village, arrived. He was going to Sandoské to trade...at Sieur Gouin's...93

The possible existence of a few Mohawks in western Area 53 in
1755 has already been noted. De Léry's observation strengthens this
possibility - the Mohawk obviously came to Anioton from the east or
south, and had therefore been wintering either in Area 53 or 54.

On March 23 De Léry left Anioton "by the Couchake road," which
started on the southeast side of the village. De Léry travelled southward about 14 leagues (35 miles) that day and the next, crossing various
branches of the "Rivière au Vermillon [Huron94]."95. On the second day he

met a Huron who told us that 20 Chaȣanons [Shawnees]
had arrived at Sandoské. I thought it might be the
ones who were going to talk at Detroit.96

From this time onward De Léry travelled southeasterly. He does not record meeting any Indians until he reached "Couchaké" (present Coshocton,
Coshocton County Ohio97), some 30 miles south of Area 54, at 6 p.m. on

123

---

93. De Léry, Journal, pp. 102, 103; Dft. Ex. A-113. Hodge, ed.,
Handbook, pt. 2, p. 1022, Dft. Ex. A-2. Note that in 1755 the French
applied the name "Sandoské" specifically to the trading post at the mouth
of Rivière du Poisson Doré (present Pickerel Creek).

94. See fn. 48, this Chapter.

95. De Léry, Journal, pp. 102-103; Dft. Ex. A-113.

96. De Léry, Journal, p. 108; Dft. Ex. A-113.

97. See pp. 48-49, this Report.

March 29, 1755. Of Conchaké as it existed in 1755 De Léry writes:

> One can still see the graves and the remains of the
> [Huron] village that was there [in the early 1750's].
> Only two of the cabins are left, one belongs to the
> Sault St. Louis savages [Caughnawaga Mohawks[98]] who
> have been there for a long time, the other belongs to
> the Five Nations.[99]

From Conchaké De Léry followed the "Naguerreconnan" or Tuscarawas

River eastward and northeast for a day and a half. About 12 leagues

(30 miles) east of Conchaké he passed "two Huron winter cabins," pro-

bably somewhere in Tuscarawas County, Ohio, a few miles south of

eastern Area 54. De Léry does not mention going as far north as

Tuscarawas, at the southeastern tip of Area 54.[100]

Another account, relating to the years 1755-1758, graphically

illustrates the manner in which Royce Areas 53 and 54 were freely used

and occupied by Indians of several different groups. The author of

124   the narrative, Col. James Smith, was a literate Pennsylvanian who in

1755, when he was 18 years old, was captured in western Pennsylvania

and lived for four years with Caughnawaga Mohawks and Wyandots, until

July, 1759.[101]

---

98. See fn. 8, this Chapter.

99. De Léry, Journal, p. 105, text and sketch; Dft. Ex. A-113.
Conchaké had evidently had some Caughnawaga Mohawks as well as
Wyandots in it, in the early 1750's.

100. De Léry, Journal, p. 105, text and sketch, and p. 107; Dft.
Ex. A-113.

101. Drake, Indian Captivities, pp. 178-181, 185, 234; Dft. Ex.
A-95.

In August, 1755 Smith was taken by his captors

> to an Indian town on the west branch of Muskingum,
> about twenty miles above the forks, which was
> called Tullihas, [and was] inhabited by Delawares,
> Caughnewagas [French Mohawks[102]] and Mohicans.[103]

This mixed town was either on the present Walhonding River, or on the lower Mohican River near its junction with the Walhonding. The town was some 15-18 miles south of Area 54.

At Tullihas Smith was formally adopted into a Caughnawaga Mohawk family. His adopted brother was a Caughnawaga "called Tontileaugo, who had married a Wyandot squaw." The two chiefs at Tullihas were "Tecanya-terighto, alias Pluggy," a warrior, and "Asallecoa, alias Mohawk Solomon." One of the Delawares at Tullihas was married to a Caughnawaga Mohawk woman. Although Smith does not explicitly say so, the various Indians he was with during his captivity were evidently all "French Indians;" their warriors raided on the frontiers of Pennsylvania and Virginia, and all trading was done with French traders.[104]

125

In October, 1755 Smith was taken north from Tullihas to Lake Erie by his adopted Caughnawaga Mohawk brother. The two went up the "west Branch of Muskingum" (Walhonding-Mohican rivers, partly in Area 54) to the headwaters, and from thence across a dividing ridge to the headwaters of

---

102. See p. 37 and fn. 8, this Chapter

103. Drake, Indian Captivities, p. 185; Dft. Ex. A-95.

104. Drake, Indian Captivities, pp. 186-188, 190-191, 195, 197, 201, 203-204, 218; Dft. Ex. A-95.

the Huron River, which Smith refers to as the "Canesadooharie."[105]
Proceeding northward and generally down the Huron River in western
Area 53, Smith and Tontileaugo "came to lake Erie about six miles west
of the mouth of Canesadooharie [Huron]." On this trip

> Tontileaugo, who was a first-rate hunter, carried a
> rifle gun, and every day killed deer, raccoons, or
> bears. We left the meat, excepting a little for
> present use, and carried the skins with us...when
> the skins were dried by the fire, we packed them up
> and carried them with us.[106]

After arriving at Lake Erie the two travellers went east along
the shore "to a large camp of Wyandots, at the mouth of Canesadooharie
[Huron] where Tontileaugo's wife was." This Wyandot camp was in
northwestern Area 53. "Here," Smith records,

126

> we were kindly received; they gave us a kind of
> rough, brown potatoes, which grew spontaneously,
> and were called by the Caughnewagas ohnenata.
> These potatoes peeled and dipped in raccoon's fat
> taste nearly like our sweet potatoes. They also
> gave us what they call caneheanta, which is a kind
> of homony, made of green corn, dried, and beans,
> mixed together.[107]

---

105. Drake, Indian Captivities, pp. 200-201; Dft. Ex. A-95.
Smith observes of the Huron River: "This river, called Canesadooharie,
interlocks with the West Branch of Muskingum, runs nearly a north
course, and empties into the south side of lake Erie, about eight miles
east from Sandusky, or betwixt Sandusky and Cayahaga."

Henry Howe, a 15th-century mid-west historian, identifies the
Canesadooharie as the Black River (Howe, Historical Collections,
vol. 2, p. 119; Dft. Ex. A-192). Howe's resumé of Smith's narrative
is, however, so full of inaccuracies that none of Howe's identifications are reliable.

106. Drake, Indian Captivities, pp. 190-191; Dft. Ex. A-95.

107. Drake, Indian Captivities, pp. 191-192; Dft. Ex. A-95. Smith
was rapidly learning to speak Mohawk at this time.

The Wyandots, Tontileaugo and his family, and Smith remained at this camp "for some time." The Indians killed

> some deer, and a great many raccoons; the raccoons here were remarkably large and fat. At length we all embarked in a large birch bark canoe...about four feet wide, and three feet deep, and about five and thirty feet long...and proceeded up Canesadooharie [Huron] a few miles, and went on shore to hunt...
>
> We kept moving and hunting up this river until we came to the falls; here we remained some weeks, and killed a number of deer, several bears, and a great many raccoons. From the mouth of this river to the falls is about five and twenty miles.[108]

At the falls of the Huron, in western Area 53, the Indians hung up the furs and skins they had accumulated, buried their large canoe, which they had been using at night as a shelter, and set out on foot to go 22 miles eastward "to a large creek that empties into lake Erie, betwixt Canesadooharie [Huron River] and Cayahaga [Cuyahoga River]." This creek was probably present Black River, in central Area 53. On Black River, in December, 1755, the party made its "winter cabin," a substantial, rectangular, multifamily structure 15 feet long and 12 feet wide, with log walls 4 feet high and a gabled roof covered with lynn bark.[109]

There were eight Indian hunters at this winter camp, and 13 "squaws, boys and children," Smith being counted as one of the "boys."

127

---

108. Drake, Indian Captivities, p. 192; Dft. Ex. A-95

109. Drake, Indian Captivities, pp. 192-194; Dft. Ex. A-95. Local tradition has it that the cabin was on Black River near present Elyria, Lorain County (Howe, Historical Collections, vol. 2, p. 119; Dft. Ex. A-192).

The party had no horses to use for transporting the game which the hunters killed at a distance from the cabin. Four of the men, therefore, decided "they would go to war even in this inclement season, in order to bring in horses." The remaining four hunters, Tontileaugo included, were to stay at the winter cabin to provide meat for the women and children.[110]

After the war party left rations in camp became short. Tontileaugo and Smith therefore set out from the cabin to hunt meat, and went southward in present Area 53, up the waters of Black River some 10-12 miles from their cabin. There they encamped "in a snug little shelter" and remained for

> about two weeks, and in this time killed four bears,
> three deer, several turkeys and a number of raccoons.
> We packed up as much meat as we could carry, and
> returned to our winter cabin. On our arrival there
> was great joy, as they were all in a starving con-
> dition, the three hunters that we had left having
> killed but very little. All that could carry a pack,
> repaired to our camp to bring in meat.[111]

During "Some time in February [1756] the four warriours returned" with two scalps and six horses they had taken on the Pennsylvania frontier. After this, Smith explains:

> The hunters could then scatter out a considerable
> distance from the winter cabin and encamp, kill meat,
> and bring it in upon horses; so that we commonly
> after this had plenty of provision.[112]

110. Drake, Indian Captivities, pp. 194-195; Dft. Ex. A-95.

111. Drake, Indian Captivities, pp. 195-197; Dft. Ex. A-95.

112. Drake, Indian Captivities, p. 197; Dft. Ex. A-95.

128

February was also the month in which the women at the winter
cabin began making maple sugar. At this time Smith and "some of the
Indian lads" trapped "raccoons, foxes, wildcats, &c."[113]

"About the latter end of March [1756]," the group

> began to prepare for moving into town, in order
> to plant corn. The squaws were they frying the
> last of their bear's fat, and making vessels to
> hold it; the vessels were made of deer-skins...
> [and] would hold about four or five gallons...
>
> When all things were ready, we moved back to
> the falls of Canesadooharie [Huron River, 25 miles
> above the mouth]...On our arrival at the falls
> (as we had brought with us on horseback about two
> hundred weight of sugar, a large quantity of bear's
> oil, skins, &c.,) the canoe we had buried was not
> sufficient to carry all; therefore we were obliged
> to make another one of elm bark.[114]

Instead of accompanying the Wyandots down the Huron River to their
town where they were to plant corn, Tontileaugo elected to go off with
Smith on a hunt. About April 1, 1756 the two "went up [south on]
Canesadooharie [Huron River] about thirty miles and encamped," to hunt
in present northwestern Area 54. In their two-weeks' stay above the
falls of Huron they had "considerable success," killing "a number of
bears, raccoons, and some beavers," and also catching a stray horse and
a colt. They then returned to the falls of the Huron, and from there
went down the river to Lake Erie, Smith on horseback and Tontileaugo in
an elm bark canoe which he had made at the falls. Reaching the shore

129

---

113. Drake, Indian Captivities, pp. 197-198; Dft. Ex. A-95.

114. Drake, Indian Captivities, pp. 198-199; Dft. Ex. A-95. The
parentheses are Smith's
No mention is made as to whether the horses used for packing as
far as the falls were kept or turned loose.

of Lake Erie, the two turned west and encamped for several days at the

mouth of a small creek. (Cold Creek?), where "a Wyandot came to our

camp" (from Ahioton?) and was given a shoulder of venison.[115]

After this Smith and Tontileaugo proceeded west and

> arrived safe at Sunyendeand, which was a Wyandot
> town that lay upon a small creek which empties
> into the little lake below [east of] the mouth of
> Sandusky.
>
> The town was about eighty rood[116] above the
> mouth of the creek, on the south side of a large
> plain, on which timber grew, and nothing more but
> grass or nettles...In this town there were also
> French traders, who purchased our skins and furs...[117]

Two years later, in 1758, Smith descended the Sandusky River, and

writes of Sunyendeand:

> When we came to the little lake [Sandusky Bay] at
> the mouth of Sandusky we called at a Wyandot town
> that was then there, called Sunyendeand. Here we
> diverted ourselves several days by catching rock
> fish in a small creek, the name of which is also
> Sunyendeand, which signifies rock fish.[118]

From these two entries we see that Sunyendeand was east of the mouth of

the Sandusky River, probably by a few miles, and that it had traders in

it. We therefore conclude that Smith's Sunyendeand or Rock Fish Creek

was De Léry's "Rivière du Poisson Doré," (present Pickerel Creek) four

---

115. Drake, Indian Captivities, pp. 199-201; Dft. Ex. A-95.

116. A rood is a linear measure varying locally, usually 7 or
8 yards, but sometimes a rod (16.5 feet). The town was, then, between
1320 and 1920 feet, or between a quarter and a third of a mile above
the mouth of the creek.

117. Drake, Indian Captivities, p. 201; Dft. Ex. A-95.

118. Drake, Indian Captivities. p. 232; Dft. Ex. A-95.

130

miles west of Area 53. It was at the village of Sunyendeand that the
Wyandots whom Smith was with had their corn fields, and this was where
he stayed during the summer and early fall of 1756.[119]

Some time in October, 1756 Smith and an older brother of Tontileaugo's, Tecaughretanego, left the Sandusky Bay region "to take a
hunt on Cayahaga [Cuyahoga River]" with a party of Caughnawaga Mohawks,
Ottawas, and Chippewas. The party assembled at the mouth of Sandusky
Bay in Area 53; the size of the group is not stated, but the members had
"four birch bark canoes, and four [mat] tents." In the party Smith met
"a Caughnawaga sister [married to a Chippewa man], and other [relatives
by adoption] I had never before seen." The group "kindly received"
Smith and his 60-year-old companion Tecaughretanego and, Smith relates

> gave us plenty of homony, and wild fowl boiled
> and roasted. As the geese, ducks, swans, &c.,
> here are well grain-fed, they were remarkably
> fat, especially the green-necked ducks.
>
> The wild fowl here feed upon a kind of wild
> rice that grows spontaneously in the shallow
> water, or wet places along the sides or in the
> corners of the lakes.

131

---

119. Drake, Indian Captivities, pp. 201-205; Dft. Ex. A-95. See
pp. 53-54, this Report.
    Rock fish is a general name for any fish that live among
rocks or on rocky bottoms; it is also a name used for the striped bass,
and the log perch. In springtime, according to Smith, the rock fish ran
up Sunyendeand Creek in great numbers.
    Joseph M. Root, a local historian of the Sandusky region,
writing in 1862 states that Smith's description of Sunyendeand "can only
apply to Pipe Creek and the Big Fields lying south-east of and about a
mile and half from the present town of Sandusky," Erie County (Firelands
Pioneer, vol. 4, June, 1863, p. 21; Dft. Ex. A-235). This puts Sunyende-
and some 20 miles east of the mouth of Sandusky River, and is at variance
with Smith's data.

> As the wind was high, and we could not pro-
> ceed on our voyage, we remained here [mouth of
> Sandusky Bay] several days, and killed abundance
> of wild fowl, and a number of raccoons.[120]

The voyage along the south shore of Lake Erie from the mouth of

Sandusky Bay to the mouth of the Cuyahoga took three days. Part of it

was made under sail; "What we used in place of sailcloth," Smith ex-

plains, "were our [rush] tent mats, which answered the purpose very

well." At the mouth of the Cuyahoga the party turned up the river on

the eastern boundary of present Area 53,

> and encamped, where we staid and hunted for several
> days; and so we kept moving and hunting until we
> came to the forks of the Cayahaga [Cuyahoga and
> Little Cuyahoga Rivers, ca. 3 miles north of Akron,
> Summit County, Ohio].
>
> This [Cuyahoga] is a very gentle river, and
> but few ripples, or swift running places, from the
> mouth to the forks. Deer here were tolerably
> plenty, large and fat; but bear and other game
> scarce...The West Branch of this river interlocks
> with the East Branch of Muskingum [present Tuscar-
> awas River], and the East Branch [of the Cuyahoga;
> present upper Cuyahoga] with the Big Beaver creek,
> that empties into the Ohio about thirty miles be-
> low Pittsburgh.
>
> From the forks of Cayahaga to the East Branch of
> Muskingum [present Tuscarawas River] there is a
> carrying place, where the Indians carry their canoes,
> &c., from the waters of lake Erie into the waters of
> the Ohio.[121]

132

---

120. Drake, Indian Captivities, pp. 205-207, 213, 215, 217, 225;
Dft. Ex. A-95.

121. Drake, Indian Captivities, pp. 207-208; Dft. Ex. A-95.

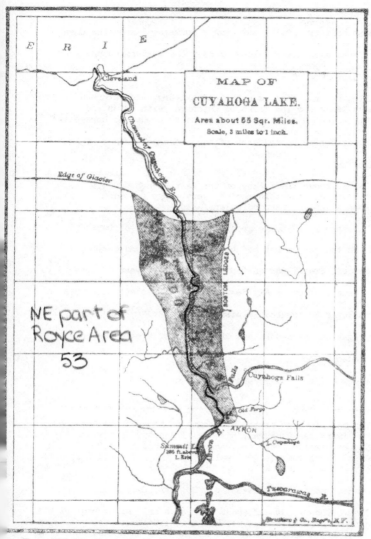

MAP OF
CUYAHOGA LAKE.
Area about 55 Sqr. Miles.
Scale, 3 miles to 1 inch.

NE part of
Royce Area
53

133

From Wright's *Ice Age in North America*; by courtesy of D. Appleton & Co., Publishers.

Fig. 2   From: **Henry Howe**
                    Historical Collections of Ohio
                    (Cincinnati, 1902) vol. 2, p. 628

With some hunters, Smith went over a portage[122] from the Cuyahoga
to the upper Tuscarawas River, along or near the eastern boundary of
Area 53. The hunters

> killed several deer, a number of beavers, and returned
> heavy laden [to the forks of Cuyahoga] with skins and
> meat, which we carried on our backs as we had no horses.[123]

The party also evidently hunted east of the eastern boundary of Area 53;
Smith mentions that

> a little above the forks, on the East Branch of Caya-
> haga, are considerable rapids, very rocky for some
> distance, but no perpendicular falls.[124]

About December 1, 1756 the group left the "forks of Cuyahoga,"
after hanging up the skins that had been accumulated and burying the
canoes, and proceeded overland on foot some 40 miles east of Area 53 to
winter on the waters of upper Big Beaver Creek in eastern Ohio, near a
little lake that was "a remarkable place for beaver."[125] In March, 1757,
after making sugar on the headwaters of Big Beaver Creek, the group, by
then heavily laden with

> all our baggage and several hundred weight of beaver

---

122. For descriptions of the two portages between the Cuyahoga
and Tuscarawas Rivers see Baughman, History of Ashland County, p. 54;
Dft. Ex. A-158; Heckewelder, Map and Description, pp. 339-340; Dft. Ex.
A-196; Howe, Historical Collections, vol. 2, p. 626; Dft. Ex. A-192; and
Ontario History, vol. 49, no. 2, p. 90; Dft. Ex. A-269.

123. Drake, Indian Captivities, p. 208; Dft. Ex. A-95.

124. Idem. The rapids end about one and a half miles east of the
eastern boundary of Area 53; see Howe, Historical Collections, vol. 2,
pp. 645-646; Dft. Ex. A-192. Smith does not seem to have gone as far up
the Cuyahoga as "Big Falls" and the other two falls above them which have
drops of 22', 16', and 12', respectively (Bierce, Historical Reminiscences, p. 62; Dft. Ex. A-233).

125. Drake, Indian Captivities, pp. 208-209; Dft. Ex. A-95.

> skins, and some deer and bear skins, all to pack on
> our backs

began moving back to the "forks of the Cuyahoga," which were some 40-50
miles westward, in eastern Area 53. Travel was "at the rate of about
five miles per day." When the party arrived at the Forks, Smith relates,

> we found that the skins we had scaffolded were all
> safe, Though this was a public place, and Indians
> frequently passing, and our skins hanging up in view,
> yet there were none stolen.[126]

The four canoes that had been buried at the Forks were taken up and
found "not damaged by the winter" and another large canoe was made of
chestnut bark, "as elm bark was not to be found." The party then

> all embarked, and had a very agreeable passage down
> the Cayahaga, and along the south side of lake Erie...

This group bypassed Sandusky Bay, and instead all its members went to

> the Wyandot town, nearly opposite to fort Detroit,
> on the north side of the [Detroit] river. Here
> we found a number of French traders, every one
> willing to deal with us for our beaver.[127]

135

No mention is made by Smith of there being any Indian towns or
trading houses on the Cuyahoga River when he went up and down it as
far as the rapids below the falls, in the fall of 1756 and spring of
1757, although Smith notes that the "forks" of Cuyahoga was "a public
place" which Indians frequently passed.

---

126. Drake, Indian Captivities, pp. 216-217; Dft. Ex. A-95.

127. Drake, Indian Captivities, p. 218; Dft. Ex. A-95.

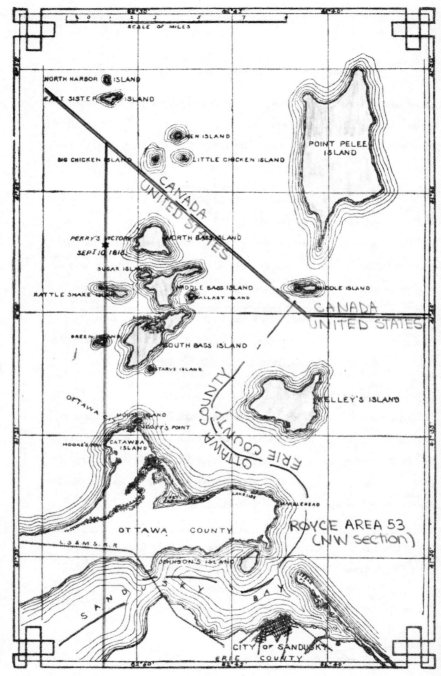

136

Fig. 3   From: Henry Howe, <u>Historical Collections of Ohio</u> (Cincinnati, 1902), vol. 2, p. 371.

Smith remained at Detroit through the summer and early fall of
1757. By the first of November, 1757, a number of Indian families
including those of his two adopted brothers, Tontileaugo and Tecaughretanego were, Smith relates:

> preparing to go on their winter hunt, and all
> agreed to cross the lake together. We encamped
> at the mouth of the [Detroit] river the first
> night, and a council was held, whether we should
> cross through by the three islands, or coast
> it round the lake. These islands lie in a line
> across the lake, and just in sight of each other.
> Some of the Wyandots, or Ottawas, frequently make
> their winter hunt on these islands; though, except-
> ing wild fowl and fish, there is scarcely any game
> here but raccoons, which are amazingly plenty, and
> exceedingly large and fat, as they feed upon the
> wild rice, which grows in abundance in wet places
> round these islands. It is said that each hunter,
> in one winter, will catch one thousand raccoons.[128]

The Indians concluded to coast around the west end of Lake Erie. Smith's
particular group, consisting of his adopted brothers' families plus two
Wyandot families, later parted from the rest of the Detroit Indian group
and went up the Sandusky River "to the falls of Sandusky" where "as
usual," they buried their birch bark canoes

137

> at a large buryingplace for that purpose, a little
> below the falls. At this place the river falls
> about eight feet over a rock, but not perpendicularly.[129]

---

128. Drake, Indian Captivities, pp. 221-222; Dft. Ex. A-95.
Emphasis ours. The three islands are present North Bass, Middle Bass and
South Bass Islands; see Map 3, facing this page. These three islands,
together with several smaller adjacent islands, form present Put-in-Bay
township, Ottawa County, Ohio. Kelley's Island, southeast of the Bass
Islands, is part of Erie County, Ohio. All four islands, together with
Pointe Peleé Island and some other small islands north of the Inter-
national Boundary line, are now sometimes called "The Wine Islands." See
Howe, Historical Collections, vol. 2, p. 367; Dft. Ex. A-192.

129. Drake Indian Captivities, p. 223; Dft. Ex. A-95.

These falls were at present Fremont, Sandusky County, some 20 miles up from the mouth of Sandusky River and some 15 miles west of Area 53. It will be noted that Smith fails to mention the existence of any town at the falls in 1757. In the spring of 1758 Smith returned down the Sandusky River and visited Sunyendeand, as already related.[130] His account after this point does not provide any additional information relevant to present Areas 53 and 54.

Additional information on use and occupancy of Royce Areas 53 and 54 in the years 1755-1756 is contained in the account of another captive, one Charles Stuart. Stuart and his wife were captured on the Pennsylvania frontier in October, 1755 and were returned to New York <u>via</u> Canada in 1757.[131] Stuart's account, in the form of a statement made after his return from captivity, is in part as follows.

In November, 1755, Stuart and Mrs Stuart were given

> 138 to the Wondot [Wyandot] Nations of Indians, and were sent off to them [from the upper Ohio region] By two Indians, one a Mingo[132] and the other a Delaware...We set off with our Two Indian Pilots & each of Us had a Horse to Ride on To the Wondot Town.[133]

---

130. Drake, Indian Captivities, pp. 232-233; Dft. Ex. A-95. Howe, Historical Collections, vol. 2, p. 522; Dft. Ex. A-119.

131. Bond, ed., The Captivity of Charles Stuart, p. 58; Dft. Ex A-92.

132. See fn. 51, this Chapter.

133. Bond, ed., The Captivity of Charles Stuart, p. 66; Dft. Ex. A-92.

The route the Stuarts took is difficult to trace. The party
crossed the "Muskingom" [Tuscarawas?] and stopped at

> the House where an Eng: Indian Trader had
> Formerly Lived and where was an Indian House
> Both of wch were deserted, S^d Two Houses were
> Close on the Bank of Muskongom where was 2
> small Springs[134]

From this spot the Stuarts and their two "pilots" travelled to
"a great Buffaloe Lick" where the party "met a Wondot Indian who had
Kill^d a Buffaloe there the day Before." This lick was in what Stuart
describes as a great "Savannah" which he judged extended "ab^t 50 miles
in Length and in general ab^t 4 or 5 miles in Bread^th," and which was
watered by a "small Creek or Brook" that emptied into the Muskingum.[135]
This savannah may have been (?) the famous "plains of Sandusky,"
immediately west of Area 54.

The next day the party

139

> set off in the Morning and Travell^d a Norwest Course
> very hard and reach^d the first Hunting Camp of the
> Wondot Nation that Night by dark, which was in the
> Fork of a Creek. At said Camp was Three Cabbins of
> the Hunters and ab^t 8 Hunters Belonging to them & here
> we got refreshment of Indian Hominy without Salt w^ch
> was very acceptable to Us...haveing Lived only on
> Meat without Salt and Frequently very scarce even at
> that--After Tarrying here one day we proceeded to the
> next Wondot Hunting came [camp[136]] wch was reach^d in
> a days hard Travel and Lay pretty near north from the
> other, here we found 3 Large Hunting Cabbins and a
> Pretty Large Creek wch seem^d to run ab^t a South West
> Course and was Probably some of the Branches of Sioto

134. Bond, ed., The Captivity of Charles Stuart, p. 68; Dft.
Ex. A-92.

135. Bond, ed., The Captivity of Charles Stuart, p. 69; Dft.
Ex. A-92.

136. Brackets by Bond, ed.

[Little Scioto River?]...At these Hunting Cabbins were
very large Quantitys of Meat consisting of Buffaloe:
Elk Deer--and Boars [bear] Meat, But there Seem^d more
of the Deers & Boars Meat than of the Elks or Buffaloes.
A good Part of their Meat was scaffolded and some part
of it was Barbacued after the Indian Manner for keeping.--
From the savannahs to this place I Judged we Travell^d
in these 2 days ab^t 36 Miles--The Ground in General was
very Level But rather descending Towards the Northwest
and North...[137]

The first and second Wyandot hunting camps may have been a few

miles west of Area 54. At the second camp, the party changed direction,

proceeding to a third camp

distant at 22 miles at wch we arriv^d ab^t an Hour after
dark with Hard Travelling from the morning. The Course
of this days Travel was to the Eastward of North East,--
We Encamp^d at a Pretty Large Creek wch run an Easterly
Course and wch I take to be the Head of Stony Creek
[Huron River[138]], here were three Hunting Cabbins
and a Large Quantity of Meat in them Consisting of
Deers Meat, Raccoon, Wild Cat, Beaver & Plenty of
Bears Meat but no Buffaloes nor Elks Flesh at this
Camp--there were 9 hunters Belonging to this Camp
Besides Women and children... here we tarried one
Night and in the morning Set off very early for
the Wondot Town wch the Indians call Canuta & the
French Sandusky.[139]

140

---

137. Bond, ed., The Captivity of Charles Stuart, pp. 69-70; Dft.
Ex. A-92.

138. So identified by Beverly Bond, editor of the Stuart document.
The fact the creek ran "an Easterly Course" argues for its being one of
the upper branches of the Huron. The name "Stony Creek" was probably
given it because the land near its mouth was full of large solid rocks
and many loose stones (Bond, ed., The Captivity of Charles Stuart, p.
71; Dft. Ex. A-92). Stuart's "Stony Creek" could not have been the
present Rocky River, in western Area 53.

139. Bond, ed., The Captivity of Charles Stuart, p. 70; Dft.
Ex. A-92. James Smith, who had gone down the Huron River a month or
so before the Stuarts went down it remarks, "In this route deer, bear,
turkeys, raccoons appeared plenty but no buffalo, and very little sign
of elks" (Drake, ed., Indian Captivities, p. 192; Dft. Ex. A-95).
(cont'd on p. 81.)

The course taken to reach Canuta was again "Eastward of North
East." The party "travelled hard" for 12 hours that day, and in the
middle of the afternoon "Came to a Chesnut Ridge of ab^t 4 miles over,"[140]
and continued

> to Stony Creek wch Creek we Cross^d and on our right
> we Left 3 Indian Hunting Cabbins Where the Indians
> then were Encamp^d to whom I was sent...[141]
> we Encamp^d this night...ab^t 5 miles from Sandusky
> and in the morning Proceeded on To Sandusky where
> we arriv^d ab^t 9 ^{o}Clock...[142] on Decr 21 1755...[143]

The last two camps Stuart visited, on a branch of the Huron and
on the Huron River itself, were both in western Area 54. The use of
the Huron River and its environs for winter hunting by Wyandots from

---

(fn. 139 cont'd) De Léry, writing in March, 1755, refers to the location
where Sieur Gouin had his trading house some 9 miles west of the small
Huron village of Anioton, as "Sandoské" (see p. 65, fn. 93, this Chapter).
Stuart's "Canuta," as we shall see, was De Léry's village of Anioton.
Stuart is therefore wrong in equating Canuta with Sandusky; or else the
latter name may have been used at times for both locations, which were
within nine miles of each other.

140. The party was probably near the falls of the Huron River.
James Smith notes that "About the falls is thin chesnut land, which is
almost the only chesnut timber I ever saw in this country" (Drake, Indian
Captivities, p. 193; Dft. Ex. A-95). Several decades later the Moravian
missionary David Zeisberger noted that Moravian Indians, then living on
the Huron River, gathered chestnuts in autumn on or near this river (Bliss,
ed., Zeisberger's Diary, vol. 1, pp. 376, 455; Dft. Ex. A-247).

141. The seeming indirection of the route taken by the Stuarts'
two "Pilots" may have been because the latter were searching among the
hunting camps for the particular Wyandots to whom the Stuarts were being
sent.

142. Bond, ed., The Captivity of Charles Stuart, p. 71; Dft. Ex.
A-92.

143. Bond, ed., The Captivity of Charles Stuart, p. 78; Dft. Ex.
A-92.

Detroit is described in some detail by Stuart, who spent the months of
January-April, 1756 with the Indians in the Sandusky region. Stuart's
description agrees in many details with James Smith's account of the
hunting trip he took with Wyandots and Caughnawaga Mohawks up the Huron
in the fall of 1755. Stuart states:

> The Hunters leave the Cheif Wondot Town
> (w[ch] is ab[t] 2 miles distant from Fort Detroit
> on the East Side of the river or Strait that
> Comes down from Lake Huron) ab[t] the Latter End
> of October and Proceed with their Familys in
> Canoes round the West End of Lake Erie keeping
> Close to the Shore Till they go Round to Stony
> Creek [Huron River]...The Hunters go up said
> Stony Creek in their Canoes wth their Familys
> &c ab[t] 18 miles from its Mouth where they dig
> Pitts for their Canoes, (w[ch] are made of Burch
> Bark) on the Dry Land and Put said Canoes in
> them Till the Spring follow[g]...From the place where
> they Leave their Canoes they disperse themselves
> into small Parties of 2 or 3 Familys To Their
> respective Hunting Camps w[ch] are scituate ab[t]
> 10 or 15 miles Distant or more according to the
> Nature of the Places where they Hunt--[144].

Concerning the town at which the Stuarts arrived on December 21,
1755, Stuart says:

> Sandusky, Call[d] by the Indians Canuta is a
> small Indian Town Containing 11 Indian Cabbins
> in it, only 3 of w[ch] are Constantly Inhabited,
> the whole were formerly Inhabited by Wondots
> who Built a Stockade Fort in it to defend them
> against the Cherokees and Catawbas,[145] but the

---

144. Bond, ed., The Captivity of Charles Stuart, pp. 72-73; Dft.
Ex. A-92.

145. The Cherokees and Catawbas were pro-English, southern Indians.
In 1755 James Smith was told at Tullihas by Mohawk Solomon, one of the
chiefs there, about the cunning the Catawbas had displayed on their war
expeditions against the Northern Indians (Drake, Indian Captivities, pp.
189-190; Dft. Ex. A-95). See also O'Callaghan, ed., Documents, vol. 6,
p. 742; Dft. Ex. A-39.

Fort is now entirely decay'd and Broke down,--
Said Sandusky is now used as the Headquarters
of the Wondot Hunters dureing the Winter Season,
who Hunt on the Head Branches of Sioto...

When they have Occasion to Hold Councils for
war or other Purposes during their Time of Hunting they give notice from one Hunting Camp to another to meet at Canuta On a Certain day, whither
they repair and there Holds Their Council,--In
time of hunting the Wondot Town is entirely Deserted Except a Few Poor Women who have no relations or Freinds to take care of them and they
are Left to Take Care of the Town and Provis[s] are
Left with them To Support on till the Hunters
return[146]--The Wondots Hunts and Traps for Beaver &c
dureing the Whole winter Season From the Latter End
of October Till the middle of April and By ab[t] the
1st of May they are generally all return[d] to their
Towns.[147]

The Stuarts stayed at Canuta from December 21, 1755 to December

25, 1755. At the latter date they were taken "to the Popish Preists

House on Little Lake [Sandusky Bay]."[148]

Stuart discounts the information given on Lewis Evans' 1755

map[149] regarding "towns" on lower Sandusky River. He states:

---

146. This description of Canuta tallies remarkably with De Léry's
March, 1755 description of Anioton. De Léry, however, does not con-
found Anioton with "Sandoské," where Sieur Gouin had his trading house.

147. Bond, ed., The Captivity of Charles Stuart, pp. 72-73; Dft.
Ex. A-92.

148. Bond, ed., The Captivity of Charles Stuart, p. 78; Dft. Ex.
A-92.

149. Evans, A General MAP; Dft. Ex. A-93.

> What is called Junundat in Evans' Map is only
> a Tradeing House and Popish Preists House where
> the Preist and Traders Live dureing the Indians
> Hunting in the Winter, and when Hunting Time Is
> over Preist & Traders return to Detroit which is
> their home--Evans Map Is prodigiously Wrong in
> makeing Indian Towns at Sandusky for there are
> None there Except the inconsiderable one at their
> Head Hunting Quarters, for the Winter Season, above
> described [Canuta]--[150]

Two Wyandot "towns" on or near the south shore of "Lake Erie
[Sandusky Bay]" were, however, apparently in existence in late April
or early May, 1758.[151] One Moses Moore, a Virginian, was taken prisoner
by nine Wyandots in Augusta County, Virginia, in April, 1758, and was
marched from Lower Shawnee Town, at the mouth of Scioto River,

> to Lake Erie [in] Six days to the first Owendat
> [Wyandot] Town[152]; next day went to another Town
> on the Lake Side, staid 3 days, cross'd a small
> part of ye Lake where they carried their Canoes,
> then to ye Owendat Town on ye other side of the
> Lake [opposite Detroit]...[153]

144

In a 1759 list of Western Indians the Wyandots are reported as
totalling "300 fighting Men," in two towns, "one at Fort D'Troit and
one at a place called Cheundea [Junundat]."[154]

---

150. Bond, ed., The Captivity of Charles Stuart, p. 80; Dft. Ex.
A-92. Stuart's statement is not entirely accurate. Stuart left the
Sandusky region in April, 1756 (ibid., pp. 78-79) and never returned; but
in the summer of 1756 the Wyandots had a village and planted corn at
Sunyendeand, according to Smith (p. 73, this Report).

151. Pennsylvania Archives, 1st ser., vol. 3, p. 632; Dft. Ex. A-105.

152. The first town was probably at the lower falls of Sandusky
River. The second town would then have been Sunyendeand at the mouth
of Pickerel Creek, opposite the south end of the portage trail that crossed
the peninsula north of Sandusky Bay.

153. Pennsylvania Archives, 1st ser., vol. 3, p. 632; Dft. Ex. A-105.

154. The Papers of Colonel Henry Bouquet, Series 21655, pp. 86, 88;
Dft. Ex. A-109. Pennsylvania Magazine of History and Biography, vol. 71,
p. 361; Dft. Ex. A-104.

In the meantime, from ca. 1755-1756 onward Delaware Indians were moving westward to establish towns on the eastern borders of Areas 53 and 54. One such town, which probably came into existence in 1755 or 1756, was at Tuscarawas, at the junction of the Tuscarawas River and Sandy Creek, near present Bolivar, Tuscarawas County, Ohio, in the southeastern tip of Area 54[155] This was where, in 1750, Gist had found a few Ottawa families living. The Delaware town is often referred to in contemporary sources as "Beaver's Town at Tuscarawas," since it was occupied by members of the Turkey division of the Delawares[156] under "King Beaver," a civil chief and brother of the noted Delaware war chief, Shingas.[157] Beaver's Town at Tuscarawas continued in existence, as we shall see, until around the end of 1763.

---

155. Pennsylvania Archives, 1st ser., vol. 3, p. 83; Dft. Ex. A-105. Pennsylvania Magazine of History and Biography, vol. 71, p. 335 and fn. 57, and p. 358; Dft. Ex. A-104. Hanna, The Wilderness Trail, vol. 1, pp. 334-335; Dft. Ex. A-70. Heckewelder, Names, pp. 388, 396; Dft. Ex. A-161. Hodge, ed., Handbook, pt. 2, p. 841; Dft. Ex. A-2.

156. The Delawares proper, in the mid-18th century, consisted of three phratries of divisions, Wolf, Turtle, and Turkey, each having its own civil chief, war chiefs, and councillors. A group closely associated with the Delawares proper, known as the Munsees, or "Munsee Delawares," has by some authorities been identified with the Wolf phratry of the Delawares, but seems rather to have been a distinct group, at least during the mid-18th century. See White, ed., Lewis Henry Morgan, pp. 51-53; Dft. Ex. A-103. Hodge, ed., Handbook, pt. 1, pp. 385-387, 957-958; Dft. Ex. A-1. Heckewelder, Names, pp. 387-396, esp. pp. 388-389, 393-394; Dft. Ex. A-161. Hanna, The Wilderness Trail, vol. 1, p. 111, fn. 1; Dft. Ex. A-70. Anthony F. C. Wallace, King of the Delawares, pp. 6-12; Dft. Ex. A-175. [Smith], Historical Account, pp. 53, 68-69; Dft. Ex. A-146. [Rupp], Early History, Appendix No. XIX, pp. 181-182; Dft. Ex. A-198. Heckewelder, Narrative, pp. 142-143; Dft. Ex. A-53. Speech from the Delawares...May 25, 1779, p. 2; Dft. Ex. A-241.

157. For biographical notices of Beaver and his brother Shingas see Heckewelder, Names, pp. 388, 396; Dft. Ex. A-161 and Hodge, ed., Handbook, pt. 2, entry "Tamaque," pp. 681-682; Dft. Ex. A-2.

A second Delaware town was established <u>ca</u>. 1756-1758 north of
Tuscarawas, on the Cuyahoga River at or near the foot of the "Big Falls"
a mile or so east of the southeastern boundary of Area 53.[158] This town
was presided over by Netawatwees or "King Newcomer,"[159] civil chief of
the Turtle division of the Delawares, and continued in existence, as we
shall see, until at least 1764. Heckewelder states that Netawatwees
removed to the Cuyahoga River on advice of the Wyandots, with whom
he had entered into a "covenant" for lands for the Delawares west
of the Ohio River.[160]

At about this same time (1758-1759) the Cuyahoga River, which
forms in part the eastern boundary of Area 53, was also serving as a
war route for Wyandots from Detroit, going to attack Fort Pitt. Warriors

---

158. Heckewelder, Names, pp. 388-389, 393; Dft. Ex. A-161. Rond-
thaler, Life of John Heckewelder, pp. 39, 46, 55-58; Dft. Ex. A-162.
Whittlesey, Early History, p. 131; Dft. Ex. A-78. Thwaites and Kellogg,
eds., Revolution on the Upper Ohio, p. 46, fn. 74; Dft. Ex. A-177.
Perrin, History of Summit County, pp. 218-219; Dft. Ex. A-234. Hanna,
The Wilderness Trail, vol. 2, p. 387; Dft. Ex. A-82. Draper Mss. 16S272;
Dft. Ex. A-268. Ontario History, vol. 49, no. 2, p. 90; Dft. Ex.
A-269.
The "Big Falls" is the most westerly of the three falls on the
Cuyahoga River; see fn. 124, this Chapter.

159. For notices of this Delaware chief see Heckewelder, Names,
pp. 388-389; Dft. Ex. A-161, and Transactions of the Moravian Historical
Society, pp. 175, 179, 345-346; Dft. Ex. A-35. Variants of Netawatwees'
name are: Nettautwaleman (Hanna, Wilderness Trail, vol. 2, p. 311; Dft.
Ex. A-82); Netawatwelomen (Zeisberger, Diary...January, 1772, p. 207; Dft.
Ex. A-36); Netalwalemut (Minutes of the Provincial Council, vol. 8, p. 618;
Dft. Ex. A-164, and Hanna, The Wilderness Trail, vol. 2, p. 241; Dft. Ex.
A-82); Noatwhelama (Hodge, ed., Handbook, pt. 2, p. 65; Dft. Ex. A-2);
Nettowhalways ([Smith], Historical Account, p. 69; Dft. Ex. A-146), etc.

160. Heckewelder, Names, p. 388; Dft. Ex. A-161.

hunted along its banks to obtain provisions for war parties while such were in transit.[161]

As the year 1759 neared its close, it was obvious that the British were winning the French and Indian War.[162] Consequently, various Indians who had been attached to the French expressed interest in trading at Fort Pitt, and announced their intentions of removing from the environs of Detroit, which was still under French command, to the region south of Lake Erie. In his journal Croghan notes, under date of November 15, 1759:

> Seven Ottawas came here [Fort Pitt] from near
> Fort D'Troit where they live & inform me their
> Nation are devided, some remaining in the French
> Interest, the others coming to settle on this
> side of the Lake [Erie] where they intend to
> hunt and Plant next Spring...[163]

Likewise, on November 29, 1759 "28 Men, and some Women and Children...of three Nations Ottawas, Cheapwas [Chippewas] and Putowatomeys" arrived at Fort Pitt, presumably from Detroit. On December 3, 1759 these Indians told Croghan

147

BROTHER

When we left home we were charged by our Nations

---

161. Pennsylvania Magazine of History and Biography, vol. 80, pp. 296-297; Dft. Ex. A-106.

162. Quebec capitulated to the British on September 18, 1759; news of the capitulation was announced to Indians of various groups gathered for a council at Fort Pitt on October 21, 1759 (Pennsylvania Magazine of History and Biography, vol. 71, p. 358; Dft. Ex. A-104).

163. Pennsylvania Magazine of History and Biography, vol. 71, p. 360; Dft. Ex. A-104.

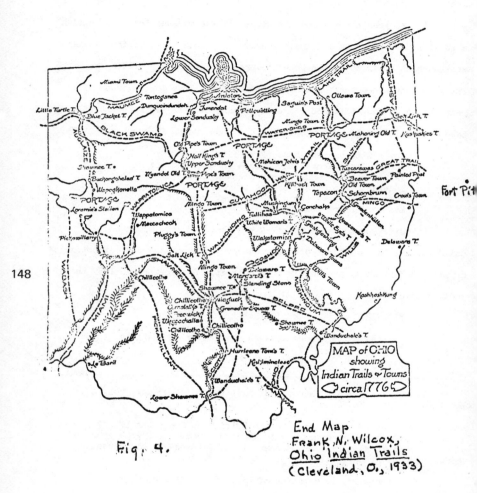

• Detroit

148

Fig. 4.

MAP of OHIO
showing
Indian Trails & Towns
◁ circa 1776 ◁

End Map
Frank N. Wilcox,
Ohio Indian Trails
(Cleveland, O., 1933)

to inform you that Numbers of them we [were][164]
coming over the Lakes to hunt this Winter, in
order to come here [Fort Pitt] and Trade next
Spring, they have made a Road, and by this Belt
which they have sent us to Deliver you, you
may be Certain of their coming here to Trade in
Peace.

Gave a Road Belt.[165]

This, Croghan replied, he was "glad to hear," and he assured the visitors
that

all Nations to the Sun Setting, that has a mind to
be admitted into Friendship with his Majesty's
Subjects will be kindly received and well Treated...[166]

4. Summary and Conclusions on Use and Occupancy of Areas 53 and
54: 1737-1759. In summary, the data presented in this chapter on
native use and occupancy of Royce Areas 53 and 54 during the years
1737-1759 are as follows.

In 1737-1738 part of an Indian group known to the French as "Hurons"
and to the English as "Wyandots" fled from the Huron Catholic mission
village on Bois Blanc Island at the mouth of the Detroit River, because
of trouble with the Detroit Ottawas, and established a village known as
"Anioton" some three miles south of the south shore of Sandusky Bay, at
or near present Castalia, Erie County, in northwestern Area 53. There
these "fugitive Hurons," together with some "Senecas" or "vagabond
Iroquois," "Loups" (Mahicans   ), Caughnawaga Mohawks, and

149

---

164. Brackets by Wainwright, editor.

165. Pennsylvania Magazine of History and Biography, vol. 71, p.
362; Dft. Ex. A-104.

166. Pennsylvania Magazine of History and Biography, vol. 71, p.
363; Dft. Ex. A-104.

perhaps some Shawnees, remained during part or all of a 10-year period, despite repeated efforts made by French authorities to induce the Hurons to return to Detroit. In 1747-1748 the Indians at Anioton numbered around 500 souls.

A few years after present northwestern Area 53 began to be occupied, northeastern Area 53 also began to be utilized by Indians. Around 1742 migrants belonging to ten different groups--Senecas, Cayugas, Onondagas, Oneidas, Mohawks, Loups (Delawares?), Moraignans (Mahicans), Ottawas, Abnakis of St. Francis, and Chippewas -- estimated by a French official as amounting to 500-600 men (2,000-2,400 persons) -- settled in two towns, "Mingo Town" and Ottawa Town, on the lower reaches of the Cuyahoga River. These various Indians apparently remained on Cuyahoga River in or close to eastern Area 53 until some time in 1752, when the French may have persuaded some of them, at least, to move to Detroit. In 1752 Wyandots were also trading with an English trader on Cuyahoga River.

In present northwestern Area 53, a succession of events in 1747 led to a withdrawal early in 1748 of the anti-French Hurons and associated Indians from their village of Anioton, near present Castalia, Erie County, and the fracturing of the "rebel Hurons" into two groups. The lesser of the two, amounting to some 30 men and their families, first went to the Cuyahoga River and then left present Area 53, to settle NEAR Kuskusky in western Pennsylvania. The larger group, which numbered 70 or more men and their families and which was led by the war chief Nicolas Orontoni, fled southward, to settle at the Forks of Muskingum, some 30 miles south of eastern Area 54. There this group established itself in a town known to the French as "Conchaké" and referred to by an

English surveyor as "Muskingum" (present Coshocton, Ohio). Conchaké was occupied by Nicolas' Hurons from 1748 to 1753, during which time its inhabitants hunted in winter throughout the western two-thirds of Areas 53 and 54, and maintained a winter depot at their former town of Anioton, near present Castalia, Erie County, in the northwestern part of Area 53. In 1753 the Hurons of Conchaké (Muskingum) returned to Detroit, but in 1755 there were three cabins of Hurons at Anioton, by then also known as
Canuta, in northwestern Area 53. Hurons also planted and had a summer village in 1756 at Sunyendeand or Sandoské, which was a quarter to a third of a mile inland from the south shore of Sandusky Bay, near the mouth of present Pickerel Creek, four miles west of Area 53.

Meanwhile, at the extreme southeastern tip of present Area 54 there were in 1750 six or eight families of Ottawas and at least one Six Nations Iroquois woman living in a small village, known as "Tuscarawas," at the junction of the Tuscarawas River and Sandy Creek near present Bolivar, northern Tuscarawas County, Ohio.

151

Beginning around 1755-1756 Delawares began moving into, or very close to, Areas 53 and 54. In 1755 or 1756 Delawares of the Turkey division established "Beavers Town at Tuscarawas" in the southeastern tip of Area 54, and ca. 1756-1758 Netawatwees, civil chief of the Turtle division of the Delawares, established his town on Cuyahoga River, close to the southeastern boundary of Area 53.

In 1755 both "Mohiccons" and "a few Mohawks" are legended on maps of that date as being in south central Area 54 and northeastern Area 53, respectively.

The period 1737-1759 ends with some of the Detroit Ottawas, Chippewas, and Potawatomis also announcing their intention to hunt and live south of Lake Erie and trade with the British at Fort Pitt.

All told, six known villages existed close to or within the eastern and western borders of Areas 53 and 54 during the period 1737-1759. The first such was Sunyendeand or Sandoské, at the mouth of present Pickerel Creek, four miles west of Area 53. This was a French trading post in 1755, and is first noticed as a Wyandot summer village in 1756. The second was Anioton or Canuta, at or near present Castalia, Erie County, Ohio, within northwestern Area 53. This village was occupied by Wyandots and other Indians between 1738-1747, destroyed by them in 1748, but later (1750-1755) used again by them, chiefly as a winter depot and a spot for occasional councils. The third village was the so-called "Mingo Town," located on the west side of the Cuyahoga River, barely within eastern Area 53. This town was occupied by a congeries of Indians from nine different groups from 1742 to 1752. The fourth village was Ottawa Town, on the east bank of the Cuyahoga River opposite Mingo Town, which was occupied from 1743 to, probably, 1752 by Ottawas. The fifth village was Tuscarawas, at the junction of the Tuscarawas River and Sandy Creek, in the southeastern tip of Area 54, where in 1750 six or eight Ottawa families and a Six Nations Indian family were living. By 1755-1756 Delawares were living at Tuscarawas. The sixth and last village was Netawatwees' Delaware town at or near the foot of the Big Falls of the Cuyahoga, immediately east of Area 53. This town was established between 1756-1758.

Despite the relatively few villages within or close to Areas 53 and
54, both Areas were extensively used in the mid-1750's by Wyandots,
Ottawas, Chippewas, and Caughnawaga Mohawks, many of whom lived outside
Areas 53 and 54, but who came to these Areas annually in the fall to
hunt during the winter and early spring months. Hunting parties ordinar-
ily consisted of 20-25 men, women. and children. Such groups, severally,
entered the mouths of main rivers, as for example the Huron and Cuyahoga
rivers in Area 53, and canoed slowly upstream, the men going ashore to
hunt every few miles. At night the canoe was drawn up on the river's
bank and used as a temporary shelter, or else small, mat-covered, domed
"tents" were set up as. sleeping quarters. Gradually the stock of furs
and hides increased, and about the beginning of December the catch was
scaffolded at well-known falls or rapids. There also, at these more or
less "public places" the canoe, or canoes, were buried, after which the
little hunting party set off, usually afoot, for a location anywhere
from 10-40 miles distant. Upon arrival at its destination the hunters
and their wives built one or more substantial winter cabins, to be
occupied for the next 3-4 months by the women and children, while the
men hunted singly as far away as 10-15 miles. When thus engaged hunters
used small shelters and camped out, until they had accumulated sufficient
meat and furs to warrant a temporary return to their families at the
winter cabin. In February large quantities of maple sugar were made
by the women at or near the winter cabin. Toward the end of March all
the furs, hides and provisions that had been accumulated in three months'
time were packed out, either on the backs of the Indians or on pack-
horses, to the spot where the canoe had been buried in the late fall
and the fall catch of furs and hides scaffolded. In case the fall and

winter hunts had been very productive, extra canoes of elm or chestnut bark were made, before the hunting party set off down the river it had ascended the previous autumn, to ultimately join other hunting parties at villages within or north of Areas 53 and 54.

There follows a summary list of more or less specific locations within the boundaries of Areas 53 and 54 only, of some of the hunting "camps" existent in these two Areas during 1755 and 1756. This list is not complete for these years; it is based on two narratives only, by White captives who happened to be in certain parts, only, of Areas 53 and 54, with certain Indians. Locations of the winter camps in Areas 53 and 54 are listed from north to south, and from west to east.

WINTER HUNTING LOCATIONS: 1755, 1756

Location	Group	Camp Shelter	Occupied	Activities
1. Bass Islands (NW Area 53)	Wyandots Ottawas	---------#	Oct. to April "frequently used"	Hunting: raccoons wild fowl Fishing
2. Mouth of Sandusky Bay, S Side (NW Area 53)	Caughna-wagas, Chippewas Ottawas (4 Canoes)	4 mat-covered tents (Ottawas)	Oct. 175 "several days"	Hunting: raccoons waterfowl
3. Mouth of Huron R. (NW Area 53)	Wyandots, Caughna-waga (1)	---------#	Oct. 1755 "for some time"	Hunting: deer raccoons
4. Lower part Huron R. (NW Area 53)	Wyandots (19) Caughna-waga (1)	Large canoe for night shelter	Oct. 1755	Hunting: meat furs hides
5. Falls of Huron R. (W Area 53) a	"	"	Nov. 1755	Hunting: deer bears raccoons

#No data given.

Location	Group	Camp Shelter	Occupied	Activities
6. Near falls of Huron R. (W Area 53)	Wyandots	"3 hunting cabins"	Dec. 20, 1755 (seen)	Hunting:
7. Upper Huron R., 30 mi. above falls (NW Area 54)	Caughnawaga hunter & White captive	-------*	April 1756 two weeks	Hunting: bears raccoons beavers
8. Head of Huron R. (NW Area 54)	Wyandots? (ca. 25?)	"3 hunting cabins"	Dec. 18, 1755 (seen)	Pelts & meat seen: deer raccoon wild cat beaver bear No buffalo or elk
9. Mouth of small creek W of Huron R. (NW Area 53)	Caughnawaga hunter & White captive	---------*	April 1756 "several days"	Hunting
10. Upper Black R. or tributary (C Area 53)	Wyandots (19) Caughnawaga (1)	1 large rectangular log cabin	Dec. 1755 to end of March 1756	House-building Hunting War party Sugar-making Trapping
11. Tributary of Black R. 10-12 mi. S of No. 10 (SC Area 53 and NC Area 54)	Caughnawaga hunter & White captive	"snug little shelter"	Jan. 1756	Hunting: turkeys bears raccoons deer
12. "Considerable distances from" No. 10 (C Areas 53, 54)	Wyandot hunters (7) Caughnawaga hunter (1)	---------*	Feb. & March 1756	Hunting: meat furs hides
13. Mouth of Cuyahoga R. (E Area 53)	Caughnawagas, Chippewas, Ottawas	4 mat-covered tents (Ottawas)	Oct. 1756 "several days"	Hunting deer (bears, etc. scarce)

*No data given.

155

Location	Group	Camp Shelter	Occupied	Activities
14. Forks of Cuyahoga R. (E Area 53)	"	"	Oct. & Nov. 1756	"
15. Upper Tuscarawas R. (NE Area 54)	Caughnawaga, Ottawa, Chippewa hunters	----------*	Oct.-Nov. 1756; "several days"	Hunting: deer beavers

In addition, during the winter of 1754-1755 one or more Mohawks wintered and hunted at an undeterminable location somewhere in central Area 53 or northern Area 54.

Our conclusions as to native use and occupancy of Royce Areas 53 and 54 during the years 1737-1759 are as follows.

Indians of several different groups--Hurons or Wyandots, Caughnawaga Mohawks from the St. Lawrence River, "Senecas" or "vagabond Iroquois" or "Six Nations Indians," "Loups" (Mahicans or Delawares), and perhaps some Shawnees-- lived and/or hunted in the western two-thirds of Areas 53 and 54 during the first decade of the period of 1737-1759. During the second decade Hurons continued to hunt in western Areas 53 and 54; Mohicans, Mohawks, and probably some Delawares also hunted in this region. The picture for the western two-thirds of both Areas during both decades is one of simultaneous utilization of the region by Indians deriving from several different groups. Of such Indians, Hurons or Wyandots may have been most numerous in the western part of Area 53. But in 1756 a party of Ottawas, Chippewas, and Caughnawaga Mohawks evidently felt free to use the natural resources along the south shore of Sandusky Bay in northwestern Area 53, and a Caughnawaga Mohawk hunted down the length of the Huron River, and

*No data given.

156

also in central Areas 53 and 54, alone as well as with Wyandots, in 1755-1756. The Bass Islands in extreme northwestern Area 53 were used at this time as winter hunting grounds by both Wyandots and Ottawas.

Non-exclusive use and/or occupancy also holds true for the eastern third of Royce Areas 53 and 54 during the period 1737-1759. Here, in or very close to the eastern boundary of Area 53, representatives of ten different groups shared use and occupancy from 1742-1752. The region was also used by other Indians; part, at least, of the rebel Hurons or Wyandots stayed in it briefly in 1748, and Wyandots traded with English traders at Cuyahoga in 1752. In 1756-1757 Ottawas, Chippewas and Caughnawaga Mohawks hunted on the Cuyahoga River and in its environs, and Wyandot warriors used the river as a war route, as well as for hunting. By 1756-1758 Delawares had established themselves on the Cuyahoga.

Farther south, in the eastern part of Area 54, a few Ottawa families had a small village at Tuscarawas (present Bolivar, Ohio), close to the southeastern tip of Area 54, in 1750, but by 1755 or 1756 Delawares were living there under a noted chief and war chief.

157

Briefly stated, our conclusions in general terms as to use and/or occupancy of all of Areas 53 and 54 are that no one group of Indians exclusively used and/or occupied any part or parts of these two Areas throughout the period 1737-1759. Use and occupancy of these two Areas either shifted during the years from one group to another, or else members of two or more groups utilized the same region for summer villages and/or for winter hunting.

158

Chapter III

Use and Occupancy of Royce Areas 53 and 54

during the British Period: 1760-1776

1. Use and Occupancy of Royce Areas 53 and 54: 1760-1764. Late
in 1759, it will be recalled, some Ottawas, Chippewas, and Potawatomis
told George Croghan, Sir William Johnson's deputy Indian agent at Fort
Pitt, that they intended to hunt and settle south of Lake Erie. This
projected move was effected, in part at least, for under date of January
13, 1760, Croghan notes in his Journal:

> Thirty three Ottawas came here [Fort Pitt]
> to Trade, and with them 18 Cheapewas they made
> some very friendly Speeches, and assure me that
> they had intirely left the French [at Detroit]
> and was come to Settle and Plant on this side
> of the Lakes.[1]

A few weeks later, in an entry for February 29, 1760, Croghan
mentions Ottawas as being at Cuyahoga specifically, in eastern Area

53. Croghan writes:

> about 40 Ottawas came here to Trade from a place
> on this side of the Lake called Gichaga [Cuya-
> hoga[2]] where they intend to plant and build a

---

1. Pennsylvania Magazine of History and Biography, vol. 71, p.
365; Dft. Ex. A-104.

2. So identified by the historian Nicholas B. Wainwright, editor
of Croghan's 1759-1763 Journal (Pennsylvania Magazine of History and
Biography, vol. 71, p. 367, fn. 98; Dft. Ex. A-104). This is correct;
elsewhere in his writings Croghan uses the names "Gichawaga Creek" and
"Guyahauga Creek" for the same stream (Pennsylvania Magazine of History
and Biography, vol. 71, p. 289; Dft. Ex. A-104. Massachusetts Historical
Collections, 4th ser., vol. 9, p. 365; Dft. Ex. A-107).

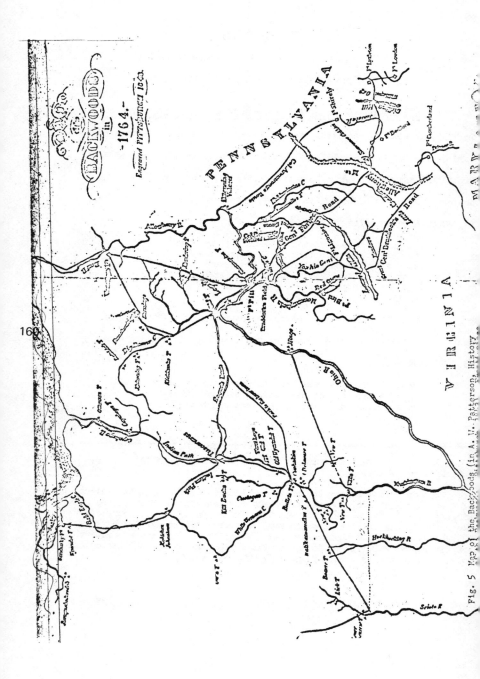

Fig. 5 Map of the Backwoods (in A. W. Patterson, History of the Backwoods. Pittsburgh, 1843) Frontispiece

Town this spring...[3]

The name of at least one Wyandot settlement on the south side of Lake Erie in 1760 is indicated in a remark of Croghan's that on June 17, 1760, "A Wyandott Indian who lives on this side of the Lake [Erie] at a place called Chenundede came here [Fort Pitt] the 15th..."[4] Also in June, 1760, Richard Peters, secretary of Pennsylvania, mentions the same town when he refers to a "great Treaty Congress of Indians which [is to meet] in one of the Owendat Towns at or near Junundat on the South West End of Lake Erie." Delaware attendees at the "Junundat" congress were first to "go to Kuskusky & Muskingum [Tuscarawas] & there take their further Rout as King Beaver shall direct," according to Peters.[5]

In a letter written in September, 1760 by Col. Henry Bouquet, a Swiss officer in service with the British, Bouquet observes that except for a few Chippewas who were at Presque Isle (Erie, Pennsylvania)

there are no other Indians settled on this side the Lake [Erie] from Niagara to Detroit, except a few wandering families who have no fixed habitations.

---

3. Pennsylvania Magazine of History and Biography, vol. 71, p. 367; Dft. Ex. A-104. Other sources mention similar intentions on the part of Indians living near Detroit. For example, on March 18, 1760 Croghan states that two Indians he had sent to Detroit the previous winter reported that numbers of the Indians there had become disaffected to the French and were "coming over the Lakes this Spring to Plant Corn and build Towns". (Pennsylvania Magazine of History and Biography, vol. 71, p. 368; Dft. Ex. A-104).

4. Pennsylvania Magazine of History and Biography, vol. 71, p. 373; Dft. Ex. A-104.

5. Massachusetts Historical Collections, 4th ser., vol. 9, pp. 258-259; Dft. Ex. A-107. "King Beaver" was at Tuscarawas at this time.

Bouquet thought that the probable reason for this dearth of Indian settlements along the south shore of Lake Erie was due to "The scarceness of game...."[6]

When George Croghan and Maj. Robert Rogers, commanding a company of Rangers, went to Detroit late in 1760 to take over that Fort for the British, both kept journals of the trip, and each also furnished Brig. Gen. Robert Monckton non-identical copies of their journals. Croghan's and Rogers' original journals, and also the copies furnished Monckton, have been published. All relevant entries in the original journals[7] and Monckton copies[8] have been compared by us, and any pertinent differences in content noted.

The Rogers-Croghan expedition sailed from Presque Isle (Erie, Pennsylvania) on November 4, 1760, met some 30 Ottawas on the south shore of Lake Erie east of Area 53 on November 5, 1760, and councilled with them.[9]

162

---

6. Massachusetts Historical Collections, 4th ser., vol. 9, p. 321; Dft. Ex. A-107.

7. Pennsylvania Magazine of History and Biography, vol. 71, pp. 387-397; Dft. Ex. A-104. Hough, ed., Journals of Robert Rogers, Dft. Ex. A-110. Unless otherwise noted, quotations in this Report are from Croghan's and Rogers' original journals.

8. Massachusetts Historical Collections, 4th ser., vol. 9, pp. 365-367, 378-379; Dft. Ex. A-107. Paltsits, ed., Journal, pp. 261-262, 266-267, 272-275; Dft. Ex. A-316.

9. Rogers' and Croghan's journals are not in agreement on where the expedition was or what happened between November 5 and 12, 1760; cp. Pennsylvania Magazine of History and Biography, vol. 71, pp. 387-390; Dft. Ex. A-104 and Hough, ed., Journals of Robert Rogers, pp. 187-188; Dft. Ex. A-110; also Paltsits, ed., Journal, pp. 266-267; Dft. Ex. A-316. Croghan's account would seem to be the more reliable; his names for rivers and distances between rivers are recognizable.

By November 12, 1760 the expedition reached the mouth of "Guyahauga Creek [Cuyahoga River]"[10] according to Croghan or "Elk River as the Indians call it" (Rogers).[11] There the British force stayed two and a half days. At the mouth of the Cuyahoga River Croghan records that he met

> some Indians Hunting being of the Ottaway Nation, who Treated us very kindly they being formerly acquainted with me.[12]

By noon of November 15, 1760 the expedition "arrived at Stoney Creek [Rocky River]" some 10 miles west of the Cuyahoga where, Croghan states:

> we met a Wyandot Indian and his Family going a hunting, he informed me he was 15 days from D'Troit...In the afternoon we came to two Creeks about 9 leagues [22.5 miles] from Guyahauga [Cuyahoga]...[13]

The next river the westward-bound expedition put into briefly, on November 18, 1760, was "Virmilion Creek [Vermilion River]."[14] From thence,

10. Pennsylvania Magazine of History and Biography, vol. 71, p. 389; Dft. Ex. A-104. In the Monckton copy of his journal Croghan refers to the creek reached on November 12, 1760 as "Gichawaga Creek where is a fine Harbour" (Massachusetts Historical Collections, 4th ser., vol. 9, p. 365; Dft. Ex. A-107).

11. Hough, ed., Journals of Robert Rogers, pp. 188-189; Dft. Ex. A-110. Elk River ("Mishaway-see-bie") was the Indian name for present Chagrin River, which empties into Lake Erie some 15 miles northeast of Cuyahoga River (Bierce, Historical Reminiscences, p. 14; Dft. Ex. A-233).

12. Pennsylvania Magazine of History and Biography, vol. 71, pp. 389-390; Dft. Ex. A-104. These were probably some of the Ottawas from Cuyahoga who had visited Croghan at Fort Pitt in February, 1760.

13. Pennsylvania Magazine of History and Biography, vol. 71, p. 390; Dft. Ex. A-104. In the Monckton copy Croghan refers to Stoney Creek as "Sinquene Thipe or Stony Creek" and also gives the name of the Wyandot Indian he met as "Togasoedy" (Massachusetts Historical Collections, 4th ser., vol. 9, pp. 365-366; Dft. Ex. A-107).

14. Referred to in the Monckton copy as "Oulame Thepy or Vermillion Creek" (Massachusetts Historical Collections, 4th ser., vol. 9, pp. 366; Dft. Ex. A-107).

Croghan records, the party

> Sailed to Nottaway thepy [Huron River]...this
> is a fine Creek 18 feet deep Running thr'o a
> Meadow...Here we met three Indians who in-
> formed me that the Deputies I sent from Fort
> Pitt passed by their Hunting Cabbins 8 days
> ago on their way to D'Troit...

The next day Croghan notes that

> Sundry Indians came down the Creek [Huron River]
> to our encampment with a Quantity of Dryed Meat
> which the[y] presented us with...[15]

The expedition sailed around the Marblehead Peninsula north of

Sandusky Bay on November 20, 1760, and encountered "a Cannoe of Wyandott

Indians." Soon afterward the British force "put into Cramberry Creek

[present Portage River]" to meet a deputation of Indians "at the

Carrying place [portage] between lake Sandusky and Lake Erie," which

ended near the mouth of Portage River, six miles west of Area 53. From

164   there Croghan and Rogers

> sent over the Carrying place to 2 Villages near
> each other on the other side [south side] of the
> Little Lake [Sandusky Bay] to call together the
> Indians living there.[16]

---

15. Pennsylvania Magazine of History and Biography, vol. 71,
pp. 390-391; Dft. Ex. A-104.

16. Pennsylvania Magazine of History and Biography, vol. 71,
p. 391; Dft. Ex. A-104. In the Monckton copy Croghan writes: "we sent
over the Carrying place to two Indian villages which are within two Miles
of each other to invite the Indians to come & meet the Deputies at our
Camp" (Massachusetts Historical Collections, 4th ser., vol. 9, pp. 366-
367; Dft. Ex. A-107). The distance between the two villages was more
than two miles; later in both his original journal and in the Monckton
copy Croghan gives it as six miles (Pennsylvania Magazine of History
and Biography, vol. 71, pp. 395-396; Dft. Ex. A-104. Massachusetts Historical Collections, 4th ser., vol. 9, p. 378; Dft. Ex. A-107).

The next day, November 21, 1760 Croghan and Rogers "were visited by some Indians from over the little Lake [Sandusky Bay]."[17] The expedition then proceeded to Detroit.

From Detroit Croghan started back to Fort Pitt on December 11, 1760. He

> Crossed the little Lake [Sandusky Bay] on the Ice
> which is about 6 Miles over to an Indian Village,
> where we got our Horses we'd sent from D'Troit--
> but very few Indians at home the rest out a hunting.[18]

Croghan's "Indian Village" was probably Smith's Sunyendeand. In his Journal entry for December 23 he calls this village "Sandusky," and locates it six miles distant from a second "Indian Village" referred to as "Junundat."

At Junundat the Indians "delivered up Six prisoners" and Croghan stayed there a day "to Reconnitre [sic] the Woods to get some Horses."[19]

---

17. Pennsylvania Magazine of History and Biography, vol. 71, p. 391; Dft. Ex. A-104. Hough, ed., Journals of Robert Rogers, p. 189; Dft. Ex. A-110.

18. Pennsylvania Magazine of History and Biography, vol. 71, pp. 395-396; Dft. Ex. A-104. In the Monckton copy Croghan writes: "there were but five Indians at home all the rest being gone a hunting" (Massachusetts Historical Collections, 4th ser., vol. 9, p. 378; Dft. Ex. A-107).

19. Pennsylvania Magazine of History and Biography, vol. 71, p. 396; Dft. Ex. A-104. In the Monckton copy Croghan's entry for December 23 is simply: "We came to Chenunda an Indian Village 6 miles from Sandusky" (Massachusetts Historical Collections, 4th ser., vol. 9, p. 378; Dft. Ex. A-107). Croghan's "Junundat" or "Chenunda" was evidently De Léry's "Anioton" and Stuart's "Canuta."
    A "Return of Prisoners from Detroit" to Fort Pitt, dated December 26, 1760, mentions one prisoner who was "Left sick at St. Duskee an Indian Town belonging to the Wyandots" (Papers of Col. Henry Bouquet, Ser. 21655, p. 103; Dft. Ex. A-109).
    In [Smith], Historical Account, p. 150; Dft. Ex. A-146, the distance between "Sandusky" and "Junundat or Wyandot town" is given as four miles. The French pronunciation of Junundat, it should be noted, approximates "Wundot."

On December 25, 1760 he left and, traveling southeastward, "came to a
Principal Mans hunting Cabbin about 16 Miles from Junundat" in present
western Area 53. The next day, still proceeding southeastwardly, he

> Marched to a Mohickon Village 30 miles, the In-
> habitants were all out a hunting except one
> family on our way Crossed several small branches
> of Muskingum...[20]

The "Mohickon Village" was in present central Area 54, probably near present Jeromeville, Ashland County.[21] Some 36 miles beyond Mohican Village, on January 1, 1761 Croghan came "to a place call'd the Sugar
Cabbins." This was probably on present Sugar Creek, in eastern Area 54,
for on January 2, 1761 Croghan travelled 12 more miles "to the Beavers
Town" at Tuscarawas, where he "Cross'd Muskingum [Tuscarawas River] and
encamped in a fine Bottom near the [present Sandy] Creek."[22]

---

20. Pennsylvania Magazine of History and Biography, vol. 71,
p. 396; Dft. Ex. A-104.

21. The historian Reuben Gold Thwaites identifies Croghan's
"Mohickon Village" as "Mohican John's Town," which he locates near present Reedsburg, western Wayne County, Ohio, in central Area 54, on "the
great path" from the Forks of the Ohio to Detroit (Thwaites, ed., Early
Western Travels, vol. 1, p. 125, fn. 90; Dft. Ex. A-148. In support,
see Ohio Archaeological and Historical Society Publications, vol. 8,
p. 276; Dft. Ex. A-117). Hanna locates Mohican John's Town farther west,
either on the Jerome Fork of the Mohican River, two miles south of
present Jeromeville, Ashland County, Ohio, or on the Black Fork of the
Mohican River (Hanna, The Wilderness Trail, vol. 2, pp. 208-210; Dft.
Ex. A-82). A. J. Baughman, a local historian, locates Mohican John's
Town or Jerometown two miles below Jeromeville, Ashland County, Ohio
(Baughman, History of Ashland County, map facing p. 12, and pp. 22, 25,
47, 49-50, 52; Dft. Ex. A-158).
    Croghan's mileages support the loca-
tion of Mohican John's Town as near present Jeromeville, on the Jerome
Fork, as do the mileages given in a table of distances from Fort Pitt,
compiled ca. 1764 ([Smith], Historical Account, p. 150; Dft. Ex. A-146).

22. Pennsylvania Magazine of History and Biography, vol. 71,
p. 396; Dft. Ex. A-104 The Monckton copy, in its entry for January 4,
1761 makes it clear that the "Creek" Croghan crossed was present Sandy
Creek (Massachusetts Historical Collections, 4th ser., vol. 9, p. 379;
Dft. Ex. A-107).

It will be noted that Croghan, except in one instance, does not identify by tribe the Indians he met west of Rocky River on his outward trip to Detroit. Nor is he more explicit when on his homeward trip, as far as concerns the Sandusky Bay region. Croghan was an Indian agent, and in his journals generally took pains to specifically identify those Indians who visited him, or whom he encountered. His repeated mention of "Indians," "sundry Indians," and "Indian towns," during his passage through the northwestern part of present Area 53 may be significant as indicating that he found the population there indistinguishably mixed by the end of 1760.

Rogers and his Rangers left Detroit for Fort Pitt 12 days after Croghan did. Rogers' group also went overland through Areas 53 and 54, but on foot. On January 2, 1761 the Rangers crossed Sandusky Bay and "came to a town of the Windot [Wyandot] Indians" where they "halted to refresh." This was probably at Smith's Sunyendeand and Croghan's "Sandusky." The following day, January 3, 1761, the Rangers travelled in a southeasterly direction for 5.5 miles and crossed a creek flowing east. One mile farther southeast they "passed through Indian houses," and three-quarters of mile farther southeast "came to a small Indian town of about ten houses" which had "a remarkably fine spring."[23] This was probably Croghan's village of Junundat, De Léry's Anioton, and Stuart's Canuta, at or close to present Castalia, Erie County, Ohio. Rogers, it will be noted, locates Junundat 7 1/4 miles southeast of the town where he "refreshed," which was Sunyendeand or

23. Hough, ed., Journals of Robert Rogers, p. 199; Dft. Ex. A-110.

Sandusky. He is the first early traveller, as far as we know, to remark on what we take to have been the present "Blue Hole" or Castalia Springs.[24] From Junundat the Rangers continued eight miles south-south-east, crossing two brooks that ran east-southeast, before they encamped in the western part of Area 53. Rogers notes that "plenty of deer and turkeys" were killed on the day's march.[25]

On January 4, 1761 Rogers' party travelled south-southeast one mile, crossed a river "about 25 yards wide," probably one of the branches of Huron River, and came to "two Indian houses [winter cabins?]." Five and a half miles southeast of these houses the party

> came to an Indian house, where there was a family
> of Windots hunting...

That day Rogers travelled almost 12 miles, and ended the day some 20 miles southeast of Junundat, in present southwestern Area 53. Rogers notes that the Rangers killed "several deer and other game" during the day.[26]

On January 5, 1761 Rogers again proceeded in a southeast direction for 12 miles and came to "Maskongom Creek." Rogers notes: "This day killed deer and turkies on our march." On January 6, 1761 the Rangers went 14 or 15 miles farther, the "general course being east-southeast,

168

---

24. For descriptions of these notable springs see Howe, Historical Collections, vol. 1, p. 584; Dft. Ex. A-191, and Wilcox, Ohio Indian Trails, pp. 24-25; Dft. Ex. A-200.

25. Hough, ed., Journals of Robert Rogers, p. 199; Dft. Ex. A-110.

26. Idem.

killed plenty of game."[27] On the 7th of January, 1761 Rogers advanced six miles to the southeast, where he crossed "Maskongom Creek running south, about twenty yards wide." By this time the Rangers had travelled 52 miles southeast from Junundat. After crossing "Maskongom Creek" Rogers came to:

> an Indian town about twenty yards from the creek, on the east side, which is called the Mingo [Mohigon[28]] Cabbins. There were but two or three Indians in the place, the rest were hunting. These Indians have plenty of cows, horses, hogs, &c.

> The 8th, halted at this town to mend our mogasons [moccasins] and kill deer...I went a hunting with ten of the Rangers, and by ten o'clock got more venison than we had occasion for.[29]

On the 9th of January, 1761 the Rangers went southeast 12 miles and "encamped by the side of a long meadow, where there were a number of Indians hunting."[30] This may have been in the vicinity of present Big Prairie on the Wayne-Holmes county line in extreme southern Area 54.   169

During the next day's march (January 10, 1761) the party killed "three bears and two elks." By January 11, 1761 Rogers had advanced

---

27. Hough, ed., Journals of Robert Rogers, p. 200; Dft. Ex. A-110.

28. In the Monckton copy of Rogers' journal the entry for January 7 reads in part: "Cross'd the Maskongom Creek running South about 20 Yards Wide; An Indian Town about 20 Yards on the East Side of the Creek, this is Called the Mohigon Cabbins, there were but two or three Indians in the place, the rest were Hunting, the Indians here had plenty of Cows, Horses & Hogs &ca" (Paltsits, ed., Journal, p. 274; Dft. Ex. A-316). This was evidently Croghan's "Mohicon Village," on the Jerome Fork of Mohican River, a tributary of the Walhonding which, in turn, is a tributary of the Muskingum River.

29. Hough, ed., Journals of Robert Rogers, p. 200; Dft. Ex. A-110.

30. Idem.

southeast of the "long meadow" (Big Prairie?) some 24 miles, into the southeastern corner of Area 54, where he found "a number of Wyandots and Six Nations Indians hunting." The next day, January 12, 1761, the Rangers went 6 miles southeast and in the evening killed several beavers. They were then a few miles south of southeastern Area 54, perhaps on present Indian Trail Creek, for in his journal entry for the next day, January 13, 1761, Rogers notes that he and his party "travelled about north-east six miles, and came to the Delaware's town, called Beaver Town."[31]

This town, as subsequent entries in Rogers' journal show, was some 84 miles, according to the route Rogers took, west of the mouth of Big Beaver Creek.[32] Rogers' description of Beaver's Town early in 1761 is as follows:

> This Indian town stands on good land, on the west side of Maskongom [Tuscarawas] River; and opposite the town, on the east-side, is a fine river [Sandy Creek] which discharges itself into it...they make a very fine stream,...running to the south-west.[33] There are about 3,000 acres of cleared ground round this place. The number of warriors in this town is about 180...At this town I staid till the 16th [of January, 1761] in the morning to refresh my party,

---

31. Hough, ed., Journals of Robert Rogers, p. 201; Dft. Ex. A-110.

32. Hough, ed., Journals of Robert Rogers, pp. 201-202; Dft. Ex. A-110. The mouth of Beaver Creek is in western Pennsylvania. On a table of distances made in ca. 1764, Tuscarawas (Beaver's Town) is noted as being 91 miles from the mouth of Beaver Creek ([Smith], Historical Account, p. 150; Dft. Ex. A-149).

33. This is the direction in which the Tuscarawas flows for about three miles below its junction with Sandy Creek. It then flows southeast for about six miles.

and procured some corn of the Indians to boil with
our venison.[34]

From this point on, Rogers travelled east of Area 54, his destinatio.
being Fort Pitt.

That the Detroit Hurons considered the Wyandot "towns" on the
south side of Sandusky Bay as of minor importance in 1761 is illustrated
in the following incident.

Early in the spring of 1761 the anti-English Senecas and other
Indians near and on the upper Ohio River proposed holding a council
with the Six Nations and Detroit Indians "at Junundat al9 Sandusky."
When Capt. Donald Campbell, British commandant at Detroit, heard of
this he ordered the British traders at Sandusky to remove themselves
and their supplies to Detroit, and he also urged the Hurons at Detroit
not to attend the proposed council. Instead, the Detroit Hurons invited
the conferees to come to their town.[35]

This led the chiefs of the various groups assembled at Junundat
to send one of their number as a spokesman to Detroit. The spokesman,
when he met with the Hurons at Detroit, admonished the latter for having let their council fire at Junundat go out, and told them that the
Indians gathered there had re-kindled it. To which the Detroit Hurons
replied:

> We are surprised at the proposal of your chiefs,
> proposing to speak to us in a land of brambles.

---

34. Hough, ed., Journals of Robert Rogers, p. 201; Dft. Ex. A-
110. This description accords with another one, written in 1764 after
Beaver's Town at Tuscarawas had been deserted ([Smith], Historical
Account, p. 50; Dft. Ex. A-146).

35. Papers of Sir William Johnson, vol. 3, pp. 695-696, 521, 448-
453; Dft. Ex. A-108. Collections of the Massachusetts Historical Society,
4th ser., vol. 9, pp. 423-424; Dft. Ex. A-107.

> We have never heard it said that there was a
> [council] fire truly lighted there.[36] It is
> true that there are a few fires lighted
> sometimes, but they are lighted by some hunters
> seeking their livelihood. We tell you we are
> not going there at all. If your Chiefs have.
> come to speak there of important affairs, we
> invite them to come here [Detroit] to tell them
> to us publicly...[37]

At about this same time the Mohawks of New York may have been nego-

tiating with the Wyandots, as the Onondagas accused them of doing, "for

a place of Settlement," since the Mohawks "had no Lands left" in New

York. Although the Mohawks denied this,[38] they were in 1761 much dis-

tressed by New Yorkers who, as Sir William Johnson, British Superintendent

of Indian Affairs for the Northern Department, remarks, were

---

36. The Eastern Woodlands Indians were accustomed to hold all
important inter-group and Indian-White councils at specified locations,
where a "council fire" had at one time been formally "lighted." The
Six Nations Iroquois, for example, had in 1761 two such council fires,
one at Onondaga and one at the Mohawk Valley residence of Sir William
Johnson, Superintendent of Indian Affairs for the Northern Department.
In 1761, when they heard that Johnson proposed to light a third council
fire for the western Indians at Detroit, they tried to persuade him not
to do so, in an effort to maintain their importance as negotiators for
all the western Indians, including those around Detroit (Papers of Sir
William Johnson, vol. 3, p. 444; Dft. Ex. A-108).

37. Papers of Col. Henry Bouquet, Ser. 21655, pp. 113-114, 123-
124; Dft. Ex. A-109.

38. The Papers of Sir William Johnson, vol. 3, pp. 701, 704-705;
Dft. Ex. A-108.

teasing them for their lands, which were now
so clipped about on every side, that they
could scarce live by hunting on what was now
left.[39]

The meeting of the several Indian groups which had been scheduled

for "Junundat al$ Sandusky" and which was actually held at Detroit in

July , 1761 was not without significance. Near the end of July, 1761

Croghan, then at Fort Pitt, learned of a plot concocted at this meeting

and agreed to by the Indians of the Ohio Valley and those around Detroit,

to destroy all the British posts in the Great Lakes-Ohio Valley region.

The newly instituted British policy of refusing to give the Western

Indians presents and ammunition for their hunting was one reason for

this projected uprising.[40] When he learned of the plot Croghan was

on the point of departing for Detroit to be present at a conference

Sir William Johnson was to hold there in the early fall of 1761 with

all the so-called "Western Indians."[41] Croghan left Fort Pitt for

Detroit in a hurry on July 28, 1761; by August 2, 1761 he was at "the

173

---

39. Stone, Life and Times, vol. 2, pp. 429-430; Dft. Ex. A-118.

40. Pennsylvania Magazine of History and Biography, vol. 71,
pp. 410-411; Dft. Ex. A-104. For a concise statement of the short-
sighted and misguided policy of Gen. Jeffrey Amherst, command-in-
chief of the British forces in America, toward the Indians in the
early 1760's, see The Papers of Sir William Johnson, vol. 3, p. 515;
Dft. Ex. A-108.

41. This conference, held in September, 1761, marked the only
time that Johnson went any farther west than Niagara, from his residence
half a mile from present Johnstown in eastern New York (O'Callaghan,
ed., Documents, vol. 7, pp. 648, 651; Dft. Ex. A-112).

Beavers Town on Muskingum" where he

> was met by Several Delaware Chiefs, who
> accompanied me to D'Troit to attend on
> the Conference to be held there by Sir
> William Johnson.[42]

On August 8, 1761 Croghan arrived at "Sandusky" where he "found but 5 Old

Chiefs at home and all their Warriors gone against the Cherokees."[43]

In the meantime orders dated August 12, 1761 from Col. Henry

Bouquet, then commanding at Fort Pitt, instructed one Lt. Elias Meyer to

proceed to "Sandusky Lake" and

> on the south side...at the most convenient Place
> ...to build a small Block House with a Pallisade
> round it, to serve as a Haltin [sic] Place for
> our Party [Sir William Johnson's] going & coming
> from Detroit.[44]

On August 31, 1761, Meyer arrived at Sandusky Bay, and on September 1,

1761 he wrote to Bouquet from "Sandusky Lake" in part as follows:

174

> yesterday afternoon [August 31, 1761], I went
> out 5 or 6 miles in a boat, to the eastern part
> of the lake, to look for a good place opposite
> the point[45] which all the boats are obliged to
> double in order to go to Detroit. But either
> the land is too low, and there is no timber, or
> the landing is too dangerous on account of rocks
> below and above water. Therefore, I have decided
> on a place here, to build a blockhouse, which is
> three miles from a village which the savages call
> Canoutout Chanondet [sic], and where all the
> horses of the merchants unloaded and loaded the

---

42. Pennsylvania Magazine of History and Biography, vol. 71,
p. 412; Dft. Ex. A-104.

43. Idem.

44. Orders for Lieut. Elias Meyer. Fort Pitt, August 12, 1761,
p. 103; Dft. Ex. A-119.

45. I.e., eastern end of present Marblehead Peninsula, the
northern enclosure of Sandusky Bay.

merchanise for Detroit. It is about in the
middle of the small Lake Sandusky.[46]

The fact that the British fort was to be, not at the entrance to
Sandusky Bay, but "about in the middle" of the "small," or what we take
to be the eastern half of Sandusky Bay puts it within extreme northwestern Area 53, probably near present Venice, Erie County, some four
miles within the western boundary of Area 53. Meyer's mention of the
village called "Canoutout Chanondet [Canuta Junundat]" also furnishes
proof for the equation of two names for the same town;[47] his location
of this village as three miles distant from the blockhouse site on the
Bay is in accord with the location of (a) "Canuta" of Charles Stuart's
1755-1756 account; (b) "Anioton," mapped by De Léry in 1755 as "one

'?.5 mile?'" inland, or south of Sandusky Bay; and (c) Croghan's
"Ju... .76(

By Septem... 4, 1761 a carpenter arrived at Meyer's camp, who had
previously "worked on a house for the Beaver King at Tuscarawas."[48]

Upon arriving at Detroit early in September, 1761, Sir William
lit a council fire, and named the Hurons or Detroit as the head of
what he termed "the Ottawa Confederacy."[49] After the Detroit council
had been concluded Johnson left Detroit to return to New York via the

175

---

46. Papers of Col. Henry Bouquet, Ser. 21647, pp. 91-94; Dft.
Ex. A-120.

47. Later Meyer refers to the village simply as "Junundat"
(Papers of Col. Henry Bouquet, Ser. 21647, pp. 130, 132, 171-172;
Dft. Ex. A-120).

48. Papers of Col. Henry Bouquet, Ser. 21647, pp. 130, 132;
Dft. Ex. A-120.

49. Stone, Life and Times, vol. 2, p. 463; Dft. Ex. A-118.

south side of Lake Erie. Reaching the mouth of present Portage River on

September 21, 1761 Johnson sent his boats around

> the point [Marblehead Peninsula] and ordered
> them encamped at the east side of the entrance
> of Lake Sandusky into Lake Erie, which is about
> a mile across--there to wait my coming.[50]

Johnson himself then crossed Marblehead Peninsula southward on the old

portage trail and came to the north shore of Sandusky Bay. From there,

he remarks, it was almost six miles directly across Sandusky Bay to

> one of the Wyandot towns [on the south shore
> of the Bay]...I sent Mr. Croghan to the Indian
> town, and went down the lake [Bay] eastward in
> a little birch canoe to the place where the
> block house is to be built by Mr. Myer. This
> place is about three leagues [7.5 miles west]
> from the mouth of Lake Sandusky, where it dis-
> embogues itself into Lake Erie...It is about
> three miles [north] from another village of
> Hurons, and fifteen miles [east] by water from
> the one opposite to the carrying-place [portage],
> and nine by land.[51] The Pennsylvania road comes
> by this post. This is one hundred and seventy
> miles from Presque Isle [Erie, Pennsylvania]
> and forty miles [by water] from Detroit.[52]

After visiting the blockhouse site Johnson went by canoe eastward

to his party's encampment at the mouth of Sandusky Bay. There were

evidently some Ottawas at this spot in northwestern Area 53; Johnson

mentions that a "Tawa [Ottawa] squaw" came into his tent "quite wet,

---

50. Stone, Life and Times, vol. 2, p. 466; Dft. Ex. A-118.

51. Johnson's mileages for the location of the Fort, 7½ miles west of the entrance to Sandusky Bay at or near present Venice, as also for the two Wyandot villages, Junundat at present Castalia and Sunyendeand at the mouth of present Pickerel Creek, 3 and 9 miles, respectively, from the Fort, are remarkably accurate.

52. Stone, Life and Times, vol. 2, p. 466; Dft. Ex. A-118. See also Papers of Col. Henry Bouquet, Ser. 21647, p. 133; Dft. Ex. A-120.

having fallen into the lake at 11 o'clock at night," and also that he gave "the Tawa's sons two silver gorgets..."[53]

Farther eastward on his journey, on October 2, 1761 Johnson encountered a party of Mohawks near the eastern end of Lake Erie. These Mohawks intended to hunt that winter at "Cherage Creek,"[54] but one of their party, named Aaron, thought that he might go farther west to Sandusky. Near Niagara Johnson also met some Cayugas who "were going a hunting to Sandusky...One of them is a Sappony..."[55]

Croghan accompanied Johnson from Detroit as far as Sandusky Bay; from thence he went overland to Fort Pitt. While Croghan was "at Sandusky [Sunyendeand]" on September 23, 1761, "the Mohiconders [Mohicans] delivered two prisoners [White captives]" to him, and the Wyandots, six prisoners. A few days later when Croghan reached Beaver's Town at Tuscarawas the Indians there delivered 16 prisoners to him.[56]

That there were Mohicans, as well as Wyandots, in northwestern Area 53 in 1761 is also evident from other accounts. On September 30, 1761, for example, Meyer wrote from his "Camp at Lake Sandusky" that

---

53. Stone, Life and Times, vol. 2, p. 467; Dft. Ex. A-118.

54. On a 1778 map the right hand branch of Grand River, east of Area 53, is legended as "Chorage Creek" (Hutchins, Map...1778; Dft. Ex. A-121).

55. Stone, Life and Times, vol. 2, p. 472; Dft. Ex. A-118.
The Saponi were an eastern Siouan-speaking group from North Carolina and Virginia who in 1753 removed north and were adopted by the Cayugas (Hodge, ed., Handbook, pt. 2, pp. 464-465; Dft. Ex. A-2).

56. Pennsylvania Magazine of History and Biography, vol. 71, p. 415; Dft. Ex. A-104.

he had made a dea.

with a certain Mohican John, a good hunter
and an honest man, who is to furnish me with
some venison, and I am to build him a house
in the village [Junundat] three miles from
here.[57]

An indication as to where Mohican John was living at this time is given
in another letter from Meyer to Bouquet, dated November 8, 1761, in which
Meyer mentions that two soldiers who had deserted from his camp were then
"at Wikenjohn's Town about 41 miles from here with one Mohican John, who
promised to bring them here."[58] Wikenjohn's Town was probably Croghan's
"Mohickon Village" cf 1760, on the Jerome Fork of the Mohican River, in
Ashland County, Ohio, in central Area 54.[59]

Meyer's camp on Sandusky Bay attracted many Indians to it in the
fall of 1761. Meyer observes, on October 22, 1761 that

178

The savages come from all directions daily in
large numbers and in state, to bother me for
provisions, ammunition and presents, (the
French have utterly spoiled them) and I have
nothing to give them. It will be fortunate if
I have no need of them.[60]

By February, 1762 Ensign H. C. Pauli was in charge of the then-
completed blockhouse or "Fort Sandusky." From the Fort Pauli reported

---

57. Papers of Col. Henry Bouquet, Ser. 21647, p. 141; Dft. Ex.
A-120.

58. Papers of Col. Henry Bouquet, Ser. 21647, p. 188, also p.
171; Dft. Ex. A-120.

59. A 1764 table of distances lists "Mohickon John's Town" as
50 miles from "Sandusky" ([Smith, Historical Account, p. 150; Dft. Ex.
A-146).

60. Papers of Col. Henry Bouquet, Ser. 21647, p. 172; Dft. Ex.
A-120. Parentheses Meyer's.

118

on February 19, 1762 that nothing extraordinary had happened since Meyer's

departure, but that

> Some of the Indians here about Shows a little
> Discondent about the Blockhous being erected,
> one in Specil who is a head [chief] of Coonu-
> duth Town [Canuta],[61] tells he'll have it burnt
> in the Spring, when hounders [hunters] comes
> home, but as I am inform'd all the rest of the
> Nations are very quit [quiet] and most of the
> young men hereabouts are gone to ware aginst
> the Cherrkees [Cherokees] I thinck nodding but
> being nonsence about it the Colonel [Bouquet]
> will be so kind and give me direction how to
> behave to this pueble [people] in case the[y]
> Should offer Insolence there has been nodding
> else but civility Showed to them.[62]

A month later in another letter of March 16, 1762 Ensign Pauli

states that the "Vindows [Wyandot]" warriors who had gone against the

Cherokees amounted to "50 men divided in 5 Companys." If all these

warriors were from the Sandusky Bay region the population there at this

time must have been over 200 souls. On their way southward the warriors   179

had met "a Party of the six nations 80 Strong" who suggested that the

Wyandots join them in striking the English. This invitation the Wyandots

refused; furthermore, they sent one of their party back to Sandusky Bay,

with news of the proposal. The intelligence was brought to Pauli by two

Indians. One of these Indians was named Kindose, and is identified by

Pauli as "an old head man" of "the Creek town near Sandusky River named

---

61. In a despatch a few months later Pauli refers to what
seems to be the same town, as "Cenundud [Junundat]" (Papers of Col.
Henry Bouquet, Ser. 21648, pt. 1, p. 123; Dft. Ex. A-122). This is
reminiscent of Lt. Meyer's "Canoutout Chanondet."

62. Papers of Colonel Henry Bouquet. Ser. 21648, pt. 1, p.
33; Dft. Ex. A-122.

Ajenevindo." The other messenger was "Erren [Aaron]," identified by
Pauli as "a Mohawk."[63]

The "Creek town near Sandusky River named Ajenevindo" where Kindose
was a head man was in all probability the village near the mouth of
present Pickerel Creek, referred to in 1756 and 1758 by James Smith as
"Sunyendeand" or "Rockfish," by Croghan in 1760 as "Sandusky" and
by Johnson in 1761 as the "Indian Town" nine miles by land west of Fort
Sandusky. Aaron, the Mohawk, was probably the same Aaron whom Johnson
had met in October, 1761, who had thought he might winter at Sandusky..

In early April, 1762 Lt. Thomas Hutchins, geographer and at this
time assistant agent for Indian affairs, set out from Fort Cumberland on
an extended tour to the west to deliver messages to the Indians at all
the British posts in the Ohio Valley-Great Lakes region.[64] Hutchins
kept a journal of his trip, and also drew a scaled map which has never
been publi. much cized. His journal entries are extremely brief; on April 19,
1762 he records that he was at "Mohican John's" and spoke to Mohican
John "and his Tribe" on the necessity of delivering the two deserters
from Meyer's former camp at Fort Sandusky, to Fort Pitt. Two days later
Hutchins "arrived at [Fort?] Sandusky."[65]

Hutchins' 1762 manuscript map provides many more details than does
his journal about sites and Indians in Areas 53 and 54 in 1762. The map

180

---

63. Papers of Col. Henry Bouquet, Ser. 21648, pt. 1, p. 51; Dft.
Ex. A-122.

64. Papers of Col. Henry Bouquet, Ser. 21655, pp. 185-186; Dft.
Ex. A-109.

65. Papers of Col. Henry Bouquet, Ser. 21655, pp. 167-168; Dft.
Ex. A-109. See also Heckewelder, History...of the Indian Nations, p.
93; Dft. Ex. A-321.

shows (1) "Beavers, Town at Tuscarawas," in the southeastern tip of Area
54. Also mapped are (2) "Mohickon John's Town" some 50 miles northwest
of "Beavers town," in south-central Area 54 on a stream we identify as
present Jerome Fork of the Mohican River; (3) "Remains of a Fort built
by the Ottawas [?]," some 20 miles north and a little west of Mohickon
John's Town, in western Area 54; (4) British Fort Sandusky on Sandusky
Bay in northwestern Area 53; and (5) "Wyandot Town" some 3-4 miles
south of Fort Sandusky, in northwestern Area 53. No town is indicated
at the mouth of Pickerel Creek. Since Hutchins did not pass through
eastern Area 53 the Cuyahoga River is not shown on his 1762 map.[66]

In marginal "Remarks" on Hutchins' 1762 map the population of
"Beavers Town at Tuscarawas" is noted as 80 warriors (ca. 320 souls).

A description by John Heckewelder, Moravian missionary, of Indian
settlements on the upper Tuscarawas River in 1762, when Heckewelder
lived on that River, adds to Hutchins' data. The "Indian town called
Tuscarawas," Heckewelder writes, consisted of "about forty wigwams."
A mile downstream from it there were also a few Indian families; a
mile upstream the trader Thomas Calhoon had his house, on the west
bank of the river. Half a mile upstream from Calhoon's cabin was
the cabin Heckewelder lived in. Nine and a half miles above (north
of) Tuscarawas, on the eastern boundary of Area 54, "there was another
Indian [Delaware?] village." Emissaries "of the Senecas and Northern
Indians" were, in the fall of 1762, according to Heckewelder, "busily
engaged in exciting the Delwares [on the Tuscarawas River] to take up

181

---

66. Hutchins, [Map of] A Tour from Fort Cumberland...1762; Dft.
Ex. A-123.

the hatchet against the English...."[67].

The presence of Mohicans in the Sandusky region, observed by Croghan and Meyer in 1761, is also noted by Hutchins, both on his 1762 map, and again in an account of his written in 1764. In the "Remarks" on his 1762 map Hutchins lists 200 Wyandot and Mohican warriors (800 persons) "At and near [the British Fort] Sandusky;" this was exclusive of the Detroit Wyandots, who are listed separately. In his 1764 account Hutchins states that "Junundat Town" alone (the "Wyandot Town" near Fort Sandusky on his 1762 map) had 70-80 warriors (280-320 souls), and "consisted of Wyandot and Mohickon Tribes."[68]

A mixed population of Wyandots and Mohicans "at or near" Fort Sandusky is also noticed by one D. Franklin, a British officer who prepared a list of the number of warriors "living at or near the several Posts" he visited in 1762. For the Fort Sandusky region Franklin lists "Wyandotts & Mohickons...200 [warriors]."[69]

Another reference locating Junundat occurs in a May, 1762 despatch from Ensign Pauli at Fort Sandusky. Pauli had called in "the Cheefs of the Indians on this side [south side] of the Lake [Sandusky Bay]" to ask

182

---

67. Rondthaler, Life of John Heckewelder, pp. 46, 56; Dft. Ex. A-162. Heckewelder, Narrative, p. 61; Dft. Ex. A-53. Paul A. W. Wallace, Thirty Thousand Miles, pp. 41, 246; Dft. Ex. A-167.
Presumably all the "Indians" mentioned by Heckewelder as living on the upper Tuscarawas River in 1762 were Delawares; had they been members of other groups Heckewelder probably would have noted the fact.

68. Hutchins, [Map of] A Tour from Fort Cumberland...1762; Dft. Ex. A-123. Hanna, The Wilderness Trail, vol. 2, pp. 202, 206, 208-209; Dft. Ex. A-82.

69. Franklin, A List, p. 1; Dft. Ex. A-125.

permission to "plant Corn" nearby. After giving the matter consideration for 12 days the chiefs finally assented, but wanted Pauli

> to plant at Cenundud [Junundat] one of their
> Towns four miles off the Blockhouse being
> better Land there; but since the Colonel [Bou-
> quet] has found proper near the Blockhouse, I
> could not allow it.[70]

Near the end of July, 1762 the Indians around British Fort Sandusky were suffering for lack of food. Pauli reports, on July 23, 1762:

> It is impossible to buy venison, as the present
> time is so hungery with the Indians that they
> [are] hardly able to keep themselves alife.[71]

During the fall and early winter of 1762 Croghan, at Fort Pitt, received reports of plans for a second native anti-British uprising.[72] There was at this time a Delaware "prophet" living at the Beaver's Town at Tuscarawas whose nativistic doctrine was attracting interest.[73] So bitter was this anti-British feeling that "King Beaver," the Delaware chief at Tuscarawas, ordered Heckwelder, then living 1 1/2 miles north of Beaver's Town, to leave the Tuscarawas region.[74]

183

---

70. Papers of Col. Henry Bouquet, Ser. 21648, pt. 1, p. 123; Dft. Ex. A-122.

71. Papers of Col. Henry Bouquet, Ser. 21648, pt. 2, p. 16; Dft. Ex. A-126. The corn crop had not yet ripened, and either the Indians had little ammunition, or their able-bodied men who did most of the hunting were off on war parties.

72. Pennsylvania Magazine of History and Biography, vol. 71, pp. 430-432; Dft. Ex. A-104. Papers of Col. Henry Bouquet, Ser. 21648, pt. 2, pp. 158, 176-177; Dft. Ex. A-126.

73. Pritts, Incidents, p. 98; Dft. Ex. A-129.

74. Rondthaler, Life of John Heckewelder, pp. 56-57; Dft. Ex. A-162. Heckewelder, Names, p. 396; Dft. Ex. A-161.

Indian discontent was also being manifested in the northwestern part of Area 53. During the early spring of 1763 Ensign Pauli was constantly being importuned for presents by Indians at Fort Sandusky. Realizing he must keep the Indians' good will, Pauli drew on his own personal funds to placate his Indian visitors.[75]

By May, 1763, the anti-British storm broke. The Ottawa leader Pontiac and his warriors laid siege to Detroit, and also persuaded the Wyandots of the Sandusky region to burn Fort Sandusky on May 16, 1763.[76]

News of Pontiac's uprising was brought to Beaver's Town at Tuscarawas on May 27, 1763. The Beaver and other Delaware leaders there notified Croghan at Fort Pitt that they did not wish to join in the uprising, and requested, since they were

> seated on the Road between you and those Nations, who have taken up the Hatchet against you,... [that] you will send no Warriors this way till we are Removed from this, which we will do as soon as we conveniently can, when we shall permit You to Pass without taking Notice, Till then we desire the Warriors may go, by the first Road You went.[77]

The Delawares at Beaver's Town also warned Thomas Calhoun, their English trader, to leave Tuscarawas, and promised they would send another trader "at Gueyahoeja [Cuyahoga]... safe Home." The population at the Beaver's Town in May, 1763 is estimated as having been about 150 warriors

184

75. Papers of Col. Henry Bouquet, Ser. 21649, pt. 1, p. 79; Dft. Ex. A-127.

76. Papers of Col. Henry Bouquet, Ser. 21649, pt. 1, pp. 117, 120-121, 129, 223; Dft. Ex. A-127. Papers of Col. Henry Bouquet, Ser. 21654, pp. 122-123; Dft. Ex. A-133.

77. Papers of Col. Henry Bouquet, Ser. 21649, pt. 1, p. 122; Dft. Ex. A-127. Emphasis ours.

124

(600 persons).[78]

During July, 1763 Junundat, the Wyandot-Mohican village in northwestern Area 53 three miles south of the by-then demolished Fort Sandusky, was burnt by English troops under the command of Capt. James Dalyell and Maj. Robert Rogers, who had been sent from Presque Isle (Erie, Pennsylvania) to relieve Detroit.[79]

A mixed Indian population continued to exist in the Sandusky Bay region, however, during the second half of the year 1763. A memorandum compiled by Sir William Johnson, dated November 18, 1763, lists "Wiandots & Mohiccons" as having "4 Villages in the Neighborhood of the Fort at Sandusky Lake which emptys into Lake Erie" with a total population of 200 men.[80] Johnson's memorandum was probably outdated when he wrote it, as an anonymous, undated French sketch map of post-July, 1763 indicates. This map shows an Indian settlement near Sandusky Bay a short distance east of the mouth of Sandusky River, but west of Area 53. The settlement is legended as "Conontia, qui ne pas habitté [Conontia, which is not inhabited]." Conontia is, obviously, the village known to

185

---

78. Papers of Col. Henry Bouquet, Ser. 21649, pt. 1, p. 121; Dft. Ex. A-127. Hanna, The Wilderness Trail, vol. 2, pp. 204, 379; Dft. Ex. A-82. [Smith], Historical Account, p. 50; Dft. Ex. A-146.

79. Col. Henry Bouquet to Gen. Jeffrey Amherst, Fort Pitt, August 27, 1763; p. 227; Dft. Ex. A-128. Bradstreet to Gage, Sandusky Lake, September 29, 1764, p. 1; Dft. Ex. A-142. Anonymous Map of Sandusky Area, 1763-1764; Dft. Ex. A-145. Papers of Sir William Johnson, vol. 10, p. 790; Dft. Ex. A-116. Dictionary of American Biography, vol. 16, p. 108; Dft. Ex. A-210.

80. Papers of Sir William Johnson, vol. 4, pp. 240, 243; Dft. Ex. A-130. O'Callaghan, ed., Documents, vol. 7, p. 583; Dft. Ex. A-112. See also Papers of Col. Henry Bouquet, Ser. 21649, pt. 2, pp. 116-117; Dft. Ex. A-132.

James Smith as Sunyendeand, which was at the mouth of present Pickerel
Creek, some four miles west of Royce Area 53. The destruction of Junundat by Dalyell is also noticed on the map.[81]

During the year 1763 shifts in population were also occurring in
eastern Areas 53 and 54. On August 5-6, 1763 Col. Henry Bouquet repulsed
an Indian attack made on his forces at Bushy Run, 25 miles east of Fort
Pitt. A White captive of the Delawares at this time, one John M'Cullough,
who was living at "Mohoning [Mahoning]," a Delaware town approximately
30 miles east of Area 53, in present eastern Ohio,[82] states that after the
battle with Bouquet at Bushy Run the Delawares of "Mohoning" moved to
"Cay-a-how-ga [Cuyahoga]," which M'Cullough refers to as "a town not far
distant from Lake Erie." In all probability this was Netawatwees' town,
at or near the "Big Falls" of the Cuyahoga River, within or close to
Area 53. However, the Delawares from Mahoning

> stayed but a short time in Cay-a-haw-ge, then
> moved across the country to the forks of Moosh-
> king-oong [Muskingum], which signifies clear
> eyes, as the river abounds with a certain kind of
> fish that have very clear eyes; from thence
> we took up the west branch [Walhonding River?]
> to its source, and from thence I know not where.
>
> Nothing remarkable happened, excepting that
> we suffered by hunger, it being in the winter
> [1763-1764].[83]

---

81. Anonymous, Map of Sandusky Area, 1763-1764 (?); Dft. Ex. A-145.
This map post-dates the destruction of Junundat in July 1763, since this
is noted. The map is not drawn to scale, and was evidently hastily
sketched.

82. For the location of Mahoning, on the Mahoning River branch of
Big Beaver Creek, see Hutchins, A Map of the Country...[1764]; Dft. Ex.
A-124.

83. Pritts, Incidents, pp. 102-103; Dft. Ex. A-129.

If the Forks of Muskingum refers, in this account, to the junction of the Walhonding and Tuscarawas rivers, as it probably does, this Delaware group spent at least part of the winter of 1763-1764 hunting in the central part of Area 54. However, in the spring of 1764 the group left Area 54 and

> returned to the west branch of Moosh-king-oong [Walhonding River], and settled in a new town which we called Kta-ho-ling, which signifies a place where roots have been dug up for food. We remained there during the summer [of 1764].[84]

Kta-ho-ling, M'Cullough states, was "ten miles from Moosh-king-oong."[85] This would put Ktaholing ten miles up Walhonding River, or about 20 miles south of Area 54.

Shifting of Delaware groups in 1763 is also noted by Gen. Thomas Gage, successor to Amherst as commander-in-chief of the British forces in America. In January, 1764 Gage wrote to Sir William Johnson:

187

> The Shawnese or rather the Delawares I hear are removed back [north] towards the South Shore of Lake Erie a Stroke made upon them or those Rascaly Thieves the Wiandots near Sandusky would be of great Consequence...[86]

Gage may have been referring to the move noted by M'Cullough, or to the abandonment of Tuscarawas Town by the Beaver. If to the latter Gage was mistaken. When the Beaver left Tuscarawas, as he had told Croghan he intended to do, he re-established his town on the head-waters of Hocking River, some 65 miles south of Area 54, either

---

84. Idem.

85. Pritts, Incidents, p. 104; Dft. Ex. A-129.

86. Papers of Sir William Johnson, vol. 4, p. 303; Dft. Ex. A-130.

late in 1763 or early in 1764.[87]

In May, 1764 Bouquet, in a letter to Sir William Johnson, lists the Delaware and Shawnee towns "over the Ohio;" Bouquet does not include those in the Sandusky region.[88] "N.W. from Fort Pitt" Bouquet names seven towns; two are in or close to eastern Area 53, namely, "Cayahga [Cuyahoga]" (the Delaware chief Netawatwees' town) and "Ottawas Town" (also on the Cuyahoga River).[89] West from Fort Pitt, "Upon the Branches of Muskingum" Bouquet lists two towns in Area 54, "Tuscarawaes," probably by then abandoned, and "Mohigon John" town, still existent in May, 1764.[90]

During the fall of 1764 Col. John Bradstreet, British officer, headed a large expedition by boat to Detroit.[91] With Bradstreet was one

---

87. Hicks, Deposition, Fort Pitt, April 14, 1764; p. 1; Dft. Ex. A-134. Hanna, The Wilderness Trail, vol. 2, pp. 194, 204; Dft. Ex. A-82. Hanna, The Wilderness Trail, vol. 1, p. 204; Dft. Ex. A-70. Hutchins, A Map of the Country...[1764]; Dft. Ex. A-124. [Smith], Historical Account, pp. 50, 150; Dft. Ex. A-146.
There had been Delawares at the head of the Hocking River as early as 1750, at least. Christopher Gist records on January 19, 1751, he arrived at "Hockhocking a small Town with only four or five Delaware Families" (Mulkearn, ed., George Mercer Papers, pp. 15, 495; Dft. Ex. A-72).

88. Papers of Sir William Johnson, vol. 4, p. 403; Dft. Ex. A-130. Papers of Col. Henry Bouquet, Ser. 21649, pt. 2, pp. 116-117; Dft. Ex. A-132.

89. Collections of the New-York Historical Society, vol. 14, p. 282; Dft. Ex. A-143.

90. Papers of Sir William Johnson, vol. 11, p. 212; Dft. Ex. A-136. Collections of the New-York Historical Society, vol. 14, p. 307; Dft. Ex. A-143.

91. Bradstreet to Gage, Presque Isle, August 14, 1764; with Enclosure; Dft. Ex. A-141.

128

Capt. John Montresor, of the Engineers Corps, whose daily journal contains several items of interest.

On the way west Bradstreet's expedition passed the mouth of the "River de Seguein [Cuyahoga River]."[92] Under date of August 18, 1764 Montresor notes:

> This [River de Seguein] is a remarkable river where the upper Nations hunt & also paddle.[sic] 6 leagues [15 miles] up this river & on the East Side & from thence march loaded to Fort du Quesne now Fort Pitt in 6 days.[93] Great party of the Ottawas hunted & saved corn here last year.[94]

On September 18, 1764 the expedition encamped half a mile west of the site of the former British Fort Sandusky on the south shore of Sandusky Bay. Montresor notes that the Indians had burnt the Fort the previous year (1763) and that the site was "a bad place for the Boats."[95] Later in September, 1764 Bradstreet encamped on the south shore of the Marblehead Peninsula, and word arrived that

189

> 40 Warriors and Chiefs exclusive of Women were on the opposite [south] side of the Lake [Sandusky Bay] at the old Village on

---

92. Saguin was the name of the French trader on the Cuyahoga in 1742. Montresor mistakenly gives "Cayahaga" as the second name for "La Grand Riviere [Grand River]," which is east of the Cuyahoga, and which the expedition had already passed.

93. References to Cuyahoga River constituting one stretch of the usual route between Fort Pitt and Detroit at this time are numerous; see, for example, Pennsylvania Magazine of History and Biography, vol. 71, p. 360; Dft. Ex. A-104.

94. Collections of the New-York Historical Society, vol. 14, p. 282; Dft. Ex. A-143. Montresor writes as though the Ottawas who had had a town on the Cuyahoga the year previously, were no longer there in 1764.

95. Collections of the New-York Historical Society, vol. 14, pp. 294-295; Dft. Ex. A-143.

the River Poisson d'ontario[96] that they had
brought some prisoners down [the Sandusky
River] with them belonging to their Band or
Party. Provisions were ordered for the
whole and sent them...[97]

The "old Village" on the Riviére du Poisson Doré, a stream first noted

by De Léry in 1755 was, as has been shown, De Léry's "Sandoské" and Col.

James Smith's Sunyendeand, on present Pickeral Creek some four miles west

of Area 53. The fact that Montresor refers to Sunyendeand as an "old

Village" indicates to us that by September, 1764 Sunyendeand had been

abandoned by the Wyandots.[98]

A final item of interest in Montresor's journal is contained in

his entry for October 13, 1764. That day an Onondaga Indian who had

been sent to Fort Pitt with messages returned to Bradstreet's camp at

Sandusky Bay with the news that

190

the Delaware Cabins where Mohican John[99]
lives were abandoned from [because of]

---

96. Later in his journal Montresor "corrects" his rendition of the
name thus: "October 10. A long Boat set off at Daylight this morning to
the river Poisson D'oré to discover the out scout..." (Collections of the
New-York Historical Society, vol. 14, p. 306; Dft. Ex. A-143).

97. Collections of the New-York Historical Society, vol. 14, p.
300; Dft. Ex. A-143.

98. The term "old Town" or "old Village" was often used on 18th-
century maps or in accounts to refer to towns no longer in existence.
Our conclusion that Sunyendeand had been abandoned by September,
1764 is further strengthened by the fact that Montresor explicitly notes
where the Wyandots were located at this time-namely, 60 miles or more up
the Sandusky River from its mouth, near present Upper Sandusky, Sandusky
County, Ohio (Collections of the New-York Historical Society, vol. 14, pp.
294-296, 306; Dft. Ex. A-143). Upper Sandusky is 23 miles west of Area 54.

99. Evidently, even as early as 1764, the Mohicans in the Ohio
Valley were becoming intermixed with the Delawares. In 1755 Henry Hamilton, Lieutenant-Governor of Detroit, refers to "Mahingan John" as a
"Delaware savage" (Thwaites and Kellogg, Revolution on the Upper Ohio,
p. 127; see also p. 62, fn. 90; Dft. Ex. A-177).

the Intelligence sent them by the 6 Nations on the day of our arrival at the
old Fort of Sandusky [September 18, 1764].[100]

Where Mohican John moved is not stated, but it is of some interest
that in 1775 an American agent noted Mohican John's arrival at a
Delaware town at present Coshocton, Ohio; he had come to Coshocton
from a Wyandot town at present Upper Sandusky, 23 miles west of Area
54.[101]

Another town, close to the eastern boundary of Area 53 was also
abandoned in 1764 because of Bradstreet's expedition - namely, Netawatwees'
town near the Big Falls of the Cuyahoga River. Learning of Bradstreet's
presence on Lake Erie Netawatwees fled south, Heckewelder states, "across
the ridge which divides the waters of the lake [Erie] from those of the
Ohio, in order to run down the Muskingum in a canoe..."[102] However, the
venerable Delaware chief met with certain personal difficulties, as we
shall see, for in the fall of 1764 Col. Henry Bouquet, at the head of
a second large British expedition, marched from Fort Pitt overland to
the Forks of Muskingum (present Coshocton) to compel the Indians to
make peace and surrender their captives.

Bouquet reached Tuscarawas, near the southeastern tip of Area 54,
on October 13, 1764, and found "the Beaver's Town" deserted. However,
while Bouquet was at Tuscarawas two messengers he despatched westward
with letters to Bradstreet at Sandusky were captured near Tuscarawas

191

100. Collections of the New-York Historical Society, vol. 14, p.
307; Dft. Ex. A-143.

101. Butler, Journal, p. 27; Dft. Ex. A-160. See also Peckham,
ed., George Croghan's Journal...1767, p. 36; Dft. Ex. A-317.
102. Heckewelder, Names, pp. 388-389; Dft. Ex. A-161. See also
Beatty, Journal, pp. 13, 14, 31, 41-52, 60-63; Dft. Ex. A-139.

and taken to a Delaware settlement "sixteen miles from hence."[103]

From Tuscarawas Bouquet marched southwestward to within a mile of the Forks of Muskingum, which are 30 miles south of Area 54. There he encamped to receive captives. Bouquet chose this location because "the principal Indians towns" in the region lay around it, "distant from seven to twenty miles..."[104]

While Bouquet was encamped near the Forks of Muskingum some of his Indian spies captured Netawatwees and brought the Delaware chief to Bouquet's camp. There Bouquet, according to Heckewelder,

> in consequence of his [Netawatwees'] not
> attending to the message he [Bouquet] had
> sent him, to come into his camp to a council
> for peace, publicly deposed him, placing
> another chief in his stead.[105]

It is very probable that the Delaware town in which Netawatwees was captured in the fall of 1764, and the Delaware town to which Bouquet's

---

103. Bouquet to Gage, Camp near Tuscarawas, October 21, 1764; Dft. Ex. A-144. Papers of Sir William Johnson, vol. 4, pp. 570-572, 583-584; Dft. Ex. A-130. [Smith], Historical Account, pp. 40, 50-51; Dft. Ex. A-146.

104. [Smith], Historical Account, p. 60; Dft. Ex. A-146. None of these "principal towns" were in Area 54 if they were within a radius of 7-20 miles from Bouquet's camp.

105. Heckewelder, Names, pp. 388-389; Dft. Ex. A-161. For brief mention of this see also [Smith], Historical Account, pp. 68-70; Dft. Ex. A-146, and Heckewelder, Narrative, p. 198, fn; Dft. Ex. A-53.
In 1773 Croghan and some Allegheny Senecas again tried to depose Netawatwees and another elderly Delaware chief, Custaloga; this attempt, however, was also unsuccessful (Papers of Sir William Johnson, vol. 12, pp. 1047-1048; Dft. Ex. A-149. Council at Pittsburgh...1776, pp. 3, 15, 27; Dft. Ex. A-193).

two messengers were taken after they had been captured near Tuscarawas
were in the fall of 1764 one and the same town. The key to the name
and location of this town lies in a 1764 map of the Ohio country drawn
by Thomas Hutchins, who accompanied Bouquet on the latter's expedition.
On his map Hutchins legends "Kill Buck's T." within present eastern
Area 54, near the headwaters of an unnamed stream, obviously present
Killbuck Creek,[106] on the west side of the Creek some 20 miles west
and a little south of "ye Beaver Town at Tuscarawas."[107] John Killbuck
Jr., or Gelelemend was for years a councillor of the Turtle division of
the Delawares,[108] the same division of which Netawatwees was the civil chief.
No documentation for Killbuck's Town exists, to our knowledge, earlier
than 1764. It is possible, therefore, that it was Netawatwees, rather
then his councillor, who had established Hutchins' so-called "Kill
Buck's Town" in the late summer or early fall of 1764, after Netawatwees
had abandoned his town on the Cuyahoga River.[109]

193

    Be this as it may, Killbuck's Town was apparently short-lived.
In 1766 one Charles Beatty, a Presbyterian missionary, found Netawatwees,

---

    106. See Hodge, ed., Handbook, pt. 1, p. 688; Dft. Ex. A-1
and Royce, Indian Land Cessions, Pl. CLVI.

    107. Hutchins, A Map of the Country...[1764]; Dft. Ex. A-124.

    108. Heckewelder, Names, pp. 388-389, 391-393; Dft. Ex. A-161;
Hodge, ed., Handbook, entry Gelelemend, pt. 1, p. 489; Dft. Ex. A-1;
Hanna, The Wilderness Trail. vol. 1, p. 111, fn. 1; Dft. Ex. A-70.

    109. Hutchins would not nave legended Kill Buck's Town as
Netawatwees' Town on his 1764 map, since Bouquet   "deposed"
Netawatwees.

(whom the Delawares had reinstated as chief immediately after Bouquet left the country,[110]) and his people firmly established at "Kighalam-pegha" or "Newcomer's Town" (present Newcomerstown, Tuscarawas County, Ohio) on the Tuscarawas River, 15 miles east of the Forks of Muskingum and 30 miles south of Area 54.[111]

Other towns besides "Kill Bucks T." in or near Areas 53 and 54 which are legended on Hutchins' 1764 map are (1) "Ottawas T." some 25 (?) miles or more up the Cuyahoga River on the east bank; (2) "Cayahoga T." on the east side of the Cuyahoga at or near the Falls; (3) "Wyandot Town" three miles south of "Fort Sandusky;" (4) "Mohickan John's Town" some 50 miles south and a little east of Fort Sandusky; and "Beavers Town at Tuscarawas."[112] However, in his description of "The Rout from Fort Pitt to Sandusky, and thence to Detroit," written in 1764 and re-

110. Heckewelder, Names, pp. 388-389; Dft. Ex. A-161. Netawatwees continued as chief "until his death in the autumn of the year 1776 being then near ninety years of age," according to Heckewelder (idem).

111. Beatty, Journal, pp. 13, 16, 31, 41-52, 63; Dft. Ex. A-139. Zeisberger, Letter No. 3...Nov. 3, 1769, p. 2; Dft. Ex. A-50. Zeisberger, Diary of the Indian Congregation...March 1771, pp. 1-7; Dft. Ex. A-163. See also McClure, Diary, pp. 61-62, 64; Dft. Ex. A-202.
    The Moravian missionaries refer to Newcomer's Town as "Gekelemukpeschunk" (Transactions of the Moravian Historical Society, vol. 12, p. 175, fn. 6, and pp. 342, 345, 348; Dft. Ex. A-35).

112. Hutchins, A Map of the Country...[1764]; Dft. Ex. A-124.

vised and added to after 1778, Hutchins recognizes that "Wyandot
Town" (referred to in his description as "Junandot"), Fort Sandusky, and
the Beaver's Town at Tuscarawas, were by 1764 no longer in existence. He likewise refers to "Mohickon John's Town" in the
past tense, remarking that it "was situated" 50 miles south by east
of Fort Sandusky and that "It consisted only of a few houses."[113]

2. Use and Occupancy of Royce Areas 53 and 54: 1765-1776. At
the end of February, 1765 George Croghan learned from some hostages at
Fort Pitt that Custaloga, chief of the Wolf division of the Delawares,[114] "& his Tribe" had been hunting that winter "near Tuscera-
was,"[115] probably in and near the southeastern corner of Area 54.
Also, in his journal for 1765 Croghan notes that Delawares, to the
number of 600 warriors (2,400 persons) were living "Between the Ohio
and Lake Erie, on the branches of Beaver Creek, Muskingum and Guyehugo
[Cuyahoga]" and that they hunted "Where they live."[116]

195

---

113. Hanna, The Wilderness Trail, vol. 2, pp. 204, 206, 209; Dft.
Ex. A-82.

114. Hanna, The Wilderness Trail, vol. 1, p. 111, fn. 1; Dft.
Ex. A-70. Heckewelder, Names, pp. 393-394; Dft. Ex. A-161. Hodge, ed.,
Handbook, pt. 1, p. 374; Dft. Ex. A-1. [Smith], Historical Account,
p. 53; Dft. Ex. A-146. See also present Chapter, fn. 6, this Report.

115. Croghan's Journals, February 28, 1765-October 8, 1765,
p. 1; Dft. Ex. A-147.

116. Thwaites, ed., Early Western Travels, vol. 1, pp. 127, 166,
168; Dft. Ex. A-148.

Re-occupation of Tuscarawas by Delawares had evidently occurred by
1766. Beatty, the Presbyterian missionary, visited "Tuscalawa Town" in
September, 1766, and was a guest of the town's headman, Apa-ma-legh-on.[117]

Beatty also visited Newcomer's town later in September, 1766 and
there met "Netatwhelman [Netawatwees], the king and head of the Delaware
nation." At Newcomer's Town Beatty was urged by the Delawares in council

> to invite the Christian Indians in New-
> Jersey ... to come to Qui-a-ha-ga [Cuya-
> hoga] a town the king [Netawatwees] and
> some of his people had lived in, about
> seventy miles northwest of this place
> [Newcomer's Town] where, as they said,
> there was good hunting...and all the
> Indians, who desired to hear the gospel,
> as they gave us to understand there was
> a number of such, might then go there
> and settle.

Further references to Cuyahoga by Beatty make it plain that no Delawares
were living there in 1766.[118]

196

In 1765 and 1766 Croghan and Sir William Johnson, respectively,
refer to Ottawas living "at Sandusky," but because of the several uses
of the name Sandusky there is no certain way of knowing whether these
Ottawas had their town within or west of Area 53.[119]

As has already been noted, in 1761 Johnson made one trip as far
west as Detroit, where he was impressed with the numbers and strength of
the Lake Indians, lit a formal council fire for them, and recognized the
Hurons as the head of what he termed the "Ottawa Confederacy." After

---

117. Beatty, Journal, pp. 37-41; Dft. Ex. A-139. See also Peckham,
ed., George Croghan's Journal...1767, pp. 33-36; Dft. Ex. A-317.
118. Beatty, Journal, pp. 43, 52,63; Dft. Ex. A-139.

119. Thwaites, ed., Early Western Travels, vol. 1, p. 161; Dft. Ex.
A-148. O'Callaghan, Documents, vol. 7, pp. 854, 864; Dft. Ex. A-112.
Papers of Sir William Johnson, vol. 5, p. 336; Dft. Ex. A-174.

Johnson visited Detroit in 1761 he ceased referring to the Lake Indians as "dependents" of the Six Nations Iroquois.[120] The same was not true as regards the Indians of the Ohio Valley, the Delawares, Shawnees, Caughnawaga Mohawks, Mohicans and Mingoes, whom Johnson continued to regard as "dependents" of the Iroquois, to be dealt with chiefly through the latter.[121] Other New York officials, among them the administrator-scholar Cadwallader Colden (1688-1776) who from 1720 to 1775 was actively concerned with New York Indian affairs,[122] questioned this policy of Johnson's. In June, 1765 Colden wrote to Johnson as follows:

> I have often thought that the Six Nations assumed too much to themselves in directing affairs with all the other Nations & that some method ought to be taken to check their ambition of having the lead everywhere. By what I have heard (the Senecas at least) had a principal part in the late general revolt [uprising of Pontiac]. They must at all times have a great influence on all the nations to the westward who pass thro' their Country to treat with you. Now that all our apprehensions of the French are removed, our Principles of negotiating with the Indians are quite changed. As the Six Nations are the most ambitious and the most Politic & have long practice in all the artifices of negociation between the English & French may it not be dangerous & impolitic to suffer them to take the lead in all public affairs. To avoid this may it not be proper for you to Treat with the distant Western Indians separately once in two years at Detroit to incourage their ambition of Independency on the Six Nations, &

197

---

120. See, for example, O'Callaghan, ed., Documents, vol. 7, pp. 572-581; Dft. Ex. A-112.

121. See, for example, Papers of Sir William Johnson, vol. 12, pp. 476, 937; Dft. Ex. A-149; Papers of Sir William Johnson, vol. 8, pp. 639-640; Dft. Ex. A-208.

122. Dictionary of American Biography, vol. 4, pp. 286-287; Dft. Ex. A-204.

by all means to prevent 'for the future such
an union among all the Indian Nations as
lately happened. For the same purposes may
it not be proper for you sometimes to meet
the Shawanese & Delawares & the nations in
that neighborhood at Fort Pitt. You are the
best judge how proper such measures may be.[123]

Despite Colden's tactful suggestions, however, Johnson never returned to

Detroit or visited Fort Pitt.

During the summer of 1766 the Mohawks of New York sent four belts

to the Huron Nation, "declaring their Desire of a strict alliance with

that nation."[124] A year later, according to Sir William Johnson, several

Mohawks had "through disgust retired to the Hurons, on account of the

Tricks & practices [of the New Yorkers] concerning Lands."[125] Where these

emigrant Mohawks settled is not stated. However, Johnson does remark

that former British Fort Sandusky, in northwestern Area 53, which had been

sacked in 1763 had not, by 1767, been re-established, since it was "not a

place of much consequence of Trade..."[126]

198

123. Collections of the New-York Historical Society, vol. 10, pp.
19-20; Dft. Ex. A-205.
        In 1940 William N. Fenton, then of the staff of the Bureau of
American Ethnology, commented on Johnson's policy as follows: "We need
not devaluate the striking power of Iroquois war parties or the range of
their raids.... However, the distribution of Iroquois villages during the
[18th century] does not show that they effectively controlled the enormous
territory that they claimed to have subjugated. Rather, Iroquois delusions
of empire were converted to Britain's advantage by Sir William Johnson, who
largely controlled the destiny of the Six Nations from the Mohawk River..."
(Smithsonian Miscellaneous Collections, vol. 100, pp. 239-240; Dft. Ex.
A-206).

124. Papers of Sir William Johnson, vol. 12, p. 122; Dft. Ex.
A-149.

125. O'Callaghan, ed., Documents, vol. 7, p. 966; Dft. Ex. A-112.

126. O'Callaghan, ed., Documents, vol. 7, p. 974; Dft. Ex. A-112.

138

At a large Indian Congress held at Fort Stanwix (present Rome, New York) in September and October, 1768, a boundary line was agreed to by the Six Nations, between the British and the New York-Ohio Valley-Great Lakes Indians. The line began at tne junction of Canada and Wood creeks, east of Lake Oneida in central New York, and ran from thence south almost to the present New York-Pennsylvania state line, thence westward along various rivers to Kittaning on the lower Allegheny River, thence to the Ohio River at Pittsburgh, and from thence down the Ohio to the mouth of the Tennessee River. All lands west and north of this "Fort Stanwix boundary line" were to be closed to White settlement, and were to be Indian lands. All lands lying east and south of the line that previously had not been purchased from the Indians were at this time ceded to the British Crown, except lands in Pennsylvania.[127] One representative from each of the Six Nations signed the Fort Stanwix agreement of 1768; no other Indians signed it[128] or received benefits from it. Present Royce Areas 53 and 54 lay west and north of the line, well within the Indian lands.

199

---

127. O'Callaghan, ed., Documents, vol. 8, pp. 135-137; Dft. Ex. A-151.
   The lands in Pennsylvania south of the boundary line, being within the grant to William Penn, could not be purchased from the Indians by the Crown, and were ceded to Pennsylvania by the Six Nations in a separate deed executed on November 5, 1768 (Deed, Six Nations to Thomas and Richard Penn; Dft. Ex. A-52).

128. O'Callaghan, ed., Documents, vol. 8, p. 137; Dft. Ex. A-151.
   Ratification by the Crown of the cession made at Fort Stanwix in 1768 was announced to the Indians by Johnson on July 21, 1770, at a Congress held at German Flatts, New York (O'Callaghan, ed., Documents, vol. 8, pp. 136-137; Dft. Ex. A-151).

A year after the Fort Stanwix Congress George Croghan, in a letter
of December 22, 1769 to Sir William Johnson, noted certain westward movements of native population, out of Pennsylvania and into the Ohio Valley.
According to Croghan, a "Party of the Ohio Senicas, Shawanese & Delwares"
had gone to Detroit in the fall of 1769, and had had

> a private Council in the Huron Village
> [near Detroit] with the Hurons, Chepawas,
> Ottawas, & Putiwatimies, in which Council
> they complain'd to these Nations, saying
> the English had made a large purchase of
> Lands from the Six Nations and that the
> Six Nations had Shamefully taken all the
> Money and Goods to themselves and not Shared
> any part thereof with them[129] tho the most
> part of the Country which was Sold was their
> Hunting Ground down the Ohio...

By this sale, the Ohio Senecas, Delawares and Shawnees stated in their
council with the Detroit Indians,

> a great Number of their people which have
> lived on the West & East Branches of
> Susquahannah [River] have been so encroached
> upon by New [English] Settlements that they
> have no Hunting Grounds left...

The Ohio Senecas, Shawnees and Delawares therefore

> requested of the Hurons to give their people
> some Lands near Quiyahaga [Cuyahoga] to
> Plant and Hunt [130]...

and promised that they (the Ohio Senecas, Delawares and Shawnees) "would
go and remove" their people from the Susquehanna River. This request
"the Hurons Granted" and gave the Ohio Senecas, Delawares and Shawnees

200

---

129. This refers, of course, to the Fort Stanwix treaty of 1768.

130. Ms. mutilated.

at the council "a large Belt [130] Wampum...."[131]

A westward removal of Indians from the Susquehanna actually took place in the early winter of 1769. In his letter of December 22, 1769 Croghan states that Alexander McKee, commissary at Fort Pitt, while on a visit to Fort Augusta and Wyoming,[132] had encountered the Indians who had come from the Ohio to take "all the Shawanese and Delawares" from the branches of Susquehanna, and that the Ohio Indians had told McKee

> thier Bussiness and he [McKee] saw above Fifty
> Families [of the Susquehanna Indians] set off
> with [the Ohio Indians] and the rest is to go
> early in the Spring [of 1770].[133]

No further details as to where the "Fifty Families" settled after removing from the Susquehanna are known to us. However, in 1770 the Delaware chief Netawatwees, at New Comer's Town, invited David Zeisberger, senior Moravian Missionary, to remove a group of Delaware, Munsee and Mahican Indian. converts, then living on the Susquehanna River and on Beaver Creek in western Pennsylvania, and settle on the Tuscarawas River. In a letter of November 2, 1771 Zeisberger remarks that his Christian Indian flock could go either to the Tuscarawas or

201

---

131. Papers of Sir William Johnson, vol. 7, p. 316; Dft. Ex. A-151. This is the second time the Hurons granted permission to other Indians to settle on or near the Cuyahoga River. In ca. 1757 they had agreed that Netawatwees, the Delaware chief, might establish his town there.

132. Fort Augusta was at the junction of the East and West branches of the Susquehanna River, at present Sunbury, Northumberland County, Pennsylvania. The region known as "Wyoming" was approximately 50 miles northeast of Fort Augusta, and was a district of which Wilkes-Barre, Luzerne County, Pennsylvania is now the center.

133. Papers of Sir William Johnson, vol. 7, p. 316; Dft. Ex. A-151.

could go a little nearer, to Cayahago, which
is near the Delamattenoos [Wyandots], the place
which was formerly assigned to us...

Around this same time another Moravian missionary, John Heckewelder, notes

that Netawatwees repeated his invitation a second time

in a more pressing manner, in which the Wyandots
(whom the Delawares call their uncles,) joined,
assuring the Christian Indians that they would
give them sufficient land, and never sell the
ground under their feet to the white people, as
the Six Nations had done to them [at the Fort
Stanwix treaty].134

Likewise, in a third message of January, 1772 Netawatwees informed the

Moravians that

the land of the Delawares is here on the
Muschingum River, from the mouth of the river
up to Cayahaga [Cuyahoga]...This stretch of
land has been given to us by the Delamattenoos
[Wyandots] and belongs to us.135

202

Later, in August, 1772 Isaac Glikhican, a Moravian Delaware convert who

had formerly been a Delaware councillor, defined the tract the Wyandots

had given the Delawares more explicitly, as consisting of

the land between Beaver creek, the Cajahaga
[Cuyahoga] river, Lake Erie, the Sandusky river,
thence to the headwaters of the Hockhocking
[Hocking] river, and then up the Ohio [River]
to Shingas Town.136

---

134. Zeisberger, Letter No. X, November 2, 1771, pp. ∧ . Dft.
a-4;
Ex. A-178. Heckewelder, Narrative, pp. 112-113, 114-115; Dft. Ex. A-53.

135. Zeisberger, Diary of the Indian Congregation, January, 1772,
pp. 207-208; Dft. Ex. A-36.

136. Heckewelder, Narrative,. p. 112; Dft. Ex. A-53. Transactions
of the Moravian Historical Society, vol. 12, pp. 345, 349-350; Dft. Ex.
A-35. Zeisberger, Letter No. 9, March 3, 1771, p. 2; Dft. Ex. A-179.
Shingas Town was at the mouth of Big Beaver Creek, which enters the Ohio
River in extreme western Pennsylvania (Hodge, ed., Handbook, pt. 2, p.
481; Dft. Ex. A-2).

This large tract included all of Royce Areas 53 and 54, as well
as lands to the east, south and west of the two Areas. Within this
tract the Moravian missionaries Zeisberger and Heckewelder obtained in
1772 from Netawatwees at Newcomer's Town a grant of land on which to
settle their Indian converts. The lands granted by the Delawares to
the Moravians were immediately south of Area 54, extending from Beaver's
former town at Tuscarawas to a point four miles above present Newcomerstown on Tuscarawas River. As soon as the Moravians and their converts
moved to this tract they sent a message to the Wyandots informing them
of their arrival, in recognition that it was from the Wyandots "that
the Delawares held what title they had to this land."[137]

Two years later, in 1774, the Delawares, seeing that the Moravian
Indian converts

> pursued agriculture, and kept much cattle,...
> enlarged the tract of land first set apart for
> them, by moving their [own] people off to a
> greater distance. And consulting their uncles,
> the Wyandots, on the subject (they being the
> nation from whom the Delawares had originally
> received the land,) these set apart, granted and
> confirmed, all that country lying between Tus-
> corawas, (old town,) and the great bend below
> Newcomerstown, a distance of upwards of thirty
> miles on the river, and including the same to the
> Christian Indians. Two large belts of wampum were
> on this occasion delivered by the Wyandots, and
> the chiefs of the Delaware nation, to the Christian
> Indians, who, in return thanked them for the gift,

203

137. Transactions of the Moravian Historical Society, vol. 12,
pp. 345-350, 359-360; Dft. Ex. A-35. Paul A. W. Wallace, Thirty
Thousand Miles, p. 98; Dft. Ex. A-167. Of the two towns the Moravians
built in 1772 on the Tuscarawas River, Thuppehunk or Schönbrunn was the
nearest to Area 54. It was 16 river miles south of the southeastern tip
of Area 54, near present New Philadelphia, Tuscarawas County. The
second town, Gnadenhutten, was some 28 miles south of Area 54, at present
Gnadenhutten, Tuscarawas County (Transactions of the Moravian Historical
Society, vol. 12, p. 350; Dft. Ex. A-35).

both verbally, and by belts and strings of wampum.[138]

This transaction between the non-Christian or "pagan" Delawares of the Tuscarawas River region, the Moravian missionaries and their Delaware and Munsee converts, and the Wyandots of Detroit in 1774 is doubtless the one referred to by John Ettwein, bishop of the Moravian Church at Bethlehem, who wrote in 1798:

> Our Society or Missionaries never made Presents to the Indian Chiefs, to gain their favour and protection! I know but one Instance, where the Indian Brethren on Muskingum collected a number of Wampums and sent them by a Solemn Message as a Present to the Wiondot or Delamatinos chiefs, (the acknowledged owners of Muskingum River) to get from them, a Confirmation of the Grant of Land, which the Delaware Chiefs had given them on Muskingum.[139]

As already noted, the tract first set apart for the Christian Indians, and the enlarged tract given them two years later, was beyond the boundaries of eastern Area 54. Of interest, however, is the fact that in the transactions between the Delawares and the Moravians, the Wyandots were consistently regarded as being the "acknowledged owners" of the lands in present northern Ohio, including Areas 53 and 54. There had not been, however, a single Wyandot settlement within either Area 53 or Area 54 after 1763, the year that Junundat, in extreme western Area 53, was destroyed.

In the meantime, Sir William Johnson continued to regard the Ohio Valley Indians as "dependents" of the Six Nations Iroquois, and the Ohio

204

---

138. Heckewelder, Narrative, p. 135; Dft. Ex. A-53.

139. Transactions of the Moravian Historical Society, vol. 21, p. 374; Dft. Ex. A-35. Ettwein uses the old name, "Muskingum," for the present Tuscarawas River throughout this passage.

Valley lands as "belonging" to the Six Nations, who were "subjects" of England. Gen. Thomas Gage, commander-in-chief of British forces in America, did not hesitate to criticise such a policy. In a letter to Johnson of October 7, 1772, Gage expressed his scepticism of the subterfuge the English were relying upon, in respect to which tribes had valid claims to the Ohio Valley lands. "It is asserted as a general Principle," Gage wrote,

> that the Six Nations having conquered such and
> such Nations their Territorys belong to them, and
> the Six Nations being the Kings Subjects which by
> treaty they have acknowledged themselves to be,
> those Lands belong to the King. I believe it is
> [was] for our Interest to lay down such principles
> especially when we were squabbling with the French
> about Territory, and they played us of [off] in
> the same stile of their Indian Subjects, and the
> right of those Indians. I never heard that Indians
> made War for the sake of Territory like Europeans,
> but that Revenge, and an eager pursuit of Martial
> reputation was the Motives which prompted one
> Nation to make War upon another. If we are to
> search for truth and examine her to the Bottom,
> I dont imagine we shall find that any conquered
> Nation ever formaly ceded their Country to their
> Conquerors, or that the latter ever required it, I
> never could learn more, than that Nations have
> yielded, and acknowledged themselves subjected to
> others, and some even have wore Badges of Subjection.
> As for the Six Nations having acknowledged them-
> selves Subjects of the English, that I conclude must
> be a very gross Mistake and am well satisfied were
> they told so, they would not be well pleased. I
> know I would not venture to treat them as Subjects,
> unless there was a Resolution to make War upon
> them, which is not very likely to happen, but I
> believe they would on such an attempt, very soon
> resolve to cut our Throats.[140]

205

140. Papers of Sir William Johnson, vol. 12, pp. 994-995; Dft. x. A-149.

Johnson's reply to Gage's letter is enlightening. He admits that

> The Truth is the 6 Nations never acknowledged
> themselves our Subjects according to the natural
> Sense of the Word; the Treatys often [quoted] on
> these occasions according to the intentions of
> the Indians [only] put themselves & Certain parts
> of their possessions under our protection, to
> prevent our people from settling thereon without
> [their] consent; so that however the contrary
> has appeared [in] Manifesto's our Right depends
> on purchase, The Question then is, whether they
> have a right to Sell those Lands, on which you
> have expressed yᵉ General Ideas of the Indians
> very Justly,...

But Johnson refused to consider any other Indians than the Six Nations
as having valid claims to the Ohio Valley lands, if for no other reason
than as a matter of expediency for the English. His letter continues:

> however with regard to the lands on Ohio, this
> much must be said that long before any public
> declaration of our Claims of Territory from
> Their Subjection, these Lands were considered
> as the property of the Six Nations, who had con-
> quered all, and actually extirpated Several of
> the Tribes there, placing the Shawanese Delawares
> &ca. on bare Toleration in their Stead, as sort
> of Frontier Dependants, [the worst] circumstance
> is that their People have [of late become more]
> powerfull by alliances & the 6 Nations less, so
> that their [Authority begins to be] disputed at
> a distance, however it may be Expedient [rather
> to] Support their Authority than encourage the
> Title of [People, who] of late form such danger-
> ous Alliances...¹⁴¹

206

---

141. Papers of Sir William Johnson, vol. 8, pp. 639-640; Dft. Ex.
A-208. All bracketed inserts in the excerpts of Johnson's reply to
Gage, quoted above, are by the editor. Johnson's copy of his letter
is badly burned; the bracketed inserts are from the letter Johnson
sent to Gage (ibid., p. 641, fn. 1; Dft. Ex. A-208).
   The "dangerous Alliances" referred to at the end of Johnson's
letter included, among others, Pontiac's quasi-successful uprising in
1763.

Johnson had been for many years an able Indian administrator. But his unwillingness near the end of his lifetime[142] to deal realistically with a situation that he himself recognized existed detracts from his stature. It is small wonder that at the outbreak of the American Revolution many of the Ohio Valley Indians were not in favor of actively supporting the British.

In the early 1770's Tuscarawas, where Delawares had lived as late as 1766, was unoccupied. In March, 1771 it was reported "uninhabited," as it also was in March, 1772, although Zeisberger notes that by then it had "been assigned [by the Delawares?] for settlement to other Indians."[143] Whether Tuscarawas was re-settled during the years 1772-1775 is, however, dubious; in 1774 Heckewelder refers to it as an "old town" and in August, 1775, when Col. Richard Butler, American Indian agent, camped overnight at Tuscarawas he met no Indians there.[144] Butler was on a tour at the time to invite all the Ohio Valley Indians to an important American peace treaty at Fort Pitt.[145] Another American messenger, Capt. James Wood, a commissioner for the proposed treaty/who in July and August,

207

---

142. Johnson died on July 11, 1774 (Papers of Sir William Johnson, vol. 12, p. 1121; Dft. Ex. A-149).

143. Zeisberger, Diary of the Indian Congregation...March, 1772, p. 218; Dft. Ex. A-159. Zeisberger, Diary of the Indian Congregation... March, 1771, p. 3; Dft. Ex. A-163.

144. Butler, Journal, August-September 1755, pp. 1-2; Dft. Ex. A-160. Papers of Sir William Johnson, vol. 12, p. 1046; Dft. Ex. A-149.

145. Loskiel, History of the Mission, pp. 109-110; Dft. Ex. A-176. Heckewelder, Narrative, p. 136; Dft. Ex. A-53. Thwaites and Kellogg, Revolution on the Upper Ohio, pp. 25-26; Dft. Ex. A-177.
     The Americans hoped to keep the Ohio Valley Indians neutral in the struggle, already begun, between the Colonies and England. The British had made even earlier attempts to secure the allegiance of these

1775 went on a mission to the Ohio Valley Indians similar to Butler's, did not treat with any Indians at Tuscarawas. Also, even more significant is the fact that neither Butler nor Wood visited any Indian towns within present Area 54.[146] Both Wood and Butler skirted the southern and western boundaries of the Area, stopping at several towns that lay between six and twenty-six miles south or west of Area 54.

Among the Delaware Indians who attended the Pittsburgh treaty in the fall of 1775 was Captain White Eyes, a prominent member of the Turtle division of the Delawares.[147] At the treaty White Eyes acquainted the Americans and the Seneca delegates present with the fact that the Wyandots, the "Uncles"[148] of the Delawares, had

---

(fn. 145 cont'd) same Indians. According to a missionary, David McClure, who visited Newcomer's Town near the Forks of Muskingum in 1772, George Croghan had at that date attempted to secure the support of the Ohio Valley Indians for the English in case a war developed (McClure, Diary, pp. 84-85; Dft. Ex. A-202).

146. Butler, Journal, August-September, 1775, pp. 1-30; Dft. Ex. A-160. Thwaites and Kellogg, eds., Revolution on the Upper Ohio, pp. 43-65; Dft. Ex. A-177. Butler had as companion on his trip a knowledgeable Seneca Indian, Kiasutha (Butler, Journal, August-September, 1775, pp. 3, 6, 10, 11; Dft. Ex. A-160. Hodge, ed., Handbook, pt. 1, p. 682; Dft. Ex. A-1). Wood was accompanied by the equally knowledgeable Simon Girty, then interpreter at Fort Pitt (Thwaites and Kellogg, eds., Revolution on the Upper Ohio, p. 43; Dft. Ex. A-177. Butterfield, History of the Girtys, pp. 35-36; Dft. Ex. A-203).

147. Heckewelder, Names, pp. 391-392; Dft. Ex. A-161. This was the division of which Netawatwees was chief. After the latter's death in 1776 White Eyes became temporary chief of the Turtle division (Heckewelder, Names, p. 391; Dft. Ex. A-161).

148. Terms of relationship are applied to tribes, as well as to individuals, by the Eastern Woodlands Indians.

> bound themselves the Shawanese Tawaas [Ottawas]
> and Delawares together and have made us as one
> People and have also given me that Tract of
> Country Beginning at the Mouth of Big Beaver
> Creek and running up the same to where it inter-
> locks with the Branches of Guyahoga [Cuyahoga]
> Creek and down the said Creek to the Mouth
> thereof where it empties into the Lake [Erie]
> along the Side of the Lake to the Mouth of San-
> duskey Creek and up the same to the head untill
> it interlocks with Muskingum down the same to
> the Mouth where it Empties into the Ohio and up
> the said River to the Place of Beginning...we
> have now Acquainted you what Lands belongs to
> us I desire you will not Permit any of your
> foolish People to set down upon it that I cannot
> suffer it least other Nations shou'd be Uneasy.[149]

Except for mention of the western branches of the Muskingum River,
rather than the Hocking River, as the southwestern boundary of the tract
granted to the Delawares, the boundaries recited by White Eyes are
essentially the same as those that were outlined by Isaac Glikhican to
the Moravian missionaries in 1772. Areas 53 and 54 lay within these
boundaries.

While White Eyes was at Pittsburgh he also took occasion to disabuse
the Seneca delegates there as to any "dependency" of the Delawares on
the Six Nations Iroquois. According to reports by the Delaware chiefs
to the Moravian missionaries after the chiefs returned home, the Seneca
delegates were chagrined that White Eyes, at the 1775 treaty, had openly
declared friendship for the Americans. Therefore the Senecas, Heckewelder states,

---

149. Thwaites and Kellogg, eds., Revolution on the Upper Ohio,
pp. 86-87; Dft. Ex. A-177. The reference to "your foolish People" is
an admonition to the Americans to respect the Indian-White boundary
line established at Fort Stanwix in 1768.

thought proper to offer a check to his [White
Eyes'] proceedings, by giving him, in a haughty
tone, a hint, intended to remind him what the
Delaware nation was in the eyes of the Six Nations,
(meaning that it had no will of its own, but was
subordinate to the Six Nations); when captain
White Eyes, long since tired of this language,
with his usual spirit, and an air of disdain, rose
and replied; that 'he well knew that the Six Nations
considered his [Delaware] nation as a conquered
people--and their inferiors.' 'You say (said he)
that you had conquered me that you had cut off my
legs--had put a petticoat on me, giving me a hoe
and cornpounder in my hands, saying; 'now woman!
your business henceforward shall be, to plant and
hoe corn, and pound the same for bread, for us
men and warriors!'--Look (continued White Eyes,)
at my legs! if, as you say, you had cut cut
[sic] them off, they have grown again to their
proper size!--the petticoat I have thrown away,
and have put on my proper dress!--the corn hoe
and pounder I have exchanged for these fire arms,
and declare that I am a man!'--Then waving his
hand in the direction of the Alleghany river, he
exclaimed, 'and all the country on the other side
of that river is <u>mine</u>.'[150]

210   However friendly White Eyes was to the Americans, some of the Dela-

wares and other Ohio Valley Indians were less so,[151] and around 1775 the

Cuyahoga River region began to be a center for British traders. In the

fall of 1774, during Lord Dunmore's War, some anti-American Mingos from

two towns west of Area 54 were prepared to flee to Cuyahoga, but were

prevented from doing so by a detachment of Virginia troops. And in 1775,

according to Heckewelder, some pro-British Munsees actually moved north-

---

150. Heckewelder, Narrative, pp. 140-141; Dft. Ex. A-53. Thwaites
is of the opinion that this speech was delivered by White Eyes at the
1775 Treaty, and was the one in which White Eyes defined the extent of
the Delawares' lands (Thwaites and Kellogg, eds., Revolution on the Upper
Ohio, p. 87, fn. 10; Dft. Ex. A-177). Heckewelder, however, definitely
implies that White Eyes' defiant address to the Senecas was not delivered
at the treaty proceedings proper (Heckewelder, Narrative, p. 140; Dft.
Ex. A-53).

151. Heckewelder, Narrative, pp. 142-143; Dft. Ex. A-53.

ward from the Muskingum River region, to a location "nearer Lake Erie."[152]
By September, 1775 one James Howell from New Jersey, who "appear'd inimi-
cal to the American Interests," was trading at Cuyahoga.[153] In August,
1776 Col. George Morgan, then serving at Pittsburgh as Indian agent
for the United States in the Middle Department.[154]

> receiv'd Intelligence that one William Forsyth
> arriv'd at Cyohogo on the 4th [of August, 1776]
> with an intention...to buy up what Cattle he can
> in order to supply our Enemies.

Morgan issued orders designed, to put an immediate stop to any such transactions.[155]

Meanwhile, at a Shawnee town west of Area 54 Matthew Elliott, a
trader,[156] was told in August, 1776 that "the Ottawas & Chippawas were
to make an attack on Pittsburg,"[157] and early in September, 1776 American
authorities at Pittsburgh were informed.

---

152. Butterfield, ed., Washington-Crawford Letters, pp. 55-56;
Dft. Ex. A-180. Heckewelder, Narrative, pp. 142-143; Dft. Ex. A-53.

153. Information from John Hamilton & John Bradley, September
13, 1776; Dft. Ex. A-181.

154. Heckewelder, Narrative, p. 150; Dft. Ex. A-53.

155. A Letter to William Wilson at Coshocton, August 11, 1776;
Dft. Ex. A-182. Letter to John Anderson, September 5, 1776; Dft. Ex.
A-184.

156. Heckewelder, Narrative, pp. 147-148; Dft. Ex. A-53.

157. Information from Matthew Elliott, August 31, 1776; p.
2; Dft. Ex. A-183.

that a great number of Ottawa, Chippewa, Delaware
& Mingoe Indians were assembled at Guyahaga with
hostile intentions

toward the Americans. Two spies, John Hamilton and John Bradley, were

therefore sent to Cuyahoga, with messages to the "Ottawas, & the Nations

Inhabiting Guyahoga."[158] Hamilton and Bradley arrived at Cuyahoga on

September 10, 1776, and the next day

assembled two Delaware [war] Chiefs, the one named
Sam Compass & the other Thomas Hickman, & two
other Indians, to hear what we had to say to
them on behalf of the United States. Hickman
appeared averse to hearing the Commissioners
Speech, but Compass was ready enough to listen
to us...

The Delawares at Cuyahoga would not, however, accept the Commissioners'

invitation to a peace treaty to be held at Fort Pitt later in the fall

of 1776 "until they heard from Capt. White Eyes, their Chief." The

212   Indians at Cuyahoga, so Hamilton and Bradley reported to Morgan,

did not appear desirous of giving us any information or cummunicating any intelligence of what
was passing among them, we are of opinion that
the Indians at Guyahoga are in the interests of
the King of England & we found this opinion on
what we have seen among them. Hickman & Compass
both told us there would be but little of a Treaty
at Pittsburgh.[159]

---

158. Speech prepared by the Commissioners, September 5, 1776; Dft.
Ex. A-185.

159. Information from John Hamilton & John Bradley, September 13,
1776; Dft. Ex. A-181. Samuel Compass is mentioned as a Delaware warrior
who was at a council at Pittsburgh in 1772 ([Rupp], Early History,
Appendix No. XX, p. 204; Dft. Ex. A-197). A Thomas Hickman, Delaware war
captain, appears on a list of Delawares present at a council at Fort
Pitt on May 9, 1765 ([Rupp], Early History, Appendix No. XVII, p. 173;
Dft. Ex. A-199).

Also, in September, 1776 news was received at Pittsburgh that "a body of Chippawas and Ottawas 1500 in number intended to rendezvous shortly at Tuscarowas." This seems to have been a false alarm, however, for during the same month several Chippewas arrived at Pittsburgh and proved to be friendly.[160] In October, 1776 the head warrior of the Wyandots of Sandusky told a Seneca chief that "The Chippawas now at Pittsburgh a e not Chiefs;--they live below [downstream from?] Guyahoga."[161]

No British forts were in existence on the south side of Lake Erie near the end of 1776, either at Sandusky or Cuyahoga, since "the Wiandots would not allow [such] but only a few traders to be there."[162] The traders at Cuyahoga in the early winter of 1776/1777 were "a Mr Graverod & a Mr Fisher late of Albany [who] were trading at Cuyahoga from Detroit." Morgan, who was anxious to prevent Cuyahoga becoming an outpost of Detroit, and a threat to Pittsburgh, invited the two traders to Pittsburgh and purchased all their goods, which were to be deposited in Fort Pitt.[163]

213

---

160. Letter from the Commissioners of Indian Affairs, September 25, 1776, pp. 1♠3; Dft. Ex. A-186. Speech Delivered by the Commissioners to the Chippewas, September 25, 1776, Dft. Ex. A-187.

161. Information from the White Mingo, October 18, 1776, p. 1; Dft. Ex. A-188.

162. Zeisberger, Letter to George Morgan, November 21, 1776, p. 3; Dft. Ex. A-189. Pennsylvania Archives, 1st ser., vol. 5, p. 287; Dft. Ex. A-236.

163. [Morgan] Letter to John Hancock, January 4, 1777, p. 1; Dft. Ex. A-190.

Two small "Mingo" or "Senneca" towns, known to traders as "Darby's
Town" and "Hell Town," both in Area 54, are noted by Heckewelder as
having been in existence "between the years 1770 and 1780."[164] Darby's
Town (referred to in another source as "Drs Town") was on the upper
Sandusky River near present Leesville, Crawford County, in extreme
western Area 54.[165] Hell Town was in southwestern Area 54, on the Clear
Fork of the Mohican River near the former village of Newville and halfway between present Perrysville, Ashland County, and present Butler,
Richland County.[166] It is probable that the Mingos living at Hell Town
in 1770 removed from this town some five years later, since in 1776 a
"new Hell Town" is reliably pinpointed as being on Sandusky River,
25 miles up that river from the Wyandot town of "Sandusky" (present

164. Ethnohistory, vol. 7, p. 72; Dft. Ex. A-153.

165. Pennsylvania Magazine of History and Biography, vol. 18,
pp. 146-147, 320; Dft. Ex. A-154. Butterfield, Historical Account,
pp. 142-144, 147-149; Dft. Ex. A-155.

166. Magazine of History, no. 10, pp. 41-42; Dft. Ex. A-156.
Pennsylvania Magazine of History and Biography, vol. 18, p. 145; Dft.
Ex. A-154. Baughman, History of Richland County, pp. 28, 425-426; Dft.
Ex. A-157. Howe, Historical Collections, vol. 1, pp. 255-256; Dft. Ex.
A-191. Paul A. W. Wallace, Thirty Thousand Miles, p. 247; Dft. Ex. A-167.
Draper Mss. 16S 289, 291; Dft. Ex. A-268.
In the Draper reference cited above Draper's informant erroneously
locates "Old Town-or Hell Town on the Black Fork of the Mohican, 10
miles due north of Mansfield, Ohio." This was the location of another
town, Snip's Town (see Collections of the State Historical Society of
Wisconsin, vol. 24, p. 152; Dft. Ex. A-226) which will be discussed in
the next Chapter of this Report.

154

Upper Sandusky, Seneca County).[167] The new Hell Town was several miles
(6-10?) west of Area 54. No Indians, apparently, were living at old
Hell Town, within Area 54, in 1776, but the Wyandots were, apparently,
negotiating at this time to have some Delawares and/or Munsees move
from Coshocton to old Hell Town.[168]

Two councils. one British and the other American, were held at
Niagara and Pittsburgh, respectively, in 1776. Kiasutha, an Allegheny
Seneca who during the previous year had accompanied the American agent
Richard Butler on his tour to the Ohio Indian towns, went to the
British council at Niagara,[169] and when he returned to Pittsburgh early
in July, 1776, informed Butler that he had been

---

167. Thwaites and Kellogg, Revolution on the Upper Ohio, pp. 48-
49 and fn. 77; Dft. Ex. A-177. Wilson, Letter to the Commissioners,
Coshocton, Aug. 13, 1776, p. 1; Dft. Ex. A-258. Wilson, Letter to the
Commissioners, Coshocton, Aug. 17, 1776, p. 2; Dft. Ex. A-259. The
Commissioners to the Committee of Congress, Aug. 18, 1776, p. 1; Dft.
Ex. A-260. Anderson, Letter to the Commissioners, Coshocton, Sept. 5,
1776, pp. 1-2; Dft. Ex. A-261. Anderson, Letter to the Commissioners,
Coshocton, Sept. 6, 1776; Dft. Ex. A-262.

168. In August, 1776 the Wyandots of Sandusky (present Upper
Sandusky) sent a message to the Delawares and Munsees in the Coshocton
region saying that they (the Wyandots) had "prepared a Bed" for the
Delawares "above Coocoosing [present Kokosing River] where we desire
you'll bring your Women & Children..." (Information from Matthew
Elliott, Aug. 31, 1776, p. 2; Dft. Ex. A-183. Speech from the Delawares, Aug. 30, 1776, p. 2; Dft. Ex. A-257). Old Hell Town was between
20 and 30 miles "above" (north) of Kokosing River. The site of the town
was notably attractive (see Pennsylvania Magazine of History and Biography, vol. 18, p. 145; Dft. Ex. A-154), and was probably the location
the Wyandots had in mind.

169. Olden Time, vol. 2, pp. 112-114; Dft. Ex. A-194. Council
at Pittsburgh...1776, pp. 33-34; Dft. Ex. A-193. See also fn. 153, this
Chapter.

215

> appointed by the Six Nations Iroquois to take
> care of this country; that is, to take care of
> the Indians on the west side of the river Ohio;
> and I desire you [Americans] will not think of
> an expedition against Detroit, for I repeat to
> you again, we will not suffer an army to march
> through our country.[170]

The second council, held by the Americans at Pittsburgh, October 15-November 6, 1776, was called to acquaint the Indians about the Revolutionary War, and to persuade them to remain neutral.[171] Six hundred and forty-four Indians came to Pittsburgh; delegates at the council included three chiefs and several warriors of the Allegheny Senecas, including Kiasutha; five Delaware chiefs and warriors from the Muskingum region; two Munsee chiefs: five Shawnee chiefs and several warriors; two Mahican messengers from the Stockbridge (Mahican) Indians of Massachusetts;[172] and one Mohawk chief.[173]

216

At this council Kiasutha, mindful of the charge given him at Niagara to "take care of the Indians on the west side of the river Ohio," proceeded to live up to his role.[174] The "authority" of the Six Nations

---

170. Olden Time, vol. 2, p. 113; Dft. Ex. A-194.

171. Council at Pittsburgh...1776, pp. 18-21; Dft. Ex. A-193.

172. See Hodge, ed., Handbook, pt. 2, pp. 637-638; Dft. Ex. A-2.

173. Council at Pittsburgh...1776, pp. 1, 3, 6, 12, 14, 27, 28, 30, 32; Dft. Ex, A-193. [Morgan] Letter to John Hancock, November 8, 1776, p. 1; Dft. Ex. A-195.

174. American Archives, 5th ser., vol. 1, p. 36; Dft. Ex. A-243. Council at Pittsburgh...1776, p. 15; Dft. Ex. A-193.

over the Delawares and over the lands west of the Ohio River was, however, again challenged at the Pittsburgh council of 1776 by the Delaware leader of the Turtle division, Captain White Eyes,[175] who at one
point called the Six Nations "Liars."[176] As further demostration of
the independence of the Delawares, White Eyes invited the Stockbridge
Mahicans, through the two Mahican messengers present at the council, to
remove westward, telling the Mahicans that if they found themselves

> too much crowded [in New England] you might come to
> us: this Land over the River [Ohio] belongs to us,
> & as we are the same people it belongs to you: The
> Warriors & Chiefs now present invite you to come &
> live among them...[177]

Summary and Conclusions on Use and Occupancy of Areas 53 and 54,
1760-1776. The data presented in this chapter on occupancy and use of
Areas 53 and 54 during the period 1760-1776 can be summarized as follows.

175. Netawatwees, aged chief of the Turtle division, died during
the council, on October 31, 1776. Captain White Eyes succeeded him
(Council at Pittsburgh...1776, p. 27; Dft. Ex. A-193. Heckewelder,
Names, pp. 1-392; Dft. Ex. A-161).

176. Council at Pittsburgh...1776, pp. 45-46; Dft. Ex. A-193.
For an after-effect of this speech see Bliss, ed., Zeisberger's Diary,
vol. 1, p. 417; Dft. Ex. A-247.

177. Council at Pittsburgh...1776, pp. 46-47; Dft. Ex. A-193.
See also Zeisberger, Letter to George Morgan, November 21,
1776, p. 1; Dft. Ex. A-189, in which John Killbuck, a councillor for
the Turtle division of the Delawares, is quoted as referring to the
Wyandots' gift of Ohio Valley lands to the Delawares.

During the first five years of this period, from 1760 to 1764, a total of eight Indian towns, some of which were fairly populous, existed in or closely adjacent to Areas 53 and 54. By the end of 1764, however, due to Pontiac's uprising in 1763 and subsequent British expeditions into the Ohio-Great Lakes region, five of these eight Indian towns are definitely known either to have been destroyed, or to have been abandoned by their occupants. Two other of the eight towns were probably abandoned by the end of the year 1764. The eighth town had a shadowy existence, being referred to by name once only, on a 1764 map.

These eight towns were:

Conontia

(1) Sandusky (Sandoské, Sunyendeand, Ajenevindo,   ), some four miles west of the northwestern boundary of Area 53, near the mouth of Pickerel Creek, in Sandusky County, Ohio. A Wyandot town, continuously occupied from 1760 through 1763 or early 1764, but an "old Village" (abandoned town) by the fall of 1764. Population: no data

218

(2) Junundat (Cenundud, Chenundede, Chanondet, Anioton, Canuta), in northwestern Area 53, at present Castalia, Erie County, Ohio. A mixed Wyandot-Mohican town, continuously occupied from 1760 until July, 1763, when it was burnt by a British force. Population: "70-80 warriors [280-320 persons] of...Wyandot and Mohickan Tribes" (1764).

(3) Mohickon John's Town (Mohickon Village, Mohigon Cabbins, Wikenjohn's Town, Delaware Cabins), in central Area 54, two miles south of present Jeromeville, Ashland County, Ohio. A Mohican Indian town, continuously occupied from 1760 until it was abandoned in September, 1764. Population: no data; "consisted only of a few houses" (1764).

(4) Killbuck's Town, on Killbuck Creek in central Area 54, 10 miles south of present Wooster, Wayne County, Ohio. A Delaware town, referred to once only, in 1764. Population: no data.

(5) <u>Tuscarawas</u> (Beaver's Town at Tuscarawas) on the Tuscarawas River close to the southeastern tip of Area 54, near present Bolivar, Tuscarawas County, Ohio. Occupied continuously by Delawares of the Turkey division under "King Beaver" from 1760 until late 1763 or early 1764; abandoned by Beaver by May, 1764. <u>Population</u>: 180 warriors or 720 persons (1760); 80 warriors or 320 persons (1762); <u>ca</u>. 150 warriors or 600 persons (1763).

(6) "<u>Indian</u> [Delaware?] <u>town</u>," on Tuscarawas River, 9 1/2 miles north of (5), in extreme eastern Area 54. Existent in 1762; probably deserted at the same time (5) was, in late 1763 or early 1764. <u>Population</u>: no data.

(7) <u>Cayahoga Town</u> (Cajahaga, Gichaga), at the "Big Falls" of Cuyahoga River a mile or so east of Area 53 in Summit County, Ohio. A Delaware town under Netawa - twees, chief of the Turtle division; occupied continuously from 1760 until the fall of 1764 when Netawatwees abandoned it. <u>Population</u>: no data; probably a sizable town.

(8) <u>Ottawa town</u>, on the east bank of the Cuyahoga River close to the eastern boundary of Area 53, and north of (7). Probably occupied continuously by Ottawas from 1760 through 1763; possibly occupied in 1764 (?). <u>Population</u>: no data; "Great party" of Ottawas there in 1763.

The above list show Wyandot, and Wyandot-Mohican occupancy of two towns, one close to and the other in northwestern Area 53; Mohican and Delaware occupancy, respectively, of two towns in central Area 54; Delaware occupancy of two towns in or close to eastern Area 54; and Delaware and Ottawa occupancy, respectively, of two towns close to extreme eastern Area 53, during the years 1760-1764. This short but turbulent period ends, however. with few if any native villages in or close to Areas 53 and 54.

During the next five years, between 1765 and 1769, there were no
new towns which can be pinpointed at new sites within Areas 53 and 54,
nor was there any return of former occupants or movement of other Indians, with only one exception, to any of the 1760-1764 village sites in
or close to the two Areas. The exception is that Delawares of the
Wolf (?) division were, in 1766, living at Tuscarawas, in the extreme
southeastern tip of Area 54, where Beaver, of the Turkey division of the
Delawares, had formerly had his town. If Killbuck's Town of Delawares
in central Area 54 continued in existence after 1764, which is dubious,
it was only for a year or so.

To a limited extent the picture changes by 1770. Tuscarawas was
by then a deserted site, but between 1770 and 1775 two small "Mingo" or
"Seneca" towns, known as Darby's Town and Hell Town, existed in Area 54.
Darby's Town was near present Leesville, Crawford County, in extreme
western Area 54, and Hell Town was on the Clear Fork of the Mohican
River, between present Perrysville, Ashland County, and present Butler,
Richland County, in south-central Area 54. Hell Town was abandoned by
the Mingos in 1775. This left Darby's Town as the only town in Areas
53 and 54 in 1776, the location of which can be pinpointed. Although
by 1776 some Delawares, Ottawas, Chippewas and Mingos were visiting
Cuyahoga, where the British had a trading post in or near northeastern
Area 53, no Indian towns can actually be pinpointed in the Cuyahoga
region in 1776.

220

Information about the use of Areas 53 and 54 for hunting during
the first few years of the period 1760-1776 is sketchy at best, and
after the winter of 176$\overset{4}{4}$-176$\overset{5}{5}$ is practically nil. In eastern Area 53
the Cuyahoga River is noted as being used by Ottawas for hunting in
the fall of 1760, and again in 1763; the "Upper Nations" (Ottawas,
Potawatomis, Chippewas and Hurons of Detroit) are also said to have
used Cuyahoga River for hunting during the early 1760's. In November,
1760 Croghan met, at the mouth of Rocky River, seven miles west of
Cuyahoga River in Area 53, "a Wyandot Indian and his Family" from
Detroit, "going a hunting." In 1766 Delawares told the missionary
Charles Beatty that there was "good hunting" at Cuyahoga.

The southeastern corner of Area 54 was also evidently a good
hunting region. In January, 1761 Rogers met "a number of Wyandots and
Six Nations Indians hunting" there, and Croghan notes that in the
winter of 1764-1765 the Delawares of the Wolf division under the chief
Custaloga were hunting "near Tuscarawas." In 1761 Croghan passed "a
placed called the Sugar Cabbins" in eastern Area 54, but fails to
state what Indians used this locale for sugar-making.

"Indians" were found hunting in south-central Area 54 in January,
1761 by Rogers, and during the winter of 1763-1764 Delawares who had
lately moved from Mahoning in eastern Pennsylvania probably hunted in
this vicinity.

In western Area 53, "Indians" were hunting on the lower Huron
River in November, 1760; in December, 1760 Croghan also found a "Principal Mans hunting Cabbin" (identity again not specified) 16 miles

221

southeast of Junundat, in western Area 53. In January, 1761 Rogers met a "Family of Windots" hunting 6 1/2 miles southeast of Junundat. Some Cayugas, a Saponi Indian, and a Mohawk are mentioned by Sir William Johnson as "going a hunting to Sandusky" in October, 1761.

Our conclusions on occupancy and use of Areas 53 and 54 during the period 1760-1776 are as follows:

Occupancy of all the towns that existed in or near Areas 53 and 54 within the period 1760-1776 was for relatively short periods of time, only, within the total period. The majority of native towns existed during the first five years of the total period, between 1760 and 1764. When the Wyandot, Mohican, Delaware and Ottawa occupants of these towns abandoned them, they established new towns at new locations anywhere from 14 to 65 miles west or south of Areas 53 and 54. From 1770 onward to 1776 both Areas 53 and 54 were devoid of any known towns, except for two small Mingo villages in western Area 54. One of these Mingo towns, Hell Town, was abandoned in 1775; this left Darby's Town, the other Mingo town, as the only Indian town in all of Areas 53 and 54 in 1776.

From the limited data relating to hunting in Royce Areas 53 and 54 during the period 1760-1776 our conclusions are that no parts of these Areas were exclusively used for hunting by one group of Indians only, during the few years for which meager data on hunting are available.

222

Chapter IV

Use and Occupancy of Royce Areas 53 and 54: 1777-1795

1. Use and Occupancy of the Eastern Half of Area 53, 1777-1795.
In January, 1777 the "Head Chief at Cuyahoga" was one Tegasah [var.
Digásu] who was, we conclude, a Delaware.[1] The British had at this
time a trading post at "Cuyahoga;" in the early spring of 1777 Daniel
Sullivan, an American spy, met Munsees who were going there to trade.[2]
In April, 1777 Sullivan went to Cuyahoga himself and "met with a few
Chippewas, Ottawas, Wiandots & Mingoes about Twenty in Number." Two
British traders had recently arrived there from Detroit "with Stores
of Indian Goods & a Cargo." The Indians at Cuyahoga were not dis-
posed to be friendly toward the Americans, Sullivan reported.[3]

223

1. Boreman, List of Enclosures...February 15, 1777, p. 1; Dft.
Ex. A-214. Heckewelder lists "Digásu, the Chief over Gajahåge" with
other Delaware chiefs, in a 1777 document (Heckewelder, Names,
p. 1; Dft. Ex. A-201).

2. Sullivan, Letter to George Morgan...March 22, 1777, pp. 1-2;
Dft. Ex. A-215

3. Sullivan, Sworn Statement to Col. John Cannon...March 20,
1778, p. 1; Dft. Ex. A-216.

By the fall of the same year (1777) Captain Pipe, by then leader of the Wolf division of the Delawares,[4] and his people, and also some Munsees, had moved to Cuyahoga, where

> the English had lately erected a Store House..
> to supply all the Indians in that Neighborhood
> with every necessary to enable them to commit
> Hostilities against the Frontier Inhabitants of
> Pennsylvania and Virginia.[5]

Some, at least, of the Delawares and Munsees at Cuyahoga were by then definitely hostile to the Americans, although Pipe himself was not.[6] His village at Cuyahoga, established in 1777, was within southeastern Area 53, on the south side of the Cuyahoga River where it turns sharply

---

4. Custaloga, old chief of the Wolf division, had died in 1776. Collections of the State Historical Society of Wisconsin, vol. 24, p. 132; Dft. Ex. A-226. Bliss, ed., David Zeisberger's Diary, vol. 1, p. 220; Dft. Ex. A-247. Ibid., vol. 2, p. 364; Dft. Ex. A-248.
   In the spring of 1777 Pipe and his Delawares had been living "at Kaskaskias [Kuskusky]" on the Big Beaver River in extreme western Pennsylvania (Message from the United States to Captain Pipe the head Chief of the Delawares at Kaskaskias...April 7, 1777, p. 1; Dft. Ex. A-217; Heckewelder, The Names of all the Different Indian Nations, p. 1; Dft. Ex. A-201).
   Prior to 1776 Pipe had had his village for a time on the Walhonding River near present Coshocton, Cushocton County, Ohio, some 20 miles south of Area 54 (Heckewelder, Narrative, p. 143; Dft. Ex. A-53; Collections of the State Historical Society of Wisconsin, vol. 23, p. 366 and fn. 1; Dft. Ex. A-225).

5. Thwaites and Kellogg, eds., Frontier Defense, pp. 178-179; Dft. Ex. A-165. Darlington, Christopher Gist's Journal, p. 215; Dft. Ex. A-224. Butterfield, ed., Washington-Crawford Letters, pp. 66-67, fn. 2; Dft. Ex. A-180

6. Darlington, Christopher Gist's Journal, p. 215; Dft. Ex. A-224. Draper Ms. IU132; Dft. Ex. A-254. Thwaites and Kellogg, pp. 164-165; Dft. Ex. A-165.

164

to flow northwestward, at a point some three miles north of present
Akron, Summit County. Heckewelder noted in 1789 that "Cayahaga Old
Town" had formerly been "a large Indian town."[7]

In February, 1778 Gen. Edward Hand, commanding at Fort Pitt, organized an American force to destroy the British stores and boats "at
Cuyahoga." Hand's expedition actually went no farther west than
extreme western Pennsylvania, however.[8]

By March, 1778 Pipe himself was among the pro-American Delawares
of the "Cooshocking" (Coshocton) region south of Area 54, to which
location Pipe's people at Cuyahoga had agreed to remove.[9] Despite
Pipe's returning to Cuyahoga in March-April, 1778 to urge that such a
move be made,[10] his Delawares, "comfortably settled" where they could

7. Heart to Harmar, January 5, 1790, pp. 5-6; Dft. Ex. A-256.
Wallace, ed., Thirty Thousand Miles, p. 253; Dft. Ex. A-167. Heckewelder, Map; Dft. Ex. A-166. Heckewelder Map and Description, pp. 339-
340; Dft. Ex. A-196. Bliss, ed., Zeisberger's Diary, vol. 1, pp. 235,
288; Dft. Ex. A-247. Howe, Historical Collections, vol. 2, p. 626; Dft.
Ex. A-192.
    Local traditions, in error on several points, connect Pipe
with "New Portage," near the head of the Tuscarawas River at present
Barberton, Summit County, Ohio (Perrin, History of Summit County,
pp. 522, 525; Dft. Ex. A-234; Baughman, History of Ashland County, p. 54;
Dft. Ex. A-158).

8. This was the so-called "Squaw Campaign;" see Butterfield, ed.,
Washington-Irvine Letters, pp. 66-67, fn. 2; Dft. Ex. A-180; also Dis-
cussion of Possible Expedition against Detroit...July 17, 1778, p. 2;
Dft. Ex. A-223.

9. White Eyes and John Killbuck, Message to George Morgan...
March 14, 1778, p. 3; Dft. Ex. A-220. American authorities at Fort
Pitt were constantly urging that all the Delawares draw together in the
Coshocton region, beyond the sphere of influence of the British post at
Detroit.

10. Message from White Eyes and Killbuck...April 6, 1778, p. 1;
Dft. Ex. A-221.

easily obtain supplies from Detroit traders, expressed unwillingness to leave,[11] and remained at Cuyahoga throughout the summer and fall of 1778. In the fall of 1778, however, American troops from Fort Pitt began building Fort Laurens at Tuscarawas, some 30 miles south of Cuyahoga Town at the extreme southeastern tip of Area 54.[12] The existence of an American fort west of the Ohio River in the "Indian lands," as designated at the British Treaty of Fort Stanwix in 1768, was resented by all the Ohio Indians, except the pro-American Delawares centered at Coshocton. Pipe's Delawares at Cuyahoga sent messengers westward to the Wyandots of "Sandusky"[13] asking for help. The Wyandots responded early in November, 1778 by sending "Horses to bring the families and effects of the Delawares to Sandusky."[14] Whether all the Delawares (and Munsees?) at Cuyahoga removed west to stay in the Wyandot town of Sandusky, some 25 miles west of Area 54, during the winter of 1778-1779 is not clear,[15] but by the following spring (1779) Pipe's Delawares had all left

226

---

11. Speeches Made by White Eyes, Teytapaukosheh, William Chilliways and Isaac Leyhickon...April 25 [1778?], pp. 1-2; Dft. Ex. A-222. Virginia Magazine of History and Biography, vol. 23, p. 345; Dft. Ex. A-230.

12. Collections of tne State Historical Society of Wisconsin, vol. 23, pp. 183-184; Dft. Ex. A-225. Bolton to Haldimand, March 24, 1799, pp. 427-428; Dft. Ex. A-232.

13. The Wyandot town of Sandusky was at this time Three miles south of present Upper Sandusky, Wyandot County, Ohio (Butterfield, Historical Account, pp. 152-154; Dft. Ex. A-155)

14. Bolton to Haldimand, November 13, 1778, p. 369; Dft. Ex. A-231. See also Thwaites and Kellogg, eds., Frontier Defense, pp. 164-165, fn. 27; Dft. Ex. A-165.

15. Collections of the State Historical Society of Wisconsin, vol. 23, p. 335; Dft. Ex. A-225.

Cuyahoga, and by 1780, and for several years thereafter, were settled
in a town some 30 miles west of Area 54.[16] No Delawares, or any other
Indians, apparently ever re-occupied the site of Pipe's Cuyahoga Town
after the Delawares left it in 1778-1779.[17]

In June, 1779 an American spy suggested to Capt. Daniel Brodhead,
commanding at Fort Pitt, that "2 [pro-American] Dellaware Men" be kept
as spies "at the Mouth of Gajahage [Cuyahoga] River, who might hunt
there without being discovered."[18]

In 1780 there may have been "Indians" living at or near present
Cuyahoga Falls, ca. two miles east of Area 53, and "In the year 1785,"
according to Heckewelder, "a Trader purchased 23 Horseloads of Peltry,
from the few Indians then hunting on [the Cuyahoga] River--"[19] Several
contemporary documents indicate, however, that there were no Indian

16. Collections of the State Historical Society of Wisconsin,
vol. 23, pp. 361-362, 266, 365-366, 367; Dft. Ex. A-225. Ibid., vol.
24, pp. 97, 109, and fn. 1, p. 219; Dft. Ex. A-226. Butterfield,
Historical Account, pp. 167-169 and fn. 7; Dft. Ex. A-155. Heckewelder,
Narrative, pp. 236, 285; Dft. Ex. A-53. Papers of the Continental Congress, Item No. 150, 1785-1788; Dft. Ex. A-250. Pennsylvania Archives,
1st Ser., vol. 10, p. 83; Dft. Ex. A-282. W.H. Smith, Life...Arthur St.
Clair, vol. 2, pp. 16-17; Dft. Ex. A-283.

17. Wallace, ed., Thirty Thousand Miles, p. 253; Dft. Ex. A-167.
Heart to Harmar, January 5, 1790, pp. 5-6; Dft. Ex. A-256. Hecke-
welder, Map; Dft. Ex. A-166. Ontario History, vol. 49, p. 90; Dft. Ex.
A-269.

18. Collections of the State Historical Society of Wisconsin,
vol. 23, p. 383; Dft. Ex. A-225. Later in 1779 Brodhead planned an expedition against Detroit via Cuyahoga, but this failed to materialize
(Pennsylvania Archives, 1st ser., vol. 12, p. 189; Dft. Ex. A-229).

19. Draper Mss. 168272, 299, 302; Dft. Ex. A-268. Bierce, Historical Reminiscences, pp. 116-117; Dft. Ex. A-233. Heckewelder, Map and
Description, p. 340; Dft. Ex. A-196.

villages on Cuyahoga River between 1782 and June, 1786.[20]

At this latter date, specifically on June 18, 1786, around 100 Christian Indian converts[21]--chiefly Delawares and Munsees, together with some Mohicans and Nanticokes--led by two Moravian missionaries, David Zeisberger and John Heckewelder,[22] came to Cuyahoga River from Detroit and built a temporary town on the east bank of the River some 20 river miles above its mouth,[23] on the site of "an old Ottawa town" near the mouth of present Tinker's Creek. They then proceeded to put in a crop opposite their town, on the west side of the Cuyahoga, within eastern Area 53. This Moravian Indian settlement became known as

---

20. A reconnoitering expedition to the mouth of Cuyahoga in 1782 fails to mention any Indians there; see Butterfield, ed., Washington-Irvine Correspondence, pp. 137-139, fn. 4; Dft. Ex. A-211. See also Draper Mss. 1NN111; Dft. Ex. A-227. A "List of the Western Nations of Indians Contiguous to the Post at Muskingum, 1785-1788" also fails to note any Indians living on Cuyahoga River (Dft. Ex. A-250, vol. (6), pp. (39-156). Moravian missionaries explicitly note that despite a diligent search, they found no one at the mouth of the Cuyahoga early in June, 1786; that upstream on this river there were no Indian settlements, and that the Cuyahoga region was "a wilderness, remote from Indian and white settlements" (Bliss, ed., Zeisberger's Diary, vol. 1, pp. 235-236, 276-278, 288-289, 314-315, 435-436; Dft. Ex. A-247).
Two maps, Thomas Hutchins' Map of 1778, Dft. Ex. A-121, and Will Cockburn's Map of the State of New York, Dft. Ex. A-264, which dates 1780-1783, legend an Ottawa town on the east bank of the Cuyahoga River, immediately east of Area 53. Much of the data on which the Hutchins Map of 1778 is based was gathered in the 1760's. Cockburn's Map, as far as Areas 53 and 54 are concerned, obviously reproduces the material on Hutchins' Map of 1778.

21. Bliss, ed., Zeisberger's Diary, vol. 1, pp. 279, 314-316; Dft. Ex. A-247.

22. Later Brother William Edwards joined the Christian congregation at Cuyahoga.

23. Heart to Harmar, January 5, 1790, p. 5; Dft. Ex. A-256. Ontario History, vol. 29, no. 2, p. 87; Dft. Ex. A-269.

"Pilgerruh" (Pilgrim's Rest).[24]

Pillgerruh was occupied by the Moravian Indians for ten months.
At the end of December, 1786 it had a total population of 96 persons.
On April 19, 1787 most of the Christian Indians abandoned the town,
and by May 4, 1787 Pilgerruh was "quite deserted."[25]

From Pilgerruh the Christian Indians did not proceed southward to
the Forks of the Muskingum region, as they had originally intended,[26]
but instead went north to the mouth of the Cuyahoga and then westward
along Lake Erie to the mouth of a stream halfway between the Cuyahoga
and the Huron Rivers--in all probability to Black River, in the extreme eastern half of Area 53. At the mouth of Black River the Mor-

---

24. Bliss, ed., Zeisberger's Diary, vol. 1, pp. 277-283, 289,
314-315; Dft. Ex. A-247. Clark, The Moravian Mission, p. 53; Dft. Ex.
A-251. Zeisberger to Ettwein, In the Huts on the River Cuyahoga, July
22, 1786; Dft. Ex. A-273. Zeisberger to Ettwein, Camp on the Bank of
the Cayahaga, June 25, 1786; Dft. Ex. A-272. Ontario History, vol.
49, p. 87; Dft. Ex. A-269.
The name of the settlement reflects its temporary nature.
The Christian Indians and their missionaries had intended, after
leaving the Detroit region in the early spring of 1786, to return to
the towns they had been forced to abandon in 1781, on the Tuscarawas
River 16-24 miles south of Area 54. But they were delayed on their
trip, and by June 18 lack of supplies and the fact that the season was
then well advanced led them to make a temporary halt. (Zeisberger to
Harmar, Cayahoga, July 12, 1786; Dft. Ex. A-225).

25. Bliss, ed., Zeisberger's Diary, vol. 1, pp. 316, 333, 338-
339; Dft. Ex. A-247.

26. See fn. 24, this Chapter.
There were two reasons for the Indians not going to the
Forks of Muskingum, south of Area 54. One was that Indian-American
hostilities continued to be a threat in this region. The other was
that the Delawares, Munsees, and Wyandots living west of Areas 53 and
54 on or near the Sandusky River were pressuring the Moravian Indians
to settle near them (Bliss, ed., Zeisberger's Diary, vol. 1, pp. 235-
236, 298, 301-304, 308, 315, 320, 322, 324-330; Dft. Ex. A-247).

(cont'd on p. 169.)

avians found pike running in great abundance on April 24, 1787. Five
miles upstream (south) from the river's mouth, a few miles north of
present Elyria, Lorain County, Ohio, the Moravian congregation found a
suitable location for a town.[27] This did not, however, please the
Delaware, Munsee and Wyandot chiefs living in the Sandusky region, who
wanted the Christian Indians to locate closer to their towns, either on
or near the Sandusky River.[28] Therefore after a total stay of only 13
days on Black River the Christian Indians and their missionaries removed
further west, out of eastern Area 53 and into the western half of Area
53.[29] Their location in western Area 53 is discussed in Section 2 of
this chapter.

(fn. 26 cont'd.) The peculiar position of the Moravian converts--the
necessity for their being under the sponsorship of at least one pagan
Indian group, and the reasons why several pagan groups wished to have the
Moravians settle near them--is frequently referred to by Zeisberger in
his Diary (Bliss, ed., vol. 1, pp. 344, 399, 405, 406, 419, 430; Dft. Ex.
A-247. Ibid., vol. 2, pp. 29-30, 65-66, 120, 136, 141-142, 191-192; Dft.
Ex. A-248).

27. Bliss, ed., Zeisberger's Diary, vol. 1, pp. 332, 334; Dft. Ex.
A-247. Zeisberger to the General Helpers' Conference, Cayahaga, April 9,
1787; Dft. Ex. A-274. Zeisberger to Ettwein, Cayahaga, April 9, 1787;
Dft. Ex. A-275.
    Present Elyria, Lorain County, is at the forks of the Black
River. Near the town are two falls having a 40' perpendicular drop
(Howe, Historical Collections, vol. 2, p. 120; Dft. Ex. A-192).

28. Bliss, ed., Zeisberger's Diary, vol. 1, pp. 335-337; Dft. Ex.
A-247.

29. Bliss, ed., Zeisberger's Diary, vol. 1, pp. 338-340; Dft. Ex.
A-247; ibid., vol. 2, p. 123; Dft. Ex. A-248.

230

The diaries and letters of the Moravian missionaries to the Ohio Indians in the late 18th century are rich primary sources on the use made of the natural resources within the eastern half of Area 53, not only by the Moravian Indians, but by Indians belonging to other groups as well. In November, 1786, for example, Zeisberger records that Christian Indian women gathered chestnuts in the vicinity of Pilgerruh, and many of the Christian Indian men returned to Pilgerruh from hunting,

> with horse-loads of venison and bear meat, and casks filled with honey they had collected in the bush, for there are many bees here...[30]

In February, 1787 the Moravian Indians made maple sugar at sugar camps located, apparently, only a few miles (4-6?) distant from Pilgerruh.[31] In May-June, 1787, after the Moravians had abandoned Pilgerruh, two of their number hunted "at Cuyahoga;"[32] in October, 1787 many Christian' Indians "went for some weeks' hunting to Cuyahoga;"[33] in mid-November, 1787, likewise, Christian Indian men "went off to their autumn hunt, some to Cuyahoga..."[34] This continued; in January, 1789 the Moravian

231

---

30. Bliss, ed., Zeisberger's Diary, vol. 1, pp. 300, 309-310; Dft. Ex. A-247. See also Zeisberger to Ettwein, In Camp on the Bank of the Cuyahoga June 25, 1786; Dft. Ex. A-272. Extract from a Letter... Fort Pitt, June 24, 1786; Dft. Ex. A-271. Zeisberger usually specifically names locations distant from Pilgerruh, but frequently uses "in the bush" for the locale near Pilgerruh.

31. Bliss, ed., Zeisberger's Diary, vol. 1, p. 324; Dft. Ex. A-247. Zeisberger apparently considered sugar camp locations 10-12 miles from town as being at a considerable distance (Bliss, ed., Zeisberger's Diary, vol. 1, p. 389; Dft. Ex. A-247).

32. Bliss, ed., Zeisberger's Diary, vol. 1, p. 347; Dft. Ex. A-247.

33. Bliss, ed., Zeisberger's Diary, vol. 1, p. 373; Dft. Ex. A-247.

34. Bliss, ed., Zeisberger's Diary, vol. 1, p. 378; Dft. Ex. A-247.

convert, "Renatus the Mohican," and a companion returned from hunting "at Cuyahoga;" in the summer of 1789 some other Christian Indians hunted at Cuyahoga; and in September, 1789 still others went hunting "in Cuyahoga."[35]

In April, 1787 Moravian Indian women "dug wild potatoes, of which there are many...a very wholesome food for Indians," five miles upstream from the mouth of Black River.[36]

Other Indians frequently mentioned by the Moravian missionaries as visiting Pilgerruh in 1786-1787 and/or utilizing the natural resources of the Cuyahoga region and other parts of the eastern half of Area 53 between the years 1786 and 1795 included "Chippewas, Ottawas, Delawares."[37]

Some 8 or 9 miles west of the Cuyahoga River, early in June, 1786 Heckewelder met "a number of Chippewas" who, like himself, "were going to the Cayahaga River" and who in fact arrived there before he did. Later, Chippewas who had been hunting along Lake Erie stole several horse-loads of flour from a storehouse belonging to White traders, at the mouth of the Cuyahoga.[38] On July 1, 1786 a group of Chippewas, including a chief and women and children, who lived "a hundred miles beyond Michili-mackinac" came up the Cuyahoga and encamped near Pilgerruh, staying there

232

---

35. Bliss, ed., Zeisberger's Diary, vol. 2, pp. 3, 50, 57; Dft. Ex. A-248.

36. Bliss, ed., Zeisberger's Diary, vol. 1, pp. 334-335; Dft. Ex. A-247.

37. Zeisberger to Ettwein, In the Huts on the River Cayahaga, July 22, 1786, p. 5; Dft. Ex. A-273.

38. Heckewelder, Narrative, pp. 370, 373; Dft. Ex. A-53. Bliss, ed., Zeisberger's Diary, vol. 1, pp. 277-279; Dft. Ex. A-247; Whittlesey, Early History, pp. 210, 363-364; Dft. Ex. A-78.

until August 6, 1786 when they "went away...down to the lake [Erie]."[39]
In the summer of 1786 some Chippewas planted "in Cuyahoga" where. Zeisberger
observes, "they never left us in peace."[40]

On October 22, 1786 "Some Chippewas came [to Pilgerruh] from the
lake [Erie]" to obtain corn. At the end of October, 1786 other Chippewas
who were going hunting up the Cuyahoga River came to Pilgerruh and encamped for two days. On November 11, 1786 Chippewas, or "six Potawatomies
and Chippewas [from Detroit?]" stayed overnight at Pilgerruh; "the next
morning however one [Indian] came after them to get them to go back
[north?] again." This party had intended "going to war, and the chiefs
wished to stop them."[41]

On January 3, 1787 "two Chippewas attended the early service" at
Pilgerruh, and on January 11, 1787 "a party of Chippewas" came to Pilgerruh
"from their hunting place, encamping nearby for several days. They were
going to their sugar-place..." Three days later these friendly Chippewas
gave the Christian Indians "a feast of bear's meat, having shot several
bears," and on January 23, 1787 the Christian Indians gave the same
Chippewas corn. The eldest man in this party was a brother of a chief
at Detroit who had previously befriended the Moravians. The Chippewas
wished to make sugar with the Christian Indians, and also, Zeisberger
observes, were "always asking" when we shall "go back home again over
the lake [Erie], thinking we stay here only for hunting, as they do."

---

39. Bliss, ed., Zeisberger's Diary, vol. 1, pp. 281, 286-287;
Dft. Ex. A-247. The men belonging to this group went on to Pittsburgh,
but the chief and the women and children stayed encamped near Pilgerruh.

40. Bliss, ed., Zeisberger's Diary, vol. 2, pp. 108-109; Dft.
Ex. A-248.

41. Bliss, ed., Zeisberger's Diary, vol. 1, pp. 306, 307, 308-
309, 310; Dft. Ex. A-247.

On February 21, 1787 these Chippewas returned to Pilgerruh "from their sugar-making very fine-looking, friendly Indians." On February 25 "Two Chippewas were present at the sermon" delivered by Zeisberger at Pilgerruh, and in a letter of April 9, 1787 Zeisberger refers to Chippewas who had been at Pilgerruh "all winter."[42]

In February, 1788, after the Moravians had left the Cuyahoga Chippewas were again hunting there; the same was true during the winters of 1788-1789, 1789-1790, and 1790-1791.[43] On November 25, 1789 Capt. Jonathan Heart, American officer, passed three Chippewa camps on the banks of Cuyahoga River, 11 miles downstream from "Cuyahoga Old Town" (Pipe's former village) in eastern Area 53.[44] In March, 1791 "a Party of Chippewas from Cayahago river on Lake Erie" killed some Americans in eastern Pennsylvania, and that same spring reports were circulated by Chippewas who had been "at Cuyahoga" that they had seen 30 American militiamen at the mouth of Cuyahoga River.[45] A surveyor's map prepared

234

---

42. Bliss, ed., Zeisberger's Diary, vol. 1, pp. 320, 321, 322, 324; Dft. Ex. A-247. Zeisberger to the General Helper's Conference, Cayahaga, April 9, 1787, p. 3; Dft. Ex. A-274.

43. Bliss, ed., Zeisberger's Diary, vol. 1, pp. 393, 419-420; Dft. Ex. A-247. Ibid., vol. 2, pp. 32, 172; Dft. Ex. A-248.

44. Heart to Harmar, Jan. 5, 1790, p. 3; Dft. Ex. A-256. Pipe's former village was in extreme eastern Area 53; see p. 163, this Report.

45. Bliss, ed., Zeisberger's Diary, vol. 2, pp. 172, 205; Dft. Ex. A-248.
As early as 1786 it was proposed to Henry Knox, Secretary of War, that the Americans build a "small post and stores at Cuyahoga," since the British were actively attempting "to prevent the passage of peltry... from that country" to Pittsburgh. A second proposal that an American fort be located at the mouth of the Cuyahoga was made in 1792. Neither of these proposals was, acted upon. See Butler to Knox, Fort Pitt, December 13, 1786; Dft. Ex. A-284. Butler to Knox, Carlisle, March 28, 1787; Dft. Ex. A-285. Carter, Territorial Papers, vol. 2, pp. 100-102; Dft. Ex. A-286. Putnam to Knox, Fort Washington, July 8, 1792; Dft. Ex. A-265. Knopf, ed., Anthony Wayne, pp. 59-61, 73, 75; Dft. Ex. A-266.

in 1791 notes two "Indian" villages on the Cuyahoga, one at its mouth, the other "about Ten Miles" upstream.[46]

The use made by Ottawas of the eastern half of Area 53 is also recorded. On November 30, 1786, according to Zeisberger, "Two Tawa Indians [Ottawas] came in [to Pilgerruh] from hunting in the bush"[47] and stayed two days. On December 12, 1786 "seven Tawas and Chippewas" who said they "lived in Sandusky on the lake [Sandusky Bay]"[48] stayed overnight in Pilgerruh. The next morning these visitors stole some flour traders had left in care of the Moravians. Later some Chippewas visiting Pilgerruh stated that all the members of the thieving party were Ottawas.[49] On April 1, 1787 three Christian Indians from Pilgerruh met "a party of Tawa Indians out hunting" on the headwaters of Black River in eastern Area 53. And on November 20, 1789 Capt. Heart found two camps of Ottawas at the Standing Stone on the Cuyahoga River near present Kent, Portage County, some 10 miles east of Area 53.[50]

The presence of some "Mingoes [?] from Niagara" who were at Cuyahoga in the late summer or early fall of 1789 is also referred to by

---

46. McNiff, A Plan of Lake Erie, Part A; Dft. Ex. A-289.

47. See fn. 30, this Chapter.

48. Zeisberger often refers to Sandusky Bay as "the lake" or "the little lake;" see Bliss, ed., Zeisberger's Diary, vol. 1. p. 87; Dft. Ex. A-247.

49. Bliss, ed., Zeisberger's Diary, vol. 1, pp. 310, 311-312, 320; Dft. Ex. A-247.

50. Bliss, ed., Zeisberger's Diary, vol. 1, p. 332; Dft. Ex. A-247. Ibid., vol. 1, pp. 419-420; Dft. Ex. A-247. Heart to Harmar, January 5, 1789, p. 2; Dft. Ex. A-256. Wallace, ed., Thirty Thousand Miles, p. 439; Dft. Ex. A-167.

Zeisberger,[51] but no details as to why the Mingos were there or what
they were doing are given.

In all probability Indians continued to frequent the Cuyahoga region for winter hunting in 1792 and subsequent years, because one Joseph
Du Shattar, a trader, maintained a post on the Cuyahoga River nine miles
upstream from its mouth from 1791 to at least 1794. However, a British
report for 1794 indicates that returns in furs from the Cuyahoga River
to Detroit were, in 1794, "of no great value."[52]

2. Use and Occupancy of the Western Half of Area 53, 1777-1795.
During the late 1770's the sources are silent as to native use and/or
occupancy of the western half of Area 53. By the early 1780's however,
Indians of several different groups are mentioned as having villages in,
or using, various parts of western Area 53--specifically, (a) the islands
north of Sandusky Bay; (b) the Sandusky Bay region; (c) the south shore
of Lake Erie and Huron River region. We will consider native use and/or
occupancy of each of these regions during the period 1777-1795, in turn.

(a) Islands North of Sandusky Bay, 1777-1795. North, Middle, and
South Bass Islands, and Kelley's Island are in the extreme northwestern
part of Area 53 (see Fig. 3). Middle Bass Island was visited by Zeisberger
and his flock of Indian converts during the early spring of 1786, while
enroute from Detroit to the south shore of Lake Erie. Bad weather

236

51. Bliss, ed., Zeisberger's Diary, vol. 2, p. 57; Dft. Ex. A-248.

52. Whittlesey, Early History, pp. III-IV, 132-133; Dft. Ex. A-78.
Cruikshank, ed., Correspondence, vol. 3, p. 55; Dft. Ex. A-296.

forced the two schooners in which the Moravians were travelling to take shelter, first on the west side of Middle Bass Island at "Pudding Bay,"[53] and later on the east side of the same Island, for 24 days. During that time the Christian Indians and their missionaries encamped ashore, hunted, gathered wild potatoes and onions, and thoroughly explored Middle Bass Island, which Zeisberger describes as "good and fertile, three miles long by two wide. South of it, about a mile off, is another [South Bass Island] much larger."[54]

After leaving middle Bass Island the Moravian party again had to take shelter, from May 23-May 30, 1786 at "Hope's Cove" (present Put-in-Bay)[55] on the northern side of South Bass Island. "Here," Zeisberger records,

> the [Christian] Indians got a new place to hunt,
> for they had already quite exhausted the game
> on the other island, and there was little more
> to be had, though there is little other game
> here than raccoons and pigeons. This island
> is as large again as the former...[56]

237

In another entry Zeisberger remarks that ginseng roots grew "in abundance, as if planted" on South Bass Island.[57] He makes no mention of the Moravian

---

53. Bliss, ed., Zeisberger's Diary, vol. 1, p. 268; Dft. Ex. A-247. Bliss is in error in identifying "Pudding Bay" as Put-in-Bay, which is on South Bass Island. See Ontario History, vol. 49, p. 80 and fns. 63, 65; Dft. Ex. A-269.

54. Bliss, ed., Zeisberger's Diary, vol. 1, pp. 268-271; Dft. Ex. A-247. North Bass Island and Middle Bass Island each contain 750 acres; South Bass Island contains 1,500 acres (Howe, Historical Collections of Ohio, vol. 2, p. 367; Dft. Ex. A-192).

55. Burton, Anthony Wayne, map facing p. 489; Dft. Ex. A-246. Ontario History, vol. 49, p. 80, fn. 65; Dft. Ex. A-269.

56. Bliss, ed., Zeisberger's Diary, vol. 1, p. 271; Dft. Ex. A-247. Zeisberger's remarks on the game available on the Island accord with James Smith's observations of 1757.

57. Bliss, ed., Zeisberger's Diary, vol. 1, p. 271; Dft. Ex. A-247.

Indians meeting any other Indians, either on Middle Bass or South Bass Islands. Nor were any Indians there, apparently, in March, 1793.[57a]

The next year, in August and September, 1787, several of the Moravian Indians, then living on the lower Huron River of Ohio, went to either Middle Bass or South Bass Island (or perhaps to both) to dig the ginseng they had seen growing there the year before.[58] Also in July, 1789 Moravian Indians again went to "the islands in the lake [Erie]" to dig ginseng, and gathered a "good quantity" of it.[59]

Abundant archaeological evidence exists of use made in the distant past of Kelley's Island, also in northwestern Area 53, but nothing is known about the use of Kelley's Island by any historic Indians.[60]

(b) The Sandusky Bay Region, 1777-1795. The "Sandusky Bay region" of western Area 53 includes the eastern half of the Marblehead Peninsula which protects Sandusky Bay on the north; it also includes Johnson's Island (formerly Bull's Island) near the mouth of the Bay, and the eastern half of Sandusky Bay's southern shore.

After the American Revolution, in 1784, two "tribes" of Ottawas and between 20 and 30 French families moved from Detroit into this region. The French families settled on the eastern end of the Marblehead Peninsula, while the Ottawas occupied the lands on the southeast shore of Sandusky

238

57a. Spencer, Indian Captivity, pp. 150-154; Dft. Ex. A-320.
58. Bliss, ed., Zeisberger's Diary, vol. 1, pp. 366, 369; Dft. Ex. A-247. The Indians sold the ginseng in order to buy clothing; a bushel of roots sold for three or four dollars. "If, then," Zeisberger observes, "they come to a place where there is a good deal of it, it repays their trouble" (ibid., vol. 1, p. 369; Dft. Ex. A-247).

59. Bliss, ed., Zeisberger's Diary, vol. 2, pp. 47, 48, 49, 50; Dft. Ex. A-248. If the roots grew in abundance, a man could gather "a good half bushel" in a day, according to Zeisberger (ibid., vol. 2, p. 48; Dft. Ex. A-248).

60. See Firelands Pioneer, vol. 4, June, 1863, pp. 30-33; Dft. Ex. A-235.

Bay, from the site of the present city of Sandusky, Erie County, in western Area 53, westward to "Old Sunyendeand," near the mouth of Pickerel Creek, four miles west of Area 53. Near Old Sunyendeand the Ottawas had their corn fields.[61]

The Indians and French families came to the Sandusky Bay region under the leadership of a Catholic-educated, highly respected Indian priest of unknown parentage, named Ogontz. Ogontz' cabin was at the present city of Sandusky, which in the early 19th century was known to traders and settlers as "Ogontz," "Ogontstown," or "the Ogontz Place."[62] The number of Ottawas who moved to Sandusky Bay in 1784 is not known, but since they consisted of two "tribes" there were probably several score of them, at least.

Ogontz and the Ottawas remained in northwestern Area 53 around present Sandusky from 1784 until the fall of 1811, when they returned to Detroit because of the impending War.[63]

239

Other accounts of the Sandusky Bay region in the 1780's provide further details on Indian use and occupancy of this region. On April 14, 1782 Zeisberger and several other Moravian missionaries set out by schooner from "Lower Sandusky" (present Fremont, Sandusky County) to go north to Detroit. The schooner sailed eastward the length of Sandusky Bay and its passengers encamped on the night of April 14, 1782 on Johnson's

---

61. Firelands Pioneer, vol. 4, June, 1863, pp. 23-29; Dft. Ex. A-235. For Sunyendeand see Chapter 2, pp. 62-63, this Report.

62. Firelands Pioneer, vol. 4, June, 1863, pp. 25-29; Dft. Ex. A-235. Howe, Historical Collections of Ohio, vol. 1, p. 567; Dft. Ex. A-191. Firelands Pioneer, vol. 2, September, 1860, pp. 34, 46; Dft. Ex. A-242; Firelands Pioneer, vol. 9, June, 1868, pp. 21, 45, 76; Dft. Ex. A-245, Bierce, Historical Reminiscences. p. 87; Dft. Ex. A-233.

63. Firelands Pioneer, vol. 4, June, 1863, p. 27; Dft. Ex. A-235.

Island (formerly Bull's Island) in the mouth of the Bay.[64] Zeisberger mentions that there were two Frenchmen living on Johnson's Island, who had been there a year or so, but says nothing of any Indians being there. However, Henry Howe, Ohio historian, states without giving his authority that Johnson's Island was

> a favorite resort of the Indians, who came here
> in the fishing season, engaged in festivities,
> and brought their captives for torture.[65]

On April 15, 1782 the schooner bearing Zeisberger and his fellow missionaries entered Lake Erie and, rounding the Marblehead Peninsula, coasted westward along the "west" (southwest) shore of the Lake, in part within western Area 53. It reached Cedar Point, Lucas County, Ohio, some 30 miles northwest of Area 53, on April 18, 1782. "Not only here [at Cedar Point]," Zeisberger notes, "but everywhere, so far as we came [from Lower Sandusky], were many Indians, Chippewas, Potawatomies, Wyandots, Tawas, etc."[66]

Four years later, at the end of May, 1786 Zeisberger was again in the neighborhood of Sandusky Bay, this time afoot and with several score Christian Indians. The group, which was on its way eastward, had been landed from two schooners, on the north shore of the Marblehead Peninsula at "Rocky Point," probably near present Catawba Island in

240

---

64. Bliss, ed., Zeisberger's Diary, vol. 1, p. 87; Dft. Ex. A-247. Firelands Pioneer, vol. 4, June, 1863, p. 24; Dft. Ex. A-235.

65. Howe, Historical Collections of Ohio, vol. 1, p. 572; Dft. Ex. A-191. In 1791 "two Indian tribes" were reported living on Johnson's(?) Island (La Rochefoucault-Liancourt, vol. 1, pp. 371-372; Dft. Ex. A-295).

66. Bliss, ed., Zeisberger's Diary, vol. 1, p. 87; Dft. Ex. A-247.

northwestern Area 53.[67] On the north shore of the Peninsula the Moravian
party met

> ten Tawas [Ottawas], out hunting...who were
> much amazed to meet such a number of people
> in a place where far and wide was no way nor
> road...We gave them food, and they shared
> their meat with us and showed us also how to
> steer through the bush to Sandusky, for near
> the lake or strand we cannot get along.[68]

The Moravian party crossed Marblehead Peninsula in a southeasterly
direction and on June 1, 1786 arrived on the northeast shore of Sandusky
Bay, at the entrance to the Bay. Zeisberger noted that "Many French live
here [southeastern shore of the Marblehead Peninsula] and on the islands
in [the eastern end of] the bay." The Frenchmen could not supply the
                                                           Bay
Moravians with boats to cross the mouth of Sandusky, so the latter "had
to turn to the Ottawas, who lived on the lake [Sandusky Bay], who were
willing to lend us their canoes, in part bark canoes, for pay." While
waiting overnight to cross the mouth of the Bay the Moravian Indians
"had many visits from Ottawas" who lived nearby. In the evening the
Ottawas, who were "pagans," had a dance, which none of the Christian
Indians attended.[69] On June 3, 1786 the Moravian party crossed the

241

---

67. Zeisberger to Dearly Beloved Brethren and Sisters, June 12,
1786, p. 3; Dft. Ex. A-276. Bliss, ed., Zeisberger's Diary, vol. 1,
p. 273; Dft. Ex. A-247. Before some of the Moravians were landed from
the schooner, Zeisberger notes, they found, at a "little island" (Rocky
Island?) the water "swarming with fish" and were able to take, with
sharp stakes, "more fish than they wanted or could bring away with
them."

68. Bliss, ed., Zeisberger's Diary, vol. 1, p. 273; Dft. Ex.
A-247.

69. Bliss, ed., Zeisberger's Diary, vol. 1, p. 274; Dft. Ex.
A-247.
      The French and Ottawas the Moravians met were some of those
who had left Detroit with Ogontz in 1784. Note that Zeisberger's remarks
confirm the respective locations of the Whites and Ottawas in the Sandusky
Bay region, as given by Ogontz.

mouth of Sandusky Bay and went that "whole day" southward and then eastward, "along the lake [Erie] shore." The travellers evidently did not
visit "Ogontz Place," at the present city of Sandusky, Erie County,
slightly west of their route.[70]

In July, 1787 some of the Moravians went to "Sandusky Island"
(Johnson's Island?) to purchase corn and other supplies; whether from
Frenchmen or Indians is not stated.[71] In 1788 Zeisberger frequently
mentions the French of Sandusky Bay, and in that year Moravian Indians
made another visit to "the island in Sandusky Bay."[72]

During July, 1790, at which time the Moravians were located near
the mouth of the Huron River of Ohio "Chippewas and Tawas [Ottawas]"
living "on Sandusky Lake [Bay]" began to shoot the Moravians' cattle.
The Moravians sent a message to one "Ekuschuwe" (var., Agushewa,
Augooshaway, etc.), an influential Ottawa chief at Detroit,[73] who from
1783 onward had befriended them,[74] asking Ekuschuwe to tell the
marauding Ottawas and Chippewas to stop their depredations. The Moravians
learned also that a message had come "from Detroit to the Chippewas and

242

70. Bliss, ed., Zeisberger's Diary, vol. 1, pp. 274-275; Dft.
Ex. A-247.

71. Bliss, eu.. Zeisberger's Diary, vol. 1, p. 360; Dft. Ex.
A-247.

72. Bliss, ed., Zeisberger's Diary, vol. 1, pp. 418, 425, 432;
Dft. Ex. A-247.

73. American State Papers, Indian Affairs, vol. 1, p. 566; Dft.
Ex. A-252; Knopf, A Surgeon's Mate, p. 43; Dft. Ex. A-253. Carter,
Territorial Papers, vol. 2, p. 537; Dft. Ex. A-286.

74. Bliss, ed., Zeisberger's Diary, vol. 1, pp. 322, 437-438,
453; Dft. Ex. A-247. Ibid., vol. 2, pp. 2, 26-28, 66, 83, 117, 119,
156, 202, 216; Dft. Ex. A-248.

182

Tawas [of Sandusky Bay], that they should keep still and not go at all to

war [against the Americans]..."[75]

In 1792 Ekuschuwe stated in a message to the Moravians that if

peace was decided upon by the Ohio-Great Lakes Indians, he intended to

remove from Detroit and "go to live not far from Sandusky Bay," presumably

to the eastward of the Bay, in western Area 53. However, since Indian-

American hostilities continued between 1792 and 1794, Ekuschuwe did not

leave Detroit and move into western Area 53.[76]

In a secondary, but oft-quoted work by Gilbert Imlay, Kentucky

land speculator who wrote in the early 1790's, there are two enumerations

of Indian groups. In the first such, "Delawares" are listed as being

> in the country between lake Erie and the head
> branches of the Muskingum...it is supposed they
> are reduced from 600 to 450.[77]

In a second listing of Indian groups in Imlay's work, Delawares are again

referred to, as "living upon the Muskingum river...on the N. W. side."[78]

Both lists are unsatisfactory, however, from the standpoint of dating and

243

---

75. Bliss, ed., Zeisberger's Diary, vol. 2, p. 114; Dft. Ex. A-248.

76. Bliss, ed., Zeisberger's Diary, vol. 2, pp. 278-279, 284-285;
Dft. Ex. A-248. Ekuschuwe was still in the Detroit region in June, 1795
(American State Papers, Indian Affairs, vol. 1, p. 566; Dft. Ex. A-252.
Knopf, A Surgeon's Mate, p. 43; Dft. Ex. A-253). His name heads the list
of Ottawa signers of the Treaty of Greenville of August 3, 1795 (7 Stats.
49:53). He died in March, 1796 (Hamtramck to Wayne, Ft. Wayne, March 22,
1796; Dft. Ex. A-299).

77. Imlay, A Topographical Description, p. 291; Dft. Ex. A-263.
This list of Imlay's probably relates to the 1760's and 1770's; see ibid.,
p. 294; Dft. Ex. A-263.

78. Imlay, A Topographical Description, p. 363; Dft. Ex. A-263.

source of information.

The majority of the Ottawas living in the Sandusky Bay region with Ogontz did not engage in anti-American hostilities. Ogontz himself stated in 1810 that he had kept most of his people from joining the Indian force which was defeated by the Legion of the United States under Gen. Anthony Wayne in the battle of Fallen Timbers on the lower Maumee River, August 20, 1794. In 1795, at the close of the period under consideration in this chapter, Ogontz and his Ottawas were still living, as they had been from ca. 1784 onward, on the southeastern shore of Sandusky Bay, within and close to western Area 53.[79]

(c) South Shore of Lake Erie and Huron River Region, 1777-1795. In July, 1785 the Moravian missionary Br. William Edwards went along the south shore of Lake Erie and passed the mouth of the "Pettquotting" or Huron River of Ohio, in western Area 53. At the Huron's mouth he met a Chippewa Indian. A year later, in early June, 1786 Zeisberger and several score Moravian Indians, on their way eastward along the southern Lake Erie shore, came to the mouth of Huron and found Chippewas encamped there. Farther east on the Lake shore, at the mouth of Vermilion River, the Moravian party passed a second Chippewa encampment.[80] There are several other references by Zeisberger to Chippewas, and also to Ottawas, on the Lake Erie shore in western Area 53 in the late 1780's and early 1790's. On October 22, 1787 he mentions

244

79. Firelands Pioneer, vol. 4, June, 1863; pp. 28-29, 25, 27; Dft. Ex. A-235.

80. Bliss, ed., Zeisberger's Diary, vol. 1, pp. 235, 274-275, 276; Dft. Ex. A-247.

184

"the Chippewas and Tawas [Ottawas], who live on the lake;" from context
it is clear the reference is to the southern shore of Lake Erie within
western Area 53.[81] In June, 1789 he also refers to a party of 20-30
Chippewas, some of whom were from the Detroit region, who went "down the
lake" (eastward), from the mouth of the Huron River. A year later, in
June, 1790 "a great party" of Chippewas "came to the lake" near the mouth
of Huron River "from hunting," and in October and November of the same
year Chippewas and Ottawas were "on the lake" or were "down at the lake,"
near the mouth of Huron River.[82] In April, 1791, Zeisberger met "Many
Ottawas and Chippewas...encamped at the lake [at the mouth of Huron River]
who were all going over [to Detroit] and waiting for a good wind;" several
days later he notes that "a multitude of Chippewas" were "encamped at the
lake," close to the mouth of Sandusky Bay.[83]

The "Huron River region," as we use the term here, includes the lower
and upper courses of the Huron River of Ohio, in the western half of Area
53. Our first notice for this region during the period 1777-1795 is for
June 3, 1786. On that date Zeisberger and several score Moravian Indians
who were on their way from Detroit to the Cuyahoga River, stopped at the
mouth of the "Pettquotting" or Huron River and learned that there was a
"Monsey town" one or two miles up the river. Many "Strange Indians"
(i.e., Indians unknown to Zeisberger) from this town visited the Moravian

245

81. Bliss, ed., Zeisberger's Diary, vol. 1, p. 370; Dft. Ex. A-247.

82. Bliss, ed., Zeisberger's Diary, vol. 1, pp. 370-371; Dft. Ex.
A-247. Ibid., vol. 2, pp. 102, 130-131, 134, 173; Dft. Ex. A-248.

83. Bliss, ed., Zeisberger's Diary, vol. 2, pp. 173, 174-177; Dft.
Ex. A-248.

Indians while the latter were encamped at the mouth of Huron River.[84]
It is quite probable that it was from this Munsee town on lower Huron
River that some "strange Monsey Indians" derived who, in mid-July, 1786,
visited the Moravians, by then settled at Pilgerruh on the Cuyahoga River.
These later Munsee visitors are identified by Zeisberger as "Indians
who, during the [Revolutionary] war had been in Niagara, and did not
know us."[85] Establishment of the Munsee town noted by Zeisberger in
1786 on the lower Huron River was therefore probably post-Revolutionary
(ca. 1784?).

Visits by Moravian Indians from Pilgerruh on the Cuyahoga to the
"Indians" (Munsees) on Huron River also occurred in the latter half of
1786, the Moravian Indians often going "to Pettquotting" (Huron River)
to obtain corn.[86] Toward the end of October, 1786 twelve Moravian
Indians of Pilgerruh, including "Luke and his family" went to live "among
the savages" at Pettquotting.[87] But by November, 1786 "all the Indians"
(Munsees) at Pettquotting had "moved thence"[88] --probably to join forces
with other Munsees living in a town in the Sandusky River region, some

246

---

84. Bliss, ed., Zeisberger's Diary, vol. 1, p. 275; Dft. Ex. A-247.

85. Bliss, ed., Zeisberger's Diary, vol. 1, pp. 285, 330; Dft.
Ex. A-247.

86. Bliss, ed., Zeisberger's Diary, vol. 1, pp. 281, 286, 288,
290, 293, 295, 300, 310; Dft. Ex. A-247.

87. Bliss, ed., Zeisberger's Diary, vol. 1, pp. 305, 315-316;
Dft. Ex. A-247.

88. Bliss, ed., Zeisberger's Diary, vol. 1, p. 310; Dft. Ex.
A-247.

20 miles west of Area 53.[89]

Another group of Munsees were on lower Huron River in May, 1787, however. These Munsees derived from a town on Tschiaque (Chatauqua?) Creek "a day's journey from the Cuyahoga eastward." Apparently they stayed at a location on Huron River two and a half miles up from the River's mouth for two years,[90] but by the spring of 1789 were no longer there.[91]

Munsees, however, were not the only Indians who planted on lower Huron River in the spring of 1787. Moravian Indians were there as well. After abandoning Pilgerruh in April 1787 and stopping briefly on the Black River in April-May, 1787 the Moravian congregation proceeded farther west, into the western half of Area 53, and in May, 1787 built a town on the east bank of Huron River at some "old fields" five and a half miles up the river from its mouth, near present Milan, Erie County, Ohio in western Area 53. This town was occupied by Moravian Indians from the middle of May, 1787 to the middle of April, 1791 and was known var-

247

---

89. The Munsee town at Sandusky, west of Area 53 had as its "captain and head man" one Titawachkim. Luke, the Moravian Indian who moved to Pettquotting in October, 1786 was, by 1787, closely associated with Titawachkam (Bliss, ed., Zeisberger's Diary, vol. 1, pp. 301, 335-336, 342; Dft. Ex. A-247. Zeisberger to Ettwein, Huron River, October 1, 1787, p. 1; Dft. Ex. A-277).

90. Bliss, ed., Zeisberger's Diary, vol. 1, pp. 345, 349, 385; Dft. Ex. A-247. In the Original Diary the name of the creek the Munsees had had their town on is unmistakably "Tschiaque" and not "Tschinque," as Bliss records it (Zeisberger, Original Diary and Schwarze Translation, entry for May 19, 1787; Dft. Ex. A-270).

91. Heckewelder, who went down the lower Huron River to its mouth in May, 1789, describes the towns he saw, but does not mention any Munsee town on the River at that time (Wallace, ed., Thirty Thousand Miles, p. 249; Dft. Ex. A-157).

iously as "Pettquotting, after a high round hill" five miles distant, or as "Salem" or "New Salem."[92]

Growth of the Indian population of New Salem was rapid. In December, 1787 it contained 123 persons (mainly Delawares and Munsees); by December, 1788, 164 persons; by December, 1789, 184 persons.[93] In March, 1790 Zeisberger observes:

> Our town grows so large and full as we
> have had nowhere else, so that we wish a chance
> to lay out another settlement, only as yet we
> know not where.[94]

In September of the same year Zeisberger again comments on the size of New Salem, "the like of which is not to be found among the [surrounding] Indians."[95] By the end of 1790 the town had a total population of 212 inhabitants, and its Indian population was becoming more and more mixed. In 1787 and 1788, for example, a Wyandot chief from Detroit and a "Mingo Mohawk" had expressed their desire to live with the Moravian Indians; in

248

92. Wallace, ed., Thirty Thousand Miles, pp. 248-249; Dft. Ex. A-167. Bliss, ed., Zeisberger's Diary, vol. 1, pp. 341-343; Dft. Ex. A-247. Ibid., vol. 2, pp. 105, 172-173, 238, 239; Dft. Ex. A-248. See also Heckewelder, Map; Dft. Ex. A-166 and Ontario History, vol. 49, pp. 81-82; Dft. Ex. A-269. In an anonymous "Journal of a Survey of the South Shore of Lake Erie made in 1789" a surveyor states that "the village [New Salem]" was "about 7 miles up the [Huron] river on a rising ground. They have in the village 3 priests [Moravian missionaries]" (Journal, p. 374; Dft. Ex. A-287).

93. Bliss, ed., Zeisberger's Diary, vol. 1, pp. 386, 464; Dft. Ex. A-247. Ibid., vol. 2, pp. 73-74; Dft. Ex. A-248. Zeisberger to Ettwein, Huron River, October 1, 1787, p. 1; Dft. Ex. A-277. A surveyor notes that the "Delaware Village" above the mouth of Huron contained "about 200 souls" in 1789 (Ford and McNiff, A Survey...taken in 1789; sheet no. 2; Dft. Ex. A-288).

94. Bliss, ed., Zeisberger's Diary, vol. 2, p. 99; Dft. Ex. A-248.

95. Bliss, ed., Zeisberger's Diary, vol. 2, p. 127; Dft. Ex. A-248.

1790 a Chippewa woman came to live at New Salem; and in 1791 a Mohican
Indian "from over the lake [Erie]" and a Mohawk woman, Mary Montour,
were granted permission to live there.[96]

The Moravian missionary Heckewelder gives a good general description of natural resources and lacks in the Huron River region as
of 1789, when he visited New Salem:

> Sugar trees, ginseng & deer are scarce in
> this vicinity. They [the Indians] trap many
> raccoons and also beaver & otter here. There
> are bears, too, and many bees in the woods.
> There are plenty of fish in the [Huron] river,
> especially very large catfish, and at times
> there are many geese & ducks. The [Moravian]
> Indians have horses, cattle, chickens & many
> pigs. They can live well if they plant enough.[97]

Zeisberger also frequently refers to food-gathering activities of
the Moravian Indians at New Salem. On June 26, 1787 he notes:

> Some sisters went to the lake [Erie] along
> the shore to seek some necessities for their
> labor, as also turtles' eggs, of which they
> have often brought home many hundreds and thou-
> sands, which for them is good food.[98]

A few days later Zeisberger observes:

> Some brethren...who were up the creek [Huron
> River] hunting came home..They brought honey
> and meat home.[99]

249

---

96. Zeisberger to Ettwein, Huron River, June 15, 1787, pp. 1-2;
Dft. Ex. A-278. Bliss, ed., Zeisberger's Diary, vol. 1, pp. 349,351,
404; Dft. Ex. A-247. Ibid., vol. 2, pp. 106, 147-149, 156-157; Dft.
Ex. A-248.
     Mary Montour's son, John Cook, was already at New Salem when
his mother asked permission to live there. Zeisberger remarks, "if more
[Iroquois] come, we must think about laying out a Mingo town."

97. Wallace, ed., Thirty Thousand Miles, p. 249; Dft. Ex. A-167.

98. Bliss, ed., Zeisberger's Diary, vol. I, p. 352; Dft. Ex. A-247.

99. Bliss, ed., Zeisberger's Diary, vol. 1, p. 353; Dft. Ex. A-247.

In January, 1788 Moravian Indian men again left the town to hunt bear and
to search for places for sugar-making. The latter were not to be found
"less than ten or twelve miles" from New Salem, the most distant locations
being all of 20 miles from the town.[100]

At the end of July, 1788, before the corn was ripe, Zeisberger notes:

> As our Indians have little to eat, they go
> industriously to the whortleberries [blue-
> berries] which are a great help for them;
> some take their children there for food,
> where they can eat their fill and have much
> pleasure too.[101]

In April, 1790 Moravian Indian women were busy digging wild potatoes near
New Salem, and in June of that year Zeisberger records that:

> Our brethren industriously brought roots
> here from down the creek [Huron River], of
> which they got many loads to town, which
> they cut thin, dry in the sun, pound and
> bake bread from, and this is now their
> principal food.[102]

250

The Moravian Indians occupied New Salem until April 14, 1791, when
they abandoned the town because of impending Indian-American hostilities.[103]
In either 1791 or 1792 "pagan" Munsees burnt all except two of the houses
of New Salem, and established a town two miles farther up the Huron River.

100. Bliss, ed., Zeisberger's Diary, vol. 1, p. 389; Dft. Ex. A-247.
Ibid., vol. 2, pp. 91-92; Dft. Ex. A-248.

101. Bliss, ed., Zeisberger's Diary, vol. 1, pp. 430, 433; Dft. Ex.
A-247.

102. Bliss, ed., Zeisberger's Diary, vol. 2, pp. 99, 109-110, also
p. 112; Dft. Ex. A-248.
Bliss suggests that the "roots" the men procured may have been
those of the yellow water lily.

103. Bliss, ed., Zeisberger's Diary, vol. 2, pp. 172-173; Dft. Ex.
A-248.

190

This Munsee town continued in existence through 1795.[104] Moravian Indians also continued to hunt in the vicinity of New Salem through 1795.[105]

Besides Munsees and Moravians groups of Chippewas and Delawares also lived on the lower Huron River between 1777-1795. The "old fields" five and a half miles up the Huron from its mouth, which the Moravians began using in May, 1787 and which Zeisberger noted as being in "a solitary place, a wilderness where nobody lived," had been planted by Chippewas the previous year.[106] Zeisberger also frequently refers to Chippewas living in the vicinity of New Salem, 1787-1791,[107] as well as to Chippewas visiting New Salem or hunting near it during these years.[108] The location of a Chippewa village on lower Huron River one and a half miles above the river's mouth, in May, 1789 is pinpointed by Heckewelder, who observes that the Chippewas at this town had "a little land cleared for planting." Heckewelder also saw a mixed village of Chippewas and Delawares at a point about a mile south of Lake Erie, on lower Huron River in May, 1789.[109]

---

104. Ontario History, vol. 49, no. 2, pp. 81-82; Dft. Ex. A-269. Bliss, ed., Zeisberger's Diary, vol. 2, p. 412; Dft. Ex. A-248.

105. Bliss, ed., Zeisberger's Diary, vol. 2, p. 417; Dft. Ex. A-248.

106. Bliss, ed., Zeisberger's Diary, vol. 1, pp. 341-343, 405, 414; Dft. Ex. A-247.

107. Bliss, ed., Zeisberger's Diary, vol. 1, pp. 405, 414, 445; Dft. Ex. A-247. Ibid., vol. 2, pp. 40, 60, 61, 105-106; Dft. Ex. A-248.

108. Bliss, ed., Zeisberger's Diary, vol. 1, pp. 369, 394, 419-420, 434, 439, 440; Dft. Ex. A-247. Ibid., vol. 2, pp. 72-75, 114, 182; Dft. Ex. A-248.

109. Wallace, Thirty Thousand Miles, p. 250; Dft. Ex. A-167.

Attendance of Delawares and Chippewas at services at New Salem in September, 1787, December, 1789 and January, 1790 is noted by Zeisberger;[110] some of these visitors may have been from the mixed Delaware-Chippewa town Heckewelder saw on lower Huron River.

Three Wyandots from Detroit, who had been hunting "in the bush" visited New Salem in June, 1787.[111] It is possible that they had been hunting in western Area 53. Other than this one reference, however, we have not found any specific record of Wyandots either living in or hunting in western Area 53 during the years 1777-1795.

3. Use and Occupancy of Area 54, 1777-1795. There may have been some Delawares in the extreme southeastern tip of Area 54 at Tuscarawas early in 1777. In a message to the pro-American Delawares at Coshocton, sent from Fort Pitt on March 29, 1777, Col. George Morgan, Indian agent 252 and a reliable source wrote that

> some of our Brothers the Delawares who live
> at Tuscarawas cross'd the Ohio to a White
> Man's house opposite Beaver Creek which they
> robb'd to a considerable value--but as the
> Family were from home they committed no Murder--
> On hearing some of our people coming up & it
> being then dark they [the marauders] made off
> in their Canoe with the Goods to the value of
> ----Bucks. I prevented our people from going
> across the River after them...[112]

The next year, in the late fall of 1778, Fort Laurens was built by American forces under Gen. Lachlan McIntosh at Tuscarawas, within south-

---

110. Bliss, ed., Zeisberger's Diary, vol. 1, p. 369; Dft. Ex. A-247. Ibid., vol. 2, pp. 72, 75; Dft. Ex. A-248.

111. Bliss, ed., Zeisberger's Diary, vol. 1, p. 349; Dft. Ex. A-247.

112. Morgan, Message to the Brethren the Delawares...March 29, 1777, p. 1; Dft. Ex. A-213. The mouth of Beaver Creek is some 55 miles due east from "Tuscarawas."

eastern Area 54. "Indians," to the number of a hundred or more men and women, visited the Fort while it was being constructed, but the accounts of several members of McIntosh's force do not mention the existence of any Indian village at or close to Tuscarawas.[113] Late in February, 1779, after Fort Laurens was completed it was besieged by 180 Indians coming from a distance; these included Wyandots, Mingos, Munsees and four Delawares. Later it was again besieged by Indians from elsewhere.[114] The Fort was finally evacuated by the Americans in August, 1779 as being too far advanced on the western frontier to supply and defend.[115]

Ephraim Douglass, a former Indian trader who was sent to the Ohio country by the Continental Congress to treat with various Indian groups in 1783, passed through Tuscarawas on his way westward, but does not mention any Indians being there. However, in 1785 some 20 or 30 Delaware (warriors?) were encamped at Tuscarawas, and in the early summer of 1786 some Cherokees and Shawnees killed four White men at Tuscarawas.[116] In

253

---

113. Collections of the State Historical Society of Wisconsin, vol. 23, pp. 157, 160, 162, 163; Dft. Ex. A-225. For the location of the Fort see Heckewelder, Map...1796; Dft. Ex. A-166.

114. Collections of the State Historical Society of Wisconsin, vol. 23, pp. 241-243, 343-344; Dft. Ex. A-225.

115. Collections of the State Historical Society of Wisconsin, vol. 24, pp.   39-40; Dft. Ex. A-226.

116. Magazine of History, No. 10, p. 40; Dft. Ex. A-156. Bliss, ed., Zeisberger's Diary, vol. 1, p. 156, fn. 1; Dft. Ex. A-247. W. H. Smith, Life...of Arthur St. Clair, vol. 2, p. 17, fn. 1; Dft. Ex. A-283. Bushnell, Journal, p. 263; Dft. Ex. A-310. The Delawares at Tuscarawas in 1785 were a group under Wingemund, a noted Delaware war chief (Draper Ms. 15S26-27; Dft. Ex. A-279).

September, 1786 and again in July, 1787 some Moravian Christian Indians hunted "in Tuscarawas, where they...had very good luck."[117] Other "Indians" were also hunting there at the latter date; in August, 1787 Zeisberger noted that "many strange Indians came [to the Moravian town of New Salem] out of the bush from their hunting in the Tuscarawas and the Muskingum." In May, 1789, Heckewelder passed near Tuscarawas, but does not mention Indians being there. However, in 1791, Zeisberger reported "Indians" hunting "on the Tuscarawas [River]," or arriving at New Salem "From Tuscarawas."[118]

On a map drawn by Heckewelder in 1796 "Tuscarawas" is legended as a location, only, at the junction of the "Muskingum [Tuscarawas] River" and Sandy Creek. No Indian towns are indicated on Heckewelder's map, along that stretch of the Tuscarawas River which forms the eastern boundary of Area 54, north of "Tuscarawas."[119]

254

So much for the eastern part of Area 54. We now turn to use and occupancy of the western half of Area 54 between 1777 and 1795.

Three or four Indian towns and one or two camps can be located with reasonable certainty as having existed for various lengths of time in the western half of Area 54 during the period 1777-1795.

It will be recalled that after the village of Hell Town in southwestern Area 54, on the Clear Fork of the Mohican River in present Ashland County, Ohio, had been abandoned by its Mingo population in 1775,

---

117. Bliss, ed., Zeisberger's Diary, vol. 1, pp. 293, 357; Dft. Ex. A-247.

118. Bliss, ed., Zeisberger's Diary, vol. 2, pp. 166, 167; Dft. Ex. A-248. Wallace, Thirty Thousand Miles, p. 246; Dft. Ex. A-167.

119. Heckewelder, Map...1796; Dft. Ex. A-166.

194

the Wyandots of Sandusky extended an invitation to the Delawares and Munsees of Coshocton to move northward.[120] In 1777 some 30 Munsee men and
their families "separated themselves" from the Delawares at Coshocton and
"moved about 30 miles higher up [north] towards the Wyandots."[121] This
virtually pinpoints these Munsees at Hell Town, which was some 30 miles
northeast of Coshocton, midway between Coshocton and the Wyandot town
of Sandusky. In June, 1778 three "Delawares" who were probably from
Hell Town attended a large council at Detroit. One of them, "Capt.
James," a war chief, promised to fight the Americans and stated he
could answer for 60 men (Delawares and Munsees?) in his village.
That same year Thomas Green, a Connecticut Tory, came to live at
Hell Town.[122]

Four years later, in the early spring of 1782, the inhabitants
of Hell Town or "Old Town" as it came to be known, fled to Sandusky.[123]
In June, 1782 Hell Town is expressly noted as a deserted, but beautiful

255

120. See Chapter III, p. 154, and fn. 168, this Report.

121. Collections of the State Historical Society of Wisconsin, vol.
23, p. 133; Dft. Ex. A-225. Account of a Meeting...April 26, 1778, pp.
1, 2; Dft. Ex. A-239. Collections of the State Historical Society of
Wisconsin, vol. 24, p. 55 and fn. 6; Dft. Ex. A-226. Bliss, ed.,
Zeisberger's Diary, vol. 1, p. 18; Dft. Ex. A-247.

122. Hamilton, Council Held at Detroit, June 14, 1778, pp. 443,
446, 449-452; Dft. Ex. A-237. Collections of the State Historical Society
of Wisconsin, vol. 23, p. 133; Dft. Ex. A-225. Hill, History of Ashland
County, pp. 34-35; Dft. Ex. A-244. Howe, Historical Collections, vol.
1, pp. 255-256; Dft. Ex. A-191. Baughman, History of Richland County,
p. 28; Dft. Ex. A-157. Baughman, History of Ashland County, pp. 21,
22, 24; Dft. Ex. A-158. Duff, History, p. 51; Dft. Ex. A-238.

123. Draper Ms. 16S289, 291; Dft. Ex. A-268. Collections of the
State Historical Society of Wisconsin, vol. 24, p. 152; Dft. Ex. A-266.
Hill, History of Ashland County, pp. 34-35; Dft. Ex. A-244. Howe,
Historical Collections, vol. 1, pp. 255-256; Dft. Ex. A-191.

natural site, close to a "large Indian trail."[124] In 1783 and again in
1789 it is also noted as deserted,[125] but according to the historian William
A. Duff it was used up to 1812 as a campsite by the "Delawares" after they
abandoned the town.[126]

The Indians of Hell Town did not stay long at Sandusky. In 1783,
with a Delaware chief named Thomas Armstrong, and with some Mingoes and
Mohawks, they established a town called "Greentown," in western Area 54.
This new town was five miles northeast of former Hell Town, on the Black
Fork of the Mohican River, two and a half miles north of present Perrys-
ville, in southern Ashland County[127] (see Fig. 6, facing p. 217, this
Report).

124. Pennsylvania Magazine of History and Biography, vol. 18, no.
2, 1894, pp. 144-145; Dft. Ex. A-154. Butterfield, Historical Account,
pp. 142-143, 147-148; Dft. Ex. A-155.
We locate Hell Town at or near the former White village of Newville, now part of the Pleasant Hill Reservoir (see Baughman, History of
Richland County, pp. 28, 425-426; Dft. Ex. A-157).
Duff states Hell Town was abandoned after the massacre early in
1782 of over 90 Moravian Indians at Gnadenhutten, a Moravian town on the
Tuscarawas River some 24 miles south of Area 54, by Pennsylvania militia
(Duff, History, p. 51; Dft. Ex. A-238. Transactions of the Moravian His-
torical Society, vol. 12, pp. 361-364; Dft. Ex. A-35). Duff is probably
correct. Another historian, Henry Howe, is in error in writing that the
Indians of Hell Town deserted their town because of Col. William Crawford's
expedition against Sandusky in June, 1782. When Crawford reached Hell
Town, on his way to Sandusky, the town had already been deserted (Howe,
Historical Collections, vol. 1, p. 256; Dft. Ex. A-191. Pennsylvania Magazine of History and Biography, vol. 18, no. 2, 1894, pp. 144-146; Dft.
Ex. A-154).

125. Magazine of History, no. 10, p. 41; Dft. Ex. A-156. Wallace,
Thirty Thousand Miles, p. 247; Dft. Ex. A-167.

126. Duff, History, p. 51; Dft. Ex. A-238.

127. Hill, History of Ashland County, pp. 34-35; Dft. Ex. A-244.
Baughman, History of Richland County, pp. 9, 28; Dft. Ex. A-157. Baughman,
History of Ashland County, pp. 23-25, 52; Dft. Ex. A-158. Duff, History,
p. 51; Dft. Ex. A-238. Howe, Historical Collections, vol. 1, p. 256; Dft.
Ex. A-191. Howe, Historical Collections, vol. 2, p. 475; Dft. Ex. A-192.
Greentown was named for Thomas Green, the Connecticut Tory who
had joined the Munsees at Hell Town in 1778 (Hill, History of Ashland
County, pp. 34-35; Dft. Ex. A-244).

Greentown was continuously occupied from 1783 to 1812. Until 1795 it was a station for captives being taken north to Detroit. Although referred to as a "Delaware" or "Delaware and Mingo" town[128] it was probably, as we have seen, a mixed Munsee-Delaware-Mingo-Mohawk town. Its population has been estimated by a local historian as averaging around 300 Indians.[129]

Darby's Town, the small Mingo town in extreme western Area 54 to which reference has already been made,[130] continued in existence in the late 1770's,[131] but by June 3, 1782 when Col. Crawford's expedition passed through Darby's Town one of Crawford's officers noted that "Drs Town," as he refers to it, had been evacuated for "some time."[132]

There were, however, some Delaware Indians very near Darby's Town early in June, 1782. According to the historian Consul W. Butterfield, a small Delaware group under Wingenund, a Delaware war chief,[133] was tem-

128. Baughman, History of Ashland County, pp. 22-24; Dft. Ex. A-158.

Howe, Historical Collections, vol. 1, p. 256; Dft. Ex. A-191. Hill, History of Ashland County, pp. 34-35; Dft. Ex. A-244.

129. Baughman, History of Ashland County, p. 23; Dft. Ex. A-158.

130. See Chapter III, p. 153, this Report.

131. Ethnohistory, vol. 6, p. 72; Dft. Ex. A-153.

132. Pennsylvania Magazine of History and Biography, vol. 18, no. 2, 1894, p. 147; Dft. Ex. A-154.

133. Heckewelder, Names, p. 395; Dft. Ex. A-161. Thwaites and Kellogg, Revolution, p. 46, fn. 75; Dft. Ex. A-177. After Capt. Pipe, Delaware chief, removed from Cuyahoga to the vicinity of Upper Sandusky in 1779 he and Wingenund were closely associated. In October, 1781 Zeisberger passed through "Pipe and Winginund's town" on his way
(cont'd. on p. 197)

porarily encamped at this time at a location "about two miles in a north-west direction from the present village of Crestline, in Crawford county," and "about three-fourths of a mile northeast of the present town of Lees-ville," Crawford County. This was in extreme western Area 54. "Crawford and his men," Butterfield states, "passed to the south of, but very near, this camp, on the 2d of June [1782], without discovering it."[134] This statement of Butterfield's is confirmed by one of Crawford's officers who noted that on June 2, 1782, when Crawford's expedition was encamped five miles from Darby's Town, "several children's & other tracks" were discovered. Crawford mistakenly supposed that these tracks had been made by Indians living at Darby's Town, not knowing until the next day that Darby's Town had been evacuated.[135]

According to an oral account given in 1860 to the historian Lyman C. Draper by the daughter of a former White captive, there was also, in 1780, a town or encampment known as "Snip's Town," at the uppermost forks of Black Creek, half a mile or so south of present Rome, Richland County, in western Area 54.[136] Snip was a well-known Wyandot war chief of the

258

(fn. 133. cont'd.) north from Upper Sandusky to Detroit (Bliss, ed., Zeisberger's Diary, vol. 1, pp. 29-30; Dft. Ex. A-247. See also Collections of the State Historical Society of Wisconsin, vol. 24, pp. 97, 217, 219; Dft. Ex. A-226, and Heckewelder, Narrative, p. 236; Dft. Ex. A-53).

134. Butterfield, Historical Account, pp. 168, 316-317; Dft. Ex. A-155. See also Brackenridge, Narratives of...Dr. Knight and John Slover, pp. 18-19; Dft. Ex. A-240.

135. Pennsylvania Magazine of History and Biography, vol. 18, no. 2, 1894, p. 147; Dft. Ex. A-154.

136. Collections of the State Historical Society of Wisconsin, vol. 24, pp. 151-152; Dft. Ex. A-226. Draper Mss. 16S289, 291; Dft. Ex. A-268. Wallace, Thirty Thousand Miles, pp. 244, 247; Dft. Ex. A-167.

1770's-1780's,[137] and the war party that stopped at his town with captives in 1780 consisted of Wyandots; hence we identify Snip's Town as a Wyandot town. In all probability, Snip's Town was established at the location mentioned above after June, 1778, since at a council held at Detroit June 14-18, 1778 Snip referred to himself and his people as "we who inhabit the little Scioto" and stated that he came "from the town situated between the two Creeks."[138]

As late as 1783 the site of the former Mohican John's Town, on the Jerome Fork of the Mohican River in present Ashland County, was a deserted site.[139] Travellers who camped overnight at "Moheeking John's Town, a place well known to the traders" on July 11, 1783 noted that they had as their companions there "a large swarm of Bees."[140]

4. Summary and Conclusions on Use and Occupancy of Areas 53 and 54, 1777-1795. Between the years 1777 and 1795 Delawares, Munsees, Mingos,

---

137. The historians Reuben Gold Thwaites and Louise Phelps Kellogg identify Snip as a Shawnee war chief (Collections of the State Historical Society of Wisconsin, vol. 24, p. 152, fn. 1; Dft. Ex. A-226). However, Snip is identified as a Wyandot war chief by the Wyandot chief Half-King and by Richard Butler, trader and Indian agent at Fort Pitt, in 1775 (Butler, Journal, August-September 1775, pp. 8-9, 14, 25; Dft. Ex. A-160)-- also by Lt. Gov. Henry Hamilton, in 1778 (Hamilton, Council Held at Detroit June 14 1778, p. 450; Dft. Ex. A-237)--and by the Moravian missionary John Heckewelder, writing in 1820 of events that occurred in 1781 (Heckewelder, Narrative, p. 254; Dft. Ex. A-53).

138. Hamilton, Council Held at Detroit, June 14, 1778, p. 450; Dft. Ex. A-237.
The Little Scioto River heads near present Bucyrus, Crawford County, six miles west of Area 54, and runs a southwesterly course parallel to the southwesterly course of the upper Sandusky River for some 10 miles, through southwestern Crawford County. Snip's locale in 1778 may have been between these "two Creeks," west of Area 54.

139. See Chapter III, p. 105 and fn. 21; also pp. 129-130, 133-134, this Report.

140. The Magazine of History, extra no. 10, p. 41; Dft. Ex. A-156.

Chippewas, Ottawas and Moravian Indian converts used and/or occupied the
Cuyahoga region of eastern Area 53 for varying lengths of time. Munsees
and Delawares of the Wolf division under Capt. Pipe had a "large" town
on the west side of the Cuyahoga River in extreme eastern Area 53 from
1777 until early in 1779. Moravian Indian converts, chiefly Delawares
and Munsees together with a few-Mohicans and Nanticokes, to the number of
100 or so, also had an encampment for 10 months on the east side of the
Cuyahoga near the outlet of Tinker's Creek, and planted on the west side
of the River within Area 53, between June, 1786 and April, 1787. Throughout the period 1777-1795 Chippewas and Ottawas from towns north of Lake
Erie crossed the lake in the fall to spend the winter and early spring
months of each year hunting and making maple sugar in the general region
of the Cuyahoga River. Three hunting camps of Chippewas, located
on the Cuyahoga River, in eastern Area 53, are specifically noted in 1789,
and in 1787 some Moravian Indian converts encountered a hunting party of
Ottawas on the headwaters of Black River, west of the Cuyahoga in Area 53.

260

The western half of Area 53 presents the same picture of fluctuating
and/or mixed occupancy during the period under consideration. For the
Bass Islands and Kelley's Island in extreme northwestern Area 53 we have
been unable to find any record of use or occupancy, except that in 1786
Moravian Indian converts encamped and hunted on Middle and South Bass
Islands for a few weeks and later, in 1787-1791, went to these Islands to
gather ginseng. Farther south, on the southeastern shore of Sandusky Bay
in northwestern Area 53, two bands of Ottawas from Detroit settled at and
near the present city of Sandusky, Erie County, and lived there from 1784
until 1811. These Ottawas hunted as far north as the Marblehead Peninsula

in northwestern Area 53. East of the Ottawas at Sandusky, along the south shore of Lake Erie, encampments of Chippewas and some Ottawas at the mouths of the Huron and Vermilion Rivers are noted for the years 1785-1786, 1790,1791. Up the Huron River a few miles from its mouth, in western Area 53 there were, between 1786 and 1791, two Munsee towns, a Moravian Indian town consisting of Delawares, Munsees, and a few Mingoes, Mohawks and Mohicans, and a mixed Delaware-Chippewa town. After 1791, when the Moravian Indian converts abandoned their town on the lower Huron River, there was a "pagan" Munsee town two miles above the former Moravian settlement; this Munsee town continued in existence for at least seven years after it was established.

In Area 54, during the years 1777-1795 native use and occupancy was almost as diverse as it was in Area 53. Small groups of Delawares are mentioned as living, or being "at Tuscarawas" in the extreme southeastern tip of Area 54 in 1777 and again in 1785. In 1786-1791 Tuscarawas is noted in several sources as a popular hunting region for "Indians," including Moravian Indian converts.

Farther west in Area 54 some Munsees, plus some Delawares, moved north in 1777 (and 1778?) to the site of the former Mingo village of Hell Town on the Clear Fork of the Mohican River in western Area 54. There these Indians stayed until 1782. In 1783 they re-established themselves, together with some Mingoes and Mohawks, in western Area 54, at a new site called Greentown, five miles northeast of Hell Town on the Black Fork of the Mohican River. Greentown, with a mixed, anti-American population, continued in existence from 1783 through 1795.

There was also, between the years 1777 and 1782, a small Mingo town known as Darby's Town in extreme western Area 54. In addition, there was in 1780 a Wyandot town or encampment known as "Snip's Town" in northwestern Area 54, and a Delaware encampment close to the site of Darby's Town in the year 1782. Mohican John's Town in central Area 54, which had been abandoned in 1764, was still in 1783 apparently a deserted site, although it was a location well known to traders.

Our conclusions are, that during the period 1777-1795 any Indians who found it expedient either to use and/or occupy Area 53 or 54 were free to do so. Chippewas and Ottawas from the Detroit region crossed Lake Erie and streamed up the rivers of Area 53 to hunt during the winter, to make maple sugar in early spring, and to encamp in late spring on the southern shore of the Lake or, if they chose, to settle in semi-permanent towns there. Munsees drifted into Area 53 from the east to establish either temporary or semi-permanent settlements at favorable locations, such as the lower Huron River. Even the Moravian Christian Indians, a mixed group, ultimately settled for varying lengths of time in Area 53, despite pressure brought to bear on them by Delawares and Wyandots to locate in the Sandusky region west of Area 53.

The same condition held true for Area 54 during the period 1777-1795. Small groups of Delawares lived at Tuscarawas during part of this period, but other Indians, as well, hunted in the region. Farther west, in central and western Area 54 Mingos, Delawares, Munsees and Wyandots had either - settlements or temporary camps for varying lengths of time between the years 1777 and 1795.

Two conclusions can be drawn regarding the native towns located within Areas 53 and 54 during the period 1777-1795. One is that none of these towns existed throughout the entire period. The only possible exception

202

to this is the essential continuity from 1777-1795 of the Hell Town-
Greentown population in western Area 54. The Munsee-Delaware group
that occupied Hell Town from 1777-to 1782, also subsequently -- augmented
by some Mingoes and Mohawks -- occupied Greentown, five miles northeast of Hell Town, from 1783 up to 1812.

Our second conclusion regarding the towns in Areas 53 and 54
during the period 1777-1795 is that Indians belonging to different
ethnic groups often lived in towns either adjacent to each other
(1-10 miles), or in the same town. This was especially true in Area
53, but also held to a certain extent in Area 54.

264

Chapter V

Use and Occupancy of Areas 53 and 54: 1796-April 24, 1806

1. Use and Occupancy of the Eastern Half of Area 53, 1796-1806.

In the summer of 1796 Gen. Moses Cleaveland, agent for the Connecticut
Land Company, negotiated with the Seneca Indians at Buffalo Creek in
western New York and met with some Missisauga Chippewas at Conneaut in
extreme northeastern Ohio, relative to lands east of Area 53. At Conneaut Creek Cleaveland was told that there were a few "Mississagos"...
"on the Cuyahogo."[1] In the summer of 1796, and again in 1797, the Conn-
necticut Land Company sent out surveying parties to lay out townships
east of Area 53, and to plat a "capital city" (present Cleveland, Ohio)
for the "State of New Connecticut" on the east bank of Cuyahoga River
at its mouth.[2]

Thus we learn that in September, 1796 a party of surveyors, upon
entering the mouth of Cuyahoga River, met "Indians, from Grand River,
who had been west hunting;" these were Senecas.[3] Chippewas and Ottawas

265

---

1. Whittlesey, Early History of Cleveland, pp. 187-188, 175-179,
181-184; Dft. Ex. A-78. Cleaveland to Phelps, Fort Independence alias
Conneaut Creek, July 5, 1796; Dft. Ex. A-140.

2. Benton, ed., Journals of Seth Pease, p. 29; Dft. Ex. A-291.
Whittlesey, Early History of Cleveland, pp. 188-189, 242, 253, 261,
275-276, 281, 338; Dft. Ex. A-78.

3. Grand River flows through northeastern Ohio to enter Lake Erie
27 miles northeast of Cleveland, at present Fairport, Lake County, Ohio.
(Con't. on p. 204)

were also on Cuyahoga River. Edward Paine, a trader who lived at the
mouth of Cuyahoga during the winter of 1796-1797, [4] wrote in 1843 that

> ...About 150 Indian Warriors and their
> families, mostly Chipewas and Ottowas,
> made their first hunting campaign after
> the peace at Greenville, on the waters of
> the Cuyahoga, scattered along on both
> banks of that river from its mouth to its
> source in the winter of '96-7. [5]

There were also "Indians" quartered at the mouth of Cuyahoga during
that winter, who constituted "by far the most numerous part" of the
population there at the time. [6]

In June, 1797 Amzi Atwater, surveyor for the Connecticut Land
Company, set up a "stores or Headquarters" on Cuyahoga River, about
a half mile above (south of) the junction of Cuyahoga and Little
Cuyahoga, on the southeastern boundary of Area 53. Seth Pease, principal
surveyor, often visited Atwater's storehouse. Both Pease and Atwater
mention that two or more "Indian hunters" were then encamped "some distance" to the north, on or near Cuyahoga River. One Indian, who spoke
a little English, frequently visited the surveyors' camp. Pease gives

266

(fn. 3 cont'd.) The Senecas from Grand River encountered by the surveyors
were living, ca. 1790 and 1796 at "Charage" (present Painesville, Lake
County, Ohio) some three miles south of the mouth of Grand River. No Indians
besides these "few families of Senecas" at Grand River, and "about 15 families" of Missisauga Chippewas at Conneaut Creek "resided on the Reserve
E. of Cuyahoga river" in 1796, according to Amzi Atwater, surveyor (Atwater
to Seaward, Mantua, Feb. 26, 1828; Dft. Ex. A-311. Whittlesey, Early History
of Cleveland, pp. 221, 244; Dft. Ex. A-78. Kent and Deardorff, John Adlum,
pp. 265, 282 and Map, p. 283; Dft. Ex. A-293).

4. Whittlesey, Early History of Cleveland, pp. 252-253; Dft. Ex. A-78.

5. Paine, Settlement of the Western Reserve, p. 6; Dft. Ex. A-312.

6. Whittlesey, Early History of Cleveland, p. 253; Dft. Ex. A-78.

this Indian's name as "Pontiock" or "Ponteeock," and states that among
the rivers Pontiock "marked out [mapped]" was one he called "Tuskenonut
[Tuscarawas]."[7] Since the Wyandot name for Tuscarawas River was "Tuscar-
abi," and the Delaware name for it was "Tuscalawi,"[8] we conclude that
Pontiock was neither a Wyandot nor a Delaware speaker. From his Indian
name, which may or may not have been identical with that of the celebrated
Ottawa war chief Pontiac, it may be that "Pontiock" was an Ottawa. If
this is correct there was, then, in the summer of 1797 a small (?)[9]
encampment of Ottawas at or near the Cuyahoga and in or very close to
eastern Area 53, "some distance" north of that point where the Cuyahoga
turns north to flow into Lake Erie.

Another Connecticut Land Company surveyor, Moses Warren, was at
"Tuscarawa landing" at the south end of the Cuyahoga-Tuscarawas portage,
on the southeastern boundary of Area 53 in July, 1797. There Warren
found "many Indian camps."[10] Whether these camps were occupied Warren
does not state, but a year later, near the end of September, 1798 Moravian
missionaries found a family of friendly Tuscaroras encamped at the same

---

7. Benton, ed., Journals of Seth Pease, pp. 76, 79-82, 88-89;
Dft. Ex. A-291. Whittlesey, Early History of Cleveland, pp. 275-276, 293,
297-300; Dft. Ex. A-78.

8. Ontario History, vol. 49, p. 91; Dft. Ex. A-269.

9. Neither Pease nor Atwater seems to have visited Pontiock's camp.
Atwater states that "two or more Indian hunters" were encamped; Pease
mentions that Pontiock's father was with him, and also refers to a visit
Pontiock paid to the surveyors' camp, accompanied by "2 other Indians--&
a Squaw & 3 papooses."

10. Whittlesey, Early History of Cleveland, pp. 275, 289, 291;
Dft. Ex. A-78.

locale, in extreme southeastern Area 53.[11]

There is some measure of agreement, in both general and particular accounts by early settlers of northeastern Ohio, by members of the Connecticut Land Company's surveying parties, and by early local historians, that Ottawas, Chippewas, Delawares, and Senecas used the Cuyahoga River and adjacent regions as hunting grounds, particularly during the winter seasons of 1796-1806. We have already quoted Paine's statement for 1796-1797. A more general statement, written in the mid-19th century by Judge John Barr, Cleveland historian, reads in part as follows:

> In the fall [of 1796 and subsequent years] the Senecas, Ottawas, Delawares and Chippewas resorted here [Cleveland]; and having procured what articles the traders had for them, dispersed to hunt through the winter, on the Cuyahoga, the Grand River,[12] Mahoning,[12] Tuscarawas,[13] Killbuck,[14] and Black[15] rivers.

---

11. Ontario History, vol. 49, pp. 90-92; Dft. Ex. A-269.
  The Tuscaroras were Iroquoian-speaking Indians who, during the early 18th century, began removing from North Carolina to join the Five Nations Iroquois in New York State. At the end of the 18th century the pro-American Tuscaroras were granted their present reservation in extreme western New York, two miles or so north of present Niagara Falls, New York, while those who had been pro-British during the Revolution were granted lands in severalty on Grand River Reserve, Ontario (Hodge, ed., Handbook, pt. 2, pp. 842, 846, 848-849; Dft. Ex. A-2).

12. For Grand River see fn. 3, this Chapter.
  The Mahoning, like the Grand River, is in extreme northeastern Ohio, east of Area 53. The Mahoning, however, flows southward into Beaver Creek, a tributary of the Ohio River, whereas the Grand River empties into Lake Erie.

13. The upper Tuscarawas bounds Area 54 on the east. The lower Tuscarawas is south of Area 54.

14. Killbuck Creek flows southward through eastern Area 54 to join the Walhonding River some six miles northwest of present Coshocton, Ohio, 25 miles or so south of eastern Area 54.

15. The Black River heads in eastern Area 53 and flows northward into Lake Erie.

In the spring they returned with their furs and
game, and after trafficking away their stock,
launched their bark canoes to repair to Sandusky
plains.[16] and the Miami prairies[17] for the summer...

While here [at present Cleveland] the Senecas
encamped at the foot of the bluff, between Vine-
yard and Superior lanes [on the east side of the
Cuyahoga]. On the west side were the Ottawas,
Delawares and Chippewas.[18]

Barr notes that in the winter of 1796-1797, among the "friendly Indians"

who supplied the first settlers at Cleveland with game were:

'OGONCE' or OGONTZ, an Ottawa; SAGAMAW, a Chippewa,
and SENECA, of the Seneca nation; all chiefs of
their respective tribes.
......

SENECA was seen here [Cleveland] in 1809, which
is the last known of him. OGONTZ was at Sandusky
in the year 1811.[19]

During the early 1800's "OGONTZ" hunted, apparently, in and around

present Hudson, Summit County, five miles east of Area 53,[20] but had his

dwelling-place, as already noted, at present Sandusky, Erie County, Ohio,

in western Area 53. A "SAWGAMAW" signed the Treaty of Fort Industry of

July 4, 1805, but as an Ottawa, not a Chippewa (7 Stat. 87:88). SENECA,

who is also often referred to as Stigwanish (var., Stig-y-Nish, Stigonish,

269

---

16. The Sandusky Plains are immediately west of Area 54 and extend
to the general region of present Upper Sandusky, Wyandot County, Ohio.

17. Maumee River region, west of Areas 53 and 54.

18. Whittlesey, Early History of Cleveland, pp. 261-262; Dft.
Ex. A-78. Copies of Historical Manuscripts, pp. 1-5; Dft. Ex. A-318

19. Whittlesey, Early History of Cleveland, p. 262; Dft. Ex. A-78.

20. Bierce, Historical Reminiscences, pp. 86-87; Dft. Ex. A-233.
Sawgamaw was an Ottawa chief who, in the early 1800's wintered with
his band on upper Cuyahoga River near Mantua, Portage Co., Ohio, some
18 miles east of Area 53 (copies of Historical Manuscripts, pp. 1, 3,
5; Dft. Ex. A-318).

208

Stygwanish) "and others of his tribe" certainly frequented the Cuyahoga
region, although one source states that Seneca's "home was in Seneca
County, Ohio," a county immediately west of Area 53.[21]

In August-September, 1798 Br. David Żeisberger and Br. Benjamin
Mortimer, Moravian missionaries, led a party of 33 Moravian Indians
from Fairfield, Ontario, across Lake Erie to the lower Tuscarawas
River region, some 20 miles south of eastern Area 54. On September 9,
1798 the Moravians passed the mouth of Vermilion River in western Area
53, and proceeded eastward "to the Chitquau or Deep river," which we
identify as Black River,[22] a stream in eastern Area 53. At Black River
the missionaries noted that there were "a few families of Mohawks" who
had lately "made a settlement" two miles up Black River from its mouth.[23]

When the Moravians arrived at the mouth of Cuyahoga River on September
11, 1798 they found two large families of New Englanders there, but no
Indians are mentioned. Proceeding southward up the Cuyahoga, the Moravians
passed the deserted site of Pilgerruh on September 17, and on September
19, 1798, farther south, the party

270

---

21. Bierce, Historical Reminiscences, pp. 38-39; Dft. Ex. A-233.
[Tappen] to Barr, Unionville, O., March 16, 1848; Dft. Ex. A-315. Whittlesey, Early History of Cleveland, pp. 416-419; Dft. Ex. A-78.
There were Senecas living in Seneca county, Ohio in the early
1800's; see Hughs, Extracts of a Journal, pp. 1, 5-6; Dft. Ex. A-294.
Scott, A Journal, p. 4; Dft. Ex. A-300.

22. Distances, as well as the group's mode of travelling (see
Ontario History, p. 76; Dft. Ex. A-269) bear out our identification of
"Deep River" as Black River. Also, in an earlier Diary Zeisberger
expressly comments on the depth of present Black River which he fails,
however, to name (Zeisberger Diary, vol. 1, pp. 332, 334; Dft. Ex.
A-247). We are at a loss to explain why Leslie A. Gray, who edited the
Diary of the 1798 trip, identifies Deep River as "Probably the one now
called Cahoon Creek near North Dover" (Ontario History, vol. 49, p. 85,
fn. 75; Dft. Ex. A-269).

23. Ontario History, vol. 49, p. 85; Dft. Ex. A-269.

passed by the so called Old Cayahaga town, which
is a place where the Delaware nation had once
their principal residence... [but] is now [1798]
quite deserted.[24]

After having traversed the Cuyahoga-Tuscarawas portage, which forms

part of the southeastern boundary of Area 53, the Moravians found on

September 22, 1798 "a family of Tuscaroras" encamped in or close to

extreme southeastern Area 53.[25] No other Indian sites, or Indians, are

mentioned as having been encountered by the Moravian group as its members

travelled and hunted along the entire length of the eastern boundary of

Area 53, from the mouth of the Cuyahoga River to the portage. Probably

Indians using the Cuyahoga region for winter hunting had not as yet arrived.

Another possible reason may lie in a general statement made by Gilman

Bryant, an early settler in Cleveland. Bryant states that ca. 1800 and

in subsequent years, as winter approached, the Indians

271

> scattered along the [Cuyahoga] river, from
> five to eight miles apart, as far [upriver]
> as the falls [present Cuyahoga Falls, Summit
> County]; they hauled their canoes above high
> water mark and covered them with bark, and
> went from three to five miles back into the
> woods [emphasis ours.] In the spring, after
> sugar making, they all packed their skins,
> sugar, bear's oil, honey and jerked venison,
> to their crafts. They frequently had to make
> more canoes, either of wood or bark, as the
> increase of their furs, &c., required. They
> would descend the [Cuyahoga] river in April,
> from sixty to eighty families, and encamp on
> the west side of the river for eight or ten
> days, take a drunken scrape and have a feast.

---

24. Ontario History, vol. 49, pp. 87, 90; Dft. Ex. A-269. This
was Capt. Pipe's old town.

25. Ontario History, vol. 49, pp. 90-92; Dft. Ex. A-269.

> I was invited to partake of a white dog...
> They erected a scaffold, and offered a large
> wooden bowlful [of dog soup] to ' Manitou,'
> prayed to him for their safety [in crossing]
> over the lake [Erie], and that they might have
> a good crop of corn, &c.[26]

From Bryant's references to the dog-sacrifice, to "manitou," and to

the prayer for a safe crossing of Lake Erie we conclude that the

Indians he refers to as using the Cuyahoga River region for winter

hunting in the early 19th century were Chippewas and/or Ottawas who lived

north of Lake Erie.

Accounts by several eyewitnesses of the murder of "Menopsy," a

"Chippewa or Ottawa" medicine man, by Big Son [Sun?], a Seneca Indian

and brother to Stigonish or Seneca in 1802 or 1803 at the mouth of

Cuyahoga River, attest to the fact that Senecas, as well as Chippewas

and Ottawas, frequented the Cuyahoga at its mouth. "The Chippewas and

Ottawas were more numerous than the Senecas," it is stated.[27]

The presence "near Cajahaga [Cuyahoga]" of an Ottawa hunting party

during the winter of 1803-1804 is referred to in a Moravian Diary. The

Ottawa party had left Detroit by the end of October, 1803, and was

expected to "return home" from "near Cajahaga" after "the sugar cooking"

was over in the spring of 1804.[28]

In May, 1806 Abraham Tappen, a surveyor, encountered the Seneca

chief, "Seneca" and his family "encamped" on Cuyahoga River at present

Peninsula, Boston Township, Summit County, in extreme eastern Area 53.

---

26. Whittlesey, Early History of Cleveland, pp. 375-376; Dft.
Ex. A-78.

27. Whittlesey, Early History of Cleveland, pp. 391-396; Dft.
Ex. A-78. [Tappen] to Barr, Unionville, O., March 16, 1848; Dft. Ex.
A-315.

28. Oppelt, Diaries, p. 2; Dft. Ex. A-301.

Gen. Lucius V. Bierce of Akron, Ohio, writing in the early 1850's, states that when the first settlers came into Boston Township in March, 1806 Senecas, "under their Chief Stygwanish or Seneca" had a settlement and orchard on the east bank of the Cuyahoga near the north line of Boston Township. The location of this village, as given by Bierce, was four or five river-miles north of the spot where Tappen saw Seneca and his family encamped.[29]

2. Use and Occupancy of the Western Half of Area 53, 1796-1806.

During the summer of 1796 six Moravian Indians from Fairfield, Ontario went to the "Pettquotting" or Huron River of Ohio, in the western half of Area 53, to get whetstones; returning to Fairfield, they reported that all the houses in New Salem, the former Moravian town on Huron River (1787-1791) had been destroyed, and that they "saw only a couple of Indians" there. In the fall of the same year two of the Moravian Indians of Fairfield again went to Huron River, this time to hunt.[30]

273

The pagan Munsees who destroyed New Salem after the Moravians left in 1791 soon afterward established, as already noted, a town of their own on the Huron, seven miles upstream from the river's mouth and two miles above the site of New Salem. This Munsee town on Huron River continued in existence throughout the years 1791/1792-1808.[31] In 1801 the town contained some 30 families "chiefly of the Munsee tribe,"

29. Bierce, Historical Reminiscences, pp. 38-39; Dft. Ex. A-233. [Tappen] to Barr, Unionville, O., March 16, 1848; Dft. Ex. A-315.

30. Bliss, ed., Zeisberger's Diary, vol. 2, pp. 451, 483, 492; Dft. Ex. A-248.

31. Denke, Diary, January-August 31, 1808, p. 9; Dft. Ex. A-306. On April 30, 1808, the chief and all the inhabitants of the town removed to "Sandusky," 20 miles or more west of Area 53.

212

according to a Presbyterian missionary. In 1804 Br. Gottfried
Sebastian Oppelt, Moravian missionary, estimated that "About 100
souls might live there." As Oppelt describes it, "Monsey Town"
extended along Huron River "for about two miles so that the cabins
on both sides of the river are standing wide apart." Most of the
inhabitants had either "been baptized by the [Moravian] brethren"
or had, "at least, lived for a time in the congregation" before
reverting to paganism.[32]

A second Indian town came into existence on the lower Huron
River of Ohio during the latter part of the period 1796-1806. This
town consisted at its founding early in June, 1804, of six families of
Moravian Indians (33 individuals) from the Moravian congregation at
Fairfield, Ontario. The Moravian Indians and their missionary, Br.
Oppelt, settled a few miles above the former New Salem, at or close
to present Milan, Erie County. The site was some ten miles upstream
from the mouth of Huron River, and two miles above "the last house"
in "Monsey Town."[33]

This early 19th-century Moravian Indian town on Huron River existed
from June, 1804 until the end of April, 1809.[34] In December, 1804 it

274

32. Ontario History, vol. 49, pp. 81-83; Dft. Ex. A-269. Hughs,
Extracts of a Journal, pp. 1-2, 8; Dft. Ex. A-294. Oppelt, Diaries,
pp. 11, 12, 67; Dft. Ex. A-301.

33. Oppelt, Diaries, pp. 1, 3-4, 12-13; Dft. Ex. A-301. Firelands
Pioneer, vol. 9, p. 106; Dft. Ex. A-245.

34. Denke, Diary, September 1, 1808-April 25, 1809, pp. 11-13; Dft.
Ex. A-307. Royce, Indian Land Cessions, Ohio 1, locates an "Old Wyandot
Vill. 1807" at Milan. We conclude he is in error, since diarist for the
first Moravian town on Huron River near Milan ("New Salem," 1787-1791;
see pp. 186-191 this Report) and for the second Moravian town at Milan
(1804-1809) do not refer to any Wyandot town on Huron River. Positively,
Moravian diarists recorded much data concerning those Indian towns that
did exist on the Huron in the late 18th and early 19th centuries.

had a population of 46 Indians; at the end of 1805 the number of Indians had increased to 61; by the end of 1806 there were 69 Indians in it.[35] No name was ever given to the town, although Br. Oppelt often requested one; letters from the town bear the address Pettquotting, and Ms. listings at the Moravian Archives in Bethlehem refer to the town as "New Salem, Pettquottink, Second Enterprise."[36]

The Diaries of Br. Oppelt for 1804-1806 at "New Salem...Second Enterprise" contain numerous references to Indians, other than Munsees and Christian Delawares, who also frequented the lower Huron River region in the early 1800's. Most of these references relate to Chippewas,[37] although Oppelt also mentions an Ottawa chief from the Detroit region who was near the mouth of the Huron River early in June, 1804, and "a certain Minque [Mingo], Tawalos, who lives here at the [Huron] river,"

275

---

35. Oppelt, Diaries, pp. 36, 66, 100; Dft. Ex. A-301.

36. Oppelt to Loskiel, Pettquotting, January 8, 1805, p. 3; Dft. Ex. A-302. Oppelt to Loskiel, Pettquotting, June 2, 1805; Dft. Ex. A-303. Oppelt to Loskiel, Pettquotting, February 20, 1806, p. 3: Dft. Ex. A-304.

37. In May, 1804, for example, Chippewas and French traders were "living around" the mouth of Huron River. On June 4, 1804 the Moravian Indians found "many Tschipue [Chippewas]" engaged in a drinking bout on lower Huron River. In April, 1805 "a horde of Tschipues who came from far away"--some 20 men, women, and children, bearing an English flag at their head--performed a begging dance at the Moravian town on the Huron and then "went away again, dancing." On May 1, 1806 Chippewas came back "from their hunting places" and encamped at the mouth of Huron. In August, 1806 Oppelt suspected that Indians seen lurking near the Moravians' fields on Huron River were hungry Chippewas intent on stealing corn. He also deplores the fact that during the years 1804-1806 Chippewas often brought liquor to Huron River to sell to the Indians (Oppelt, Diaries, pp. 11-12, 44-45, 74, 86, 101; Dft. Ex. A-301).

and who visited Oppelt in February, 1805.[38] However, aside from Munsees and Moravian Delawares the Indians who made most use of the Huron River region in the early 1800's were undoubtedly Chippewas, who encamped in the region chiefly during the late spring months. Some Chippewas also seem to have been settled, on a more permanent basis, around the mouth of Huron, where French traders were established.[39]

Hunting was very poor on the lower Huron River in 1804-1806;[40] consequently Moravian Indian hunters usually had to go "far away" or "several days' journey away" from their town to obtain deer and other game,[41] but where they went is not recorded. During the middle of April large fish ran in abundance in Huron River and the Indians secured them in quantity.[42] grew at a distance upstream, Sugar maple trees ~~were suddenly plentiful,~~ and early each spring all the Indians living along the Huron made sugar. Munsee sugar camps were, apparently, located upriver (south) from the Moravian settlement; the

38. Oppelt, Diaries, pp. 11-12, 39; Dft. Ex. A-301.

39. French traders who lived at the mouth of Huron are noticed frequently in Oppelt's Diaries. Three such were a "Mr. Borrel" and his brother (or son?), and a "Mr. Flemming." Borrel, at least, maintained his post at Huron River on a year-round basis during 1804-1806 (Oppelt, Diaries, pp. 11, 15-17, 19, 27, 32-33, 38, 42-43, 46, 54-55, 59, 62, 90, 96; Dft. Ex. A-301).

40. Oppelt, Diaries, pp. 37, 59, 60, 84, 93; Dft. Ex. A-301. Oppelt to Loskiel, Pettquotting, Feb. 10, 1806, pp. 1-4; Dft. Ex. A-304.

41. Oppelt, Diaries, pp. 34, 53, 59; Dft. Ex. A-301. Oppelt to Loskiel, Pettquotting, November 1, 1804, p. 4; Dft. Ex. A-305. Oppelt to Loskiel, Pettquotting, January 8, 1805, p. 3; Dft. Ex. A-302.

42. Oppelt, Diaries, pp. 45, 73; Dft. Ex. A-301.

Christian Indians had their camps anywhere from one to six miles distant from their town. The quantity of sugar the Indians made depended on the weather; too-warm weather caused the sap to flow too quickly.[43]

Other wild foods obtainable close to lower Huron River included huckleberries, which grew in abundance two miles from the Moravian town and were gathered in quantity in midsummer;[44] "cramberries [cranberries?]";[45] nettles, hops, bulbs, Indian hemp and rampio;[46] hickory nuts, walnuts, chestnuts, and honey from bee trees.[47] Both the Munsees and the Moravians on the Huron River cultivated corn; the Moravian missionaries, at least, also raised potatoes, turnips, cabbages, pumpkins, tobacco, and other garden crops.[48] The Munsees and Moravians had horses and pigs, and the Moravians also had cattle and chickens.[49]

Farther west in western Area 53, during the entire period 1796-1806 the two "bands" of Ottawas that had removed from the Detroit region with Ogontz in 1784[50] continued to live at or near present Sandusky, Erie County, on the southeastern shore of Sandusky Bay. There were also

277

---

43. Oppelt, Diaries, pp. 40, 43, 69-72; Dft. Ex. A-301.

44. Oppelt, Diaries, pp. 13, 16, 83; Dft. Ex. A-301.

45. Oppelt, Diaries, pp. 73, 75; Dft. Ex. A-301.

46. Oppelt, Diaries, pp. 13, 30, 47, 51; Dft. Ex. A-301.

47. Oppelt, Diaries, pp. 13, 30, 39; Dft. Ex. A-301.

48. Oppelt, Diaries, pp. 14-15, 28, 30-32, 35, 38, 46, 48-49, 51-55, 58-65; Dft. Ex. A-301.

49. Oppelt, Diaries, pp. 13-16, 28-29, 32-34, 37-38, 45, 47, 52-53, 58, 62-63; Dft. Ex. A-301.

50. See Chapter IV, this Report, pp. 177-178.

"several Indian families," probably Ottawas, as well as a French family,
living on the north shore of Sandusky Bay, nearly opposite Sandusky, in
1796.[51]

The Bass Islands, in extreme northwestern Area 54, were visited by
the English traveller Isaac Weld, Jr., in September, 1796, and also by
Br. Oppelt in September, 1804. Weld made many personal observations
while he was on the Bass Islands, but neither he nor Oppelt mentions the
presence of any Indians on the Islands.[52]

2. Use and Occupancy of Area 54, 1796-1806. On July 2, 1797
Rufus Putnam, surveyor, "arrived at the crossing of the Muskingum [Tus-
carawas River] above Fort Laurence [Laurens]," in the extreme southeastern corner of Area 54. No mention is made by Putnam of any Indians
being there.[53] The next year, early in October, 1798, Moravian missionaries and 33 Christian Indians travelled southward along the entire eastern boundary of Area 54. Progress was necessarily slow; one day the
group buried an Indian child who had died on the way; during two other
days some of the Moravian brethren made a large canoe, while the rest
"were very successful on the chace;" whenever a bee tree was found the
honey was secured. But no mention is made of the Moravians finding any

278

---

51. Whittlesey, Early History of Cleveland, pp. 336-337; Dft. Ex.
A-78.

52. Weld, Travels, pp. 407-412; Dft. Ex. A-280. Oppelt, Diaries,
pp. 24-25; Dft. Ex. A-301.

53. Carter, Territorial Papers, vol. 2, p. 615; Dft. Ex. A-286.

MAP OF

SHLAND CO.

OHIO.

HURON CO.   LORAIN CO.

HURON CO.

RUGGLES CENTER

RUGGLES

TROY

TROY

SULLIVAN

SULLIVAN

MEDINA CO.

PERRYSBURG

R. SAVANNAH

CLEAR CREEK

Vermilion lake

ORANGE

ORANGE

Polk

JACKSON

LAFAYETTE

CO.

CO.

MILTON

ASHLAND

MONTGOMERY

ROWSBURG

PERRY

Jerome

JEROMEVILLE

JEROMETOWN INDIAN TOWN

MIFFLIN

HAYESVILLE

Mifflin Lakes

MIFFLIN VERMILLION

MOHICAN

WAYNE

MOHICANVILLE

MCKAY P O

GREEN

LAKE

CO.

OLD GREEN TOWN

PERRYSVILLE

P FT W & C R R

LOUDONVILLE

Rocky Fork

HANOVER

HOLMES CO.

RICHLAND

Black Fork

ntispiece
rge William Hill
story of Ashland County
io
shland, O., 1880)

Fig. 6

Indian encampments or hunting parties at Tuscarawas or, for that matter, at any other point on the eastern boundary of Area 54.[54]

Greentown, the mixed Indian town which had been established in western Area 54 in 1783,[55] continued in existence through the years 1796-1812. Moravian missionaries knew this town in the early 19th century, and refer to it as "Samboing" or "Sambosink," "Armstrong's Town," "Pemaxit's Town," and "Green Town," and to its chief as "Pemaxit" or "Armstrong." The Moravians do not explicitly say it was a Delaware town, but several local historians do. Hill refers to it as a "Delaware and Mingo village."[56]

A second town, the existence of which prior to 1806 is less satisfactorily documented than is that of Greentown, was a small trading post settlement known as Jerometown or Mohican John's Town, located on the Jerome Fork of the Mohican River a mile or so southwest of present Jeromesville, Ashland County, and ca. 8 miles northeast of Greentown, in central Area 54. When Ashland County was surveyed in 1807 the surveyors noted an Indian village containing "about fifteen" persons at this site.[57] The well

280

---

54. Ontario History, vol. 49, p. 93; Dft. Ex. A-269.

55. See Chapter IV, pp. 195-196, this Report.

56. Oppelt, Diary, Jan. 1-June 1, 1807, p. 117; Dft. Ex. A-313. Denke, Diary, May 30-Dec. 30, 1807, pp. 1, 3, 10-11, 16; Dft. Ex. A-314. Denke, Diary, Jan.1-Aug. 31, 1808, p. 8; Dft. Ex. A-306. Moravian Historical Society Transactions, vol. 10, p. 396, Dft. Ex. A-281. American State Papers, Indian Affairs, vol. 1, p. 744; Dft. Ex. A-252. Baughman, History of Ashland County, p. 24; Dft. Ex. A-158. Howe, Historical Collections, p. 255; Dft. Ex. A-191. Duff, History, p. 51; Dft. Ex. A-238. Hill, History of Ashland County, p. 34; Dft. Ex. A-244. Emphasis Hill's.

57. Baughman, History of Ashland County, pp. 21, 25, 47, 50, 52; Dft. Ex. A-158. Hill, History of Ashland County, p. 23, fn., 45-46; Dft. Ex. A-244. Howe, Historical Collections, vol. 1, pp. 255-256; Dft. Ex. A-191.
Hill, a local historian, estimates the town probably contained some 50-60 persons in 1807, but that most of its occupants were away

(cont'd. on next page)

known Captain Pipe of Revolutionary and post- Revolutionary war fame[58] was, according to local tradition, chief at Jerometown,[59] but here local tradition is in error, since the Captain Pipe active in the 1770's and 1780's died in July, 1794.[60] There was, however, a "Captain Pipe," a Delaware, living in 1808 and 1814, who was probably the first Captain Pipe's son, and who was associated with the Jerometown Indians.[61]

A petition dated Dec. 6, 1806, presented to Congress on behalf of the Indians comprising the "Delaware nation," and living in "two towns about ten miles apart" in a recently ceded area, would seem to be the most convincing documentation for the existence of Jerometown as a small Indian village by 1806.[62] Various entries in the 1804-1807 diaries of two Moravian missionaries living at the Moravian town on lower Huron River also provide data about Jerometown. In 1804 Dr. Gottfried Sebastian Oppelt spent several days at a trading post "about

(fn. 57 cont'd.) hunting when the surveyors were there (Hill, History of Ashland County, p. 45; Dft. Ex. A-244).

58. See Chapter IV, pp. 163-166, this Report; also Heckewelder, Names, pp. 393-394; Dft. Ex. A-161.

59. Howe, Historical Collections, vol. 1, p. 255; Dft. Ex. A-191. Baughman, History of Ashland County, pp. 21, 25; Dft. Ex. A-158.

60. Bliss, ed., Zeisberger's Diaries, vol. 2, p. 364; Dft. Ex. A-248.

61. Baughman, History of Ashland County, pp. 25, 50, 52; Dft. Ex. A-158. Hill, History of Ashland County, p. 46, fn; Dft. Ex. A-244. A "Captain Pipe" signed a Treaty of Peace at Greenville, Ohio, on July 22, 1814, as a Delaware (7 Stat. 118:119).

62. American State Papers, Indian Affairs, vol. 1, p. 744; Dft. Ex. A-252. Thwaites and Kellogg, eds., Revolution, p. 28, fn. 57; Dft. Ex. A-177. Jerometown and Greentown were ca. 10 miles apart; see Figs. 6 and 7, this Report.

half way" between the Moravian town on lower Huron River and the Moravian mission at Goshen on the lower Tuscarawas River.[63] At the trading post Oppelt visited were two French traders, one of them named "Mr. Jerome." Both traders, Oppelt records,

> have Indian women who have been baptised
> by the brethren; Ma. Elis., daughter of
> the old Renatus and Johanne, John Cook's
> grandchild. The Traders as well as their
> women were very friendly...[64]

Oppelt does not give any native name for Jerome's post, nor mention that there was an Indian village at or near it. However, Br. Christian Denke, who succeeded Oppelt at the Huron mission village in 1807, makes it reasonably clear that Indians were living at a location called "Echquitehanek," fairly close to Sambosink (Greentown).[65] Echquitehanek was, we conclude, the native name for Jerometown.

282

Late in 1806 it was estimated by a member of "the Delaware nation"
-all that remained of the Delaware nation-
that 47, "or at most" 50 Delaware men/lived in the "two towns about ten miles apart. The lowest town [Greentown] contains much the greatest number of inhabitants..."[66]

---

63. Jerometown was approximately halfway between these two Moravian towns.

64. Oppelt, Diaries, pp. 17-18; Dft. Ex. A-301. Renatus was a Mohican; John Cook an Iroquois; see pp. 170-171, 188, fn. 96, this Report.

65. Denke, Diary, May 30-Dec. 31, 1807, pp. 3, 5, 10-11; Dft. Ex. A-314. Denke, Diary, Sept. 1, 1808-April 25, 1809, p. 5; Dft. Ex. A-307. When the Jerometown Indians were evacuated in 1812, Jerome's wife and daughter were among the evacuees (Hill, p. 55; Dft. Ex. A-244).

66. American State Papers, Indian Affairs, vol. 1, p. 744; Dft. Ex. A-252. Thwaites and Kellogg, eds., Revolution, p. 28, fn. 57; Dft. Ex. A-177. Royce, Ohio 1, locates a "Lower Delaware Town" (undated) at the head of Jerome Fork of Mohican River; this town is noticed in Horne, ed.,
(cont'd. on next page)

An undocumented statement by George W. Hill, M. D., writing in the 1870's, reads that in 1807, when Ashland County (central Area 54) was first surveyed, all that County "was used as a free hunting ground by the Wyandots, Ottawas, Delawares, Mohegans and Mingoes."[67] Hill was apparently a conscientious chronicler; he interviewed many early settlers and had access to records of the 1807 surveys of Ashland County.[68]

In eastern Area 54 Royce, Ohio 1, legends "Beaver Hat's Village" (undated) on Apple Creek, at present Wooster, Wayne County. Royce probably noted this village on the authority of two mid-19th century historians, Henry Howe and Gen. Lucius V. Bierce, who also do not date the village, but state that Beaver Hat or Paupelenan was an "Indian chief" who lived, with a few other Indians, in Wooster (which was laid out in 1808)[69] at a "camp or residence called by him Apple Chauquecake or Apple Orchard." Beaver Hat was "a bitter enemy of the whites" and was probably killed by one George Harter,[70] some time after 1808. The fact that "Pappellelond, or Beaver Hat" was one of the four "Munsee and Delaware" signers of the Treaty of July 4, 1805 (7 Stat. 87:89) identifies him as either a Delaware or a Munsee Indian. Since our information about him is so scanty we cannot be certain that Beaver Hat was at Apple

283

(fn. 65 cont'd.) Handbook, pt. 1, p. 776; Dft. Ex. A-1, on Royce's authority. We know of no other secondary, much less any primary, documentation for the existence of any town at this location. Royce legends Greentown and Jerometown as "(Delaware 1812)."

67. Hill, History of Ashland County, p. 45; Dft. Ex. A-244. Emphasis Hill's.

68. Hill, History of Ashland County, pp. 34, 35 and fns., pp. 45, 46, 52, 54, 55; Dft. Ex. A-244.

69. Howe, Historical Collections, vol. 2, p. 832; Dft. Ex. A-192.

70. Bierce, Historical Reminiscences, p. 82; Dft. Ex. A-233. Howe, Historical Collections, vol. 2, p. 831; Dft. Ex. A-192.

Orchard in 1806 or the years prior to then, although from the tenor of
the two references we have concerning him this may have been the fact.

4. Summary and Conclusions on Use and Occupancy of Areas 53 and
54, 1796-April 24, 1806. In regard to Area 53: during the years 1796-
1806 no part of the eastern half of Area 53 was, we conclude, exclusively
used and occupied by any one group of Indians. Ottawas, Chippewas,
Delawares, and Senecas hunted in winter in the Cuyahoga region on the
eastern boundary of Area 53, from the mouth of Cuyahoga River southward,
and also hunted up the Black River in the central portion of Area 53.
Some Senecas, Ottawas, Tuscaroras, and Mohawks had settlements or "camps'
in or close to the eastern half of Area 53 during this period. To wit:
around 15-20 river miles up the Cuyahoga Senecas had a village on the
east bank of the River in 1806 and an "encampment" a few miles farther
up-river; in the summer of 1796 some Ottawas had a "camp" on the Cuyahoga,
somewhere between its mouth and the junction of Cuyahoga and Little
Cuyahoga; in 1798 Tuscaroras were encamped at the south end of the
Cuyahoga-Tuscarawas portage; in 1798 a few families of Mohawks had recently
settled two miles up Black River. In spring, from 1797 onward, the mouth
of the Cuyahoga was a rallying point for Ottawa, Chippewa, Delaware and
Seneca hunters and their families.

The western half of Area 53 was also, we conclude, largely a region
of mixed use and occupancy during the period 1796-1806. This was especially true of the Huron River region, where Munsee Indians and Moravian
Christian Indians had towns within two miles of each other, and where
Chippewa Indians hunted in relatively large numbers on the Huron during
the winter months. Some Chippewas also probably lived, more or less permanently, at the mouth of Huron below the Moravian and Munsee towns, dur-

284

ing the years 1796-1806. Not only did Indians of several groups live and
plant on the Huron River but they also, according to Moravian diarists,
utilized whatever natural resources were available within several miles
of their villages, as well as hunting at more distant locations.

A few miles west of the Huron River, in that part of the Sandusky
Bay region within western Area 53, two bands of Ottawas who had come
to Sandusky Bay in 1784 continued living there during the years 1796-1806,
as did also some French families. The Bass Islands, in extreme northwestern Area 53 were apparently, in 1796-1806, unused and unoccupied.

As regards Area 54: the eastern third of Area 54 was, we conclude
from the few references we have been able to find concerning it, chiefly
used for winter hunting by several different Indian groups of Senecas,
Ottawas, Delawares, Chippewas, who after stopping at Cleveland in the
autumn dispersed to hunt, some going to the Tuscarawas and Killbuck
rivers in eastern Area 54.

Very few, if any, Indians lived in eastern Area 54 -- there may
have been, in 1806, a single small Indian encampment at Wooster, Wayne
County. Here Beaver Hat or Pappellelond, one of the four "Munsee and
Delaware" signers of the Treaty of July 4, 1805 (7 Stat. 87:89), plus
"a few Indians" had a camp known to early settlers of Wooster as "Apple
Orchard." We are at a loss as to how to identify the Indians at this
camp. It may be that Beaver Hat himself was a Munsee, since late in
1806 all the Delawares remaining of the "Delaware nation" were reported
by a member of that nation as living farther west in Area 54, at "two
towns" identified by us as Greentown and Jerometown.

The central third of Area 54 was definitely, we conclude, a region of mixed Indian use and occupancy. By 1806 there were two Indian villages in it, both in Ashland County and about ten miles apart. The larger of the two villages was Greentown or Sambosink, founded in 1783 and continuously occupied from then through 1806. Its chief was Pemaxit or Thomas Armstrong, a Delaware. The ethnic composition of Greentown during the years 1796-1806 is difficult to determine. However, since its population at the time it was founded was mixed Munsee-Delaware-Mohawk-Mingo, and we know of no later populational changes having occurred, we conclude that it probably continued as a mixed town through 1806. Various references to Greentown identify it as a "Delaware" town, or a "Delaware and Mingo" town, or a town containing (in whole or in part is not stated) an unstated number of men belonging to "the Delaware nation" and their families.

286

The second town in central Area 54 was Jerometown or Echquitehanek. Its existence in 1804, except as a trading post, is dubious, but in December, 1806 a small town, probably Jerometown, is reported as having Delawares in it. We accept Jerometown, questionably, as a Delaware town. Our doubts arise from the fact that the two Indian wives of the two traders at Jerome's post in 1804 are reliably reported as of Mohican and Iroquois ancestry. At least one of these women and her daughter were among the Indian evacuees of Jerometown in 1812.

Not only did Ashland County, in central Area 54, have two Indian towns in it by 1806, but all of Ashland County was, at this time, "a free hunting ground" for the Wyandots, Ottawas, Delawares, Mohegans and Mingoes.

For the western third of Area 54 during the years 1796-1806 we
have little or no data on which to base any firm conclusions. We
do know, however, that Indians in the mixed village of Greentown,
in central Area 54, used the deserted site of Hell Town, five
miles southwest of Greentown in Richland County, as a camp site
during hunting trips, up to 1812. This would seem to indicate
that the western third of Area 54 was also probably a region in
hich Indians belonging to several different ethnic groups hunted,
oetween 1796 and 1806.

Dft. Ex. No.

A-1   Frederick Webb Hodge, ed., Handbook of American Indians North
       of Mexico, 2 Pts. (Washington, 1907-1910). Pt. I, pp. 220, 374,
       385-387, 430-432, 489, 584-591, 682, 688, 867-868, 957-958, 776.

A-2   Frederick Webb Hodge, ed., Handbook of American Indians North
       of Mexico, 2 Pts. (Washington, 1907-1910). Pt. II, pp. 58,
       65, 464-465, 481, 507, 637-638, 681-682, 755-756, 841-842, 846,
       848-849, 1022, 1026, 1050-1051, 1057, 1083, 1094, 1109-1110,
       1134, 1162, 1164, 594.

A-3   Reuben Gold Thwaites, ed., The Jesuit Relations and Allied
       Documents, 73 vols. (Cleveland, 1896-1901). Vol. XXI, pp. 39,
       187, 189, 191.

A-4   Reuben Gold Thwaites, ed., The Jesuit Relations and Allied
       Documents, 73 vols. (Cleveland, 1896-1901). Vol. XXXIII, p. 63.

A-5   Reuben Gold Thwaites, ed., The Jesuit Relations and Allied
       Documents, 73 vols. (Cleveland, 1896-1901). Vol. XLII, pp.
       49, 53, 57, 85, 87, 97, 111, 113, 129, 137, 177, 181, 183, 191,
       193, 201, 179.

A-6   Reuben Gold Thwaites, ed., The Jesuit Relations and Allied
       Documents, 73 vols. (Cleveland, 1896-1901). Vol. XLV, pp.
       205, 207.

A-7   Reuben Gold Thwaites, ed., A New Discovery of a Vast Country
       in America, by Father Louis Hennepin, 2 vols. (Chicago, 1903).
       Vol. I, pp. xiii-xliii, 58-59, 76-109.

A-8   Reuben Gold Thwaites, ed., New Voyages to North-America, by
       the Baron de Lahontan, 2 vols. (Chicago, 1905). Vol. I, pp.
       x-xxix, xxxvi-xlix, 25, 46-47, 135-149, 152-166, 264, 297, 319-
       320, 340-341.

A-9   Reuben Gold Thwaites, ed., New Voyages to North-America, by
       the Baron de Lahontan, 2 vols. (Chicago, 1905). Vol. II, pp.
       732-733.

A-10   Sara Jones Tucker, Indian Villages of the Illinois Country
       (Springfield, Ill., 1942). Pp. 4, 6, 9, 10.

A-11   Map: Franquelin, Carte de la Louisiane (in: Reuben Gold
       Thwaites, ed., The Jesuit Relations and Allied Documents,
       73 vols., Cleveland, 1896-1901, vol. 63, frontispiece.)

289

Dft. Ex. No.

A-12   George Peter Murdock, Clark Wissler, 1870-1947 (in: American Anthropologist, vol. 50, pp. 292-304. Menasha, Wis., 1948

A-13   Clark Wissler, Indians of the United States (Garden City, 1954) pp. v-vi, 108-131.

A-14   [Zenobius Membré?], Official Account of the Enterprise of Cavelier de la Salle from 1679-1681. (In: English Translation of Margry, vol. I, pp. 546-550, 553, 561, 569-570. Microfilm copy in the files of the Great Lakes-Ohio Valley Research Project.)

A-15   Map: Henry Popple, Map of the British Empire in North America, 1733 (in: Lloyd Arnold Brown, Early Maps of the Ohio Valley, Pittsburgh, 1959). Pl. 14.

A-16   E. B. O'Callaghan, ed., Documents Relative to the Colonial History of the State of New-York, 15 vols. (Albany, 1853-1887). Vol. IV, pp. 337, 647-652, 781-782, 796-797, 888-889, 896-911.

A-17   Evarts B. Greene and Virginia D. Harrington, American Population Before the Federal Census of 1790. (New York, 1932). Pp. 194-195.

290

A-18   Charles Howard McIlwain, ed., An Abridgment of the Indian Affairs..., by Peter Wraxall (Cambridge, 1915). Pp. ix, xxxvi-xxxix, lxi-lxiv, lxxvi-lxxviii, c-cii, cxvi-cxvii, 9-16, 33-34.

A-19   Cadillac, Detroit is Founded (in: Historical Collections... Michigan Pioneer and Historical Society, 39 vols., Lansing, 1877-1915, vol. XXXIII, pp. 96-100).

A-20   Callières, Cadillac Starts for Detroit (in: Historical Collections...Michigan Pioneer and Historical Society, 39 vols., Lansing, 1877-1915, vol. XXXIII, p. 107).

A-21   Callières, Detroit in Charge of the Company of Canada (in: Historical Collections...Michigan Pioneer and Historical Society, 39 vols., Lansing, 1877-1915, vol. XXXIII, pp. 108-110).

A-22   E. B. O'Callaghan, ed., Documents Relative to the Colonial History of the State of New-York, 15 vols. (Albany, 1853-1887). Vol. IX, pp. 44-47, 75-85, 263-265, 296-297, 336-344, 704-711, 722-725, 1052-1058, 1099-1100, 1111-1112.

Dft. Ex. No.

A-23   Map: Samuel Clowes, Map of 1701 (Library of Congress).

A-24   Allen W. Trelease, Indian Affairs in Colonial New York: The Seventeenth Century (Ithaca, 1960). Pp. 251-253, 260, 292-294.

A-25   D'Aigremont, Letter (in: Historical Collections... Michigan Pioneer and Historical Society, 39 vols., Lansing, 1877-1915, vol. XXXIII, p. 431).

A-26   Cadillac, Report of Detroit in 1703 (in: Historical Collections...Michigan Pioneer and Historical Society, 39 vols., Lansing, 1877-1915, vol. XXXIII, pp. 161-163, 170-171, 184).

A-27   Cadillac, Memorandum (in: Historical Collections... Michigan Pioneer and Historical Society, 39 vols., Lansing, 1877-1915, vol. XXXIII, p. 207).

A-28   List of Indian Tribes in the West (in: Historical Collections...Michigan Pioneer and Historical Society, 39 vols., Lansing, 1877-1915, vol. XXXIII, pp. 552-553).

A-29   Sabrevois, Memoir on the Savages of Canada as Far as The Mississippi River... (in: Collections of the State Historical Society of Wisconsin, 31 vols., Madison, 1855-1931, Reuben Gold Thwaites, ed., vol. XVI, The French Regime in Wisconsin-I, 1634-1727, pp. 363-376).

A-30   Cadillac Complains of Vaudreuil (in: Historical Collections...Michigan Pioneer and Historical Society, 39 vols., Lansing, 1877-1915, vol. XXXIII, pp. 336-341).

A-31   State of Canada in 1730 (in: Historical Collections... Michigan Pioneer and Historical Society, 39 vols., Lansing, 1877-1915, vol. XXXIV, pp. 73-76).

A-32   Sylvester K. Stevens and Donald H. Kent, Wilderness Chronicles of Northwestern Pennsylvania (Harrisburg, 1941), pp. 3-6.

A-33   Samuel Hazard, ed., The Register of Pennsylvania (Philadelphia), vol. III, January to July 1829, pp. 211-212.

A-34   Map: Daniel Coxe, A Section from A Map of Carolana and the River Meschacebe, London, 1726 (in: Lloyd Arnold Brown, Early Maps of the Ohio Valley, Pittsburgh, 1959). Pl. 11.

A-35 Transactions of the Moravian Historical Society, vol.
XII, Parts III and IV, Bethlehem, Pa., 1940. Pp. 175,
179, 341-351, 358-364, 371-374.

A-36 David Zeisberger, Diary of the Indian Congregation in
Lancundoutenunk [Friedenstadt], January 1772 (in: Moravian
Archives, Bethlehem, Pa., pp. 205-210).

A-37 Map: Guillaume Delisle, Carte de la Louisiane et du Cours
du Mississipi, 1718 (in: Indian Villages of the Illinois
Country, vol. II, Part I, by Sara Jones Tucker, Springfield,
1942). Pl. XV.

A-38 E. B. O'Callaghan, ed., Documents Relative to the Colonial
History of the State of New-York, 15 vols. (Albany, 1853-
1887). Vol. V, pp. 445-446, 570-572, 641-642, 704-705, 726-
733, 799-804.

A-39 E. B. O'Callaghan, ed., Documents Relative to the Colonial
History of the State of New-York, 15 vols. (Albany, 1853-
1887?). Vol. VI, pp. 532-533, 703-704, 706-707, 731-733,
735-736, 738, 742, 747, 825, 853, 885-888.

A-40 P. de Charlevoix, Journal of a Voyage to North-America, 2
vols. (London, 1761). Vol. II, pp. 1-2.

A-41 E. B. O'Callaghan, ed., Documents Relative to the Colonial
History of the State of New-York, 15 vols. (Albany, 1853-
1887). Vol. III, pp. 121-127, 250-252, 347, 363, 389-395,
447-449, 464, 503-504, 533-536.

A-42 E. B. O'Callaghan, ed., Documents Relative to the Colonial
History of the State of New-York, 15 vols. (Albany, 1853-
1887). General Index, p. 312.

A-43 Map: LeClercq, Carte Generalle de la Nouvelle France, 1692
(in: First Establishment of the Faith, by Chrétien LeClercq,
trans. by J. G. Shea, New York, 1881, 2 vols.) Vol. 2,
frontispiece.

A-44 John Gilmary Shea, Discovery and Exploration of the Mississippi
Valley (New York, 1852). Pp. 78, 79-82.

A-45 Map: Louis de la Porte de Louvigny, Carte du Fleuve Missisipi,
1697 (in: Indian Villages of the Illinois Country, vol. II,
Part I, by Sara Jones Tucker, Springfield, 1942). Pl. 14.

A-46   Claude Charles LeRoy Bacqueville de la Potherie, Histoire de
        l'Amérique Septentrionale (Paris, 1722). English translation
        in the files of Great Lakes-Ohio Valley Research Project.
        Letter XII, vol. IV, pp. 193-266.

A-47   Map: Father Louis Hennepin, A Map of a Large Country...(in:
        Reuben Gold Thwaites, ed., A New Discovery of a Vast Country
        in America, by Father Louis Hennepin, reprinted from the second
        London issue, 1698, Chicago, 1903, 2 vols.). Vol. 1, facing
        p. 22.

A-48   Map: Baron de Lahontan, A General Map of New France (in:
        Reuben Gold Thwaites, ed., New Voyages to North-America, by
        the Baron de Lahontan, 2 vols., Chicago, 1905). Vol. I, p. 156.

A-49   Reuben Gold Thwaites, ed., New Voyages to North-America, by the
        Baron de Lahontan, 2 vols. (Chicago, 1905). Vol. I, map
        facing p. 1.

A-50   David Zeisberger, Letter No. 3, November 3, 1769 (Moravian
        Archives, Bethlehem, Pa.). 2 pp.

A-51   Map: An Anonymous Map of the Five Indian Nations, ca. 1730
        (in: Lloyd Arnold Brown, Early Maps of the Ohio Valley,
        Pittsburgh, 1959). Pl. 13.

A-52   Deed from the Sachems or Chiefs of the Six Indian Nations to
        Thomas Penn and Richard Penn... (in: Lancaster County, Pa.,
        Record Book L, p. 406).

293

A-53   John Heckewelder, A Narrative of the Mission of the United
        Brethren among the Delaware and Mohegan Indians... (Philadelphia,
        1820). Pp. 59-61, 111-115, 135, 140-143, 147-148, 150, 197-198,
        236, 254, 285, 368-374.

A-54   Louise Phelps Kellogg, Early Narratives of the Northwest, 1634-
        1699 (New York, 1917). Pp. 163-166, 176-180, 195-198, 208-209.

A-55   Reuben Gold Thwaites, ed., The Jesuit Relations and Allied
        Documents, 73 vols. (Cleveland, 1896-1901). Vol. 50, p. 307.

A-56   Cadwallader Colden, The History of the Five Indian Nations...
        (Ithaca, 1958). Pp. xviii-xix, 17-20, 49-57.

A-57   Cadillac, Description of Detroit; Advantages Found There (in:
        Historical Collections...Michigan Pioneer and Historical Society,
        39 vols., Lansing, 1877-1915, pp. 133, 136-138, 140-141, Vol. XXXIV.

A-58   Map: William Hack, Nouvelle France (Wapping, 1684, in: the J. P. Baxter Collection, Library of Congress).

A-59   Robert F. Bauman, Claims vs Realities: The Anglo-Iroquois Partnership (in: Northwest Ohio Quarterly, vol. XXXII, No. 3, pp. 81, 87-101).

A-60   Henri de Tonty to Cabart de Villermont, Montreal, September 11, 1694 (in: English Translation of Margry, vol. IV, pp. 99-101. Microfilm copy in the files of the Great Lakes-Ohio Valley Research Project.).

A-61   English Translation of Margry, vol. V, pp. 245-246, 321-322, 409-411, 413-414, 449-450.

A-62   W. Eugene Shiels, The Jesuits in Ohio in the Eighteenth Century (in: Mid-America, vol. 18, no. 1, pp. 27-47).

A-63   Johannes Megapolensis, Short Sketch... (in: Collections of the New-York Historical Society, New-York, 1868-, Second Series, vol. III, part I, pp. 153, 157).

A-64   Adriaen Van de Donck, Description of the New Netherlands, trans. by Jeremiah Johnson (in: Collections of the New-York Historical Society, New-York, 1868-, Second Series, vol. I, pp. 126, 128, 138, 211, 221).

A-65   E. B. O'Callaghan, ed., Documents Relative to the Colonial History of the State of New-York, 15 vols. (Albany, 1853-1887). Vol. I, pp. 150, 182.

A-66   The Huron of Detroit Desire to Migrate (in: Collections of the State Historical Society of Wisconsin, 31 vols., Madison, 1855-1931, vol. XVII, The French Regime in Wisconsin--II, 1727-1748, pp. 279-288).

A-67   De Noyelle to Beauharnois, February 1, 1739 (in: Historical Collections...Michigan Pioneer and Historical Society, 39 vols., Lansing, 1877-1915, vol. XXXIV, pp. 163-164).

A-68   Instructions to the Chevalier de Beauharnois (in: Collections of the State Historical Society of Wisconsin, 31 vols., Madison, 1855-1931, vol. XVII, The French Regime in Wisconsin--II, 1727-1748, pp. 346-348).

A-69   E. B. O'Callaghan, ed., Documents Relative to the Colonial History of the State of New-York, 15 vols. (Albany, 1853-1887). Vol. X, pp. 83-89, 114-115, 137-138, 141, 162, 178, 181-182, 240-241, 245-251, 145-146, 148, 150-151, 156-157.

Dft. Ex. No.

A-70   Charles A. Hanna, The Wilderness Trail..., 2 vols. (New York, 1911). Vol. I, pp. 12, 111, 204, 315-340.

A-71   Lawrence Henry Gipson, The British Empire before the American Revolution, 7 vols. (New York, 1939). Vol. IV, North America, South of the Great Lakes Region, 1748-1754, pp. 169-171.

A-72   Lois Mulkearn, ed., George Mercer Papers Relating to the Ohio Company of Virginia (Pittsburgh, 1954). Pp. 7, 11, 13-15, 143, 225, 237, 411-412, 486-492, 495, 526-527, 577-578.

A-73   Pennsylvania Archives, First Series, (Philadelphia, 1852-1856). Vol. I, pp. 741-742.

A-74   Raymond, Memoir on English Encroachments, November 2, 1747 (in: Collections of the State Historical Society of Wisconsin, 31 vols., Madison, 1855-1931, vol. XVII, The French Regime in Wisconsin--II, 1727-1748, pp. 474-477).

A-75   Anonymous Diary of a Trip from Detroit to the Ohio River (in: Archives of the Seminary of Quebec, V-V 17:1). Pp. 1-2.

A-76   Minutes of the Provincial Council of Pennsylvania...(Harrisburg, 1851). Vol. V, pp. 145-151, 348-358, 438-439, 470, 477-478, 599-600, 684, 731-732.

A-77   Kenneth P. Bailey, The Ohio Company Papers, 1753-1817 (Arcata, Cal., 1947). Pp. 36-37, 110, 113-114, 137-138, 70-71.

A-78   Charles Whittlesey, Early History of Cleveland, Ohio (Cleveland, 1867). Pp. iii-iv, 131-133, 175-179, 181-184, 187-189, 210, 215, 221, 242-244, 252-253, 261-262, 275-276, 281, 289-291, 293, 297-300, 333-338, 345-346, 363-366, 375-376, 391-396, 416-419.

A-79   Vaudreuil to Maurepas, March 22, 1747 (in: Collections of the Illinois State Historical Library, Springfield, 1903 — , vol. XXIX, Illinois on the Eve of the Seven Years' War, 1747-1755, pp. 12-22, 31-35).

A-80   La Jonquière to Rouillé, September 27, 1751 (in: Collections of the Illinois State Historical Library, Springfield, 1903—, vol. XXIX, Illinois on the Eve of the Seven Years' War, 1747-1755, pp. 369-372).

Dft. Ex. No.

A-81   Conrad Weiser, Notes appended to his Reise Diarium, 1748
(Moravian Provincial Archives, Bethlehem, Pa.).

A-82   Charles A. Hanna, The Wilderness Trail...2 vols. (New York,
1911). Vol. II, pp. 142-145, 167-168, 172, 192-211, 241,
310-311, 362, 368, 379, 387, 176-177.

A-83   E. R. Ott, ed., Documents--Selections from the Diary and
Gazette of Father Pierre Potier, S. J. (1708-1781) (in:
Mid-America, vol. 18, no. 4, pp. 260-265).

A-84   Reuben Gold Thwaites, ed., The Jesuit Relations and Allied
Documents, 73 vols. (Cleveland, 1896-1901). Vol. LXX, pp.
63, 65.

A-85   Map: John Mercer, Map of the Ohio Company Lands (ca. 1754),
Library of Congress.

A-86   Céloron to Vaudreuil, April 23, 1751 (in: Collections of
the Illinois State Historical Library, Springfield, 1903 — ,
vol. XXIX, Illinois on the Eve of the Seven Years' War,
1747-1755, pp. 244-246).

A-87   Céloron to Vaudreuil, August 4, 1751 (in: Collections of
the Illinois State Historical Library, Springfield, 1903 —,
vol. XXIX, Illinois on the Eve of the Seven Years' War, 1747-
1755, pp. 283-289).

A-88   Céloron, Journal, 1749 (in: English Translation of Margry,
vol. 6, pp. 686-688, 692-694. Microfilm copy in the files
of the Great Lakes-Ohio Valley Research Project).

A-89   La Jonquière and Bigot to the French Minister, October 5,
1749 (in: Collections of the State Historical Society of
Wisconsin, 31 vols., Madison, 1855-1901, vol. XVIII, The
French Regime in Wisconsin, 1743-1760, pp. 30-32).

A-90   Reuben Gold Thwaites, ed., The Jesuit Relations and Allied
Documents, 73 vols. (Cleveland, 1896-1901). Vol. LXIX, pp.
151, 177, 179, 181, 183, 297-299.

A-91   Duquesne to Rouillé, October 31, 1753 (in: Collections of
the Illinois State Historical Library, Springfield, 1903 —,
vol. XXIX, Illinois on the Eve of the Seven Years' War, 1747-
1755, pp. 843, 849-850).

Dft. Ex. No.

A-92　　Beverley W. Bond Jr., ed., The Captivity of Charles Stuart,
1755-57 (in: The Mississippi Valley Historical Review, vol.
XIII, pp. 58, 66, 68-73, 78-80).

A-93　　Map: Lewis Evans, A General MAP of the Middle British
Colonies in America (1755) (Library of Congress).

A-94　　Lewis Evans, An Analysis of a General MAP of the Middle
British Colonies in America; and of the COUNTRY of the
Confederate Indians (Philadelphia, 1755). Pp. iv, 13.

A-95　　Samuel G. Drake, Indian Captivities... (New York, 1856).
Pp. 178-181, 185-209, 212-218, 221-223, 232-234.

A-96　　Map: Map of the Western Parts of the Colony of Virginia as far
as the Mississipi (1754) (in: Lloyd Arnold Brown, Early Maps
of the Ohio Valley, Pittsburgh, 1959). Pl. 19.

A-97　　Lloyd Arnold Brown, Early Maps of the Ohio Valley... (Pittsburgh, 1959). Pp. ix-xi, 83-85, 91-92, 94-97.

A-98　　Evans, Lewis (in: Dictionary of American Biography, 21 vols.,
New York, 1937). Vol. VI, pp. 206-207.

A-99　　John Mitchell, A Map of the British and French Dominions
in North America (1755) (National Archives, Record Group
76, Mitchell Map No. 2, in 8 sections). Part of Section 3.

A-100　Map: Anonymous, A Draft of the Ohio from an Indian Account
(ca. 1755) (in: Lloyd Arnold Brown, Early Maps of the Ohio
Valley, Pittsburgh, 1959). Pl. 22.

A-101　Edmund de Schweinitz, trans., The Narrative of Marie Le Roy and
Barbara Leininger, for Three Years Captives among the Indians
(in: The Pennsylvania Magazine of History and Biography, vol.
XXIX, Philadelphia, 1905). Pp. 407-420.

A-102　Map: [John Pattin?], A Trader's Map of the Ohio Country, 1750-
1752 (Library of Congress).

A-103　Leslie A. White, ed., The Indian Journals, 1859-62, by Lewis
Henry Morgan (Ann Arbor, 1959). Pp. v, 51-53.

A-104　Nicholas B. Wainwright, ed., George Croghan's Journal, 1759-
1763, Pt. 1 (in: The Pennsylvania Magazine of History and
Biography, vol. LXXI, no. 4).

A-105   Pennsylvania Archives, First Series, (Philadelphia, 1853-1856).
Vol. 3, pp. 632-633, 83.

A-106   Howard W. Peckham, ed., Thomas Gist's Indian Captivity, 1758-
1759 (in: The Pennsylvania Magazine of History and Biography,
vol. LXXX, pp. 285, 296-297).

A-107   Collections of the Massachusetts Historical Society, Fourth
Series, 10 vols. (Boston, 1852-1871). Vol. 9, pp. 258-259,
321, 365-367, 378-379. 423-424.

A-108   The Papers of Sir William Johnson (Albany, 1921 ──). Vol.
III, pp. 133, 276-277, 442-444, 448-453, 514-516, 521, 690,
695-696, 701, 704-705.

A-109   Sylvester K. Stevens and Donald H. Kent, eds., The Papers of
Col. Henry Bouquet, Harrisburg, 1941-1943, Series 21655, pp.
85-86, 88. 103. 113-114, 123-124, 167-168. 185-186.

A-110   Franklin B. Hough, ed., Journals of Major Robert Rogers (Albany,
1883). Pp. 187-189, 198-202.

A-111   William P. Palmer, ed., Calendar of Virginia State Papers...,
1652-1781. (Richmond, 1875). Vol. I, pp. 245-247.

298   A-112   E. B. O'Callaghan, ed., Documents Relative to the Colonial
History of the State of New-York, 15 vols. (Albany, 1853-
1887). Vol. VII, pp. 582-584, 648-651, 854, 864, 953-956,
958, 966, 974, 985, 572-581.

A-113   Sylvester K. Stevens and Donald H. Kent, eds., Journal of
Chaussegros de Léry (Harrisburg, 1940). Introduction and
pp. 47-56, 62, 93-108, 72-73.

A-114   Nicholas B. Wainwright, George Croghan and the Indian Uprising
of 1747 (in: Pennsylvania History, vol. XXI. no. 1, pp. 21-23).

A-115   Nicholas B. Wainwright, George Croghan, Wilderness Diplomat
(Chapel Hill, 1959). Pp. 6. 40-43

A-116   The Papers of Sir William Johnson, (Albany, 1921 ──). Vol.
X, pp. 790-791.

A-117   Archer Butler Hulbert, The Indian Thoroughfares of Ohio (in:
Ohio Archaeological and Historical Publications (Columbus.
1900). Vol. VIII, pp. 264, 276.

Dft. Ex. No.

A-118   William L. Stone, The Life and Times of Sir William Johnson,
         Bart., 2 vols. (Albany, 1865). Vol. II, pp. 429-430, 460,
         463, 466-467, 469-470, 472.

A-119   Orders for Lieut Elias Meyer, Fort Pitt, August 12, 1761 (in:
         Historical Collections...Michigan Pioneer and Historical   ,105
         Society, 39 vols., Lansing, 1877-1915, Vol. XIX, pp. 102-103).

A-120   Sylvester K. Stevens and Donald H. Kent, eds., The Papers of
         Col. Henry Bouquet, (Harrisburg, 1941-1943). Series 21647,
         pp. 91-94, 130-133, 139-141, 168-172, 186-188.

A-121   Map: Thomas Hutchins, A New Map of the Western Parts of
         Virginia, Pennsylvania, Maryland & North Carolina (London,
         1778). 2 sections. Library of Congress.

A-122   Sylvester K. Stevens and Donald H. Kent, eds., The Papers of
         Col. Henry Bouquet, (Harrisburg, 1941-1943). Series 21648,
         part I, pp. 33, 51, 123.

A-123   Map: Thomas Hutchins, A Tour from Fort Cumberland North West
         ward round part of the Lakes Erie, Huron and Michigan...1762
         (Ms. map from the Henry E. Huntington Library). 2 sections.

A-124   Thomas Hutchins, 1764 Map of the Ohio Country (in: The Wild-   299
         erness Trail, by Charles A. Hanna, vol. II, New York, 1911,
         p. 202, from copy in the Library of Congress).

A-125   D. Franklin, A List of the Number of Fighting Men of the differ-
         ent Nations of Indians...1762 (in: Shelburne Papers, vol. 48,
         p. 411, William L. Clements Library).

A-126   Sylvester K. Stevens and Donald H. Kent, eds., The Papers of
         Col. Henry Bouquet, (Harrisburg, 1941-1943). Series 21648,
         part II, pp. 16, 158, 176-177.

A-127   Sylvester K. Stevens and Donald H. Kent, eds., The Papers of
         Col. Henry Bouquet, (Harrisburg, 1941-1943). Series 21649,
         part I, pp. 76-79, 115-117, 120-122, 129, 219, 223, 226.

A-128   Col. Henry Bouquet to Gen. Jeffery Amherst, Fort Pitt, August 27,
         1763 (in: Historical Collections...Michigan Pioneer and
         Historical Society, 39 vols. Lansing, 1877-1915, vol. XIX,
         p. 227).

A-129   John M'Cullough, A Narrative of the Captivity of John M'Cullough
         (in: Incidents of Border Life..., [by Joseph Pritts], Chambers-
         burg, Pa., 1839, pp. 87, 98, 100-104).

Dft. Ex. No.

A-130   The Papers of Sir William Johnson, (Albany, 1921 ——). Vol.
         IV, pp. 240, 243, 302-303, 401-404, 570-572, 583-584.

A-131   Howard N. Eavenson, Who Made the "Trader's Map"? (in:
         Pennsylvania Magazine of History and Biography, Vol. LXV,
         pp. 420-438).

A-132   Sylvester K. Stevens and Donald H. Kent, eds., The Papers of
         Col. Henry Bouquet, (Harrisburg, 1941-1943). Series 21649,
         part II, pp. 115-117.

A-133   A Return of Indian Traders and Servants Killed or Made Prisoners
         by the Indians [Fort Pitt, September 5, 1763] (in: Sylvester
         K. Stevens and Donald H. Kent, eds., The Papers of Col. Henry
         Bouquet, (Harrisburg, 1941-1943). Series 21654, pp. 122-123).

A-134   Garshum Hicks, Deposition, Fort Pitt, April 14, 1764 (enclosed
         in Grant to Gage, April 15, 1764, Gage Papers, American Series,
         William L. Clements Library). P. 1.

A-135   Gladwin to Bradstreet, Detroit, July 12, 1764 (enclosed in
         Bradstreet to Gage, August 8, 1764, Gage Papers, American
         Series, William L. Clements Library).

A-136   The Papers of Sir William Johnson, (Albany, 1921 ——). Vol.
         XI, pp. 210-213.

A-137   Gage to Gladwin, New York, April 23, 1764 (in: Gage Papers,
         American Series, William L. Clements Library).

A-138   Letter, Detroit, June 9, 1764 (enclosed in Gladwin to Gage,
         June 11, 1764, Gage Papers, American Series, William L.
         Clements Library).

A-139   Charles Beatty, The Journal of a Two Months Tour... (London,
         1764). Pp. 9, 13, 14, 16, 31-56, 60-63.

A-140   Cleaveland to Phelps, Fort Independence, Coneaut Creek,
         July 5, 1796 (Western Reserve Historical Society, Ms.
         No. 2988, pp. 1-3)

A-141   Bradstreet to Gage, Presque Isle, August 14, 1764, with
         enclosure (in: Gage Papers, American Series, William L.
         Clements Library).

A-142   Bradstreet to Gage, Sandusky Lake, September 29, 1764, with
         enclosure (in: Gage Papers, American Series, William L.
         Clements Library).

Dft. Ex. No.

A-143   John Montresor, Journals (in: Collections of the New-York
         Historical Society,New York 1868 —). Vol. XIV, pp. 282,
         294-297, 300, 302-304, 306-307.

A-144   Bouquet to Gage, Camp near Tuscorawas, October 21, 1764 (in:
         Gage Papers, American Series, William L. Clements Library).

A-145   Map: Anonymous, Map of the Sandusky Area and Detroit River
         Region, 1763-1764 [?] (British Museum).

A-146   [William Smith], Historical Account of Bouquet's Expedition...
         (Cincinnati, 1868). Pp. 40, 50-51, 53, 60, 68-70, 81, 149-150,
         152.

A-147   George Croghan, Journals, February 28, 1765-October 8, 1765
         (in: Collections of the Illinois State Historical Library,
         The New Regime, 1765-1767, Springfield, 1903 —). Vol. XI,
         p. 1.

A-148   Reuben Gold Thwaites, ed., Early Western Travels, 1748-1846,
         32 vols. (Cleveland, 1904-1907). Vol. 1, pp. 124-125, 127,
         161, 166-168.

A-149   The Papers of Sir William Johnson, (Albany, 1921 —). Vol.
         XII, pp. 121-122, 476-478, 937-938, 994-995, 1044-1048, 1121-
         1124, 150.

A-150   Emerson D. Fite and Archibald Freeman, A Book of Old Maps
         (Cambridge, 1926). Pp. 181-183.

A-151   E. B. O'Callaghan, ed., Documents Relative to the Colonial
         History or the State of New-York, 15 vols. (Albany, 1853-1887).
         Vol. VIII, pp. 135-137, 233, 235-237.

A-152   The Papers of Sir William Johnson, (Albany, 1921 —). Vol.
         VII, pp. 315-317.

A-153   Erminie Wheeler-Voegelin, ed., John Heckewelder to Peter S. Du
         Ponceau, Bethlehem, 12th Aug 1818 (in: Ethnohistory, Vol.
         VI, No. 1, pp. 70, 72, 78).

A-154   F. D. Stone, ed., Journal of a Volunteer Expedition to Sandusky...
         (in: The Pennsylvania Magazine of History and Biography, Vol.
         XVIII, No. 2, pp. 129-131, 133, 144-147, 318-320).

A-155   Consul W. Butterfield, An Historical Account of the Expedition
         against Sandusky... (Cincinnati, 1873). Pp. 142-144, 147-149,
         162-163, 167-169, 316-317, 152-155.

301

A-156   Clarence Monroe Burton, ed., Ephraim Douglass and His Times...
(in: The Magazine of History, Extra No. 10, pp. 39-42).

A-157   A. J. Baughman, History of Richland County Ohio...2 vols.
(Chicago, 1908). Vol. I, pp. 9, 28, 312, 316-317, 370, 425-
426.

A-158   A. J. Baughman, History of Ashland County, Ohio (Chicago,
1909). Pp. 7, 21-25, 47, 49-52, 54, and map facing p. 12.

A-159   David Zeisberger, Dairy of the Indian Congregation in Lan-
cundoutenůnk [Friedenstadt], March 1772 (Moravian Archives,
Bethlehem, Pa.). Pp. 216-221.

A-160   Richard Butler, Journal, August 22-September 20, 1775 (in:
collections of The Historical Society of Pennsylvania).

A-161   John Heckewelder, Names which the Lenni Lenape or Delaware
Indians...had given to Rivers, Streams, Places...; and also
Names of Chieftains and distinguished Men of that Nation...
(in: Transactions of the American Philosophical Society,
New Series, Philadelphia, 1818-1898). Vol. IV, pp. 387-396.

A-162   E. H. Coates, ed., Life of John Heckewelder, by the Rev. Edward
Rondthaler (Philadelphia, 1847). Pp. 35-39, 46-58

A-163   David Zeisberger, Diary of the Indian Congregation in Langun-
toutenunk-on-Ohio [Friedenstadt], March, 1771 (Moravian
Archives, Bethlehem, Pa.). Pp. 151-162.

A-164   Minutes of the Provincial Council of Pennsylvania...(Harrisburg, 1852-1853). Vol. VIII. pp. 618-619.

A-165   Reuben Gold Thwaites and Louise Phelps Kellogg, eds., Frontier
Defense on the Upper Ohio, 1777-1778 (Madison, 1912). Pp.
164-167, 178-179, 193, 215-216.

A-166   Map: John Heckewelder, Map of Northeastern Ohio, 1796 (in:
Western Reserve and Northern Ohio Historical Society, Tract
64, November, 1884).

A-167   Paul A. W. Wallace, ed., Thirty Thousand Miles with John
Heckewelder (Pittsburgh, 1958). Pp. 41, 98, 212-213, 234,
244, 246-254, 305, 439.

A-168   Reuben Gold Thwaites, ed., The Jesuit Relations and Allied
Documents, 73 vols. (Cleveland. 1896-1901). Vol. XLI, p. 221.

302

Dft. Ex. No.

A-169   Reuben Gold Thwaites, ed., The Jesuit Relations and Allied
         Documents, 73 vols. (Cleveland, 1896-1901). Vol. XLIX, pp.
         109, 111, 113, 115, 257, 259.

A-170   Reuben Gold Thwaites, ed., The Jesuit Relations and Allied
         Documents, 73 vols. (Cleveland, 1896-1901). Vol. XVIII, pp.
         233, 235.

A-171   Reuben Gold Thwaites, ed., The Jesuit Relations and Allied
         Documents, 73 vols. (Cleveland, 1896-1901). Vol. LXVII, pp.
         145, 147.

A-172   Reuben Gold Thwaites, ed., The Jesuit Relations and Allied
         Documents, 73, vols. (Cleveland, 1896-1901). Vol. LXIII, pp.
         139, 141, 143, 145, 147, 149, 151, 153, 155.

A-173   Reuben Gold Thwaites, ed., The Jesuit Relations and Allied
         Documents, 73 vols. (Cleveland, 1896-1901). Vol. XVI, pp.
         225, 227.

A-174   The Papers of Sir William Johnson, (Albany, 1921-). Vol.
         V, p. 336.

A-175   Anthony F. C. Wallace, King of the Delawares: Teedyuscung...
         (Philadelphia, 1949). Pp. 6-12, 298.

A-176   George Henry Loskiel, History of the Mission of the United
         Brethren among the Indians of North America, trans, by
         Christian Ignatius La Trobe (London, 1794). Pp. 109-110.

A-177   Reuben Gold Thwaites and Louise Phelps Kellogg, eds., The
         Revolution on the Upper Ohio, 1775-1777 (Madison, 1908).
         Pp. 25-28, 34, 43-67, 78-80, 82, 86-87, 127.

A-178   David Zeisberger, Letter No. X, Langontoutenunk, November 2,
         1771 (Moravian Archives, Bethlehem, Pa.). Pp. 1-6.

A-179   David Zeisberger, Letter No. IX, Langontoutenunk, March 3,
         1771 (Moravian Archives, Bethlehem, Pa.). Pp. 1-2.

A-180   Consul W. Butterfield, ed., The Washington-Crawford Letters...
         (Cincinnati, 1877). Pp. 54-57, 66-67.

A-181   John Hamilton and John Bradley, Information to the Commission-
         ers, Pittsburgh, September 13, 1776 (in: Col. George Morgan's
         Letter Books, Book 2, Carnegie Library of Pittsburgh). Pp. 1-2.

A-182   Letter to William Wilson at Coshocton, Pittsburgh, August 11, 1776 (in: Col. George Morgan's Letter Books, Book 2, Carnegie Library of Pittsburgh). 1 p.

A-183   Matthew Elliott, Information to the Commissioners, Pittsburgh, August 31, 1776 (in: Col. George Morgan's Letter Books, Book 2, Carnegie Library of Pittsburgh). Pp. 1-3.

A-184   The Commissioners to John Anderson, Pittsburgh, September 5, 1776 (in: Col. George Morgan's Letter Books, Book 2, Carnegie Library of Pittsburgh). 1 p.

A-185   Speech prepared by the Commissioners, Pittsburgh, September 5, 1776 (in: Col. George Morgan's Letter Books, Book 2, Carnegie Library of Pittsburgh). Pp. 1-2.

A-186   The Commissioners to the Committee or Congress for Indian Affairs, Pittsburgh, September 25, 1776 (in: Col. George Morgan's Letter Books, Book 2, Carnegie Library of Pittsburgh). Pp. 1-4.

A-187   Speech delivered by the Commissioners to the Chippewas, Pittsburgh, September 25, 1776 (in: Col. George Morgan's Letter Books, Book 2, Carnegie Library of Pittsburgh). Pp. 1-4.

304

A-188   The White Mingo, Information to the Commissioners, October 18, 1776 (in: Col. George Morgan's Letter Books, Book 2, Carnegie Library of Pittsburgh). Pp. 1-3.

A-189   Zeisberger to Morgan, Cushaghkunk, November 21, 1776 (in: Col. George Morgan's Letter Books, Book 1, Carnegie Library of Pittsburgh). Pp. 1-5.

A-190   [Morgan] to Hancock, Baltimore, January 4, 1777 (in: Col. George Morgan's Letter Books, Book 1, Carnegie Library of Pittsburgh). Pp. 1-3.

A-191   Henry Howe, Historical Collections of Ohio, 2 vols. (Cincinnati, 1902). Vol. I, pp. 255-258, 567, 572, 584.

A-192   Henry Howe, Historical Collections of Ohio, 2 vols. (Cincinnati, 1902). Vol. II, pp. 119-120, 367-368, 475, 522, 626, 645-646, 831-832.

A-193   Council at Pittsburgh, October 15-November 6, 1776 (in: Yeates Collection, the Historical Society of Pennsylvania). Pp. 1-56.

Dft. Ex. No.

A-194   Neville B. Craig, ed., The Olden Time...2 vols. (Cincinnati, 1876). Vol. II, pp. 97-104, 112-114.

A-195   [Morgan] to Hancock, Pittsburgh, November 8, 1776 (in: Col. George Morgan's Letter Books, Book 1, Carnegie Library of Pittsburgh). Pp. 1-2.

A-196   John Heckewelder, Map and Description of Northeastern Ohio... 1796 (Cleveland, 1864). Pp. 335, 339-340.

A-197   [D. Rupp], Early History of Western Pennsylvania, and of the West...With an Appendix (Pittsburgh and Harrisburg, 1850). Appendix XX, pp. 203-204.

A-198   [D. Rupp], Early History of Western Pennsylvania, and of the West...With an Appendix (Pittsburgh and Harrisburg, 1850). Appendix XIX, pp. 181-182.

A-199   [D. Rupp], Early History of Western Pennsylvania, and of the West...With an Appendix (Pittsburgh and Harrisburg, 1850). Appendix XVII, p. 173.

A-200   Frank N. Wilcox, Ohio Indian Trails (Cleveland, 1933). Pp. 24-25.

A-201   John Heckewelder, The Names of All the Different Indian Nations in North America [1777] (Ms., Box: Moravian Indian Missions, Heckeweller, Moravian Archives, Bethlehem, Pa.). Pp. 1-3.

A-202   Franklin B. Dexter, ed., Diary of David McClure, Doctor of Philosophy, 1748-1820 (New York, 1899). Pp. 61, 62, 63, 64, 75, 76, 77, 82, 83, 84, 85, 86, 92, 93, 94, 99.

A-203   Consul W. Butterfield, History of the Girtys (Cincinnati, 1890). Pp. 35-36.

A-204   Colden, Cadwallader (in: Dictionary of American Biography, 21 vols., New York, 1937). Vol. IV, pp. 286-287.

A-205   Collections of the New-York Historical Society, (New York, 1868 —). Vol. 70, pp. 19-20.

A-206   William N. Fenton, Problems Arising from the Historic Northeastern Position of the Iroquois (in: Smithsonian Miscellaneous Collections, Washington, 1862 —). Vol. 100, Essays in Historical Anthropology of North America, pp. 159, 239-240.

A-207   Deposition of Thomas Bourke, March 2, 1752 (in: Collections of the Illinois State Historical Library, Springfield 1903 ——, Vol. XXIX, Illinois on the Eve of the Seven Years' War, 1747-1755, pp. 503-504).

A-208   The Papers of Sir William Johnson, (Albany, 1921 ——). Vol. VIII, pp. 638-641.

A-209   The Detroit Huron (in: Collections of the State Historical Society of Wisconsin, 31 vols., Madison, 1855-1931). Vol. XVII, The French Regime in Wisconsin, II, 1727-1748, pp. 328-335.

A-210   Rogers, Robert (in: Dictionary of American Biography, 21 vols., New York, 1937). Vol. XVI, pp. 108-109.

A-211   Consul W. Butterfield, ed., Washington-Irvine Correspondence... (Madison, 1882). Pp. 137-139.

A-212   N. B. Craig, Statement (in: Draper Mss, 4S10. State Historical Society of Wisconsin).

A-213   George Morgan, Message to the Brethren of the Delawares Meeting in Council at Coochocking, March 29, 1777 (in: Col. George Morgan's Letter Books, Book 1, Carnegie Library of Pittsburgh). Pp. 1-2.

A-214   List of Enclosures to Congress Sent by Mr. Boreman, February 15, 1777 (in: Col. George Morgan's Letter Books, Book 1, Carnegie Library of Pittsburgh). Pp. 1-2.

A-215   Sullivan to Morgan, Fort Pitt, March 22, 1777 (in: Col. George Morgan's Letter Books, Book 1, Carnegie Library of Pittsburgh). Pp. 1-3.

A-216   Sullivan, Sworn Statement to Col. John Cannon, Fort Pitt, March 20, 1778 (in: Col. George Morgan's Letter Books, Book 3, Carnegie Library of Pittsburgh). Pp. 1-3.

A-217   Message from the United American States to Ct. Pipe the Head Chief of the Delawares at Kaskaskias, Fort Pitt, April 7, 1777 (in: Col. George Morgan's Letter Books, Book 1, Carnegie Library of Pittsburgh). Pp. 1-3.

A-218   Message to Taimenend from Delawares and Senecas, April 5, 1777 (in: Col. George Morgan's Letter Books, Book 1, Carnegie Library of Pittsburgh). Pp. 1-3.

Dft. Ex. No.

A-219   S. P. Hildreth, Pioneer History... (Cincinnati, 1848). Pp. 159, 160, 163.

A-220   White Eyes and John Killbuck, Message to Morgan, Coshocton, March 14, 1778 (in: Col. George Morgan's Letter Books, Book 3, Carnegie Library of Pittsburgh). Pp. 1-4.

A-221   White Eyes and John Killbuck, Message to Morgan and the Commissioners, Coshocton, April 6, 1778 (in: Col. George George Morgan's Letter Books, Book 3, Carnegie Library of Pittsburgh). Pp. 1-2.

A-222   Speeches made by White Eyes, Teytapaukosheh, William Chilla- ways and Isaac Leyhhickon, Fort Pitt, April 25, [1778?] (in: Col. George Morgan's Letter Books, Book 3, Carnegie Library of Pittsburgh). Pp. 1-3.

A-223   Discussion of possible expedition against Detroit..., July 17, 1778 (in: Col. George Morgan's Letter Books, Book 3, Carnegie Library of Pittsburgh). Pp. 1-2.

A-224   William M. Darlington, ed., Christopher Gist's Journals... (Pittsburgh, 1893). Pp. 105, 214-216, 271-272.

A-225   Louise Phelps Kellogg, ed., Collections of the State Histori- cal Society of Wisconsin, 31 vols., (Madison, 1855-1931) Vol. XXIII, Frontier Advance on the Upper Ohio, 1778-1779, pp. 132- 133, 157-164, 183-184, 214, 241-243, 265-266, 334-335, 343-344, 349, 361-362, 365-367, 382-383.

307

A-226   Louise Phelps Kellogg, ed., Collections of the State Histori- cal Society of Wisconsin, 31 vols., (Madison, 1855-1931) Vol. XXIV, Frontier Retreat on the Upper Ohio, 1779-1781, pp. 55, 39-40, 97, 109, 132, 150-154, 217-219.

A-227   Baron de Rosenthal's Intended Marriage, Cayahoga Trip of 1782... (in: Drpaer Mss. 1NN111, State Historical Society of Wisconsin).

A-228   Gen. George Clark to Officers in Westmoreland Co., Crossings, June 3, 1781 (in: Pennsylvania Archives, First Series, Vol. IX, Philadelphia, 1854). P. 189.

A-229   Brodhead to Taylor, Pittsburgh, November 21, 1779, and Brod- head to Washington, Pittsburgh, November 22, 1779 (in: Pennsylvania Archives, Philadelphia, 1852-1856, First Series, Vol. XII, pp. 188-189.

A-230   William Wilson, An Account of the Indian Towns and Nations
        in the Western Department... (August 4, 1778) (in: The
        Virginia Magazine of History and Biography, Vol. XXIII, pp.
        345-346).

A-231   Bolton to Haldimand, Niagara, November 13, 1778 (in: Col-
        lections of the Illinois State Historical Library, Spring-
        field, 1903 ——, Vol. I, pp. 369-370).

A-232   Bolton to Haldimand, Niagara, March 24, 1779 (in: Histor-
        ical Collections...Michigan Pioneer and Historical Society,
        39 vols., Lansing, 1877-1915, Vol. IX, pp. 427-429).

A-233   Lucius V. Bierce, Historical Reminiscences of Summit County,
        (Akron, 1854). Pp. 13-14, 39, 62, 85-87, 116-117, 120-122, 82.

A-234   William H. Perrin, History of Summit County...(Chicago, 1881).
        Pp. 218-219, 522, 525.

A-235   The Fire Lands Pioneer, Vol. IV, June, 1863, pp. 21-33.

A-236   Pennsylvania Archives, Philadelphia, 1852-1856, First Series,
        Vol. V, p. 287.

A-237   Henry Hamilton, Council Held at Detroit June 14th 1778...
        (in: Historical Collections...Michigan Pioneer and Histori-
        cal Society, 39 vols., Lansing, 1877-1915, Vol. IX, pp.
        442-452).

A-238   William A. Duff, History of North-Central Ohio (Topeka-
        Indianapolis, 1931). P. 51.

A-239   Account of a Meeting between the Commissioners and Others
        with the Delaware Indians, April 26, 1778 (in: Col. George
        Morgan's Letter Books, Book 3, Carnegie Library of Pittsburgh).
        Pp. 1-4.

A-240   Hugh H. Brackinridge, ed., Narratives of the Perils and
        Sufferings of Dr. Knight and John Slover... (Cincinnati,
        1867). Pp. 18-19.

A-241   Speech from the Delawares..., Philadelphia, May 25, 1779
        (in: Col. George Morgan's Letter Books, Book 3, Carnegie
        Library of Pittsburgh). Pp. 1-2.

A-242   The Fire Lands Pioneer, Vol. 2, No. 3, September, 1860,
        pp. 11-12, 22, 34, 46-48.

Dft. Ex. No.

A-243   Conference with Indians at Fort Pitt, July 6, 1776 (in:
         American Archives..., edited by Peter Force, Washington, 1837-
         1853, Fifth Series, Vol. I, pp. 36-37.

A-244   George W. Hill, History of Ashland County, Ohio... (1880).
         Pp. 23-24, 28, 34-35, 45-46, 50-52, 54-55.

A-245   The Fire Lands Pioneer, Vol. IX, June, 1868, pp. 21, 45, 76,
         106.

A-246   Map: Robert Pilkington, A Sketch of the Bass Islands, Miamis
         Bay and a Part of the Miamis River 1794 (in: Historical
         Collections...Michigan Pioneer and Historical Society, 39
         vols., Lansing, 1877-1915). Vol. XXI, facing p. 489.

A-247   Eugene F. Bliss, ed., Diary of David Zeisberger...2 vols.
         (Cincinnati, 1885). Vol. I, pp. v-ix, 17-18, 87, 156, 220,
         235-236, 267-290, 292-295, 298, 300-316, 320-330, 332-349,
         351-357, 359-361, 364-366, 369-371, 373, 376, 378, 384-387,
         389-390, 393-394, 399, 403-408, 414, 417-420, 425, 427-428,
         430, 432-440, 445, 452-457, 462-464, 29-30.

A-248   Eugene F. Bliss, ed., Diary of David Zeisberger...2 vols.
         (Cincinnati, 1885). Vol. II, pp. 2-3, 7-11, 13, 15-18,
         20-21, 25-30, 32-33, 39-40, 47-50, 52-55, 57-58, 60-61,
         65-66, 68-70, 72-75, 78-84, 91-92, 99-103, 106, 108-110,
         112-120, 123-127, 130-131, 134-136, 141-143, 146-153,
         155-159, 163-164, 166-169, 172-179, 182, 191-192, 197-198,
         202, 205, 216, 234, 238-239, 278-279, 284-285, 350, 364,
         372, 412, 417, 451, 454, 483, 492, 502.

A-249   Alfred T. Goodman, ed., Journal of Captain William Trent from
         Logstown to Pickawillany A. D. 1752 (Cincinnati, 1871). P. 85.

A-250   A List of the Western Nations of Indians Contiguous to the
         Post at Muskingum (in: Papers of the Continental Congress,
         National Archives, Microcopy 247, Reel 164). Item No. 150,
         1785-1788, Vol. I, pp. 155-156.

A-251   David Sanders Clark, The Moravian Mission of Pilgerruh (in:
         Transactions of the Moravian Historical Society, Vol. XII, Pt.
         II, Bethlehem, Pa., 1940). P. 53.

A-252   American State Papers, Indian Affairs, (Washington, 1832).
         Vol. I, pp. 566, 744, 676.

A-253   Richard C. Knopf, ed., A Surgeon's Mate at Fort Defiance...
         (Columbus, 1957). P. 43.

Dft. Ex. No.

A-254 Gibson to Hand, Fort Pitt, December 10, 1777 (in: Draper Mss. 1U132-132₁, State Historical Society of Wisconsin).

A-255 Zeisberger to Harmar, Cayahoga, July 12, 1786 (in: Harmar Papers, Vol. 3, William L. Clements Library). Pp. 1-2.

A-256 Heart to Harmar, Fort Harmar, January 5, 1790, with 2 enclosures (in: Wayne Papers, Reel 5, Pennsylvania Historical Society). Pp. 1-7.

A-257 Speech from the Delawares to the Commissioners, Cooshaughking, August 30, 1776 (in: Yeates Collection...1776, Historical Society of Pennsylvania). Pp. 1-2.

A-258 Wilson to the Commissioners, Coochocking, August 13, 1776 (in: Yeates Collection...1776, Historical Society of Pennsylvania). Pp. 1-3.

A-259 Wilson to the Commissioners, Cooshaughking, August 17, 1776 (in: Yeates Collection...1776, Historical Society of Pennsylvani Pp. 1-2.

A-260 The Commissioners to the Committee of Congress for Indian Affairs, Pittsburgh, August 18, 1776 (in: Yeates Collection... 1776, Historical Society of Pennsylvania). Pp. 1-3.

A-261 John Anderson to the Commissioners, Cooshocton, September 5, 1776 (in: Yeates Collection...1776, Historical Society of Pennsylvania). Pp. 1-2.

A-262 John Anderson to the Commissioners, Coshocton, September 6, 1776 (in: Yeates Collection...1776, Historical Society of Pennsylvania). 1 p.

A-263 Gilbert Imlay, A Topographical Description of the Western Territory of North America (London, 1797). Pp. 291, 294, 363.

A-264 Will Cockburn, Map of the State of New York and Parts adjacent (1783) (Lake Erie portion) (New York State Library).

A-265 Putnam to Knox, Fort Washington, July 8, 1792 (in: Wayne Papers, Historical Society of Pennsylvania). Pp. 1-8.

A-266 Richard C. Knopf, ed., Anthony Wayne... (Pittsburgh, 1960). Pp. 59-61, 71-75.

Dft. Ex. No.

A-267 Joncaire to Baby, [March 11, 1752] (in: Collection Baby, University of Montreal). Pp. 1-2.

A-268 Draper Mss. 16S, State Historical Society of Wisconsin. Pp. 272-274, 277, 280, 285, 286, 289, 291, 292, 299, 302.

A-269 Leslie R. Gray, ed., From Fairfield to Schönbrun--1798 (in: Ontario History, Vol. XLIX, No. 2, 1957, pp. 63-65, 74-95).

A-270 David Zeisberger, Original Diary, May 19, 1787 (photostat, with translation by William N. Schwarze, in: Archives of the Moravian Church, Bethlehem, Pa., Box 153, Folders 2 and 9). 1 p.

A-271 Schebosch to Ettwein, Fort Pitt, June 24, 1786 (extract, in: Archives of the Moravian Church, Bethlehem, Pa., Box 153, Folder 10). 1 p.

A-272 Zeisberger to Ettwein, Camp on the Bank of the Cayahaga, June 25, 1786 (in: Archives of the Moravian Church, Bethlehem, Pa., Box 53, Folder 10). Pp. 1-2.

A-273 Zeisberger to Ettwein, In the Huts on the River Cayahaga, July 22, 1786 (in: Archives of the Moravian Church, Bethlehem, Pa., Box 153, Folder 10). Pp. 1-6.

A-274 Zeisberger to the General Helpers' Conference, Cayahaga, April 9, 1787 (in: Archives of the Moravian Church, Bethlehem, Pa., Box 153, Folder 10). Pp. 1-4.

A-275 Zeisberger to Ettwein, Cayahaga, April 9, 1787 (in: Archives of the Moravian Church, Bethlehem, Pa., Box 153, Folder 10). Pp. 1-3.

A-276 Zeisberger to "Dearly Beloved Brethren and Sisters," Camp at the Mouth of the Cayahaga, June 12, 1786 (in: Archives of the Moravian Church, Bethlehem, Pa., Box 153, Folder 10). Pp. 1-5.

A-277 Zeisberger to Ettwein, Huron River, October 1, 1787 (in: Archives of the Moravian Church, Bethlehem, Pa., Box 153, Folder 10). Pp. 1-2.

A-278 Zeisberger to Ettwein, Huron River, June 15, 1787 (in: Archives of the Moravian Church, Bethlehem, Pa., Box 153, Folder 10). Pp. 1-2.

A-279 Draper Mss. 15S26-28, State Historical Society of Wisconsin.

A-280   Isaac Weld, Junior, Travels through The States of North America...￼
(London, 1800). Pp. 17, 407-412, 546.

A-281   The Autobiography of Abraham Luckenbach, translated by H. E.
Stocker (in: Transactions of the Moravian Historical Society,
Vol. X, Parts III and IV, Bethlehem, Pa., 1917). Pp. 359, 396.

A-282   Pennsylvania Archives, (Philadelphia, 1852-1856). First Series,
Vol. X, p. 83.

A-283   William H. Smith, ed., The Life...of Arthur St. Clair...2
vols. (Cincinnati, 1882). Pp. 16-17, Vol. II.

A-284   Butler to Knox, Fort Pitt, December 13, 1786 (in: Papers
of the Continental Congress, National Archives, Microcopy
247). Series 150, II, pp. 115-118.

A-285   Butler to Knox, Carlisle, March 28, 1787 (in: Papers of the
Continental Congress, National Archives). Series 150, II,
pp. 287-298.

A-286   Clarence E. Carter, ed., The Territorial Papers of the United
States, (Washington, 1934). Vol. II, The Territory Northwest of the River Ohio, 1787-1803, pp. 100-102, 537, 614-615.

312   A-287   Journal of a Survey of Lake Erie, 1789 (in: Publications
of the Buffalo Historical Society, Buffalo, 1879 —), Vol.
VII, p. 374.

A-288   Map: P. McNiff and H. Ford, A Survey of the South Shore of
Lake Erie...taken in 1789, in 5 sections (Public Archives
of Canada). Sections 2, 3, 5.

A-289   Map: P. McNiff, A Plan of Lake Erie...1791, in 3 sections
(Public Archives of Canada). Sections A and C.

A-290   Butler to Sir John Johnson, Niagara, April 24, 1791 (in:
Historical Collections...Michigan Pioneer and Historical
Society, 39 vols., Lansing, 1877-1915). Vol. XXIV, p.
212.

A-291   The Journals of Seth Pease to and from New Connecticut, 1796-
98, Part II (in: Tract No. 94, The Western Reserve Historical Society, Cleveland, November, 1914). Pp. 27, 29-31, 76,
79-82, 88-89.

A-292   Charles Whittlesey, A Sketch...of Cleveland (in: The American
Pioneer, Vol. II, Cincinnati, 1843). Pp. 22-27, 33.

Dft. Ex. No.

A-293 Donald H. Kent and Merle H. Deardorff, eds., <u>John Adlum on the</u>
<u>Allegheny: Memoirs for the Year 1794</u> (in: <u>The Pennsylvania</u>
<u>Magazine of History and Biography</u>, Vol. LXXXIV, Nos. 3 and 4,
pp. 265, 282-283).

A-294 Extracts from the Rev. Thomas Hughs' Journals (in: <u>Western</u>
<u>Missionary Magazine</u>, April 1803, pp. 91-98, The Presbyterian
Historical Society). Pp. 1, 2, 5, 6, 8 of transcription.

A-295 La Rochfoucault Liancourt, <u>Travels through the United States</u>
<u>of North America</u>...2 vols. (London, 1800). Vol. I, pp.
371-372.

A-296 E. A. Cruikshank, ed., <u>The Correspondence of Lieut. Governor</u>
<u>John Graves Simcoe</u>...5 vols. (Toronto, 1925). Vol. III, pp.
52, 55.

A-297 Extracts from the Letter Books of the Marquis de Vaudreuil
(contemporary translations in the handwriting of John Appy,
Loudoun Collection, Henry E. Huntington Library). Pp. 22-23.

A-298 <u>Collections of the Illinois State Historical Library</u>,(Springfield, 1903). Vol. XXIX, <u>Illinois on the Eve of the Seven</u>
<u>Years' War, 1747-1755</u>, pp. 23, 96-99, 105-108.

A-299 Hamtramck to Wayne, Fort Wayne, March 22, 1796 (in: Wayne   313
Papers, Pennsylvania Historical Society, Vol. 44). 1 p.

A-300 George Scott, <u>Journal of a Missionary Tour</u>... (in: <u>Western</u>
<u>Missionary Magazine</u>, October, 1803, pp. 339-345, The Presbyter-
ian Historical Society). Pp. 1, 4 of transcription.

A-301 Gottfried Sebastian Oppelt, <u>Diaries of the Indian Congregation</u>
<u>in Pettquotting</u>, October 1803-December 31, 1806 (Mss. in the
Archives of the Moravian Church, Bethlehem, Pa.). Pp. 1-102.

A-302 Oppelt to Loskiel, Pettquotting, January 8, 1805 (Archives of
the Moravian Church, Bethlehem, Pa., Box 157, File 7, Item 1).
Pp. 1-3.

A-303 Oppelt to Loskiel, Pettquotting, June 2, 1805 (Archives of
the Moravian Church, Bethlehem, Pa., Box 157, Folder 7,
Item 5). 1 p.

             Feb. 20, 1806

A-304 Oppelt to Loskiel, Pettquotting, ⌄   (Archives
of the Moravian Church, Bethlehem, Pa., Box 157, Folder 7,
Item 3). Pp. 1-4.

Dft. Ex. No.

A-305   Oppelt to Loskiel, Pettquotting, November 1, 1804 (Archives of the Moravian Church, Bethlehem, Pa., Box 157, Folder 6, Item 6). Pp. 1-6.

A-306   Christian Friedrich Denke, Diary, January-August 31, 1808 (Archives of the Moravian Church, Bethlehem, Pa., Box 157, Folder 5). Pp. 1, 8, 9.

A-307   Christian Friedrich Denke, Diary, September 1808-April 1809 (Archives of the Moravian Church, Bethlehem, Pa., Box 157, Folder 5). Pp. 1, 5, 11-13.

A-308   Henry B. Curtis, Pioneer Days in Central Ohio (in: Ohio Archaeological and Historical Publications. (Columbus, 1887-1910). Vol. I, pp. 243, 247-248, 253-254.

A-309   Susan Martha Reed, British Cartography of the Mississippi Valley in the Eighteenth Century (in: The Mississippi Valley Historical Review, Vol. 2, No. 2, pp. 213-224).

A-310   David I. Bushnell, Jr., ed., Journal of Samuel Montgomery (in: The Mississippi Valley Historical Review, Vol. 2, No. 2, pp. 261-263).

A-311   Atwater to Seaward, Mantua, February 26, 1828, with enclosure (Ms. No. 749, Western Reserve Historical Society, pp. 1, 4-5).

A-312   Edward Paine, Settlement of the Western Reserve (Ms., Western Reserve Historical Society, Vol. II. Book 3, p. 1-7).

A-313   Gottfried Sebastian Oppelt, Diary, January 1-June 1, 1807 (Archives of the Moravian Church, Bethlehem, Pa., Box 157, Folder 4). Pp. 103, 117.

A-314   Christian Friedrich Denke, Diary, May 30, 1807-December 31, 1807 (Archives of the Moravian Church, Bethlehem, Pa., Box 157. Folder 1). Pp. 1, 3, 5, 10-11, 16.

A-315   [Tappen] to Barr, Unionville, Ohio, March 15, 1848 (Ms., Western Reserve Historical Society, Vol. 11, Book 4, pp. 5-7)

A-316   Victor H. Paltsits, ed., Journal of Robert Rogers... (in: Bulletin of the New York Public Library, Vol. 37, New York, 1933). Pp. 261-262, 266-267, 272-275.

A-317   Howard H. Peckham, ed., George Croghan's Journal of His Trip to Detroit in 1767 (Ann Arbor, 1939). Pp. 31-45.

Dft. Ex. No.

A-318   Copies of Historical Manuscripts mostly unpublished appertaining to the Early History of the Western Reserve and especially of the township of Mantua Portage Co Ohio (Ms. No. 1589, Western Reserve Historical Society). Typed excerpts, pp. 1-5.

A-319   Howard H. Peckham, Pontiac and the Indian Uprising (Princeton, 1947). P. 33.

A-320   Milo M. Quaife, ed., The Indian Captivity of O. M. Spencer (Chicago, 1917). Pp. xxiii, xxiv, 146-147, 150-154.

A-321   Reichel, William C., ed., History, Manners, and Customs of The Indian Nations..., by John Heckewelder (Philadelphia, 1876). P. 93.

THE LOCATION OF INDIAN
TRIBES IN SOUTHEASTERN MICHIGAN
AND NORTHERN OHIO
1700 - 1817

Helen Hornbeck Tanner
Ann Arbor, 1963

318

The purpose of this research report is to present an account of the tribes and bands of Indians occupying southeastern Michigan and northern Ohio in historic times, with particular emphasis on the period following the establishment of the French fort at Detroit in 1701 and continuing through the period when the tribes ceded land by treaty in 1805, 1807 and 1817. The principle area involved is that designated by the numbers 53, 54, 66, 87 and 88 on Royce's maps in the Eighteenth Annual Report of the Bureau of American Ethnology. Frequent reference will also be made to Royce #11, southern and eastern Ohio. The Indians with a major interest in this area are tribes or bands of Wyandot, Delaware and Shawnee, Ottawa, Pottawatomi and Chippewa, as well as splinter groups who left the Six Nations organization.

As a necessary background, the preliminary discussion begins with the Iroquois wars of conquest in 1648, which forced the migration of some tribes and the obliteration of other tribes within and adjacent to this area. At the time of first European contact, most of these tribes were distributed over a large expanse in the Great Lakes region, although the Delaware were still in eastern Pennsylvania and part of the Shawnee were probably on the Ohio river. South of Lake Ontario, between the Hudson and Niagara rivers, were the Five Nations of the Iroquois: the Mohawks, Oneidas, Cayugas, Onandagas and Senecas. This organization became the Six Nations in 1722 with the addition of the Tuscararas, who lived on Beaver Creek near the Pennsylvania-Chio line.

The early French explorers found a tribe which they called the Huron north of Lake Ontario, extending to the Georgian Bay region of Lake Huron. South of the Huron, along the north shore of Lake Erie near the Niagara river were the Neutrals, so identified by the French because of their intermediate position between the rival Huron and Iroquois tribes. To the west and southwest of the country of the Huron proper lay that of the Tiononotati, sometimes called the Tobacco Huron.[1] This group probably extended into southeastern Michigan.[2] It is the combined remnants of Hurons, Tiononotati and Neutrals who were called the Huron during the early years of the settlement at Detroit, and by about 1750 were called the Wyandot of Detroit Michigan and Sandusky Ohio . The Erie were on the south shore of the lake that bears their name and had their central headquarters near the eastern end. All these tribes, i.e., the Five Nations, Huron, Tiononotati, Neutral and Erie belong to the Iroquois-Huron linguistic group, one of the two principal language groups in the Great Lakes region.

320

The other tribes involved in the story of the Indian occupation of southern Michigan and northern Ohio all belong to the Algonkin language group. Three of these tribes, the Chippewa - an adaptation of the more accurate name Ojibwa-, the Ottawa and Pottawatomi had

---

[1]W. Vernon Kinietz, The Indians of the Western Great Lakes, 1615-1760. (Ann Arbor, 1940), p. 1.

[2]See Map I adapted from George Peter Murdock Ethnographic Bibliography of North America, 3rd ed. (New Haven, 1960), p. 220. See also, Ernest J. Lajeunesse, The Windsor Border Region (Toronto, 1960), p. 27, Document B 8, an extract from Charlevoix's journal for June 8, 1721. Exhibit No. 134.

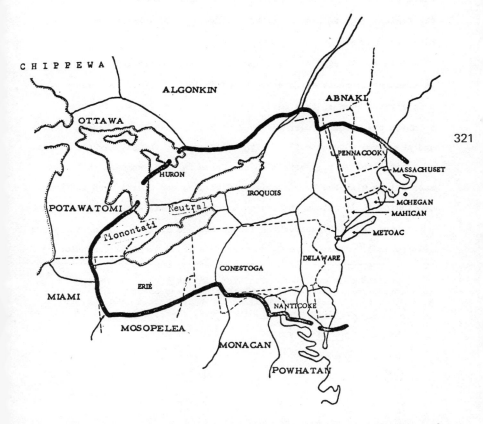

Map I, adapted from George Peter Murdock, <u>Ethnographic Bibliography of North America</u>, 3rd Edition, New Haven, 1960, page 220.

a tradition of closer association at some time in their past history,
referring to this older relationship as the 'three fires." From the
information secured by French explorers and missionaries, early in the
seventeenth century, the Ottawas occupied the region north of Georgian
Bay and Lake Huron, including some of the islands. Their name was
given to the Ottawa river, the important artery for carrying furs
eastward to the French trading center at Montreal. The Pottawatomi
had moved into the lower peninsula of Michigan. The Chippewa occupied
the region north of Lake Superior, but were apparently in the process
of moving southward.

This territorial distribution was altered permanently by the
destructive Iroquois warfare beginning in 1648. One of the causes of
hostilities, even at this early date, was rivalry for the fur trade,
in which the Iroquois were involved with the Dutch on the Hudson river,
and the Huron were associated with the French on the St. Lawrence river.[3]

322

After the initial attack on the Huron in 1648, some of the Huron
took refuge with the Tionontati and Neutrals, and others with the Erie.
Continuing their raids, the Iroquois raized the villages, massacred the
population and took captive the Tionontati and Neutrals during the years
1649 to 1651.[4] The Erie were destroyed in 1655, with the exception of

---

[3]England took over the Dutch trade in 1664, when the Duke of
York forced the surrender of New Netherlands and changed the name to
New York. See Samuel Eliot Morrison and Henry Steele Commager, The
Growth of the American Republic, (New York, 1942), Vol. I, p. 72.

[4]Kinietz, op. cit., p. 2.

a fragment that, according to tradition, fled west of the Mississippi river.[5] Survivers of the Huron, Neutrals and Tionontati escaped by way of Mackinac Island to the northwest shore of Lake Michigan. Fear of the Iroquois invaders impelled the Ottawa and Pottawatomi also to move westward.

The Huron, Ottawa and Pottawatomi Indians spent several years in the vicinity of Green Bay, Wisconsin and a portion of the Pottawatomi located there. The westward migration was halted in the upper waters of the Mississippi river by contact with the Sioux, on whose territory they were encroaching. In 1660, the Chippewa attacked the Iroquois, who were pursuing the Ottawa and Huron, near Sault Ste. Marie and brought an end to the Iroquois raids in that area.[6] The Ottawa and Huron turned eastward again to the southern shore of Lake Superior. These two tribes, and the Chippewa from the Lake Superior region, were drawn to the eastern end of the upper peninsula of Michigan when the Jesuit missions were founded at Sault Ste. Marie in 1668, and at St. Ignace on the Mackinac Straits in 1671.

323

Mackinac Straits, an important juncture of many routes of water transportation, was the central point for the expanding French fur trade in the Great Lakes area. The hunters and trappers who collected furs during the winter brought them to the trading posts at the Straits of Mackinac, to be transported by way of the Ottawa river to Montreal

---

[5]Relation of Blacksnake, chief of the Senecas, printed in the Buffalo Commercial of July, 1845, and quoted in Charles Whittlesey, Early History of Cleveland, (Cleveland, 1867), p. 69.

[6]Cyril Thomas, The Indians of North America in Historic Times, (London, 1903), p. 291.

in the spring. In the early years, this route was used because the presence of the Iroquois, who were partisans of the English, on the shores of Lake Ontario made it unsafe for the French to traverse the eastern end of the Great Lakes chain. France's foothold in central North America was strengthened in 1690 with the establishment of a military fort, Fort Buade, at Mackinac Straits to protect the missionaries and traders.

The establishment of the French on the Straits of Mackinac, with their Indian allies - Chippewa, Ottawa and Huron - was a preliminary step to the founding of a fort at Detroit, on the straits between Lake Huron and Lake Erie. LaSalle made the first investigation of this region in 1679, when he built the Griffin on the north shore of Lake Erie, probably near the Cuyahoga river, and thereafter sailed the length of Lake Erie, through the Detroit river, Lake St. Clair, Lake Huron and the Straits of Mackinac to Lake Michigan. In the course of this voyage, he encountered isolated Indians along the Detroit river whose inhabitants were Huron speaking people. LaSalle reported the name of a Huron village as Teuchsaygrondie.[7] French interest in lower Michigan developed slowly. For two years, 1686-1688, a fort existed near modern Port Huron, at the southern outlet to Lake Huron. No permanent settlement existed, however, until Antoine de la Motte Cadillac, commander of Fort Buade from 1695 to 1699, convinced the French colonial minister of the need for a military post on the strategically located Detroit river. Cadillac was the last commander of Fort Buade.

324

---

[7]E. M. Sheldon, Early History of Michigan, (New York, 1856), p. 40-42.

In France in 1700, Cadillac presented his case for the establishment of a fort at Detroit. It was written in the form of an
interview with Count Ponchartrain, the French colonial minister.
His remarks indicate his reasons for founding Detroit, and forecast
the contentions between the French and the English during the next
sixty years, involving their Indian allies in Michigan and Ohio.
Excerpts of his argument follow:

> "It is incontestable that all the waters of the Great
> Lakes pass through this strait, i.e. Detroit , and this is
> the only practicable path by which the English can carry on
> their trade with the savage nations, which have correspondence
> with the French.... The English use every possible means to
> obtain trade, but, if that post were fortified in form, the
> English would entirely abandon the hope of depriving us of
> its advantages.... If Detroit is not established, sir, we
> shall soon see all the savages of the country going to the
> English, or inviting them to come and establish themselves
> in the Indian country.... One cannot deny that our savages
> hitherto hunted north of Lake St. Clair, but by this estab-
> lishment i.e. Detroit , they would pursue the chase as far
> as two hundred leagues south of Lake Erie, toward the sea..."[8]

325

Cadillac was aware that English goods were often cheaper than
French trade goods, and that British traders could sometimes offer
better prices for furs. But he also knew that the personal relationship existing between the French hunters and trappers, the coureurs
de bois, was a factor influencing the Indians to adhere to the French.

> "... they French traders are too cunning to allow
> his [the Indian's] furs to escape, especially when they
> succeed in making him eat and drink with them."[9]

---

[8] Ibid., p. 86, 87, 88.

[9] Ibid., p. 88.

Convinced by these arguments, Count Ponchartrain directed the
establishment of a fort at Detroit, which Cadillac appropriately named
Fort Ponchartrain. Returning from France, Cadillac reached his destination in July, 1701 by the "old route," traveling up the Ottawa
river from Montreal to Lake Nipissing, and down the French river to
Georgian Bay, and Lake Huron. In August of that year, the French made
peace with the Iroquois, a new circumstance that made travel safe from
Montreal to Detroit by way of the St. Lawrence river, Lake Ontario and
Lake Erie. Following the conclusion of peace with the Iroquois, Madame
Cadillac left Montreal in September, 1701, on the first French vessel
to take the new route.[10]

It is important at this point in the discussion to indicate the
significance of the establishment of the new French outpost, Detroit,
which became the base for penetration of the region south to the Ohio
river and eastward to the foothills of the Appalachian mountains.
In 1700, prior to the founding of Detroit, no Indian tribal group was
settled in the region south of Detroit on the western and southern
shores of Lake Erie. Mounds, earthworks and artifacts in Ohio indicated
the existence of an aboriginal population over a thousand years earlier,
but that culture had disappeared. The eastern Ohio border had been
inhabited by a little known tribe, called the Andastes, who lived south
of the Erie, and were destroyed by the Iroquois after the Iroquois
destroyed the Erie. Part of the Shawnee, living near the Ohio river

326

---

[10]Lajeunesse, Ibid., p. xlii.

in the southeastern part of the state, were driven south in 1672 by the Iroquois wave of conquest.[11] Detroit was founded on the fringe of an apparently vacant area. The word "apparently" is inserted because any wilderness is apt to contain renegades, refugees, or exiles, removed from normal tribal associations. Parties of Iroquois occasionally ventured into the regions.

The founding of Detroit marked an important advance in the history of the French frontier in North America. Knowing that his isolated fort was insecure without Indian allies, Cadillac issued an invitation for midwestern tribes to settle in Detroit. Indian allies provided protection for the fort, food from Indian gardens for the military personnel, and furs for the traders at the fort. Among the first Indians to accept Cadillac's invitation were the Huron from Michilimackinac who in June, 1703, joined the Huron-speaking Tionontati already living at Detroit.[12]

327

The exploitation of the area south of the Great Lakes began immediately after the founding of Detroit. By 1703, Cadillac reported that all the Iroquois had been driven out of that hunting area, and the proceeds of the hunt were being brought to French traders in Detroit.[13] In other words, Iroquois hunters were prevented from collecting furs south of Lake Erie and taking them to rival English traders in Albany.

---

[11]Thomas, op. cit., p. 262.

[12]Cadillac to Ponchartrain, August 31, 1703, in <u>Michigan Historical Collections</u>, Vol. XXXIII (Lansing, 1904), p. 161 et ff. Exhibit No. 139.

[13]<u>Ibid.</u>, p. 171.

In response to Cadillac's invitation, some Ottawa also moved to Detroit, but many remained at Mackinac until 1742 when they transferred permanently to a new settlement, L'Arbre Croche, on the northeastern shore of Lake Michigan. In addition, two Chippewa bands, the Salteur and the Missisaugi arrived and were encouraged by Cadillac to form a single village. A group of Potawatomi and Miami came from the St. Joseph river on the southeastern shore of Lake Michigan. Cadillac also mentioned a group of Openango, or Wolves, probably a Delaware clan. By 1705, there were 2,000 Indians including 400 warriors living close to Detroit.[14]

These assorted Indian groups were not able to live in harmony. In 1706, during Cadillac's absence, a fight broke out which involved the Ottawas, Hurons and Miamis. Cadillac's method of settling the dispute was unsatisfactory to the Miami, who killed three Frenchmen in retaliation. In 1708, Cadillac brought about the subjection of the Miami by using military force. Not long afterward, the Miami moved back to more familiar territory on the Wabash river in present day Indiana, and invited British traders to visit them.[15] A more serious outbreak occurred at Detroit during the winter of 1711-1712, when a thousand Fox, Sac and Mascouten arrived from Wisconsin intending to settle near Detroit. They were acting on Cadillac's invitation, issued several years previously, but they arrived after Cadillac left Detroit.

328

---

[14]Sheldon, op. cit., p. 150. Report of Cadillac to Count Ponchartrain at Quebec in 1705.

[15]Howard H. Peckham, Pontiac and the Indian Uprising, (Princeton, 1947), p. 8.

His successor tried to get the Fox and their allies to return to
Wisconsin, and soon warfare broke out. The Fox besieged the French
fort in May, 1712, while the Ottawa and Huron were still off on a
winter hunt, but the garrison was soon strengthened by the arrival
of reinforcements. The Fox retreated twelve miles north of Detroi
and built their own fort, where they were in turn besieged for
nineteen days.[16] Trying to escape on a stormy night, they were
overtaken by Huron, Ottawa and Pottawatomi and about ninety percent
were massacred.[17]

By 1712, therefore, the Indians in the vicinity of Detroit were
limited to four tribes, the Chippewa, Ottawa, Pottawatomi and Huron.
In subsequent years, these four groups were often referred to as
"the Detroit Indians." Actually, only the Ottawa, Pottawatomi and
Huron remained in villages close to the fort. The Missisaugi-
Chippewa soon located in the Thames river in Canada, east of Lake St.
Clair. The remaining Chippewa moved about Lake St. Clair, and the
lower tip of Lake Huron, and became known eventually as the Chippewa
of Saginaw Bay.

329

The religious issue created a division in the Hurons. Cadillac
was strongly opposed to the Jesuits, and permitted no mission establishment during his residence in Detroit. The huron Indians, who had
been attached to a mission at Mackinac, requested in 1726 that a

[16]F. Clever Bald, Michigan in Four Centuries, (New York, 1954),
p. 56.

[17]Michigan Historical Collections, Vol. XXXIII, p. 553-555.
Letter of Father Marest, Missionary at Michilimackinac to M.
Vandreuil, Governor-General of Canada, June 21, 1712. Exhibit
No. 139.

Catholic priest be sent to them in Detroit. A Jesuit mission among the Huron, founded in 1728, continued until 1781 and was the last Jesuit mission in North America.[18] But not all Hurons were associated with the mission community. Some adhered to their own native religious beliefs.

Relative harmony prevailed among the four groups of Indians associated with the French post at Detroit. Apparently, by 1720, they agreed on a distribution of the hunting territory surrounding Detroit. Peter Dooyentate Clarke, in his Original and Traditional History of the Wyandots, reports:

> "About this time [the close of the second decade of the eighteenth century] the four nations (the French being a fifth party) of Indians having already formed an alliance for their mutual protection against the incursions of the roving savages of the West, the four nations now entered into an arrangement about their country, as follows:--
> The Wyandots to occupy and take charge of the regions from the River Thames, north, to the shores of Lake Erie, south. The Chippewas to hold the regions from the Thames to the shores of Lake Huron, and beyond. The Ottawas to occupy and take charge of the country from Detroit to the confluence of Lake Huron, with the St. Clair river, thence north-west to Michilimackinac, and all around there. And the Potawatamies the regions south and west of Detroit. Such was the grand division mutually agreed upon (as was proposed by the Chippewas and Ottawas), by the four nations of the then vast "howling wilderness". But it was understood among them, at the same time, that each of the four nations should have the privilege of hunting on one another's territory. It was also decided that the Wyandotts should be the keeper of the international council fire; the locality of which was to be figuratively represented by a column of smoke, reaching to the skies, and which was to be observed and acknowledged by all Indian nations in and around this part of North America."[19]

330

---

[18]Lajeunesse, op. cit., p. xlvi and xciv.

[19]Peter Dooyentate Clarke, Origin and Traditional History of the Wyandotts, (Toronto, 1870), p. 17-18. Exhibit No. 143.

See Map II, red lines

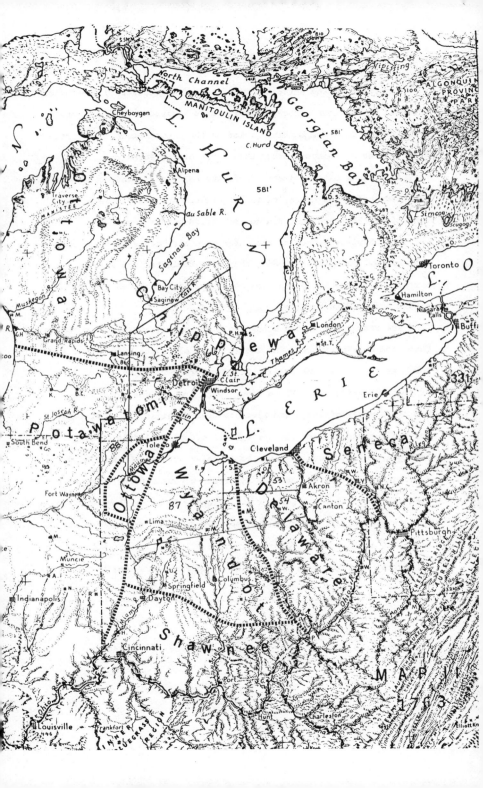

The terms of the agreement describe fairly accurately the regions occupied by the four tribes, with a single exception: Ottawas at Detroit established a hunting ground on the Maumee River in a corridor south of the Potawatomi rather than north of the Potawatomi.[20] Naturally, some minor adjustments in the pattern of land occupation occurred during the course of the eighteenth and early nineteenth centuries. The agreement did not set rigid borderlines.

The Chippewa tended to concentrate on the rivers emptying into Saginaw Bay. Within Royce #66, they also dominated the streams emptying into the St. Clair river and Lake St. Clair, as far south as the modern Clinton river.

The Potawatomi hunted along the River Rouge, and upstream on the Huron and Raisin Rivers. The Indian trail along the Huron river was known as the Potawatomi trail. These rivers were important arteries of transportation. The Huron river, with a short portage, led by way of branches of the Grand River to Lake Michigan. More important for the Potawatomi were the portages in modern Hillsdale county, Michigan. Here it was possible to transfer between the Raisin river, flowing into Lake Erie, and two important rivers flowing into Lake Michigan, the Kalamazoo and the St. Joseph. From the same cross roads Portage area in Hillsdale county, southward travel was provided by access to the Little St. Joseph river, a tributary of the Wabash.[21] Potawatomi villages were located on all these rivers, which cross part

332

---

[20] See Map II.

[21] See Wilbert B. Hinsdale, *Archaeological Atlas of Michigan*, (Ann Arbor, 1931), Map 3, "Principal Indian Portages"; and Map 1, "Counties of Michigan." Exhibit No. 154.

of northern Ohio and Indiana as well as southern Michigan.[22]   (See
Royce #66 and #88).

To follow the development of Indian hunting grounds in Ohio, it
is necessary to understand the principle topographical features of
the area, (Royce 87, 53, 54 and 11). Most important are rivers which
form three principal north-south water transportation routes connecting
Lake Erie with the Ohio River. From east to west these are: 1) the
Cuyahoga-Tuscarawas-Muskingum, 2) the Sandusky-Scioto, and 3) the
Maumee-An Glaize or St. Mary's-Great Miami. The Maumee also led to
the Ohio by way of the Wabash river, an important hunting region in
Indiana. Short portages were required on all these routes. The most
important of these routes in Ohio was the Sandusky-Scioto. Traveling
in canoes from Detroit, the Indians could follow a line of islands
across Lake Erie to the mouth of Sandusky bay, and go up the Sandusky   333
river to reach the interior hunting region. This route was also used
by war parties going to attack the southern Indians.

The Sandusky-Scioto region formed the central core of the
Wyandot hunting grounds in Ohio, which extended from the Maumee river
to the Cuyahoga in the north and from the waters of the Little Miami
to the Muskingum in the south. The Wyandot villages established in
these hunting grounds beginning in 1739 on the Sandusky bay were the
first continuous Indian settlements in northern Ohio in the eighteenth
century. Reasons for the establishment of the new villages are

---

[22]Ibid., Map 2, "Indian Villages of Michigan, of which the
Names and Locations are Known." Hinsdale's map is helpful to use
in conjunction with the Royce maps.

summarized in the following account based on French correspondence:

"The quarrel between the Hurons (Wyandots) and the
Ottawas broke out in the spring of 1738. During a council
at Detroit, the Huron chief gave a belt to the Ottawas,
announcing that the Hurons had made peace with the Flatheads
of the West (Chickasaws). The Ottawas rejected the belt,
and proclaimed their bitter hatred of the Flatheads. They
were upheld by the Pottawatomi and Saulteurs; and sent a
small war party against their southern enemy. On its return,
the Hurons were accused of having sent information of the
expedition to the Flatheads, which prevented the Ottawas
from surprising one of their villages."[23]

As a result of this quarrel, numbers of the Huron withdrew from
Detroit to their winter hunting ground near Sandusky, in 1739.

The decade of the 1740's heralded a rapid change in the Ohio
country, during which this area ceased being only a hunting ground,
and became the permanent homeland for the Wyandots, Delaware, Shawnee
and detached groups from the Six Nations, principally Senecas. Part
of the Miami from the Wabash-Maumee area briefly occupied a site on
the Great Miami, a town called Pickawillany near present-day Piqua,
Ohio, where they traded with the British. This settlement, established
in 1747, was destroyed in a bloody massacre in 1753 led by the French-
Ottawa chief from northern Michigan, Charles Michel Langlade.[24]

In surveying the activity along the Ohio borders in the 1740's,
the most difficult area to analyze is the zone east of the Cuyahoga.
Here congregated bands from the Six Nations, including several
dissident factions; Delaware who left their former hunting grounds

334

---

[23]Charles A. Hanna, The Wilderness Trail, 2 Vols., (New York,
1911), Vol. II, p. 165. Exhibit No. 137.

[24]Ibid., p. 261.

on the Susquehanna river in Pennsylvania; Ottawa from Detroit; and
Missisaugi-Chippewa from modern Ontario. In 1743, and for a short
period thereafter, Saguin's French trading post stood on the west bank
of the Cuyahoga river. Further upstream, on the opposite shore, was
an Ottawa town. The situation along the Cuyahoga river in 1743 was
reported by Robert Navarre, a French official in Detroit from 1730 to
1760, who made an official inspection tour of the region. Excerpts of
a translation of his "Memoire" include the following statements:

> "There are ten different tribes settled upon that river,
> numbering altogether about five or six hundred men, namely,
> the Senecas, Cuyayugas, Oneidas, Onondagas, Mohawks, Loups,
> Delaware, Moraignans, Ottawas, Abenakis of St. Francis,
> and the Salteux Chippewa of the lower end of Lake Ontario...

> "The number of Indians who have settled on this river
> increases every day; since hunting there is abundant; while
> on the other hand, at their former homes, there is no more
> game...

> "The powder and balls which Saguin asks that we send him,
> are very necessary, as ammunition is scarce at this time, when
> deer hunting begins; while besides, there have come from afar
> some Indians loaded with peltries, in order to buy powder
> from Saguin. He made them wait, telling them that some was
> then coming from Detroit, where he had written for it..." [25]

335

Concerning the Ottawa, Navarre reported:

> "There was found there of that nation five or six cabins,
> who have asked the Iroquois Senecas for a small piece of land,
> in order to light a little fire; which has been granted them.
> The greater part of these Ottawas are bad people who only
> established themselves in this place in order to be able to
> go more easily to Choueghen [Oswego, N.Y.,] a trading post
> No one can prevent them. The people of Detroit to whom they
> owe money can never catch them and make them pay."[26]

---

[25] Ibid., Vol. I, p. 315-318. Exhibit No. 136.

[26] Ibid., Vol. I, p. 321.

The influx of the Iroquois to the Cuyahoga border zone was temporary; and the small group remaining there became known as Mingos.
Saguin's post, and the Ottawa town, were both gone by 1755, when an
informative observer, James Smith, traveled up and down the Cuyahoga.[27]
In 1786, a group of Christian Delaware Indians settled briefly on the
site of the old Ottawa town on the east bank of the Cuyahoga, north of
the mouth of Tinkers' Creek.[28] On arriving at this location, the Christian Indians found "neither White person nor Indian" about the place.
The mouth of the Cuyahoga was being used as a supply depot, however, by
Detroit contractors.[29]

More permanent residents in Ohio were the Shawnee bands that in
the 1740's filtered into southern Ohio from two directions, from western
Pennsylvania and from the Cumberland valley of Tennessee. They located
their villages on the lower branches of the Scioto river and still
claimed Kentucky as their hunting ground. About the same time, the
Delaware began moving into the Muskingum valley, in eastern Ohio.
The early settlements of both tribes were in the area identified as
Royce #11.

Peter Dooyentate Clarke has preserved the story of the Wyandot's
first encounter with the Shawnee. According to tradition, the meeting
took place in the late 1730's, when the Wyandot were encamped on the
Ohio river at the mouth of the Scioto. On seeing a part of strange
Indians in canoes, the Wyandot made friendly signals, and after inquiring

336

---

[28] Ibid., Vol. I, p. 334.

[29] John Heckenwelder to John Askin, June 9, 1786, in The John Askin Papers,
2 Vols. ed. by M. M. Quaife (Detroit, 1931) Vol. II, p. 247. Exhibit
No. 151.

the identity of the newcomers, learned that they were Shawnee who had been driven from their former homes. Clarke continues:

> "Come ashore," said the Wyandott, "and we will protect you." You can," he continued, "go up this stream," which he indicated with his hand, "and take possession of the country, for your future homes." And the Shawnee nation did go up the Scioto, and thereafter became occupants of some of the interior parts of Ohio and Indiana territories."[30]

The Wyandots who moved from Detroit to Sandusky in 1739 created serious problems for the civil and religious authorities at Detroit in 1747. A Jesuit father who visited Sandusky in 1746 strongly advised his superiors to send back to Detroit a priest, who had been unusually influential among the Huron, with the object of persuading the Sandusky warriors to return to their former home.[31] The activities of British traders along the Cuyahoga river and at Sandusky were particularly alarming to the French authorities. Nicolas (or Oronntony), the leading Wyandot chief at Sandusky, organized a coalition of tribes, including the Chippewa and Ottawa, to remove the French from Detroit. In April of 1747, his warriors attacked and set fire to the Huron mission on Bois Blanc Island at the entrance to the Detroit river. According to reports, a Huron squaw managed to inform the commandant at the fort and Nicolas' attempt was thwarted. In September of 1747, the French commandant indicated his fears that Nicolas would afford the English facilities for establishments along Lake Erie as far as the Maumee river.[32]

337

---

[30] Peter D. Clarke, Ibid., p. 35 and 36. Exhibit No. 143.

[31] Lajeunesse, op. cit., p. xivii. Exhibit No. 134.

[32] Ibid., p. 29-30. "Extract from the Journal of the Most Interesting Occurrences in Canada, 1746-47." See also, Hanna, op. cit., vol. II, pp. 165-167 for reports of French correspondence. Exhibit No. 137.

Later in the spring of 1747, five French traders were murdered at Sandusky where they had stopped on their return trip to Detroit from the Cuyahoga river. The traders were seized and killed when English traders were at Sandusky, and there is some evidence that the English actually instigated the attack in order to secure the French peltry.[33]

A year later, in the spring of 1748, Nicolas burned his fort and village, and with 119 warriors and their families set out for the Cuyahoga river, beginning an odyssey that lasted until about 1753. This group established villages on the Shenango branch of Beaver Creek, a stream which flows into the Ohio River at Beaver, Pennsylvania.[34] They also had a village called Conchake at the forks of the Muskingum in a region later occupied by several Delaware towns. In 1751-1752, small pox took a heavy toll among the Wyandot fugitives at Conchake.[35]

Living in the eastern border zone of Ohio, this Wyandot band became closely associated with the Ohio valley tribes. At an Indian council in Logtown in May, 1748, Conrad Weiser, Pennsylvania Indian agent, asked for a census of the Ohio valley tribes. Their warrior strength was reported as: Senecas, 163; Shawnee, 162, Wyandots, 100; Tisangechroanu, 40; Mohawks, 74 (among whom were 27 French Mohawks); Mohicans, 15; Onandagas, 35; Cayugas, 20; Oneidas, 15; Delawares, 165; in all, 789.[36]

338

---

[33]Randolph C. Downes, Council Fires on the Upper Ohio, Pittsburgh, 1940, p. 47.

[34]Ibid., p. 43.

[35]Hanna, op. cit., vol. II, p. 178. From "Journal of Lieutenant Joseph Gaspart Chaussegros de Lery," March 30, 1755. Exhibit No. 137.

[36]Ibid., Vol. I, p. 331. Exhibit No. 136.

Not all the Wyandot abandoned the Sandusky settlements in 1748. While at Conchake, Nicolas' followers referred to another group of 70 warriors who were living at some distance from them along with some Ottawa. Kinousaki, an Ottawa chief from Detroit, was at Sandusky in 1748 trying to get members of his tribe to return to Detroit and he appears to have been successful. Father Poitier of the Jesuit mission in Detroit tried until 1751 to get the Wyandot fugitives to move back to Detroit, but his pleas were unavailing.[37]

About 1753, the fugitive Wyandot returned to the Sandusky river. Here, the Wyandot carried on their traditional pattern of living, planting corn and other crops at their villages in the spring for late summer harvest, then dispersing for winter hunting. In this latter activity, the Wyandots of Sandusky and Detroit participated jointly. A picture of Sandusky in 1755 comes from Charles Stuart, who was captured in a Delaware-Mingo-Shawnee raid near modern McConnelsburg, Pennsylvania, and turned over to the Wyandot. Ultimately he was ransomed in Detroit and made his way back to New York by way of Quebec and England. Part of his account, with the spelling modernized, states:

> ..... Sandusky, called by the Indians Canuta is a small Indian town containing 11 cabins in it, only 3 of which are constantly inhabited, the whole were formerly inhabited by Wyandots who built a stockade fort in it to defend them against the Cherokees and Catawbas, but the fort is now entirely decayed and broke down...Said Sandusky is now used as a headquarters of the Wyandot hunters during the winter season, who hunt on the head branches of Scioto. The hunters leave the chief Wyandot town (which is about 2 miles distant from Fort Detroit on the East side of the river or strait that comes down from Lake Huron) about the latter end of October and proceed with their families in canoes round the west end of Lake Erie...

339

----

[37]Lajeunesse, op. cit., p. xlviii.

In time of hunting the Wyandot town (Sandusky) is entirely
deserted except a few poor women who have no relations to take
care of them and they are left to take care of the town and
provisions are left with them to support on till the hunters
return...The Wyandot hunting ground begins at the west end
of Lake Erie where the river that comes from Fort St. Joseph
emties into the lake, about 40 miles from the mouth of the Strait
that comes from Detroit to Lake Erie.[38] This river from St.
Joseph divides the hunting ground of the Wyandots from the Hunting
ground of the Ottawas. The Wyandots hunt and trap for beaver,
etc. during the whole winter season from the latter end of October till the middle of April and by about the first of May they
are generally all returned to their towns...[39]

Interesting evidence of Wyandot (or Huron) winter activity in the

territory east of Sandusky comes from the journal of British Major Robert

Rogers, who traveled from Detroit to Pittsburgh across central Ohio in

January, 1761. He was returning from his mission to transfer Detroit

from French to British rule, an event that took place with all formali-

ties on November 29, 1760.[40] Near Sandusky Bay, he saw the town called

Junundat, inhabited by Wyandots. A few miles beyond, he found an Indian

town of ten houses, undoubtedly also Wyandots, at Cold Spring in Erie

County. The following day he noted two Indian houses near the Huron

river, and an isolated dwelling where a family of Wyandot was hunting.

Roberts also passed through the community called Mohican John's town,

in Ashland County, in which Mingoes were settled. At that time, Rogers

observed only two or three Indians were present, since all the rest

were hunting. He said they had plenty of cows, horses, hogs, etc. On

January 9, Rogers came near unidentified Indians hunting on the Long

340

---

[38]Stuart had mistakenly assumed that the St. Joseph, a tributary
of the Maumee river, is identical with the river of the same name which
flows westward into Lake Michigan. Fort St. Joseph was located on the
latter river. Stuart's "river from St. Joseph" is actually the Maumee river.

[39]Lajeunesse, op. cit., p. 59. Exhibit No. 134.

[40]Bald, op. cit., p. 62.

Prarie in Wayne county. Two days later, on January 11, he met a group

of Wyandots and Six Nations Indians hunting together. On January 13,

1761, Rogers reached his first Delaware town, that of King Beaver on

the Tuscarawas river in lower Stark county.[41]

The Delaware population in Ohio increased after the tribe's lands

in western Pennsylvania were ceded by the Iroquois in 1754. They

secured new hunting grounds in Ohio from the Wyandot.[42] The boundaries

of their new lands, largely in Royce #53 and #54, were described by the

Delaware chief White Eyes in a speech delivered October 9, 1775, at a

council in Pittsburgh. The speech was addressed to commissioners of

the American Congress and commissioners from Virginia.

> "I now also acquaint you that my Uncles the Wyandots have
> bound themselves and the Shawanese, Tawas, and Delawares together
> and have made us as one people and have also given me that tract
> of country beginning at the mouth of the Big Beaver Creek and
> running up the same to where it interlocks with the branches of
> Guyahoga Creek and down said creek to the mouth thereof where it
> empties into the lake along the side of the lake to the mouth of
> Sandusky Creek and up the same to the head until it interlocks
> with the Muskingum down the same to the mouth where it empties
> into the Ohio and up the said river to the place of beginning.
> I also now acquaint my Uncles the Six Nations that my Uncles the
> Wyandots have given me that tract of country."[43]

341

Of the tribes under discussion in this report, the Ottawa were

the last to make permanent settlements in Ohio in the eighteenth cen-

tury. Following Pontiac's unsuccessful attempt to remove the English

from Detroit in the summer of 1763, he and his Ottawa followers moved

---

[41] Hanna, op. cit., p. 184-185. Exhibit No. 137.

[42] See Map II.

[43] Journal of the Treaty of Pittsburgh, September 12 to October 21,
1775, printed in Reuben Gold Thwaites and Louise Kellogg, Revolution in
the Upper Ohio (Madison, 1908), page 25-127. This speech of White Eyes
is on pages 86-87. Exhibit No. 145.

to the Maumee river, above the rapids. Howard H. Peckham in his recent
publication, <u>Pontiac</u> <u>and</u> <u>the</u> <u>Indian</u> <u>War</u>, has assembled the documents
indicating the interest of the Ottawas of Detroit in this region. A
section of a lengthy footnote on page 17 reads as follows:

"A memoir on the western Indians dated 1736 implies,
indeed, that the river valley was then uninhabited.

"Thirty miles up the river (from Lake Erie) is a place
called La Glaise where Buffaloes are always found; they eat
the clay and wallow in it. The Miamis are sixty leagues from
Lake Erie, and number 400..." (<u>Documents</u> <u>Relating</u> <u>to</u> <u>the</u>
<u>Colonial</u> <u>History</u> <u>of</u> <u>New</u> <u>York</u>., IX, 891). In 1748 Kinousaki,
an Ottawa chief, reported at Detroit that some Ottawas who
were at Sandusky told him they wished to settle at the lower
end of the Maumee (<u>Ibid</u>., p. 162). Yet in March, 1750, a Miami
reported to the French that the Ottawa of Detroit were to make
their village at La Roche de Bout (in the Maumee just above
Waterville, Ohio) to be closer to the English of Great Miami
River who have promised to sustain them and to supply all
their needs. The English have been several times with forty or
fifty horse loads of goods to the upper part of the river at
Grand Chaize, where the greater part of the tribes have wintered." (<u>Illinois</u> <u>Historical</u> <u>Collections</u>, 168).

342

The intention of the Ottawas was not carried out until the fall
of 1763. All during the summer of 1763, Pontiac tried to assemble
Indian allies to force the English to abandon their newly-acquired
fort at Detroit. Toward the end of this period, many Indians were
inclined to make peace. His siege ended abruptly after an early snow
on October 31 forecast the approach of winter.[44] Almost immediately,
Indians departed in canoes for their winter hunting grounds. Pontiac
and many Ottawa families, plus some discontented French, left the
Detroit area at this time. The Ottawa formed two villages on the
Maumee, one on the north bank, opposite Roche de Bout Island, near
Waterville, was under chief Atawang.[45] Pontiac had his settlement

[44]Peckham, <u>op</u>. <u>cit</u>., p. 236.
[45]<u>Ibid</u>., p. 243.

farther up on an island, which is now divided in two, Indianola Island and Vollmar's Island.[46] After moving to the Maumee river, Pontiac hunted in the Wabash-White River section of Indiana until he died in 1769.[47] As other evidence concerning these new settlements, Peckham cites C. E. Slocum's History of the Maumee River Basin, page 122, where Slocum says that the Ottawa Village on the north bank was on the site of the town of Providence, about eight miles up river from these islands, but these villages moved frequently. Ottawas lived there in 1800.

The above paragraphs clarify the origin of the Ottawa band, identified by their new geographic location as the Ottawa of the Maumee.

In August, 1765, the Indian trader George Crochan observed the new Ottawa towns on a trip up the Wabash and Maumee rivers to Detroit. A portion of his journal includes the following statements:

> "About ninety miles from the Miamis or Twightwee, we came to where the large river that heads in a large lick [probably the Au Glaize] falls into the Miami (Maumee) river. This they call the Forks. The Ottawas claim this country and hunt here, where game is very plenty. From hence we proceeded to the Ottawa village. This nation formerly lived at Detroit, but is now settled here, on account of the richness of the country, where game is always to be found in plenty. Here we were obliged to get out of our canoes, and drag them eighteen miles, on account of the rifts, which interrupt the navigation. At the end of these rifts, we came to a village of the Wyandots, who received us very kindly, and from thence we proceeded to the mouth of this river, where it falls into Lake Erie. From the Miamis to the lake is computed one hundred and eighty miles, and from the entrance of that river into the lake at Detroit, is sixty miles--that is, forty-two miles upon the lake, and eighteen miles up the Detroit river to the garrison of that name."[48]

343

---

[46]Ibid., p. 252. Exhibit No. 133.

[47]Ibid., p. 299 and 308.

[48]George Croghan's "Journals", in Reuben Gold Thwaites (ed.), Early Western Travels, Vol. I, (Cleveland, 1904), p. 151-152. Exhibit No. 142.

The period from 1739 to 1763, which encompasses the time of village expansion into the Ohio area under discussion, was far from tranquil for these Indian tribes. They were involved in the imperial struggle between France and England. As Cadillac had explained in 1700, the principle motivation for founding Detroit was the potential fur trade south of Lake Erie. English merchants of New York, Pennsylvania and Virginia also were interested in tapping the resources of this area. The economic contest between the merchants was intensified by political rivalry between the English and French monarchs whose objective was control of the interior of eastern North America. International conflicts of the two European powers were always fought with Indian allies.

Following the founding of Detroit in 1701, three European wars affected the Indians of the Michigan-Ohio region. In American history, these are termed: Queen Anne's War (1702-1713). King George's War or the "Old French War" (1744-1748), and the French and Indian War (1754-1762). In between these periods of official hostilities, intermittent raids were frequent, particularly in the border region along the Ohio and Allegheny rivers. This focus of tension was created in 1749 when France launched a program for effective occupation of the area north of the Ohio river and west of the Appalachian mountains. The campaign enjoyed brief success. Resentful of newly-established forts, some Indians sought the aid of the English in preventing the advance of the French into their hunting lands. Although temporarily partial to the English in the 1740's, the majority of the Michigan and Ohio Indians fought with the French in the French and Indian War, either because they preferred the trade relations with the French or because they thought that the French would be victorious.

344

The actual outcome of the warfare was decided in other theatres of action, notably Manila and Havana, but the post-war settlement forecast significant changes in the Michigan-Ohio region of North America. As part of the general European peace negotiations at the Treaty of Paris in 1763, France surrendered to England the province of Canada, including the region north of the Ohio river. This transfer of political sovereignty over the Michigan-Ohio region concludes the first phase of warfare affecting the movement and distribution of the Indian tribes in that area. Consequently, it might be advisable to survey the pattern of Indian occupation at that time, when the situation was relatively stable.

By 1763, the Indian tribes who later ceded land in southeastern Michigan and northern Ohio were all settled in this territory. Villages and hunting grounds have been identified, and data exist for determining with reasonable confidence the location of the Wyandot, Shawnee, Delaware, Chippewa, Potawatomi and Ottawa. Some of the documentary information on the subject has already been cited. In the summary which follows, additional documentation will be supplied.

At the outset, one must recognize the priority exercised by the Wyandot in this region. This may be attributed to the fact that Huron-speaking Indian, probably Tionontati, already were living in Detroit and hunting in the Sandusky-Scioto river system when the new Indian groups began to gather near the fort in 1703. The Huron refugees from the Straits of Mackinac settled in the Huron village already existing on the Detroit river, and joined in hunting in an established hunting ground south of Lake Erie. Indications are that the Cuyahoga, the Maumee and the Ohio rivers, were accepted border lines, although Indians generally divide territory by waterheads rather than by river courses.

345

During the period of hostilities and tension in 1747, the Wyandot of Sandusky entrench themselves on the west bank of the Cuyahoga, reportedly to observe the behavior of the Iroquois, who were temporarily concentrated in the border zone east of the Cuyahoga.[49] From this action, it is reasonable to conclude that the Wyandot entrenched themselves on the border of their hunting grounds. The Wyandot assigned this eastern portion of their territory to the Delaware before 1763. The testimony of the Delaware chief, White Eyes, has already been cited.

After the Shawnee occupied southern Ohio, the Wyandot still claimed ultimate jurisdiction over the area, which was part of Royce #11. The Wyandot strongly objected to the treaty negotiated separately between the Shawnee and the American government in 1786. Their objections are reported in Arthur St. Clair's letter to President George Washington written in May, 1789 after the Treaty of Fort Harmar:

346

> "The claim of the Wyandot nation to the lands reserved to the Shawnese was strongly insisted upon by them, and to be made an article of the treaty--to that I could not consent; but, to satisfy them, and that it might be kept in remembrance, it is inserted at the bottom of it, by way of memorandum. It seems that this is a claim that has always been held up, and the reason it was so much insisted on at this time, they said, was that they were sure that the Shawnese, and the Cherokees inforcorated with them, would continue to give us trouble; that it could not be expected to be born with much longer; that they would be driven out of the country, and then it would be claimed and held by the United States by right of conquest..."[50]

At the request of the Wyandots, therefore, St. Clair added to the Treaty of Fort Harmar the following article:

---

[49] Hanna, Vol. I, French correspondence, Exhibit No. 136.

[50] American State Papers, Indian Affairs, Vol. I (Washington, 1832) p. 10. Exhibit No. 147.

"Be it remembered that the Wyandots have laid claim to
the lands that were granted to the Shawnees at the treaty held
at the Miami; and have declared, that, as the Shawnees have been
so restless, and caused so much trouble, both to them and to the
United States, if they will not now be at peace, they will dis-
posses them, and take back the country into their own hands; for
that the country is theirs by right, and the Shawnees are only
living upon it by their permission. They further lay claim to
all the country west [east?] of the Miami boundary, from the village
[Miami?] to Lake Erie and declare that it is now under their manage-
ment and direction."[51]

To be sure, the Six Nations tried to exert a claim on the area

south of Lake Erie based on their conquest of the Erie in 1655, but by

1763 this claim could not be considered valid. Sir William Johnson,

the famous British Indian superintendent, commented on this situation

in a letter dated November 13, 1763, to the Board of Trade:

"My Lords: In obedience to your Lordships' commands of
the 5th of August last, I am now to lay before you the claims
of the Nations mentioned in the State of the Confederacies.....
"As original proprietors, this Confederacy claim the
country of their residence, south of Lake Ontario to the great
Ridge of the blue Mountains, with all the Western Part of the
Province of New York toward the Hudson River, west of the Cat-
skill, thence to Lake Champlain, and from Regioghne, a Rock at
the east side of said lake, to Oswegatche or LeGallette, on the
St. Lawrence (having long since ceded their claim north of said
line in favor of the Canada Indians, as hunting-ground,) thence
up the River St. Lawrence, and along the South side of Lake
Ontario to Niagra.
"In right of conquest, they claim all the country (compre-
hending the Ohio) along the great Ridge or blue Mountains at
the back of Virginia thence to the head of Kentucky River, and
down the same to the Ohio above the Rifts, thence Northerly to the
South end of Lake Michigan, then along the Eastern shore of said
lake to Michillimackinac, thence Easterly across the North end
of Lake Huron to the great Ottawa River, (including the
Chippewa or Mississagey Country,) and down the said river to the
island of Montreal. However, these more distant claims being
possessed by many powerful nations, the inhabitants have long begun
to render themselves independent, by the assistance of the French,
and the great decrease of the Six Nations..."[52]

347

---

[51]Ibid., p. 7.

[52]Francis Parkman, The Conspiracy of Pontiac, (Boston, 1855) pp.
575-576.

Among the Wyandot and Delaware in Ohio were living individuals and
groups detached from the tribes of the Six Nations, and other eastern
tribes. But these splinter-groups were affiliated with the Wyandot and
subject to their leadership.

The foregoing paragraphs deal mainly with the Wyandot claims to land
between the Maumee and Cuyahoga rivers in Ohio, in Royce #53, #54 and #87.
Their territory between Detroit and the Maumee river in Royce #66 remains
to be delineated. Here, their towns were located in an area assigned to
the Potawatomi, according to Peter Dooyentate's description of the
original agreement between the four tribes before 1720. As might be
expected, the modifications of the original agreement all occur close to
Detroit, on both sides of the river. Clarks points out some of these
adjustments:

> "The Ottawas and Chippewas continued to occupy portions of the
> territory set apart for the Wyandotts(in Canada). The Potawatamies
> silently permitted the Wyandots to make their villages and
> cornfields within the territory assigned to them (Michigan). About
> this time, a part of the Wyandotts took permanent possession of
> the River Aux Canord Country, on the Canada side, and extended
> their place of abode to the mouth of the Detroit river and down
> along the shores of Lake Erie."

348

> "At the commencement of the fifth decade, (between the years
> 1740 and 1751) the principal portion of the Wyandotts had taken
> permanent possession of the country between Fort Detroit, and the
> River Huron, in Michigan. Their main village was at the place now
> called Gibraltar, and about Amherstburg, on the main land, where
> they erected their council house. In this village was kept their
> archives and international council fire."

> "Their main village was on the River Huron and near its
> confluence with the lake, and between what is now Sandusky City and
> Cleveland."[53]

---

[53]Peter Dooyentate Clarke, op. cit., pp. 35-37, passim, p. 54.
Exhibit No. 143.

The traditional account of Peter Dooyentate Clarke is substantiated
by the well-known authority, Colonel E. L. Taylor, who published the
results of his research on Ohio Indians in 1898. Concerning the Wyandot,
whose leadership is the key to regional Indian affairs, Colonel Taylor
makes the following summary statement:

> "They took possession of the country from Lake St.
> Clair south along the Detroit river, across Lake Erie to the mouth of the
> Sandusky river, thence up that river to the ridge of the State in
> Wyandot, Marion and Crawford counties, in which territory they had
> their principal villages.
>
> "They extended their occupance of the country south as far at
> least as the Shawnee settlements on the lower Scioto. They hunted
> and trapped all the streams between the Little Miami and the
> Muskingum. They also expanded to the west of this general line
> along the southern shore of Lake Erie as far as the Maumee river;
> and to the east almost if not quite to the eastern boundary of the
> State, which last region had once been the home of the Eries....
>
> "The Wyandots were admitted to be the leading tribe among the
> Indians in the territory of the Northwest. To them was intrusted
> the grand calumet which united all the tribes in that territory
> in a confederacy for mutual protection and gave them the right
> to assemble the tribes in council and to kindle the council fire..."[54]   349

The Wyandot established only a foothold on the western shore of the
Detroit river and Lake Erie, a slender connecting link between the two
principal settlements of the tribe, on the Detroit and Sandusky rivers.
The interior region of southern Michigan, below Lake St. Clair, was
Potawatomi territory. A sampling of early Indian land grants indicates
that the European settlers made agreements with the Potawatomi to secure
land on the River Rouge, River Ecorse, the Huron River and the River
Raisin.[55]   The Potawatomi also granted the land on Grosse Isle, the

---

[54]E. L. Taylor, "The Ohio Indians," Ohio Archaeological Society
Publications, Vol. 6, 1898, pp. 79.

[55]See The John Askin Papers, Vol. II, pp. 25-28, 46-47 (fn.), 174-177,
211-215, 249-250. Exhibit No. 151.

largest of the islands in the Detroit river.[56] This marks the eastern
boundary of Potawatomi territory.

The Chippewa, who traditionally remained north of the other tribes,
settled in this same relative position in lower Michigan after 1703.
Actually, they extended their occupation south of the area assigned to
them, according to Peter Dooyentate Clarke's definition of the original
agreement between the four tribes. As a result, they took over the narrow
corridor of land which appears to have been intended for the Ottawa,
Chippewa territory, therefore bordered directly on that of the Potawatomi,
in Royce #66.

It is not easy to set a precise line for the southern border of
Chippewa territory in 1763, but helpful information comes from a later
source, entries for the years 1782 and 1784 in the diary of David Zeisberger,
missionary among the Delaware. Following an attack on the Moravian Indian
settlements in southern Ohio in 1781, this Delaware group sought refuge
away from the Ohio valley battle zone, and settled a short time on the
Clinton river, which empties into Lake St. Clair. To settle there
originally, they sought permission from the Chippewa; and they left at the
request of the Chippewa.[57] It seems reasonable to conclude that the Moravian
Delaware were living on the edge of Chippewa territory, and the watershed
between the Clinton river and the River Rouge may be used as a borderline.
(See Map   ).

Although the Ottawa had no association with the area south of Lake

350

---

[56]Copy of Deed from The Burton Collection, Detroit Public Library.
Exhibit No.

[57]Diary of David Zeisberger, ed. by B. F. Bliss, 2 vols., (Cincinnati,
1885) Vol. I, pp. 91, 93, 205-207. Exhibit No. 135.

Erie prior to their settlement at Fort Detroit, by 1750, they were hunting
both east and west of the Wyandot in Ohio. In 1763, one group of Ottawa -
the followers of Pontiac - established villages above the rapids either
on islands or on the north bank of the Maumee river, in territory
previously used only for hunting. They hunted around the juncture of the
Auglaize and Maumee rivers. In their new location, the Ottawa were
situated between the Potawatomi and the Wyandot. There is no evidence
that the Potawatomi resented this intrusion, or that the Wyandot objected
to the Ottawa's hunting in the borderzone territory south of the Maumee
river. The speech of White Eyes at Pittsburgh in 1775 suggests that the
Ottawa had reached some earlier agreement with the Wyandot, and were also
responsible to Wyandot leadership. An estimate of the area utilized by
the Ottawa in Royce 66, 87 and 88, in 1763, is shown on Map II.

Following the French and Indian war, the tribes northwest of the
Ohio river enjoyed ten years of relative peace. The last campaign on the
frontier took place in 1764, when Colonel Henry Bouquet led a punitive
expedition up the Muskingum river to subdue Indians who had supported the
French during the recent war. The basis for a new period of hostilities
was the treaty in 1768 between the British government and representatives
of the Six Nations, whereby Kentucky was ceded to the British crown.
Since Kentucky had been the principal hunting ground for the Shawnee, who
did not consent to the cession, the treaty aroused the animosity of the
Shawnee against the white hunters and settlers who entered the area.

Mutual antipathy between the Shawnee and frontiersmen flared into
open warfare in the series of engagements known as Dunmore's war, which
commenced in the spring of 1774. The decisive battle of the war was the

defeat of the Shawnee and their allies by militia units on October 10,
1774 at Point Pleasant, a projection of land at the juncture of the
Great Kanawha and Ohio rivers. Lord Dunmore, last British royal governor
of Virginia, negotiated the peace treaty near the Shawnee towns not far
from modern Circleville, Ohio. By the terms of the treaty, the Shawnee
agreed to recognize the Ohio river borderline which had been established
in the Treaty of 1768 to separate the lands for European settlement from
the lands permanently to be retained by the Indians.[58]

Lord Dunmore expected to follow up his peace negotiations with a
general Indian council at Pittsburgh, but the outbreak of the American
Revolution disrupted his plans. Nevertheless, in the fall of 1775, an
Indian council was held under the joint auspices of commissioners from the
Continental Congress and the Virginia legislature. By the Treaty of
Pittsburgh in 1775, the Ohio river border was reaffirmed by the new
American government. This treaty, along with the treaty of 1768, forms the
basis for Indian claims to the validity of the Ohio river as the boundary
between the area of white occupancy and Indian lands.

352

But treaties were meaningless documents to frontier inhabitants.
Dunmore's war in 1774 was the beginning of twenty years of warfare, during
which the Indians were successful in repelling the periodic frontier
invasions until the advent of Anthony Wayne. After military defeat in 1794,
the Indians were forced to accept the dictates of their conqueror,
Anthony Wayne, and grant to Americans the right to occupy land north of

---

[58]Reuben Gold Thwaites and Louise Phelps Kellogg (editors), Dunmore's
War (Madison, 1905), p. 386.

the Ohio river. This first significant land cession took place at the Treaty of Greenville, 1795. Having established military superiority, American authorities maintained the upper hand in all subsequent dealings with Indians to acquire more of their land in Ohio and Michigan.

Lord Dunmore clearly understood the problems of maintaining any set boundary to frontier expansion. After returning from the expedition to the Shawnee towns in 1774, he included the following paragraph in a letter to the British Ministry:

> I have had, My Lord, frequent opportunities to reflect upon the emigrating spirit of the Americans, since my arrival to this government. There are considerable bodies of inhabitants settled at greater and less distances from the regular frontiers of, I believe, all the colonies. In this colony (Virginia) proclamations have been published from time to time to restrain them. But impressed from their earliest infancy with sentiments and habits, very different from those acquired by persons of a similar condition in England, they do not conceive that Government had any right to forbid their taking possession of a vast tract of Country, either uninhabited, or which serves only as a shelter to a few scattered tribes of Indians. Nor can they be easily brought to entertain any belief of the permanent obligation of treaties made with these people, whom they consider, as but little removed from the brute creation."[59]

353

In the summer of 1774, during Dunmore's war, Virginia militiamen began the series of destructive raids against the Indian towns across the Ohio river. The first settlement to be attacked was Waketomica, eastern-most of the Shawnee towns on the Muskingum river. Reporting the results of his expedition, Major Angus McDonald wrote:

> "I and my party attacked the Upper Shawnese towns; I destroyed their corn fields, burnt their cabins, took three scalps and made one prisoner...."

---

[59]Dunmore to Dartmouth, Williamsburg, December 24, 1774, *Ibid.*, p. 371.

The toll of destruction included five towns, seventy acres of standing corn and four hundred bushels of dried corn.[60]

After Lord Dunmore concluded his preliminary peace negotiations with the Shawnee in November, 1774, he authorized an expedition against the towns of the Mingo, who had refused to joint the parley. Major William Crawford, who had participated in the McDonald raid earlier, organized this action which destroyed six Mingo towns near present day Columbus, Ohio. Booty taken was sold for 305 pounds, 15 shillings, and the proceeds divided among Crawford's men. The booty taken by McDonald's men at Waketomica was only 35 pounds, 11 shillings, 3 pence.[61]

The treaty of Pittsburgh in 1775 did succeed in setting a policy of neutrality for the northwest Indians at the outset of the American Revolution. Tribes who united in pledges of peace and friendship with the new American government were: the Wyandot, Shawnee, Mingo, Ottawa, Delaware, and Seneca from the Upper Allegheny river. Yet as the American Revolution progressed, the Indian tribes found they were caught between the opposing influences of the Americans at Pittsburgh and the British at Detroit. This was the same predicament they had faced during the French and Indian War, when the French were at Detroit and the British at Pittsburgh.

By 1779, the majority of Indians were convinced that their interests were more closely allied with the British objectives in the war. Three factors may be cited. In the first place, the British home government in 1774 established the Ohio river as the southern border of Canada, creating

354

---

[60]Ibid., p. 152.

[61]Ibid., p. 304, fn 18.

a common line of defense for the British and Indian warriors. Secondly, the Indians were apprehensive when the Continental army erected Fort McIntosh on the lower Ohio river in 1778, and Fort Laurens on the Tuscarawas in 1779. These advance posts existed only in 1778 and 1779, but were intended to spearhead a military offense through the Indian territory toward the British in Detroit. But the most important element in solidifying the Indian sympathies with the British was the departure of three key Indian agents from Pittsburgh. In March of 1778, Alexander McKee, Matthew Elliot and Simon Girty left for Detroit. McKee immediately became captain in the Indian Department of the British army, and all three men were extremely influential with the northwestern tribes for the rest of the century.[62]

As the Indians abandoned their neutral position, Kentucky and Pennsylvania militia units renewed their campaigns against Indian towns northwest of the Ohio river. The following incidents cover major campaigns for the balance of the Revolutionary War period. In 1779, a campaign directed against the Seneca on the upper Allegheny resulted in the obliteration of eight towns. At the most northern town, 130 horses and 500 acres of growing corn were destroyed and over thirty thousand dollars worth of plunder taken. Additional Delaware towns were added to the list on the return trip.[63] Kentuckians hit the Shawnee towns in southern Ohio in May of 1779.[64]

355

---

[62]Reuben Gold Thwaites and Louise Phelps Kellogg (editors), The Revolution on the Upper Ohio, 1775 - 1777 (Madison, 1908), p. 74, fn 3.

[63]Downes, op. cit., p. 252.

[64]Ibid., p. 225.

The Delaware became targets for decisive action in 1781, when their central town, Coshocton, on the Tuscarawas river was destroyed along with the neighboring Moravian village of Lichtenau. In this action, fifteen warriors were killed after they had been captured, twenty prisoners were seized, and plunder in the form of livestock and peltry carried back to Wheeling, where it was sold for 80,000 pounds.[65] As a result of this blow, many of the Delaware migrated to the Sandusky river during the year 1781.[66]

More tragic for the Delaware was the year 1782, when some of the tribe returned to Gnadhutten, one of the Moravian settlements, to salvage some stores which they had concealed in their hasty departure. Cornered by an American militia unit on March 8, 1782, ninety Christian Delaware Indians were beaten to death with Mallets.[67] This atrocity surpassed even the murder of the family of Logan, the Mingo chief, at Yellow Creek in April of 1774 just before the outbreak of Dunmore's War.

But the Delaware had an opportunity for vengeance three months afterwards. In June, 1782, the same militia unit reached the Upper Sandusky region, trying to strike at the Indian towns which had provided a rendezvous for warriors sympathetic to the British. During the retreat, Colonel William Crawford fell into the hands of Delaware Indians and was shortly thereafter slowly roasted to death.[68] Crawford had earlier

---

[65]Ibid., p. 265.

[66]Ibid., p. 271.

[67]Warren King Moorehead, "The Indian Tribes of Ohio," Ohio Archaeo-logical and Historical Society Publications, Vol. 7, 1899, p. 69.

[68]Ibid., p. 274.

participated in raids against Shwanee and Mingo towns in Ohio during Dunmore's war, as well as the more recent Moravian massacre.

During the later years of the Revolutionary War, additional attacks also took place against the Shawnee. In these raids, a conspicuous role was played by George Rogers Clarke, another veteran of action in the Mingo raids during Dunmore's War. Following engagements in 1780 and 1781, Clarke and his Kentucky volunteers advanced to Chillicothe, near modern Piqua, Ohio, in early November, 1782. A total of five villages were burned and ten thousand bushels of corn were destroyed.[69] The official end of the American Revolution brought no cessation of hostilities on the frontier. Kentuckians, under orders from George Rogers Clarke, burned seven Shawnee towns on the Great Miami river in October of 1786, killed ten chiefs and did great damage to crops and cattle.[70]

As a result of military activity concurrent with the American Revolution, increasing numbers of Delaware, Shawnee, Seneca and Mingo sought refuge with the Wyandot, in Northern Ohio. The Seneca of Sandusky and the Delaware towns closely associated with the Wyandot in Ohio, came into existence during this period. Crawford's expedition against Sandusky in 1782 marked the first occasion in which American troops penetrated Royce area 87.

357

When the American Revolution ended, the Indian tribes assumed that the Ohio river borderline would be respected. But after American commissioners tried to secure territory northwest of the Ohio river by

---

[69]Ibid., p. 278.

[70]Ibid., p. 298.

negotiation, and their questionable Indian treaties renounced, the war
for the Ohio border began again. In 1786, leading Indian chiefs entreated
the American government to prevent surveyors from operating north of the
Ohio river.[71] Yet in 1787, the American Congress passed Northwest
Ordinance to organize that territory. In 1788, the seat of government,
Marietta, was established. In 1789, Fort Washington (modern Cincinnati)
was built; and became the departure point for the three final expeditions
against the northwest Indians.

By 1790, the Wyandot in central Ohio seemed inclined to compromise
on some peaceful settlement with the American government, so that Upper
Sandusky no longer was a military objective. Instead, between 1790 and
1794, American armies directed operations primarily against the "hostile
tribes" on the Maumee river. In October, 1790, General Josiah Harmar
advanced to the head of the Maumee river. Before Harmar suffered disastrous
defeat, his army destroyed five temporarily vacated Miami Indian towns
near modern Fort Wayne. In the following year, General Arthur St. Clair
tried to reach the rapids of the Maumee river, but was repulsed far short
of his goal by a confederated Indian army led by the Miami chief, Little
Turtle.[72]

358

---

[71]_American State Papers_, IV, Indian Affairs, Vol. II, pp. 8 and 9.
"Speech of the United Indian Nations" at their Confederate Council, held
near the mouth of the Detroit river, Nov. 28 and Dec. 18, 1786. It is
signed by the Five Nations, Hurons, Ottawas, Twichtwees, Shawnees,
Chippewas, Cherokees, Delawares, Potawatomies, and the Wabash Confederates.
Exhibit No. 147.

[72]Downes, op. cit., pp. 315, 318.

In spite of the fact that these campaigns were unsuccessful, they did affect the activities of the Indians who lived and hunted in the area designated for invasion. Consequently, it is important to indicate the rather abnormal situation which prevailed in 1792 along the Maumee river, on the borders of Royce #87, #88 and #66.

Most unusual is the absence of references to the Ottawa on the Maumee and AuGlaize rivers during the years just prior to Wayne's victory in 1794. Instead of the Ottawa, records indicate the presence of Shawnee, Miami, Delaware and Wyandot villages. The Ottawa's old hunting ground at the juncture of the AuGlaize and Maumee rivers is occupied in 1792 by two Shawnee villages, one of them the headquarters of the famous Shawnee chief, Blue Jacket. A few miles west is the town of Little Turtle, a Miami chief whose villages at the head of the Maumee were destroyed by General Harmar in 1790. South on the AuGlaize river, is a third Shawnee town, Wapakonetta. Detailed information concerning life in these towns comes from O. M. Spencer's report of his captivity in the year 1792.[73]

359

Similar information concerning the Delaware on the Maumee river comes from another former Indian captive, John Brickell, who lived with the Delaware chief Big Cat from 1791 until 1795.[74] A Delaware town, opposite the British Fort Miami, appears on maps of Wayne's battle scene.[75] When O. M. Spencer left the Shawnee towns late in 1792, he travelled downstream on the Maumee river, and noted a Wyandot village at the lower rapids and

---

[73]Milo M. Quaife (ed.) The Indian Captivity of O. M. Spencer (Chicago, 1917), pp. 73-75, et. ff. Exhibit No. 153.

[74] Horace S. Knapp, History of the Maumee Valley (Toledo, 1872), pp. 585-587. Exhibit No. 146.

[75] Richard C. Knopf (ed.) Anthony Wayne (Pittsburgh, 1960), Map facing p. 377. See also p. 362, where Wayne mentions a Delaware town fifteen miles from Grand Glaize.

a Wyandot encampment at the entrance to Lake Michigan.[76]

In April of 1794, when Lieutenant Governor John Graves Simcoe came from Canada to meet the Indians gathered at AuGlaize, he talked to delegates of the Miami, Shawnee, Delaware, Mingo and Wabash tribes. A month later, the "hostile tribes" sent a message to Simcoe saying, "When you filled the Pipe of the three Nations (Miami, Delawares, and Shawnee), you told them you would rise & go along with us; make haste then & get up & bring your children with you, as we expect they (the Americans) are all now collected at Greenville."

By June of 1794, Wayne's scouts had advanced north of the Maumee river near the AuGlaize and taken some Potawatomi prisoners who were brought back to Fort Greenville for interrogation.[77] In mid-August, General Wayne's army reached the juncture of the AuGlaize and Maumee rivers, where he later built Fort Defiance. He immediately commenced preparations for the final battle which took place at the foot of the rapids on August 20, 1794. Although volunteers and British militia from Detroit were present, the British closed the gates of Fort Miami, denying protection to the Indians. This incident was never forgotten by the northwest tribes.

Wayne's military victory was accompanied by the usual "scorched earth" policy. For three days prior to the Battle of Fallen Timbers on August 20, houses and cornfields were destroyed above and below the British fort. Wayne's report continued:

360

---

[76]Quaife, Ibid., p. 135.

[77]Knopf, op. cit., p. 339. Wayne to Knox, June 10, 1794.

"The army returned to this place [AuGlaize] on the 27th by easy marches laying waste the Villages & Corn fields for about Fifty miles on each side of the Miamis [Maumee] -- there remains yet a number of Villages & a great Quantity of Corn to be consumed or destroyed upon AuGlaize & the Miamis above this place which will be effected in the course of a few days."[78]

Wayne's campaign was a turning point in the history of the northwest Indian frontier. After 1794, the tribes were on the defensive. They had suffered severe economic loss, as well as loss of leadership, and loss of faith in the British. They were forced to accede to the American demands, whose justice they had denied for ten years. In 1795, they obediently gathered at Greenville to sign a treaty ceding the first land north of the Ohio river. By this time news had arrived of Jay's Treaty, whereby Detroit and the northwest military posts would be transferred from British to American command in 1796.

The period of readjustment following Wayne's campaign brought some permanent changes to northern Ohio. The Wyandot towns on the lower Maumee disappeared. The Ottawa returned to the river, and established villages near the river mouth as well as upstream. The Miami moved back to Indiana, and the Shawnee retreated southward to the headwaters of the AuGlaize and Great Miami rivers in western Ohio.

Changes took place also in eastern Ohio, where Connecticut Land Company representatives founded Cleveland on the east bank of the Cuyahoga river in 1796. Before establishing the new town, the prospective settlers first made an agreement with the Six Nations concerning rights to the land only as far as the Cuyahoga river. They also made additional negotiations

361

---

[78]Ibid., p. 354. Wayne to Knox, August 28, 1784.

with the Missisagi Indians living on Conneaut Creek, east of the Grand
river.[79] The establishment of trading facilities at Cleveland in 1798,
and a distillery in 1800 increased the popularity of the location.[80]
The development of commercial relations with the Maumee valley and Detroit,
as well as eastern centers, increased the economic strength of the new
community.

Cleveland became the trading post for diverse groups of Indians.
Extracts from the Barr Manuscripts, included in Whittlesey's Early History
of Cleveland, include the following interesting information:

> "In the fall, the Senecas, Ottawas, Delaware and Chippewas
> resorted here; and having procured what articles the traders had
> for them, dispersed to hunt through the winter, on the Cuyahoga,
> the Grand river, Mahoning, Tuscarawas, Killbuck and Black rivers.
> In the spring they returned with their furs and game, and after
> trafficking away their stock, launched their bark canoes to repair
> to Sandusky plains and the Miami prairies, for the summer. Here
> they planted corn, beans, and potatoes, around their villages.

> "While here the Senecas encamped at the foot of the bluff....
> On the west side were the Ottawas, Delawares and Chippewas."[81]

With the founding of Cleveland, interest mounted in northern Ohio
lands. John Askins, British fur trader and merchant in Detroit tried to
forestall American land speculators by arranging a "purchase" of the land
between the Cuyahoga and Maumee rivers in January, 1796.[82] He hoped that
his agreement with the Chippewa, Ottawa and Missisaugi Indians, known as
the "Cuyahoga Purchase," would be recognized by the American government.

362

---

[79]Charles Whittlesey, Early History of Cleveland (Cleveland, 1867),
p. 183, "Extract from the Journal of General Moses Cleveland." Exhibit No.14

[80]Ibid., p. 395, "Statement of Alonzo Carter;" and p. 372, "Letter of
Gilman Bryant."

[81]Whittlesey, Ibid., pp. 261-262.

[82]The John Askin Papers, II, pp. 5-8. "Deed to Cuyahoga Purchase."
Exhibit No. 151.

Joseph Brant, the Six Nations chief, later advised him to renegotiate the "sale," and be certain to secure Wyandot assent.[83] By this time, most of the Delaware had moved out of Ohio.

Askins had sent his half-Indian son, born at the Ottawa town of L'Arbre Croche, to attend the treaty council at Greeneville and secure Wayne's endorsement for the land dealings of Askins and his associates. But General Wayne, wary of young Askins' influence with the Indians, locked him up until the critical portion of negotiations had been completed.[84]

But Askins' project was doomed to failure when enterprising William Dean, representing the Connecticut Land Company, secured government cooperation in "extinguishing the Indian claims" to approximately the area of the Cuyahoga Purchase, Royce #53 and #54. Working against a deadline, Dean and Indian agent, Charles Jouett, hastily made arrangements for the Treaty of Fort Industry, which took place near modern Toledo on July 4, 1805.[85] The Indians who signed were members of the Wyandot, Ottawa, Chippewa, Delaware, Shawnee and Potawatomi Nations. In protest against the negotiations, John Askins sent two representatives to the council, but they returned with only a six hundred dollar settlement intended to "extinguish" the Cuyahoga Associates' claims to the land.[86]

363

An interesting unofficial account of the Treaty of Fort Industry in 1805 is found in the reminiscences of Abraham Tappen, who recalled

---

[83]The John Askin Papers, I, p. 311-312. Brant to Askins, Aug. 30, 1800. Exhibit No. 150.

[84]Ibid., pp. 552-565. Askins to Henry, July 9, 1795; and Report to Colonel on Mission to Greenville, Aug. 18, 1795.

[85]Relative documents are: Exhibits 1 and 47; and American State Papers, IV, Indian Affairs, I, pp. 702-705.

[86]F. Clever Bald, Detroit's First American Decade (Ann Arbor, 1948), pp. 233-234.

that unsuccessful attempts were made earlier to hold the treaty council
in Cleveland or Sandusky. Money for the payments at the treaty appears
to have been conveyed to western Lake Erie by way of Pittsburgh, Warren
and Cleveland. Tappan also reports:

> "It is said by those who attended this treaty, that the
> Indians in parting with and making sale of the above lands to the
> whites, did so with much reluctance, and after the treaty was signed,
> many of them wept."[87]

In the year the Treaty of Fort Industry was signed, 1805, the Michigan
Territory was organized. One of the first tasks faced by the governor,
William Hull, was the acquisition of land for the Indians to encourage
American settlers. He was delayed by the need for rebuilding Detroit,
which had been virtually destroyed by fire shortly before Hull's arrival
364 at his governmental post.[88] He was also hampered in his dealings by the
activities of the British Indian authorities, who exerted their influence
from their headquarters in Malden, across the Detroit river south of the
American town. In 1807, Hull's plans for a treaty were further thwarted
by the rising influence of the Shawnee prophet, who exhorted his followers
not to deal with Americans.[89]

Nevertheless, by patient effort, and such special inducements as
presenting a horse to the recalcitrant Chippewa chief, Little Cedar,
Governor Hull managed to secure a cession of land in November of 1807.
Discussions were held in a Council House erected for this special purpose.
The cession was not as large as he had hoped. The Indians were adamant

---

[87]Whittlesey, op. cit., pp. 401-403.

[88]Bald, op. cit., pp. 239-240.

[89]Michigan Historical Collections, Vol. XL, (Lansing, 1929), pp. 212-214
Hull to Dearborn, Nov. 4, 1807.

in their refusal to give up land between the Maumee river and the Connecticut Land Company purchases. Also, the Chippewa refused to cede land on Saginaw Bay. The resulting diagonal line, the border of Royce #66 in Michigan, was intended to strike the watershead up the middle of the thumb district in Michigan.[90] Surveying the boundaries was not carried out until after the War of 1812, so that the division between white and Indian territory in Michigan did not arouse any initial animosity. Indians remained in their customary habitats in southeastern Michigan.

Indians were on the move, however, as war between England and the United States became imminent. Factions in many of the tribes remained unreconciled to the constriction of their hunting grounds by white intrusion. These factions, gathered under the banner of Tecumseh, were defeated at the Battle of Tippecanoe in 1811. But Tecumseh and his partisans joined the British cause in the War of 1812, and the tide of Indian warfare, which had extended to the Maumee river in 1795, now advanced across the river into Canada. After Perry's naval victory on Lake Erie, the certain American victory took place at the Battle of the Thames on October 5, 1813. Never again did any Indian leader look to the British for military support.

365

As in the case of Wayne's war, the campaigns of 1812 and 1813 caused severe loss of life and property in northern Ohio, and in the Detroit section as well. Armies to a certain extent live off the land. Harrison's army assembled at Lower Sandusky for the advance against the British who temporarily held Detroit.[91] At one time, Tecumseh had an estimated four

---

[90]Ibid., Hull to Dearborn, November 25, 1807.

[91]Carl F. Klinck, ed., Tecumseh (Englewood Cliffs, N. J., 1961), p. 182, Proctor to Prevost, Aug. 8, 1813.

thousand warriors between the Maumee and Sandusky rivers, trying to capture the American fort at Lower Sandusky. Just before the battle of the Thames, many of the Wyandots near Detroit abandoned their homes and crossed to the British side of the river, taking cattle and supplies for the British army.

When peace was announced, the readjustment was more difficult than after Wayne's war. In addition to the rapid influx of settlers, the disbanded soldiers and stragglers encamped on the land. The Indians of southeastern Michigan and northern Ohio were thoroughly dispirited. The more sophisticated of their leaders realized that the Indians had to adopt the economic system of white settlers, or move further west. The Wyandots and Shawnee in particular had made agricultural progress in the years before the War of 1812, but their accomplishments were destroyed during the interval of hostilities. Since hunting no longer provided adequate means for supporting a family (particularly with white settlers as rival hunters), the government annuities offered by treaties seemed the only means of subsistence.

366

In the treaty of 1817, an effort was made to allot land to each Indian family group involved in the cession in Royce 87. Some special dispensations also were handed out.[92] The significance of the treaty is best seen in the letter written by Lewis Cass at the conclusion of the council. The following quotations are selected from that letter written at Fort Meigs on October 2, 1817:

"The country ceded by this treaty to the United States includes nearly all of the land within the state of Ohio, to which the Indians have any claim, a small tract in the state of Inaiana and probably a small tract in the Michigan Territory.".....

"The Wyandots who own it and the Shawanese and Senecas who live upon it are fully aware of its importance to us and to them....The ancestors of some of these Indianas have occuped it for many generations, which bind men White or Red to their Country.

"Its acquisition was also rendered more difficult because it is the last tract of land in the possession of the Wyandots, once a pwerful and still a high spirited people. Its cession to the United States will make necessary for those Indians to change the manners and customs of their whole nation.

"From this day they cease to be hunters and must depend upon their own Inudstry and the produce of their reservations for support.... When therefore we demand of the Indians an absolute relinquishment of everything, which gives rest to savage life, we must expect that this demand will be received with regret and obeyed with reluctance. In fact the whole of the Wyandots and those of the Shawnese & Senecas in his quarter have made the last struggle to preserve the inheritance of manners or of land transmitted to them by their ancestors. They now feel that settlements are surrounding them and that the chase furnishes a scanty and precarious supply. They will cease to be hunters and will, we trust, become farmers....

"Under these circumstances we judged it expedient to consider these persons, as the heads of Indian families and to make the provision which is found in the treaty. It will be perceived that the greater part of them live upon or near the Land secured to them and it would have been equally impolitick and unjust to have attempted their exclusion."[93]

367

---

[92] Concerning presents and special concessions, see particularly Exhibit Nos. 89 and 93. Preparations for the Treaty of 1817 are in Exhibits 78 thru 96.

[93] Exhibit No. 104

When the Senate refused to ratify the treaty, modification in the nature of land tenure had to be made, and this was accomplished in 1818. From the correspondence, it appears that altering the treaty was a very difficult assignment. A sum of $7000 was requested, to be expended to bring tribal leaders into agreement concerning the necessary changes. [94]

In retrospect, it is interesting to observe that the Maumee river border played an important part in the framing of the Treaty of 1817. The so-called "northern tribes," Chippewa, Ottawa and Potawatomi were considered as having claims only to the area identified as Royce 88, north of the Maumee river. The Wyandots alone ceded the area identified as Royce 87, although the correspondence cited recognizes that Shawnee and Senecas were living within these boundaries. (By this time, almost all of the Delaware had moved into Indiana.) The Ottawa were assigned to a reservation south of the Maumee river, probably because land on the river was desired by American settlers. The clause at the end of Article 6 of the Treaty say specifically that the reservation is for the use of the Ottawa Indians, "but not granted to them."

368

---

[94] Exhibit 108

By 1817, the Indian tribes of southeastern Michigan and northern Ohio were crowded much closer together than they had been a half a century earlier. Their meager hunting lands clearly had to overlap; and most villages had minorities of refugees from the long period of warfare.[95] The example of Anthony Shane is probably not unusual in this intertribal environment. Anthony Shane's mother was an Ottawa, but he resided with the Shawnee for many years and served as an interpreter for this tribe. His wife, on the other hand, a Delaware, lived with the Shawnee.[96] The maps indicating the approximate location of the tribes at the time of these treaties therefore include rather arbitrary boundaries.[97] Nevertheless, the relative position of the various tribes can be established.

369

[95] Warren K. Moorhead, "Indian Tribes of Ohio," Ohio Archaeological and Historical Society Publications, Vol. VII, 1899, p. 108. "Out of curiosity to ascertain the number of Indians and Whites killed in Ohio, or by war parties sent out from Ohio against the frontiers of Pennsylvania, Virginia and Kentucky, from earliest times through the War of 1812, and including the last settler killed by an Indian in northern Ohio in 1825, I occupied most of the winter 1893--1894 in computing from military records, histories, etc., and obtained this result: Whites killed by Indians: 12,002; Indians killed by whites, 7,837.

[96] See Exhibit No. 131

[97] See Maps III and IV

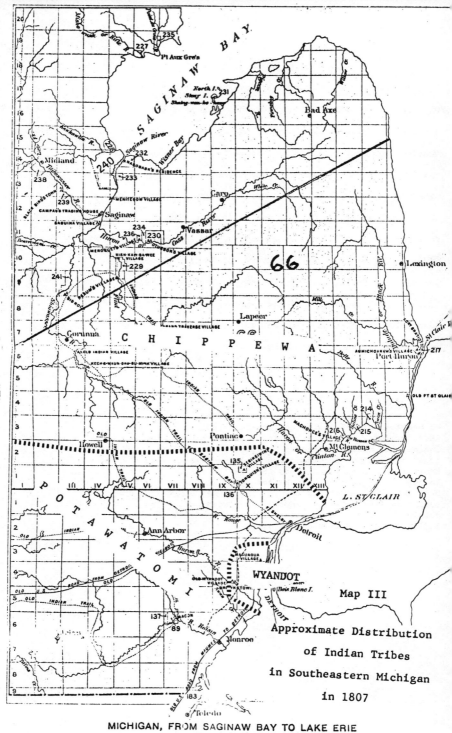

Map III

Approximate Distribution

of Indian Tribes

in Southeastern Michigan

in 1807

MICHIGAN, FROM SAGINAW BAY TO LAKE ERIE

SCALE 35 MILES TO 1 INCH

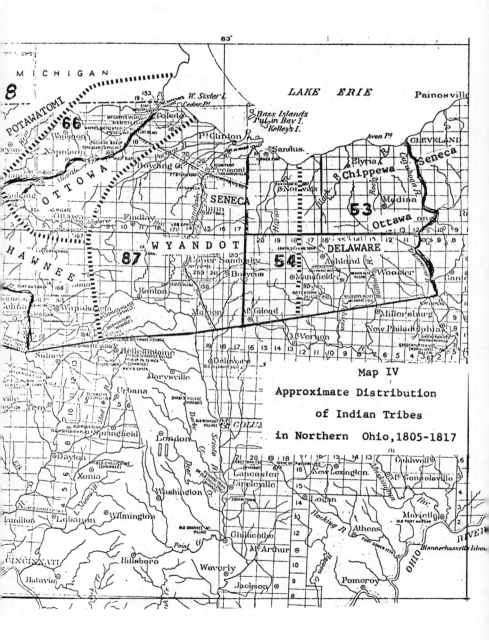

Map IV

Approximate Distribution

of Indian Tribes

in Northern Ohio, 1805-1817

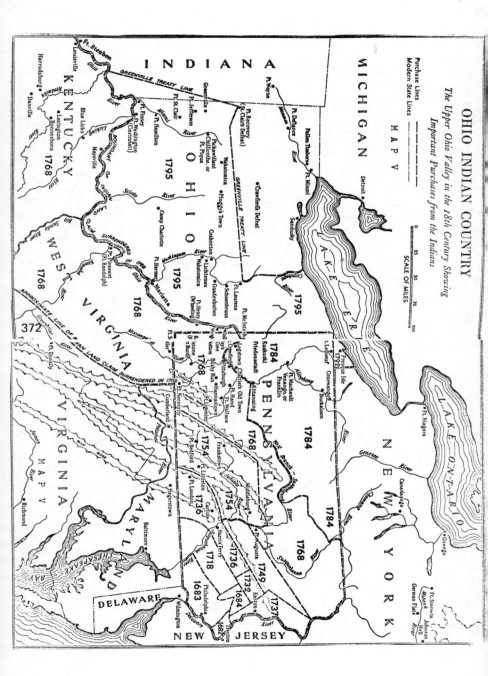

OHIO INDIAN COUNTRY

The Upper Ohio Valley in the 18th Century Showing Important Purchases from the Indians

Purchase Lines ————
Modern State Lines ————

MAP V

SCALE OF MILES

372

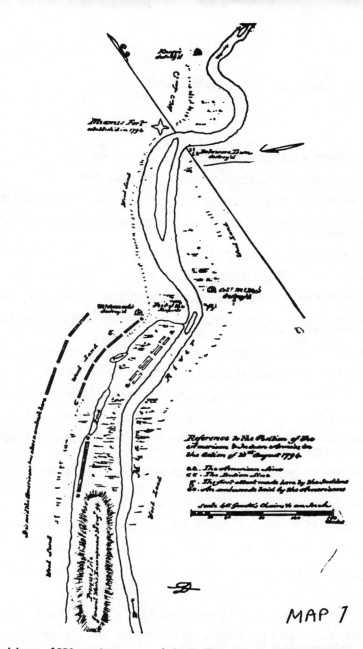

373

MAP 7

Positions of Wayne's army and the Indians, August 20, 1794, showing
major actions in the Battle of Fallen Timbers, from E. A. Cruikshank,
The Correspondence of John Graves Simcoe.

BIBLIOGRAPHY

BOOKS

Bald, F. Clever. Detroit's First American Decade. Ann Arbor: 1948.

_____. Michigan in Four Centuries. New York: 1954.

Bliss, B. F., ed. Diary of David Zeisberger. 2 Vols. Cincinnati: 1885.

Clarke, Peter Dooyentate. Origin and Traditional History of the Wyandotts.
      Toronto: 1870.

Downes, Randolph C. Council Fires on the Upper Ohio. Pittsburgh: 1940.

Hanna, Charles A. The Wilderness Trail. 2 Vols. New York: 1911.

Hinsdale, Wilbert B. Archaelogical Atlas of Michigan. Ann Arbor: 1931.

Kinietz, W. Vernon. The Indians of the Western Great Lakes, 1615-1760.
      Ann Arbor: 1940.

Klinck, Carl F., ed. Tecumseh. Englewood Cliffs, N. J.: 1961.

Knapp, Horace S. History of the Maumee Valley. Toledo: 1872.

Knopf. Richard C., ed. Anthony Wayne. Pittsburgh: 1960.

Lajeunesse, Ernest J. The Windsor Border Region. Toronto: 1960.

Morrison, Samuel Eliot and Commager, Henry Steele. The Growth of the
      American Republic. New York: 1942.

Murdock, George Peter. Ethnographic Bibliography of North America.
      3rd Ed. New Haven: 1960.

Parkman, Francis. The Conspiracy of Pontiac. Boston: 1855.

Peckham, Howard H. Pontiac and the Indian Uprising. Princeton: 1947.

Quaife, M. M., ed. The John Askin Papers. 2 Vols. Detroit: 1931.

_____. O. M. Spencer, Chicago: 1917.

Sheldon, E. M. Early History of Michigan. New York: 1856.

Thomas, Cyril. The Indians of North America in Historic Times. London: 1903.

Thwaites, Reuben Gold and Kellogg, Louise Phelps, eds. Dunmore's War.
      Madison: 1905.

374

Thwaites, Reuben Gold and Kellogg, Louise Philps, eds. <u>Early Western Travels</u>. Vols. Cleveland: 1904.

_____. <u>Revolution in the Upper Ohio</u>. Madison: 1908.

Whittlesey, Charles. <u>Early History of Cleveland</u>. Cleveland: 1867.

ARTICLES & PERIODICALS

Moorehead, Warren King. "The Indian Tribes of Ohio," <u>Ohio Archaeological and Historical Society Publications</u>, Vol. 7, 1899.

Taylor, E. L. "The Ohio Indians," <u>Ohio Archaeological Society Publications</u>, Vol. 6, 1898.

PUBLIC DOCUMENTS

<u>American State Papers</u>, Indian Affairs, Washington: 1832.

The State of Michigan. <u>Michigan Historical Collections</u>, Vols. XXXIII and XL. Lansing: 1904, 1929.